I0188117

☩SH

The
Saint
Helena
Breviary

Personal Edition

CHURCH PUBLISHING
An Imprint of Church Publishing Incorporated, New York

Copyright © 2006 by The Order of Saint Helena, Inc. All rights reserved.

The quotations from the Bible that are used in *The Saint Helena Breviary* are based on the NRSV. Some adjustments have been made for meter and for inclusive language.

Collects for St. Paul (January 25), St. Vincent (January 22), Thomas Aquinas (January 28), St. Athanasius (May 2), the Visitation (May 31), St. Alban (June 22), and Hugh of Lincoln (November 17): excerpted from *For All The Saints: Prayers and Readers for Saints' Days*, compiled by Stephen Reynolds, copyright © 1994, General Synod of the Anglican Church of Canada; published by ABC Publishing, Anglican Book Centre; used with permission.

"Song of the Soul that is glad to know God" by John of the Cross, from *Celebrating the Saints: Devotional Readings for Saints' Days*, copyright © 2001 by Robert Atwell and Christopher L. Webber, used by permission of Morehouse Publishing.

"O Felix Anima" or "O Happy Soul", from *Hildegard of Bingen's Book of Divine Works, with letters and songs*, edited and introduced by Matthew Fox, copyright © Inner Traditions – Bear & Company, Rochester, VT 05767, www.InnerTraditions.com, used by permission.

"Christ, our redeemer and our heart's fulfillment...", and "God of almighty changeless energy, creation's secret source...", two hymns adapted from the breviary of the Benedictine Sisters of West Malling Abbey, Kent, England. Used by permission.

"It is I who am the strength and goodness of Fatherhood...", by Julian of Norwich, adapted from *Revelations of Divine Love*, translated by Clifton Wolters, copyright © 1966, the estate of Clifton Wolters, used by permission.

Hymn 545 from *The Hymnal 1982* © 1985 the Church Pension Fund. All rights reserved. Used by permission of Church Publishing Incorporated, New York, NY. Words: *Translations and Paraphrases*, 1745, alt.; para. of Hebrews 12:1-3; alt. Order of St. Helena, 2005.

Hymn 474 from *The Hymnal 1982* © 1985 the Church Pension Fund. All rights reserved. Used by permission of Church Publishing Incorporated, New York, NY. Words: Isaac Watts (1674-1748); alt. Order of St. Helena, 2005.

Doxology, Benedicite, Magnificat, Benedictus, Dignus es, Te Deum, Canticles B, F, H, N, P, R, S from *Enriching Our Worship 1*, © 1998 the Church Pension Fund. All rights reserved. Used by permission of Church Publishing Incorporated, New York, NY.

Library of Congress Cataloging-in-Publication Data
Episcopal Church.
  [Breviary]
  The Saint Helena breviary. — Personal ed.
    p. cm.
  ISBN-13: 978-0-89869-516-8
  ISBN-10: 0-89869-516-3
  1. Breviaries—Texts. 2. Episcopal Church—Liturgy—Texts. 3. Anglican Communion—Liturgy—Texts.
  4. Order of St. Helena—Prayer-books and devotions—English. 5. Monastic and religious orders for women—Prayer-books and devotions—English. I. Order of St. Helena. II. Title.
  BX5947.B8E827 2006
  264'.03—dc22
                        2006014595

Church Publishing Incorporated
445 Fifth Avenue
New York NY 10016
www.churchpublishing.org
5 4 3 2 1

TABLE OF CONTENTS

PREFACE TO THE SAINT HELENA BREVIARY PERSONAL EDITION

Watching the *Saint Helena Breviary* take shape has been an enriching and rewarding experience. From the early days in the 1980s when we St. Helena sisters began to feel the frustration of the masculine language in the psalms, we knew something had to change. But we also knew that whatever changes we made could not be purely academic or intellectual; they would have to grow out of our shared prayer in community.

We knew we wanted to stay within our own tradition of worship based on the Episcopal 1979 Book of Common Prayer, and we knew we wanted to stay within the mainstream of the wider church's movement in both inclusive and expansive language. But we also knew that we needed to experience whatever changes we made within the context of living prayer over a long period of time before we could consider publication.

We began with the psalms. As a community we had been singing (or chanting) the psalms in the 1979 Book of Common Prayer since 1976. We knew that version to be poetic and singable, and we did not want to lose that quality even as we adjusted the language to be non-gender specific. We worked on the psalms for four years, praying them faithfully in all our Offices. Church Publishing, Inc. accepted the *Saint Helena Psalter* and published it in 2004, and it has been widely circulated throughout the church and received with enthusiasm in many quarters.

However, we began to feel excitement about new avenues of worship beyond the psalter. By the late 1990s, a wealth of material was available and many new ideas were circulating to stimulate and challenge us. *Enriching Our Worship* was offered to the church in 1997 with the express purpose of providing "additional resources to assist worshiping communities wishing to expand the language, images and metaphors used in worship." This is exactly what we were trying to do.

Antiphons, canticles, and hymns were provided for Ordinary Time, but what about the other seasons of the church year, which needed relevant materials, as well? We began to fill in those gaps, providing lovely new canticles for the seasons of Christmas, Lent, and Easter. Since we are now living in the space age, it seemed appropriate to include reference to that in our praise of God. The hymn for Monday Vespers, for example, says, "Creator of all time and space / you made the earth your dwelling place." And the hymn for Trinity Sunday now says, "The hosts of interstellar space / adore and sing your wondrous grace".

We began experimenting with broader ways of imaging God. Seeing God as a mother was not a new idea; from Augustine of Hippo, through Sts. Bernard and Anselm, the maternal side of both the first and second persons of the Trinity has been evoked. Julian of Norwich referred to "Jesus our Mother" in the early fifteenth century. However, only with the publication of the Franciscan *Celebrating Common Prayer* in 1992 did such images appear in liturgical worship. What was specifically new for us was using material from Dame Julian's writings in the form of canticles which we assigned to the season of Advent—a celebration of motherhood as we await the celebration of the birth of Jesus.

Inspired by Julian's words, we explored the works of the great mystics of the Middle Ages and incorporated material from Hildegard of Bingen for another one of our new canticles.

What was also new for us was to bring into our worship more passages from scripture that showed the active participation of women in salvation history, as, for example, on the Feast of the Presentation (February 2) we honor Anna's presence in the temple praising God and speaking of the child who was to come *[Luke 2:37-38]*.

Also, many people question why the western church has been reluctant to give appropriate recognition to Mary Magdalene, who was the first one to whom Jesus appeared on the morning of his Resurrection *[Mark 16:8* and *John 20:11-18]*. We opted to honor Mary Magdalene (July 22) with new antiphons and hymns which celebrate her as the one so chosen by Jesus.

Over the years of increased scrutiny of our worship, and as we prayed through the cycle of the church year and the Calendar of Saints, we began to pay closer attention to the collects assigned to the different saints. Some of these were so generic that they could be applied to any saint merely by changing the name. We began to realize that often we paid no attention to the collects because "they didn't say anything" and were frankly tedious. So, with renewed energy, we decided to re-write a number of them. We studied the collects from other liturgical churches as well as the biographies of the saints themselves, and where it seemed appropriate, we either adapted a collect from another tradition or completely re-wrote it. What we have come up with, we think, is a collection of engaging collects that speak to the saint being honored. They also include a petition that we may in some way emulate that holy life.

Despite all that is new, we have never departed from the basic framework of the Daily Office, inherited from Archbishop Cranmer in the sixteenth century and been prayed in Anglican and many other churches worldwide ever since. Not only is it familiar, but it has stood the test of time. We have also done our best, in all cases, to maintain the language and style of the Book of Common Prayer, respecting its time-honored richness and dignity. Only by remaining faithful to what has lasted so long could we feel confident that our work, too, would last and find wide appeal among others who want to pray the Daily Office.

The truly rewarding aspect of all this work has been the renewed energy in our worship. Guests who visit and pray with us are quick to comment how much the vitality in the services means to them. We are convinced that this has come about for two important reasons: first, the work has been done by the entire community, not by a committee of a few sisters working behind closed doors. Of course there was a task force doing the actual daily work, yet every sister has been a part of the development of *The Saint Helena Breviary*. And secondly, we have not done any of it hastily; every experiment, every change, every new idea, has been prayed in the Office for at least one, more often two or even three full cycles of the liturgical year.

We hope there will be many, regardless of individual faith tradition, who will find this book a useful tool in their own personal prayer life. The Daily Office is for everyone, regardless of faith tradition, and there is enough richness and variety here to appeal to many different worship styles. It is enough to know that wherever and whenever this form of the Daily Office is used, we are all united by our prayer to the one, holy, and living God. May we all be blessed by our common prayer together.

Sister Cintra Pemberton, OSH
for the Sisters of St. Helena

Eastertide 2006

INTRODUCTION

"OUR MOUTH SHALL PROCLAIM YOUR PRAISE"—
HOW TO PRAY THIS BREVIARY

This edition of *The Saint Helena Breviary* is offered by the Sisters of St. Helena as a gift to the church at large so that anyone may take the opportunity to join in these ancient prayers. The Sisters have reworked them in language that is both highly traditional and fresh, expressing the concerns of our time for inclusivity and reminding us always of God's love for creation which exceeds anything we can fully imagine. The book follows the general order for offices of daily prayer as arranged in the Book of Common Prayer, 1979. With *The Saint Helena Breviary* and a Bible or lectionary for Morning and Evening Prayer, you can easily learn to pray with it. Breviaries contain forms of daily prayer which hark back to ancient Hebrew daily liturgies. They were further developed during the Middle Ages by cathedral congregations and religious orders. They help us order our day with prayer and praise and turn our minds to God. The heart of these prayers lies in the recitation of psalms, followed by lessons from the Hebrew Scripture and the New Testament. The addition of canticles and hymns provide a kind of commentary on the lessons from Scripture, in which we join our voices in praise with the whole church throughout the ages. During the Middle Ages, clergy, monks and nuns began to dominate "the work of prayer," assuming that laity were otherwise occupied with secular labors. However, the Reformers, including Archbishop of Canterbury Thomas Cranmer, realized the importance of all Christians claiming prayer as something incumbent upon "the priesthood of all people," not merely ordained or dedicated orders.

The major difference between using this (or another) breviary, and saying the offices in the Book of Common Prayer is the addition of antiphons (short passages, generally of Scripture, recited before and after a psalm or selection of psalms or a canticle) and the expansion of available canticles (songs of prayer, generally from Scripture, but sometimes from the writings of saints, or, in the case of the *Te Deum*, traditional to the church). A hymn is also included at every office. Although you will likely not be singing, these hymns are treasures of the church which comment in some way on the rest of the office. Reading them will be edifying, and you may even want to fit the rhythms to a familiar hymn tune you know.

To pray with this book, begin with the four hours of daily prayer, Matins (morning), Diurnum (noonday), Vespers (early evening) and Compline (nighttime, before going to bed). A few general points: you will see passages marked Officiant and Response. Read both parts of these (except for "God be with you/and also with you"). Begin at your comfort level. If you only have time to say one office a day, do that. However, as the rhythm of the office becomes more familiar, you will probably find yourself wanting to take on another, and the time spent in worship will order the rest of your day and make it more meaningful. Similarly, as you begin to familiarize yourself with the breviary, start simply, using the forms for Ordinary Time. Then, as you fall into the rhythm of the office, add the seasonal (Advent, Lent, etc.) and major saints' days. For minor saints' days you may want to omit them altogether, just use the collect, or use the appropriate common (indicated with the collect).

Note that this version of *The Saint Helena Breviary* is arranged in the following sections:
- Matins, Diurnum, Vespers and Compline
- The Seasons of the Church year (Advent, Christmas, Lent, etc.) with weekly collects
- Commons of the Saints (these are special forms for feast days)
- The collects for Saints' Days and Holy Days
- The Psalter
- A Lectionary (schedule of readings) to pray the office in a two-year cycle

Ribbon markers will help you keep your place as you pray the office.

How to Pray an Office

Say you plan to begin with Matins.
- If this is *Ordinary Time* ("Green" seasons), turn to the beginning of the office with the salutation: "O God, open our lips, and our mouth shall proclaim your praise."
- Chose one of the "antiphons" suitable for the day of the week. Then say the "Venite" which is used except during Eastertide, when the "Pascha Nostrum" is used instead. Antiphons are short selections, generally from Scripture, recited before and after a psalm or canticle.
- You will notice that Matins is arranged by days of the week: Sunday through Saturday. The other offices follow the same pattern, except for Vespers which begins on Saturday, in anticipation of Sunday.
- Choose one of the antiphons provided for the psalm(s) in ordinary time.

- The Psalter is in the back of the book. You have three choices, depending on the time you have to spend. 1) The Sisters recite the entire Psalter over two weeks. Their table for doing so is printed in the back, on p. 547. Each set of psalms is arranged so as to express our need, followed by God's response and our gratitude. In addition, this arrangement assigns certain themes to days of the week: worship and thanksgiving for Sundays and Thursdays, penitence for Wednesdays and Fridays, and the Incarnation for Saturdays. 2) The Prayer Book has traditionally divided the Psalter so that it may be recited over the course of a month at morning and evening. You will find these designations printed within the Psalter itself (see p. 369, for example). 3) The Lectionary for Morning and Evening Prayer, beginning on p. 552, assigns a shorter portion of psalms for each office. In this method, the psalms are arranged in a seven-week pattern. (Certain psalms appropriate for Diurnum and Compline are indicated in those offices.)
- After the psalm(s), read the first lesson for the day.
- This is followed by the appointed canticle, arranged for the appropriate day of the week. In Advent and Lent or for major festal periods like Christmastide and Eastertide, special canticles are appointed. (The seasons of Christmas and Easter have additional enrichments in special sections called the "Ordinary" of those seasons, with easy directions for their use.)
- After the canticle, read the second lesson for the day.
- This is followed by the appointed hymn.
- The Benedictus is the traditional second canticle for Matins. It is found on p. 31 with its appropriate antiphons.
- The Apostles' Creed (optional), Kyrie and Lord's Prayer follow, with suffrages and closing collects. The collect for the week (the previous Sunday) or feast or saint's day may be used. Collects for Sundays can be found beginning on p. 95. The collects for Saints' Days and Major Holy Days begin on p. 271. "Commons" for special occasions or particular saints begin on p. 213.
- Of course, you may add your own prayers and petitions for those you wish to lift up before God before the close of Matins.

The other offices follow similar patterns. Vespers for the following Sunday is traditionally said Saturday evening. Similarly, before major feasts, Vespers is said the evening before (this is why the office of Vespers begins with Saturday instead of with Sunday, as the others do).

A Word about Years A, B, and C

On Sundays, beginning with the First Sunday of Advent (p. 95) you will see antiphons on the New Testament canticles with an A, B, or C designation. These letters refer to the three-year thematic Sunday lectionary (not the Daily Office lectionary) of the Book of Common Prayer. If you wish to use these antiphons in order as part of your Sunday observance, Year C begins on the First Sunday of Advent 2006, Year A begins on the First Sunday of Advent 2007, and so on.

❖　　❖　　❖

The Sisters of St. Helena celebrate certain special feasts associated with their patron, Helena, the Emperor Constantine's mother (c. 255-c. 350). A Christian, she made a pilgrimage to the Holy Land where she identified many of the sites associated with Jesus; she also believed she had found the true cross. One of the riches of this breviary is the special material provided for these feasts: The Finding of the Cross (May 3); St. Helena (August 18); Exaltation of the Holy Cross (September 14); and the Founding of the Order of St. Helena (November 8). Among other non-Prayer Book Feasts celebrated by the Sisters, you will find Ministering Angels and the Birth of the Virgin Mary. Mary Magdalene is kept as a major feast because of a growing awareness of her importance, not only as a disciple of Jesus, but also of the honor paid her by various traditions in the church throughout history. You will find other riches from saints throughout history, along with fresh, new collects for each feast.

Any use of this breviary will enrich your daily prayers. You may well find as you attune your prayers to the ancient rhythms of this manner of prayer that even though you are alone in a room, you feel yourself part of a vast community of Christians throughout the world, lifting up before God the words of Scripture and of holy women and men and of their own hearts, praising God, "Source of all being, Incarnate Word and Holy Spirit" alive throughout all ages.

MATINS

Officiant:	O God, open our lips.
Response:	And our mouth shall proclaim your praise.
All:	Glory to the holy and undivided Trinity, one God, * as it was in the beginning, is now and will be forever. Amen. Alleluia.

The Alleluia is omitted throughout Lent.

THE INVITATORY

The opening canticle throughout the year except in Eastertide is the Venite below, with additional verses that may be included during Lent.

During Eastertide, the opening canticle is Christ Our Passover (Pascha nostrum) on p. 3.

The invitatory antiphons are according to the Saint or Season.

Invitatory Antiphons

Ordinary Time:

Sunday:	Our God has created all things: *
Monday:	Our God orders all things well: *
Tuesday:	Our God's bounty fills the earth: *
Wednesday:	Our God is praised by all creation: *
Thursday:	Our God ever reigns on high: *
Friday:	Our God has redeemed the world: *
Saturday:	Our God is the Source to whom all things return: *
Response:	O come, let us worship.

Advent:

Invitatory:	Alleluia, our God and Savior now draws near:
Response:	O come, let us worship, alleluia.

For Christmas, see p. 109.

From Ash Wednesday through the Week of Lent III:
Invitatory: Our God is full of compassion and mercy:
Response: O come, let us worship.

From Saturday Vespers of Lent IV until Maundy Thursday:
Invitatory: Christ is reigning from the tree:
Response: O come, let us worship.

For the Triduum of Holy Week, see p. 148.

VENITE

PSALM 95:1-7

Come, let us sing to the Holy One; *
    let us shout for joy to the Rock of our salvation.

Let us come before God's presence with thanksgiving, *
    and raise a loud shout with psalms.

For you, O God, are a great God; *
    you are great above all gods.

In your hand are the caverns of the earth, *
    and the heights of the hills are yours also.

The sea is yours, for you made it, *
    and your hands have molded the dry land.

Come, let us bow down and bend the knee, *
    and kneel before God, our Maker,

For you are our God,
    and we are the people of your pasture and the sheep of your hand. *
Oh, that today we would hearken to your voice!

The invitatory antiphon is repeated, except during Lent when the following verses may be added.

Harden not your hearts,
>   as your forebears did in the wilderness, *
>>   at Meribah, and on that day at Massah,
>>   when they tempted me;

They put me to the test, *
>   though they had seen my works.

Forty years long I detested that generation and said, *
>   "This people are wayward in their hearts;
>   they do not know my ways."

So I swore in my wrath, *
>   "They shall not enter into my rest."

The invitatory antiphon is repeated.

CHRIST OUR PASSOVER (PASCHA NOSTRUM)

For use during Eastertide.

Invitatory antiphon: Alleluia, Christ is risen indeed:
Response: O come, let us worship, alleluia.

1 CORINTHIANS 5:7-8; ROMANS 6:8-11; 1 CORINTHIANS 15:20-22

Alleluia,
>   Christ our Passover has been sacrificed for us; *
>   therefore let us keep the feast,

Not with the old leaven, the leaven of malice and evil, *
>   but with the unleavened bread of sincerity and truth. Alleluia.

Christ being raised from the dead will never die again; *
>   death no longer has dominion.

The death that Christ died was death to sin, once for all; *
>   but the life Christ lives, is life to God.

So also consider yourselves dead to sin, *
>   and alive to God in Christ Jesus. Alleluia.

Christ has been raised from the dead, *
>   the first fruits of those who have fallen asleep.

For since by a human being came death, *
>   by a human being has come also the resurrection of the dead.

For as in Adam all die, *
>   so also in Christ shall all be made alive. Alleluia.

The invitatory antiphon is repeated.

Other invitatory antiphons are according to the appointed Saint.

THE PSALMS OF THE DAY

The St. Helena schedule of Psalm readings or one of the Prayer Book schedules may be used. See pp. 547 and 550 for instructions. The following antiphons may be used with the Psalms. The antiphons for Monday through Saturday begin on page 9.

Sunday Matins

Antiphons for Psalms

Ordinary Time:
> On this day God has acted; *
> we will rejoice and be glad in it.

or

> I will offer to you, O God, the sacrifice of thanksgiving *
> and call upon your holy Name.

Other antiphons for Sundays are appointed according to the Saint or Season.

After the psalm(s) is said:.
> Glory to God, Source of all being, Incarnate Word, and Holy Spirit, *
> as it was in the beginning, is now and will be forever. Amen.

The antiphon is repeated.

THE LESSONS

Matins continues with the First Lesson, followed by the appointed canticle.

Sunday Matins Canticle   PHILIPPIANS 2:5-11

> The divine nature was Christ's from the first.*
> Yet Christ did not think to snatch at equality with God,

> but became nothing, assuming the nature of a slave, *
> bearing the human likeness, revealed in human shape.

Jesus humbled himself, and in obedience *
   accepted even death, death on a cross,

and therefore was raised to the heights*
   and given the name above all names,

that at the name of Jesus every knee should bow,*
   in heaven, on earth, and in the depths,

and every tongue confess, "Jesus Christ is Savior",*
   to the glory of God the Almighty.

Matins continues with the Second Lesson, followed by the hymn below, or as appointed.

Sunday Matins Hymn

Other hymns for Matins are according to the Saint or Season.
   O blest Creator of the light,
   you made the day with radiance bright,
   and with the birth of light began
   to form creation to your plan.

   Your wisdom joined the sun's first ray
   to eventide and named it day;
   so now the light of morning's star
   pierces the dusk and shines afar.

   Let us this day with joy arise;
   daybreak renews our heavy eyes,
   awakes who still in sleep would lie,
   and bids them praise our God most high.

   Shed through our hearts your warming ray;
   our souls' dull slumber drive away;
   your name be first on every tongue;
   to you our earliest hymns be sung.

   To you all glory, Trinity,
   all laud, O Holy Unity;
   to you on this new day we raise
   our grateful hearts in songs of praise. Amen.

Seasonal Hymns for Matins

The following hymns are appropriate throughout the week of their respective seasons.

Advent:

A thrilling voice by Jordan rings
proclaiming new and wondrous things;
trembling, the powers of evil fly
as Christ in might shines forth on high.

The Lamb descends from heaven above
to conquer sin with freest love;
for such compassion let us raise
our hearts in grateful hymns of praise.

Now let the joyless soul arise
that wounded or in darkness lies;
see, the new Star's resplendent ray
shall drive despair and gloom away.

Laud, honor, praise and glory be
this Advent and eternally
to God, who was before all days,
and is, and is to be always. Amen.

For Christmas, see p. 116.

From Ash Wednesday Through the Third Week of Lent:

The fast as taught by sacred lore,
we come to celebrate once more,
as every year in prayer and praise
we keep these holy forty days.

The law and prophets had foretold
this Lent in many ways of old,
which Christ, who governs all our time,
in blest observance made sublime.

Then let us also keep this Lent
with watchful and devout intent,
that, vigilant, we may prepare
our hearts for God's redeeming care.

As by our lapses we offend
O you who love us, truest friend;
forgive us, Jesus, our offense;
teach us a new obedience.

Let all the world for evermore
you, gracious Trinity, adore;
and may we spend these forty days
in seeking you and singing praise. Amen.

or

O Christ, true Sun of righteousness,
let dawn our darkened spirits bless;
the light of grace to us restore
while day to earth returns once more.

This is th'accepted time when we
should mourn for our iniquity,
and let your gift of pardoning grace
our grievous sinfulness efface.

Thoughts, words and deeds we now review,
what we did ill or failed to do;
and, as we would be pure within,
repent, confess, and fast from sin.

Soon will that day, your day, appear
and all things with its brightness cheer;
then we, renewed, will celebrate
the victory of your risen state.

Let all the world for evermore
you, gracious Trinity, adore;
and may we spend these forty days
in seeking you and singing praise. Amen.

From Vespers of Lent IV through Holy Week:

This hymn is sung in its entirety during Holy Week. At other times marked verses may be omitted.

Sing, my tongue, the glorious battle,
sing the winning of the fray;
now above the cross, the trophy,
sound the high triumphal lay:
tell how Jesus, our redeemer,
through surrender won the day.

Thirty years among us dwelling,
his appointed time fulfilled;
born for this, he met his passion,
which he saw and freely willed;
on the cross he was uplifted,
where his lifeblood then was spilled.

He endured the nails, the spitting,
vinegar and spear and reed;
from his holy body broken,
blood and water forth proceed;
earth and stars and sky and ocean
by that flood from stain are freed.

Faithful cross, above all other,
one and only noble tree,
none in foliage, none in blossom,
none in fruit your peer may be;
sweetest wood and nails together
bearing sweetest majesty.

Bend your boughs, O tree of glory,
your relaxing sinews bend;
for awhile the ancient rigor
that your birth bestowed, suspend,
and the body of our Savior
on your bosom gently tend.

You alone were counted worthy
this world's ransom to sustain,
with the sacred blood anointed
of the Lamb for sinners slain,
that a shipwrecked race forever
might a port of refuge gain.

For Easter season, see p. 173.

Matins continues with the Benedictus, found on p. 31.

Monday Matins

Antiphons for psalms

Ordinary Time:
> I will give thanks to you, O God, with my whole heart; *
> I will tell of all your marvelous works.

or
> The righteous will rejoice and put their trust in God, *
> and all who are true of heart will glory.

Advent:
> Behold, the desire of all nations will come, *
> and the house of God will be filled with glory, alleluia.

For Christmas, see p. 115.

From Ash Wednesday through the Third Week of Lent:
> Examine yourselves: are you living the life of faith? *
> Put yourselves to the test.

From Lent IV until Maundy Thursday:
> Purge me from my sin, and I shall be pure; *
> wash me, and I shall be clean indeed.

From Easter season, see p. 171.

Other antiphons are appointed according to the Saint or Season.

After the psalm(s) is said:
> Glory to God, Source of all being, Incarnate Word, and Holy Spirit, *
> as it was in the beginning, is now and will be forever. Amen.

The antiphon is repeated.

Matins continues with the First Lesson, followed by the canticle below, or as appointed.

Monday Matins Canticle

Ordinary Time: ISAIAH 12: 2-6

Surely God is my salvation; *
  I will trust and will not be afraid,

For God is my strength and my might *
  and will be my Savior.

Therefore you shall draw water with rejoicing
from the springs of salvation, *
  and on that day you shall say,
Give thanks and call upon God's name;

Make known God's deeds among the peoples; *
  proclaim that God's name is exalted;

Sing praises to the Most High who has done great things; *
  let this be known in all the world.

Shout aloud and sing for joy, O inhabitants of Zion, *
  for great in your midst is the Holy One of Israel.

Advent: ADAPTED FROM JULIAN OF NORWICH

You, O Christ, are the One: *
  the might and goodness of fatherhood.

You are the One: *
  the wisdom and kindness of motherhood.

You, O Christ, are the One:
the light and grace of all blessed love; *
  you are Trinity; you are Unity.

You, O Christ, are the One: *
  the high sovereign goodness of all manner of things.

You are the One who makes us to love; *
  you are the One who makes us to long.

You, O Christ, are the One: *
  the endless fulfilling of all our true desires.

For Christmas, see p. 115.

Lent: JONAH 2:2-7

I called to you, O God, in my distress, *
  and you answered me;

Out of the belly of Sheol I cried for help, *
  and you heard my cry.

You cast me into the depths, far out at sea,
and the flood closed round about me; *
  all your waves, all your billows, passed over me.

I thought I was banished from your sight *
  and should never see your holy temple again.

Weeds twined around my head in the troughs of the mountains; *
  I was sinking into a world whose bars would hold me fast forever;

But you brought me up alive from the pit, O my God; *
  as my senses failed me, I remembered you,
  and my prayer reached you in your holy temple.

For Easter season, see p. 171.

Matins continues with the Second Lesson, followed by the hymn below or as appointed.

Monday Matins Hymn

Other hymns for Matins are according to the Saint or Season. For seasonal hymns, see Sunday Matins.

O brightness of the Maker's ray,
true Light of light and Day of day,
light's fountain and eternal spring,
shine forth, the morn illumining.

Eternal Sun, on us your light
let fall in royal splendor bright;
the Spirit's sanctifying beam
upon our earthly senses stream.

Creator of perpetual light,
enlighten us to choose aright,
that with your gift of loving grace,
we may all grievous sin efface.

Now prosper all we nobly do;
let love all envy now subdue;
make our ill fortune turn to fair
and give us grace our wrongs to bear.

To you all glory, Trinity,
all laud, O Holy Unity;
to you on this new day we raise
our grateful hearts in songs of praise. Amen.

Matins continues with the Benedictus, found on p. 31.

Tuesday Matins

Antiphons for psalms

Ordinary Time:
Be merciful to me, O God, be merciful, *
for I have taken refuge in you.

or

Yours, O God, is an everlasting reign; *
your dominion endures throughout all ages.

Advent:
Behold, our Savior will appear in the clouds of heaven, *
with power and great glory, alleluia.

For Christmas, see p. 115.

From Ash Wednesday through the Third Week of Lent:
If we confess our sins, God is just and may be trusted to forgive our sins *
and cleanse us from every kind of wrong.

From Lent IV until Maundy Thursday.
Create in me a clean heart, O God, *
and renew a right spirit within me.

For Easter season, see p. 172.

After the psalm(s) is said:

Glory to God, Source of all being, Incarnate Word, and Holy Spirit, *
as it was in the beginning, is now and will be forever. Amen.

The antiphon is repeated.

Other antiphons are appointed according to the Saint or Season.

Matins continues with the First Lesson, followed by the canticle below, or as appointed.

Tuesday Matins Canticle

Ordinary Time: SONG OF SOLOMON 8:6-7

Set me as a seal upon your heart, *
as a seal upon your arm.

For love is strong as death, passion fierce as the grave; *
its flashes are flashes of fire, a raging flame. Many waters cannot
quench love, *
neither can the floods drown it.

If all the wealth of our house were offered for love, *
it would be utterly scorned.

Advent: ADAPTED FROM JULIAN OF NORWICH

God chose to be our mother in all things *
and in the fullness of time
took human form in the womb of Mary.

God, the perfect wisdom of all, *
chose to be arrayed in this humble place.

Christ came in our poor flesh *
to share a mother's care.

Our mothers bear us for pain and for death; *
our true mother, Jesus, bears us for joy and endless life.

Jesus carried us within him in love and travail, *
until the full time of his passion.

And when all was completed, and we were carried so for joy, *
still, all this could not satisfy the power of God's wonderful love.

All that we owe is redeemed in truly loving God, *
    for the love of Christ works in us;
    Christ is the one whom we love.

For Christmas, see p. 115.

Lent: ISAIAH 49:14-17

Zion says, God has forsaken me; *
    my God has forgotten me.

Can a woman forget the infant at her breast, *
    or a loving mother the child of her womb?

Even these forget, yet I will not forget you; *
    your walls are always before my eyes;
    I have engraved them on the palms of my hands.

Those who are to rebuild you make better speed

than those who pulled you down, *
    while those who laid you waste depart.

For Easter season, see p. 172.

Matins continues with the Second Lesson, followed by the hymn.

Tuesday Matins Hymn

Other hymns for Matins are according to the Saint or Season. For seasonal hymns, see Sunday Matins.

Behold, another day is given
    for us to journey on toward heaven,
    when Christ invites us to awake,
    to work and love for Love's own sake.

Greet the new day, the Savior cries
    to each who still in slumber lies;
    in justice and in virtue stand,
    and watch, my coming is at hand.

Help us, O Christ, your call to heed
    that we may recognize our need;
    may longing hope for you inspire
    in us unquenchable desire.

So may you, Christ, our slumbers wake,
from us the chains of evil break;
with clarity reveal your way,
and make us zealous to obey.

To you all glory, Trinity,
all laud, O Holy Unity;
to you on this new day we raise
our grateful hearts in songs of praise. Amen.

Matins continues with the Benedictus, found on p. 31.

Wednesday Matins

Antiphons for psalms

Ordinary Time:

> Restore us, O God of hosts; *
> show the light of your countenance, and we shall be saved.

Or

> You, O God, will build up Zion, *
> and your glory will appear.

Advent:

> Behold, our God comes, with all the saints together, *
> and there will be in that day a great light, alleluia.

For Christmas, see p. 115.

From Ash Wednesday through the Third Week of Lent:

> You must work out your own salvation in fear and trembling, *
> for it is God who works in you, inspiring both the will and the deed.

From Lent IV until Maundy Thursday:

> The sacrifice acceptable to God is a troubled spirit; *
> a broken and contrite heart, O God, you will not despise.

For Easter season, see p. 171.

Other antiphons are appointed according to the Saint or Season.

After the psalm(s) is said:

Glory to God, Source of all being, Incarnate Word, and Holy Spirit, *
as it was in the beginning, is now and will be forever. Amen.

The antiphon is repeated.

Matins continues with the First Lesson, followed by the canticle below, or as appointed.

Wednesday Matins Canticle

Ordinary Time: 1 Samuel 2:-1-8

My heart rejoices in God; *
in God my head is lifted up.

Derision for my foes is on my lips, *
for God's deliverance has made me glad.

There is no Holy One like our God; *
there is no one besides you;
there is no rock like our God.

Speak boastfully no longer, *
nor let arrogance come out of your mouth;

For our God is a God of knowledge, *
to whom all deeds are manifest.

The Most High strips away possessions, *
and likewise gives abundance.

God raises the poor from the dust *
and lifts the needy out of the ashes,

To give them a seat among those of noble birth, *
a place of honor for their inheritance.

To God belong the pillars of the earth, *
and the world is set upon them.

Christ revealed our frailty and our falling, *
our trespasses and our humiliations.

Christ also revealed God's blessed power, *
such blessed wisdom and love.

Christ protects us as tenderly and as sweetly
when we are in greatest need; *
Christ raises us in spirit
and turns everything to glory and joy without ending.
God is the ground and the substance,

the very essence of nature; *
God is the true father and mother of natures.

We are all bound to God by nature; *
we are all bound to God by grace.

And this grace is for all the world, *
because it is our precious mother, Christ.

For this fair nature was prepared by Christ *
for the honor and nobility of all,
and for the joy and bliss of salvation.

For Christmas, see p. 115.

Lent: LAMENTATIONS 1:12,16; 3:19,21-24,26

Is it nothing to you, all you who pass by? *
Look and see if there is any sorrow like my sorrow,

Which was brought upon me, *
inflicted by God's fierce anger.

For these things I weep; my eyes flow with tears, *
for a comforter is far from me,
one to revive my courage.

Remember my affliction and my bitterness, *
wormwood and gall!

But this I call to mind *
and therefore I have hope:

The steadfast love of God never ceases; *
  God's mercies never end.

They are new every morning; *
  great is your faithfulness.

"God is my portion," says my soul, *
  "therefore I will hope in God."

It is good that we should wait quietly *
  for the coming of God's salvation.

For Easter season, see p. 172.

Matins continues with the Second Lesson, followed by the hymn below or as appointed.

Wednesday Matins Hymn

Other hymns for Matins are according to the Saint or Season.
For seasonal hymns see Sunday Matins.

O great Creator of the light,
from your effulgence, calm and bright,
soon as the hours of night have gone,
we greet the loveliness of dawn.

Earth's dusky veil is torn away,
pierced by the sparkling beams of day;
the world resumes its hues apace
when Daystar shows its radiant face.

Your love, O Christ, alone we seek
with conscience pure and temper meek;
in faith and hope we humbly pray
that you will guide us through this day.

Light of the Morning Star, illume,
serenely shining, all our gloom,
and with your love our lives refine,
that we may with your glory shine.

To you all glory, Trinity,
all laud, O Holy Unity;
to you on this new day we raise
our grateful hearts in songs of praise. Amen.

Matins continues with the Benedictus, found on p. 31.

Thursday Matins

Antiphons for psalms

Ordinary Time:
To you, O God, will I offer an oblation
  with sounds of great gladness; *
    I will sing and make music to you.

or

  Ascribe due honor to God's holy Name; *
    worship the Most High in the beauty of holiness.

Advent:
  Behold, the desire of all nations will come, *
    and the house of God will be filled with glory, alleluia.

For Christmas, see p. 115.

From Ash Wednesday through the Third Week of Lent:
  Examine yourselves: are you living the life of faith? *
    Put yourselves to the test.

From Lent IV through Maundy Thursday:
  Purge me from my sin, and I shall be pure; *
    wash me, and I shall be clean indeed.

For Maundy Thursday, see p. 148.

From Easter season, see p. 171.

Other antiphons are appointed according to the Saint or Season.
After the psalm(s) is said:
  Glory to God, Source of all being, Incarnate Word, and Holy Spirit, *
    as it was in the beginning, is now and will be forever. Amen.

The antiphon is repeated.

Matins continues with the First Lesson, followed by the canticle below, or as appointed.

Thursday Matins Canticle

Ordinary Time: SIRACH 51:13-18; 21

Before I ventured forth,
    even while I was very young, *
      I sought wisdom openly in my prayer.

In the forecourts of the temple I asked for wisdom, *
    and this I will seek until the end.

From first blossom to early fruit, *
    wisdom has been the delight of my heart.

My foot has kept firmly to the path of truth; *
    I have diligently pursued this from my youth.

I inclined my ear a little and became receptive; *
    I found for myself much wisdom, and in this I became adept.

To the one who gives me wisdom will I give glory, *
    for I have resolved to live according to this way.

As my reward the Almighty has given me the gift of language, *
    and with it I will offer praise to God.

Advent: ADAPTED FROM JULIAN OF NORWICH

You, O Christ, are the One: *
    the might and goodness of fatherhood.

You are the One: *
    the wisdom and kindness of motherhood.

You, O Christ, are the One:
the light and grace of all blessed love; *
    you are Trinity; you are Unity.

You, O Christ, are the One: *
    the high sovereign goodness of all manner of things.

You are the One who makes us to love; *
    you are the One who makes us to long.

You, O Christ, are the One: *
    the endless fulfilling of all our true desires.

For Christmas, see p. 115.

For Christmas, see p. 115.

Lent: JONAH 2:2-7

I called to you, O God, in my distress, *
   and you answered me;

Out of the belly of Sheol I cried for help, *
   and you heard my cry.

You cast me into the depths, far out at sea,
and the flood closed round about me; *
   all your waves, all your billows, passed over me.

I thought I was banished from your sight *
   and should never see your holy temple again.

Weeds twined around my head in the troughs of the mountains; *
   I was sinking into a world whose bars would hold me fast forever;

But you brought me up alive from the pit, O my God; *
   as my senses failed me, I remembered you,
   and my prayer reached you in your holy temple.

For Easter season, see p. 171.

Matins continues with the Second Lesson, followed by the hymn below or as appointed.

Thursday Matins Hymn

Other hymns for Matins are according to the Saint or Season.
For seasonal hymns, see Sunday Matins.

As darkness flees before the sun
when its bright journey has begun,
so Christ, with love's redemptive power,
expels all evil at this hour.

May this new day be calmly passed,
may we keep faith while it shall last,
nor let our lips from truth depart,
nor evil thoughts engage the heart.

From life's beginning to its end
may we ourselves in service spend;
so Christ's example be preserved,
who came to serve, not to be served.

For God, all-seeing from on high,
surveys us with a loving eye
and knows our needs before we pray,
from dawn until the close of day.

To you all glory, Trinity,
all laud, O Holy Unity;
to you on this new day we raise
our grateful hearts in songs of praise. Amen

Matins continues with the Benedictus, found on p. 31.

Friday Matins

Antiphon for psalms

Ordinary Time:
Be not far away, O God; *
    you are my strength; hasten to help me.

or

Create in me a clean heart, O God, *
    and renew a right spirit within me.

Advent:
Behold, our Savior will appear in the clouds of heaven, *
    with power and great glory, alleluia.

For Christmas, see p. 115.

From Ash Wednesday through the Third Week of Lent:
If we confess our sins, God is just and may be trusted to forgive our sins *
    and cleanse us from every kind of wrong.

From Lent IV until Maundy Thursday:
Create in me a clean heart, O God, *
    and renew a right spirit within me.

For Good Friday, see p. 151.

For Easter season, see p. 171.

Other antiphons are appointed according to the Saint or Season.

After the psalm(s) is said:

> Glory to God, Source of all being, Incarnate Word, and Holy Spirit, *
> as it was in the beginning, is now and will be forever. Amen.

The antiphon is repeated.

Matins continues with the First Lesson, followed by the canticle below, or as appointed.

Friday Matins Canticle

Ordinary Time: HABAKKUK 3:2-3, 13A, 17-19

> O God, I have heard of your renown; *
> I stand in awe of all you have made.

> In our own time make all your work known; *
> in our own time revive it,
> and in wrath may you remember mercy.

> O God, you came from Teman, *
> from Mount Paran, O Holy One.

> Your radiance overspreads the skies, *
> and your splendor fills the earth.

> You come forth to save your people; *
> you come to save your anointed.

> Although the figtree does not blossom, *
> the vines bear no fruit, the olive crop fails,
> the orchards yield no food;

> The flock is cut off from its fold, *
> and there are no cattle in the stalls,

> Yet I will exult in you, O Most High, *
> and rejoice in you, O God of my salvation,

> For you are my strength; *
> you make my feet nimble as a mountain goat's,
> and set me to range the heights.

God chose to be our mother in all things *
and in the fullness of time
took human form in the womb of Mary.

God, the perfect wisdom of all, *
chose to be arrayed in this humble place.

Christ came in our poor flesh *
to share a mother's care.

Our mothers bear us for pain and for death; *
our true mother, Jesus, bears us for joy and endless life.

Jesus carried us within him in love and travail, *
until the full time of his passion.

And when all was completed, and we were carried so for joy, *
still, all this could not satisfy the power of God's wonderful love.

All that we owe is redeemed in truly loving God, *
for the love of Christ works in us;
Christ is the one whom we love.

For Christmas, see p. 115.

Lent: ISAIAH 49:14-17

Zion says, God has forsaken me; *
my God has forgotten me.

Can a woman forget the infant at her breast, *
or a loving mother the child of her womb?

Even these forget, yet I will not forget you; *
your walls are always before my eyes;
I have engraved them on the palms of my hands.

Those who are to rebuild you make better speed
than those who pulled you down, *
while those who laid you waste depart.

For Easter season, see p. 172.

Matins continues with the Second Lesson, followed by the hymn below or as appointed.

Other hymns for Matins are according to the Saint or Season.
For seasonal hymns, see Sunday Matins.

Eternal glory of the sky,
blest hope of frail humanity,
from Mary you were humbly born,
yet reign the Sun of every morn.

Uplift us with your arm of might,
and let our hearts rise pure and bright;
in love and gratitude we pray
for all your blessings through the day.

The Daystar's rays are shining clear
and tell that day itself is here;
so, holy Light, illume the heart,
and to us all your gifts impart.

The faith that first must be possessed
root deep within our inmost breast,
and joyous hope in second place,
then holy love, your greatest grace.

To you all glory, Trinity,
all laud, O Holy Unity;
to you on this new day we raise
our grateful hearts in songs of praise. Amen.

Matins continues with the Benedictus, found on p. 31.

Saturday Matins

Antiphon for psalms:

Ordinary Time:

O praise God, who has exalted blessed Mary, *
and made her the joyful Mother of the Savior.

or

Praise God, who chose blessed Mary *
to be the mother of the Incarnate Word.

Advent:

Behold, our God comes, with all the saints together, *
and there will be in that day a great light, alleluia.

For Christmas, see p. 115.

From Ash Wednesday through the Third Week of Lent:

You must work out your own salvation in fear and trembling, *
for it is God who works in you, inspiring both the will and the deed.

From Lent IV until Maundy Thursday:

The sacrifice acceptable to God is a troubled spirit; *
a broken and contrite heart, O God, you will not despise.

For Holy Saturday, see p. 154.

For Easter season, see p. 171.

Other antiphons are appointed according to the Saint or Season.

At the end of the psalm(s) is said:

Glory to God, Source of all being, Incarnate Word, and Holy Spirit, *
as it was in the beginning, is now and will be forever. Amen.

The antiphon is repeated.

Matins continues with the (First) Lesson, followed by the canticle below, or as appointed.

Saturday Matins Canticle

Ordinary Time: SIRACH 39:13-16

Listen to me, my faithful children, *
and blossom like a rose growing by a stream of water.

Send out fragrance like incense
and sing a hymn of praise; *
bless our God for all creation.

Ascribe majesty to the Most High;
  give thanks with praise, *
    with harps, and with songs on your lips.

All God's works are good, *
  and whatever God commands will be done.

Advent: ADAPTED FROM JULIAN OF NORWICH

  Christ revealed our frailty and our falling, *
    our trespasses and our humiliations.

  Christ also revealed God's blessed power, *
    such blessed wisdom and love.

Christ protects us as tenderly and as sweetly
  when we are in greatest need; *
    Christ raises us in spirit
    and turns everything to glory and joy without ending.

God is the ground and the substance,
  the very essence of nature; *
    God is the true father and mother of natures.

  We are all bound to God by nature; *
    we are all bound to God by grace.

  And this grace is for all the world, *
    because it is our precious mother, Christ.

  For this fair nature was prepared by Christ *
    for the honor and nobility of all,
    and for the joy and bliss of salvation.

For Christmas, see p. 115.

Is it nothing to you, all you who pass by? *
Look and see if there is any sorrow like my sorrow,

Which was brought upon me, *
inflicted by God's fierce anger.

For these things I weep; my eyes flow with tears, *
for a comforter is far from me,
one to revive my courage.

Remember my affliction and my bitterness, *
wormwood and gall!

But this I call to mind *
and therefore I have hope:

The steadfast love of God never ceases; *
God's mercies never end.

They are new every morning; *
great is your faithfulness.

"God is my portion," says my soul, *
"therefore I will hope in God."

It is good that we should wait quietly *
for the coming of God's salvation.

For Easter season, see p. 172.

Matins continues with the Second Lesson, followed by the hymn below or as appointed.

Saturday Matins Hymn

Other hymns for Matins are according to the Saint or Season.
For seasonal hymns, see Sunday Matins.

The dawn has filled the east with light,
day over earth is gliding bright;
as shades of darkness fade away,
with strength renewed we greet the day.

For of a woman humbly born
into a world by evil torn,
the Maker's brightness shone ablaze
to guide us through our earthly days.

So let this day in joy pass on,
our hope spread like the early dawn,
our faith like noontide splendor glow,
our souls a gentle twilight know.

And when the world at last shall end,
and Christ appears as judge and friend,
may we be welcomed by that light
and dwell forever in God's sight.

To you all glory, Trinity,
all laud, O Holy Unity;
to you on this new day we raise
our grateful hearts in songs of praise. Amen.

Matins continues with the Benedictus below.

Antiphons during Ordinary Time:

Sunday: *As appointed in the Proper.*

Monday: Zechariah's tongue was freed, and he praised God; *
he was filled with the Holy Spirit and spoke this prophecy.

Tuesday: O God, you have raised up for us a mighty Savior, *
born of the house of your servant David.

Wednesday: You have saved us from our enemies, O God, *
from the hands of all who hate us.

Thursday: Set us free, O God, from the hands of our enemies, *
that we may worship you without fear.

Friday: In your tender compassion, O God, *
the dawn from on high shall break upon us.

Saturday: From this day forth, O Mary, *
all generations will count you blest.

Advent:

Monday and Thursday

Behold, our God will surely come and will not tarry *
and will be made manifest to all nations, alleluia.

Tuesday and Friday

Blow the trumpet in Zion, for the day of Messiah is near at hand; *
behold, God comes to save us, alleluia.

Wednesdays

God shall shine over you, O Jerusalem, *
and over you shall God's glory appear, alleluia.

Saturdays

God has been gracious to you, Mary;
you will conceive and bear a son, *
and you shall give him the name Jesus, alleluia.

On December 23

Behold, all things are fulfilled *
which were spoken by the angel to Mary, alleluia.

For Christmas, see p. 116.

Antiphons for Lent:

Ash Wednesday through the Third Week of Lent

Monday and Thursday

Put on all the armor that God provides, *
so that you may be able to stand firm against the devices of the devil.

Tuesday and Friday

Give yourselves wholly to prayer and entreaty; *
pray on every occasion in the power of the Spirit.

Wednesday and Saturday

You must work out your own salvation in fear and trembling, *
for it is God who works in you, inspiring both the will and the deed.

From Vespers of Lent IV to Maundy Thursday:

Monday and Thursday

As the time approached when Jesus was to be taken up to heaven, *
he set his face resolutely toward Jerusalem.

Tuesday and Friday

Jesus must be lifted up, *
as the serpent was lifted up by Moses in the wilderness.

Wednesday and Saturday

Christ died for us while we were yet sinners, *
and that is God's own proof of love toward us.

For the Triduum of Holy Week, see p. 148.

For Easter season, see p. 174.

Other antiphons are appointed according to the Saint or Season.

BENEDICTUS

Luke 1:68-79

Blest are you, O God of Israel; *
you have come to your people and set them free.

You have raised up for us a mighty Savior, *
born of the house of your servant David.

Through your holy prophets you promised of old,
that you would save us from our enemies, *
from the hands of all who hate us.

You promised to show mercy to our forebears *
and to remember your holy covenant.

This was the oath you swore to Sarah and Abraham, *
to set us free from the hands of our enemies,

Free to worship you without fear, *
holy and righteous before you all the days of our life.

And you, child, shall be called the prophet of the Most High, *
for you will go before the Promised One to prepare the way,

To give all people knowledge of salvation, *
by the forgiveness of their sins.

In the tender compassion of our God, *
the dawn from on high shall break upon us,

To shine on those who dwell in darkness and the shadow of death, *
and to guide our feet into the way of peace.

Glory to God, Source of all being, Incarnate Word, and Holy Spirit, *
as it was in the beginning, is now and will be forever. Amen.

The antiphon is repeated.

APOSTLES' CREED

On occasion the Creed may be omitted.

All recite together:

I believe in God, the Father almighty,
   creator of heaven and earth.

I believe in Jesus Christ, his only Son, our Lord.

He was conceived by the power of the Holy Spirit,
   and born of the Virgin Mary.

He suffered under Pontius Pilate,
   was crucified, died and was buried;

He descended to the dead.

On the third day he rose again;
   he ascended into heaven,
         and is seated at the right hand of the Father.

He will come again to judge the living and the dead.

I believe in the Holy Spirit,
   the holy catholic Church,
   the communion of saints,
   the forgiveness of sins,
   the resurrection of the body,
   and the life everlasting. Amen.

MATINS CLOSING PRAYERS

Officiant:	Lord, have mercy.		Kyrie eleison.
Response:	Christ, have mercy.	*or*	Christe eleison.
All:	Lord, have mercy.		Kyrie eleison.

All recite together:

Our Father in heaven,
　hallowed be your Name,
　your kingdom come,
　your will be done,
　　　on earth as in heaven.

Give us today our daily bread.

Forgive us our sins
　as we forgive those who sin against us.

Save us from the time of trial,
　and deliver us from evil.

SUFFRAGES

The Suffrages are recited on all Sundays and feasts.

A

v.　Help us, O God our Savior;
r.　deliver us and forgive us our sins.

v.　Look upon your congregation;
r.　give to your people the blessing of peace.

v.　Declare your glory among the nations;
r.　and your wonders among all peoples.

v.　Let not the oppressed be shamed and turned away;
r.　never forget the lives of your poor.

v.　Continue your loving-kindness to those who know you;
r.　and your favor to those who are true of heart.

v.　Satisfy us by your loving kindness in the morning;
r.　so shall we rejoice and be glad all the days of our life.

B

v.　Save your people, O God, and bless your inheritance;
r.　govern and uphold them now and always.

v.　Day by day we bless you;
r.　we praise your name forever.

v. O God, keep us without sin today;

r. have mercy on us, O God, have mercy.

v. Show us your love and mercy;

r. for we put our trust in you.

v. In you, O God, is our hope;

r. and we shall never hope in vain.

Matins Collects

For feasts, the Common Collect in the common of the day may be used.

A Collect for Sundays:

O God, you make us glad with the weekly remembrance of the glorious resurrection of our Savior: Give us this day such blessing through our worship of you, that the week to come may be spent in your favor; through our Redeemer, Jesus Christ. *Amen.*

A Collect for Fridays:

Almighty God, whose most dear One went not up to joy before suffering pain, and entered not into glory before being crucified: Mercifully grant that we, walking in the way of the cross, may find it none other than the way of life and peace; through Jesus Christ our Redeemer. *Amen.*

A Collect for Saturdays:

Almighty God, who after the creation of the world rested from all your works and sanctified a day of rest for all your creatures: Grant that we, putting away all earthly anxieties, may be duly prepared for the service of your sanctuary, and that our rest here upon earth may be a preparation for the eternal rest promised to your people in heaven; through our Savior Jesus Christ. *Amen.*

A Collect for the Renewal of Life:

O God, the Sovereign eternal, whose light divides the day from the night and turns the shadow of death into the morning: Drive far from us all wrong desires, incline our hearts to keep your law, and guide our feet into the way of peace; that, having done your will with cheerfulness during the day, we may, when night comes, rejoice to give you thanks; through Jesus Christ our Savior. *Amen.*

A Collect for Peace:

O God, the author of peace and lover of concord, to know you is eternal life and to serve you is perfect freedom: Defend us, your humble servants, in all assaults of our enemies; that we, surely trusting in your defense, may not fear the power of any adversaries; through the might of our Savior Jesus Christ. *Amen.*

A Collect for Grace:

O God in heaven, almighty and everlasting, you have brought us in safety to this new day: Preserve us with your mighty power, that we may not fall into sin nor be overcome by adversity; and in all we do, direct us to the fulfilling of your purpose; through Jesus Christ our Savior. *Amen.*

A Collect for Guidance:

O God, our Creator and Sustainer, in you we live and move and have our being: We humbly pray you so to guide and govern us by your Holy Spirit, that in all the cares and occupations of our life we may not forget you, but may remember that we are ever walking in your sight; through Jesus Christ our Savior. *Amen.*

A Collect for Morning:

O Christ, our true and only Light: Receive our morning prayers and illumine the secrets of our hearts with your healing goodness, that no evil desires may possess us who are made new in the light of your heavenly grace, through Jesus Christ our Savior. *Amen. (Gelasian Sacramentary)*

A Collect for Protection:

O God, our shield and armor of light, whom we adore with all the angelic host: Defend us from evil; watch over any who are in danger this day and give your angels charge over them; and grant that we may always rejoice in your heavenly protection and serve you bravely in the world; through Jesus Christ our Savior. *Amen.*

A Collect of Dedication:

Beloved God: As we offer ourselves to you this day, guide and stir us with your Holy Spirit, that we may become one body, one spirit in Jesus Christ our Savior. *Amen.*

Cantor:	Let us bless our God.
Response:	To God be thanks for ever.

Matins concludes with one of the following:

Officiant:

The grace of our Savior Jesus Christ, and the love of God, and the communion of the Holy Spirit, be with us all evermore. *Amen.*

May the God of hope fill us with all joy and peace in believing through the power of the Holy Spirit. *Amen.*

Glory to God, whose power working in us can do infinitely more than we can ask or imagine. Glory to God from generation to generation in the church, and in Christ Jesus for ever and ever. *Amen.*

Diurnum

Officiant:	O God, make speed to save us.
Response:	O God, make haste to help us.
All:	Glory to the holy and undivided Trinity, one God: as it was in the beginning, is now, and will be forever. Amen. Alleluia.

The Alleluia is omitted throughout Lent.

Then follows the hymn, psalm, and lesson, according to the day.

Sunday

Sunday Diurnum Hymn

> To God who orders all our days,
> we lift our hearts in grateful praise
> that God, with an almighty arm,
> would keep us free from any harm;
>
> Would keep our inmost conscience pure;
> our souls from folly would secure;
> would bid us check the pride of sense
> with due and holy abstinence.
>
> So we, when each new day is gone,
> and night in turn is drawing on,
> with conscience by the world unstained
> shall praise God's name for victory gained.
>
> Creator, let our prayers be heard
> through Jesus, your Eternal Word,
> who, with the Spirit and with you,
> shall live and reign all ages through. Amen.

To you, our Maker, thanks and praise
for this, the first and dawn of days:
the day when you, creation's spring,
did light and life from chaos bring;

The day when Christ rose from the grave,
new life for us that victory gave;
the day on which your Spirit came,
your gift to us, in wind and flame.

Creator, let our prayers be heard
through Jesus, your Eternal Word,
who, with the Spirit and with you,
shall live and reign all ages through. Amen.

Antiphons for Psalm

Ordinary Time:

How happy are they who dwell in your house; *
they will always be praising you.

or

You spread a table, O God, before me; *
you have anointed my head, and my cup is running over

Other antiphons for Sundays are appointed according to the Saint or Season.

Sunday Diurnum Psalm

Psalm 23, page 390.

After the psalm is said:

Glory to the holy and undivided Trinity, one God, *
as it was in the beginning, is now and will be forever. Amen.

The antiphon is repeated.

Other antiphons are appointed according to the Saint or Season.

Sunday Diurnum Lesson   1 TIMOTHY 1:1-7

Reader: To the Ruler of ages, immortal, invisible, the only God, be honor
and glory for ever. Amen.

Response: Thanks be to God.

Sunday Diurnum Respond

Cantor: Great are you, O God, and great is your power.

Response: Yes, and your wisdom is infinite.

The Office continues with the Closing Prayers in the Ordinary of Diurnum, p. 55.

MONDAY

Monday Diurnum Hymn

O come, Creator Spirit, come
and find within our hearts a home,
shed forth your grace within our breast,
and dwell with us, a welcome guest.

By every power, by heart and tongue,
by act and deed your praise be sung;
inflame with perfect love each sense,
that other souls may kindle thence.

Creator, let our prayers be heard
through Jesus, your Eternal Word,
who with the Spirit and with you
shall live and reign all ages through. Amen.

Antiphons for Psalm

Ordinary Time:

Happy are they who seek God with all their hearts, *
and always walk in the ways of the Holy One.

or

God shall ever watch over your going out and your coming in, *
from this time forth for ever more.

Advent:

The law was given by Moses, *
but grace and truth came by Jesus Christ.

For Christmas, see p. 117.

From Ash Wednesday through the Week of Lent III
> Turn my eyes from watching what is worthless; *
> give me life in your way.

From Lent IV through Holy Week:
> Take from me the way of lying; *
> let me find grace through your law.

For Easter season, see p. 176.

Other antiphons are appointed according to the Saint or Season.

Monday Diurnum Psalm

Psalm 119: 105-112, page 515.

After the psalm is said:
> Glory to the holy and undivided Trinity, one God, *
> as it was in the beginning, is now and will be forever. Amen.

The antiphon is repeated.

Monday Diurnum Lesson

Reader: God is love; those who abide in love abide in God,
            and God in them.

Response: Thanks be to God.

Monday Diurnum Respond

Response: Do not forsake me, O God of my salvation.

Advent:

Lesson and Respond   JEREMIAH 23:5-6

> The days are surely coming, says God, when I will raise up for David a
> righteous Branch, who shall execute justice and righteousness in the land.
> Then Judah will be saved and Israel will live in safety.

Response: Thanks be to God.

    v. Stir up your strength, and come to help us, O God of hosts.
    r. Show the light of your countenance, and we shall be saved.

For Christmas, see p. 117.

From Ash Wednesday through the Week of Lent III:

Lesson and Respond   ISAIAH 58:1

Shout aloud without restraint; lift up your voice like a trumpet. Call my people to account for their transgressions and the house of Jacob for their sins.

Response: Thanks be to God.

    v. God shall deliver you from the snare of the hunter,
    r. And from the deadly pestilence.

From Lent IV through Holy Week:

Lesson and Respond   ROMANS 3:23-24

All alike have sinned and are deprived of the divine splendor, and all are justified by God's free grace alone, through the act of liberation in the person of Jesus Christ.

Response: Thanks be to God.

    v. Deliver me from my sins, O God of my salvation,
    r. And my tongue shall sing of your righteousness

For Easter season, see p. 176.

The Office continues with the Closing Prayers in the Ordinary of Diurnum, p. 55.

TUESDAY

Tuesday Diurnum Hymn

> O God of truth, O God of might,
> you order time and change aright,
> and send the early morning ray,
> and light the glow of perfect day.
>
> From all transgression set us free
> and banish our iniquity,
> and while you keep the body whole,
> shed forth your peace upon the soul.
>
> Creator, let our prayers be heard
> through Jesus, your Eternal Word,
> who with the Spirit and with you,
> shall live and reign all ages through. Amen.

Antiphons for Psalm:

Ordinary Time:

> For with you, O God, is the well of life, *
> and in your light we see light.

or

> You are my refuge and shield, O God; *
> my hope is in your word.

Advent:

> Christ is our lawgiver; Christ is our Redeemer; *
> Christ our God will come and save us.

For Christmas, see p. 117.

From Ash Wednesday through the Week of Lent III:

> I have confessed my ways, and you answered me; *
> instruct me in your statutes.

From Lent IV through Holy Week:

> If my delight had not been in your law, *
> I should have perished in my affliction.

For Easter season, see p. 176.

Other antiphons are appointed according to the Saint or Season.

Tuesday Diurnum Psalm

Psalm 121, page 520.

After the psalm is said:

> Glory to the holy and undivided Trinity, one God, *
>   as it was in the beginning, is now and will be forever. Amen.

The antiphon is repeated.

Tuesday Diurnum Lesson

Reader: Owe no one anything except to love one another,
              for to love the other is to fulfill the law.

Response: Thanks be to God.

Tuesday Diurnum Respond

Reader: Incline my heart, O God, to walk in your ways.

Response: Turn my eyes from looking at vanities.

Advent:

Lesson and Respond   Isaiah 25:9

> It will be said on that day, Lo, this is our God for whom we have waited
> so that we might be saved; this is the One we have looked for; let us be
> glad and rejoice in the coming salvation of God.

Response: Thanks be to God.

> *v.* Show us your mercy, O God, and grant us your salvation.
> *r.* Remember us with the favor you have for your people.

For Christmas, see p. 117.

From Ash Wednesday through Lent III:

Lesson and Respond   JOEL 2:12-14

Yet even now, says God, return to me with all your heart; rend your hearts and not your garments. Return to me, your God, for I am gracious and merciful, slow to anger, and abounding in steadfast love.

Response: Thanks be to God.

v. You shall find refuge under God's wings;
r. You shall be covered with God's pinions.

From Lent IV through Holy Week:

Lesson and Respond   1 PETER 3:18

Christ suffered for our sins once for all, the righteous for the unrighteous, in order to bring us to God.

Response: Thanks be to God.

v. Jesus was pierced for our offenses; by his stripes we are healed.
r. The chastisement that he bore makes us whole.

For Easter season, see p. 176.

The Office continues with the Closing Prayers in the Ordinary of Diurnum, p. 55.

WEDNESDAY

Wednesday Diurnum Hymn

> O God, creation's secret force,
> yourself unmoved, all motion's source,
> you from the morn till evening's ray
> through all its changes guide the day.
>
> Grant us, when this short life is past,
> the glorious evening that shall last,
> that, by a holy death attained,
> eternal glory may be gained.

Creator, let our prayers be heard
through Jesus, your Eternal Word,
who, with the Spirit and with you,
shall live and reign all ages through. Amen.

Antiphons for Psalm

Ordinary Time:
Teach me, O God, the way of your statutes, *
and I shall keep it to the end.

or

Rescue me from those who oppress me, O God, *
and I will keep your commandments.

Advent:
Let us live in righteousness and godliness, *
as we look forward to the fulfilling of our hope in the coming
of our Savior.

For Christmas, see p. 117.

From Ash Wednesday through the Week of Lent III:
Turn my eyes from watching what is worthless; *
give me life in your way.

From Lent IV through Holy Week:
We sink down into the dust; our body cleaves to the ground. *
Rise up and help us, for the sake of your love.

For Easter, see p.176.

Other antiphons are appointed according to the Saint or Season.

Wednesday Diurnum Psalm

Psalm 126, page 523.

After the psalm is said:
Glory to the holy and undivided Trinity, one God, *
as it was in the beginning, is now and will be forever. Amen.

The antiphon is repeated.

Wednesday Diurnum Lesson JEREMIAH 17:1-4

Reader: Heal me, O God, that I may be healed; save me that I may be saved, for it is you whom I praise.

Response: Thanks be to God.

Wednesday Diurnum Respond

Reader: I said, O God, be gracious to me.

Response: Heal me, for I have sinned against you.

Advent:

Lesson and Respond ISAIAH 13:23, 14:1

The time draws very near and the days have not long to run. The Holy One will show compassion for Jacob and will once again make Israel God's choice.

Response: Thanks be to God.

v. God will shine forth upon you, O Jerusalem;
r. Then God's glory will be seen.

For Christmas, see p. 117.

From Ash Wednesday through Lent III:

Lesson and Respond ISAIAH 1:18-19

Though your sins are like scarlet, they shall be like snow; though they are red like crimson, they shall become like wool. If you are willing and obedient, you shall eat the good of the land.

Response: Thanks be to God.

v. God will send the angels to watch over you,
r. To keep you in all your ways.

From Lent IV through Holy Week:

Lesson and Respond   COLOSSIANS 1:21-22

You, who were once estranged and hostile in mind, doing evil deeds, Jesus has now reconciled in his body of flesh by his death, in order to present you holy and blameless and irreproachable before God.

Response: Thanks be to God.

v. With your blood you have redeemed us from every race and nation;

r. You have made us to be priests ever serving God.

For Easter season, see p. 177.

The Office continues with the Closing Prayers in the Ordinary of Diurnum, p. 55.

THURSDAY

Thursday Diurnum Hymn

> O Holy Spirit, guide and guest,
> with Maker and Redeemer blest,
> our long-resisting hearts inspire
> with spreading warmth and heavenly fire.
>
> Let flesh and heart and lips and mind
> send forth your word to humankind,
> and last light up our mortal frame,
> till others catch the living flame.
>
> Creator, let our prayers be heard
> through Jesus, your eternal Word,
> whom with the Spirit we adore,
> one only God for evermore. Amen.

Antiphons for Psalm

Ordinary Time:

Let Mount Zion be glad and the cities of Judah rejoice, *
because of your judgments, O God.

or

God has done great things for us, *
and we are glad indeed.

Advent:

The law was given by Moses, *
but grace and truth came by Jesus Christ.

For Christmas, see p. 117.

From Ash Wednesday through the Week of Lent III:

Turn my eyes from watching what is worthless; *
give me life in your way.

From Vespers of Lent IV to Maundy Thursday:

Take from me the way of lying; *
let me find grace through your law.

For Maundy Thursday, see p. 149.

For Easter season, see p. 176.

Thursday Diurnum Psalm

Psalm 119:105-112, page 515.

After the psalm is said:

Glory to the holy and undivided Trinity, one God, *
as it was in the beginning, is now and will be forever. Amen.

The antiphon is repeated.

Thursday Diurnum Lesson
2 THESSALONIANS 3:5

Reader: May your hearts be directed to the love of God and to the
steadfastness of Christ.

Response: Thanks be to God.

Thursday Diurnum Respond

Reader: Your word endures for ever, O God.

Response: Your truth remains from one generation to another.

Advent:

Lesson and Respond   JEREMIAH 23:5-6

The days are surely coming, says God, when I will raise up for David a righteous Branch, who shall execute justice and righteousness in the land. Then Judah will be saved and Israel will live in safety.

Response: Thanks be to God.

v. Stir up your strength, and come to help us, O God of hosts.
r. Show the light of your countenance, and we shall be saved.

For Christmas, see p. 117.

From Ash Wednesday through the Week of Lent III:

Lesson and Respond   ISAIAH 1:18-19

Though your sins are like scarlet, they shall be like snow; though they are red like crimson, they shall become like wool. If you are willing and obedient, you shall eat the good of the land.

Response: Thanks be to God.

v. God will send the angels to watch over you,
r. To keep you in all your ways.

From of Lent IV through Holy Week:

Lesson and Respond   ROMANS 3:23-24

All alike have sinned and are deprived of the divine splendor and all are justified by God's free grace alone, through the act of liberation in the person of Jesus Christ.

Response: Thanks be to God.

v. Deliver me from my sins, O God of my salvation,
r. And my tongue shall sing of your righteousness.

For Easter season, see p. 176.

The Office continues with the Closing Prayers in the Ordinary of Diurnum, p. 55

FRIDAY

Friday Diurnum Hymn

Almighty Ruler, God of Truth,
from whom the ordered seasons flow,
the splendor of the morning sun,
the noonday heat which you bestow.

Put out the flames of strife, and bid
the heat of passion to depart;
grant us the gift of health, O God,
for every one true peace of heart.

To you, Incarnate One, be praise;
to you, Creator, glory be:
to you, O Spirit, hymns we raise,
one God through all eternity. Amen.

Antiphons for Psalm

Ordinary Time:

Your hands have made me and fashioned me; *
give me understanding, that I may learn your commandments.

or

I have hoped for your salvation, O God, *
and I have fulfilled your Commandments.

Advent:

Christ is our lawgiver; Christ is our Redeemer; *
Christ our God will come and save us.

For Christmas, see p. 117.

From Ash Wednesday through the Week of Lent III:

I have confessed my ways, and you answered me; *
   instruct me in your statutes.

From Lent IV through Friday of Lent V:
   If my delight had not been in your law, *
   I should have perished in my affliction.

For Good Friday, see p. 152.

For Easter season, see p. 176.

Other antiphons are appointed according to the Saint or Season.

Friday Diurnum Psalm

Psalm 121, page 520.

After the psalm is said:
   Glory to the holy and undivided Trinity, one God, *
   as it was in the beginning, is now and will be forever. Amen.

The antiphon is repeated.

Friday Diurnum Lesson   1 CORINTHIANS 6:19B-20

Reader: Do you not know that your body is a temple of the Holy Spirit within
               you, which you have from God, and that you are not your own? For
               you were bought with a price; therefore glorify God in your body.

Response: Thanks be to God.

Friday Diurnum Respond

Reader: I will bless you, O God, at all times.

Response: Your praise shall ever be in my mouth.

Advent:

Lesson and Respond   ISAIAH 25:9

   It will be said on that day, Lo, this is our God for whom we have waited
   so that we might be saved; this is the One we have looked for; let us be
   glad and rejoice in the coming salvation of God.

Response: Thanks be to God.

   v. Show us your mercy, O God, and grant us your salvation.
   r. Remember us with the favor you have for your people.

From Ash Wednesday through the Week of Lent III:

Lesson and Respond   JOEL 2:12-14

Yet even now, says God, return to me with all your heart; rend your hearts and not your garments. Return to me, your God, for I am gracious and merciful, slow to anger, and abounding in steadfast love.

Response: Thanks be to God.

   v. You shall find refuge under God's wings;
   r. You shall be covered with God's pinions.

From Lent IV through Holy Week:

Lesson and Respond   1 PETER 3:18

Christ suffered for our sins once for all, the righteous for the unrighteous, in order to bring us to God.

Response: Thanks be to God.

   v. Jesus was pierced for our offenses; by his stripes we are healed.
   r. The chastisement that he bore makes us whole.

For Easter season, see p. 176.

The Office continues with the Closing Prayers in the Ordinary of Diurnum, p. 55.

SATURDAY

Saturday Diurnum Hymn

> Christ yesterday and Christ today,
> for all eternity the same,
> the image of our hidden God:
> Divine Redeemer is your name.
>
> Your truth remains from age to age,
> the saving truth for which you died,
> a cloud by day, a flame by night
> to go before us as our guide.

To you, Incarnate One, be praise;
to you, Creator, glory be;
to you, O Spirit, hymns we raise:
one God through all eternity. Amen

Antiphons for Psalm

Ordinary Time

You have rescued my soul from death, *
that I may walk before you in the light of the living.

or

Every day we glory in God, *
and we will praise your name for ever.

Advent:

Let us live in righteousness and godliness, *
as we look forward to the fulfilling of our hope in the coming
of our Savior.

From Ash Wednesday through the Week of Lent III:

I said, "I will confess my transgressions to God"; *
then you forgave me the guilt of my sin.

From Lent IV through Saturday of Lent V:

We sink down into the dust; our body cleaves to the ground. *
Rise up and help us, for the sake of your love.

For Holy Saturday, see p. 155.

For Easter season, see p. 177.

Other antiphons are appointed according to the Saint or Season.

Saturday Diurnum Psalm

Psalm 126, page 523.

After the psalm is said:

Glory to the holy and undivided Trinity, one God, *
as it was in the beginning, is now and will be forever. Amen.

The antiphon is repeated.

Saturday Diurnum Lesson

Reader: Help carry one another's burdens; in that way you will fulfill the law of Christ.

Response: Thanks be to God.

Saturday Diurnum Respond

Reader: How wonderful are your works, O God.

Response: In wisdom you have made them all.

Advent:

Lesson and Respond   Isaiah 13:23, 14:1

The time draws very near and the days have not long to run. The Holy One will show compassion for Jacob and will once again make Israel God's choice.

Response: Thanks be to God.

> *v.* God will shine forth upon you, O Jerusalem;
> *r.* Then God's glory will be seen.

For Christmas, see p. 117.

From Ash Wednesday through the Week of Lent III:

Lesson and Respond   Isaiah 1:18-19

Though your sins are like scarlet, they shall be like snow; though they are red like crimson, they shall become like wool. If you are willing and obedient, you shall eat the good of the land.

Response: Thanks be to God.

> *v.* God will send the angels to watch over you,
> *r.* To keep you in all your ways.

From Lent IV through Holy Week:

Lesson and Respond COLOSSIANS 1:21-22

You, who were once estranged and hostile in mind, doing evil deeds, Jesus has now reconciled in his body of flesh by his death, in order to present you holy and blameless and irreproachable before God.

Response: Thanks be to God.

v. With your blood you have redeemed us from every race and nation;
r. You have made us to be priests ever serving God.

For Easter season, see p. 177.

For Easter season, see p. 177.

The Office continues with the Closing Prayers in the Ordinary of Diurnum, below.

A period of intercessions may follow. If so, the response to close intercessions may be:

Officiant: O God, hear our prayer,

Response: And let our cry come to you.

DIURNUM CLOSING PRAYERS

Officiant:	Kyrie eleison,		Lord, have mercy,
Response:	Christe eleison,	*or*	Christ, have mercy,
All:	Kyrie eleison.		Lord, have mercy.

All recite together:

Our Father in heaven,
   hallowed be your Name,
   your kingdom come,
   your will be done,
      on earth as in heaven.

Give us today our daily bread.

Forgive us our sins
   as we forgive those who sin against us.

Save us from the time of trial,
   and deliver us from evil.

DIURNUM COLLECTS

The Officiant recites the collect appointed for the day, one of those below, or some other suitable collect. No commemoration is ever made at Diurnum.

Almighty God, send your Holy Spirit into our hearts, to direct and rule us according to your will, to comfort us in all our afflictions, to defend us from all error, and to lead us into all truth; through our Savior Jesus Christ. *Amen.*

Blessed Savior, at this hour you hung upon the cross, stretching out your loving arms: Grant that all the peoples of the earth may look to you and be saved; for your tender mercies' sake. *Amen.*

Almighty Savior, who at noonday called your servant Paul to be an apostle to the Gentiles: We pray you to illumine the world with the radiance of your glory, that all nations may come and worship you; for you live and reign for ever and ever. *Amen.*

O Jesus Christ, you said to your apostles, "Peace I give to you; my own peace I leave with you:" Regard not our sins, but the faith of your Church, and give to us the peace and unity of that heavenly City, where with the Creator and the Holy Spirit you live and reign, now and for ever. *Amen.*

Holy Wisdom, in your loving kindness you created and restored us when we were lost: Inspire us with your truth, that we may love you with our whole minds and run to you with open hearts; through Christ our Savior. *Amen.* *(Alcuin of York, Mass of Wisdom)*

O God, our rock and refuge: Keep us safe in your care and strengthen us with your grace, that we may pray faithfully to you and love one another boldly, following the example of Jesus; who with you and the Holy Spirit lives and reigns for ever and ever. *Amen.* *(Veronese Sacramentary)*

Reader:	Let us bless our God.
Response:	To God be thanks for ever.
Officiant:	May the souls of the departed, through the mercy of God, rest in peace.
Response:	Amen.

VESPERS

Officiant: O God, make speed to save us.

Response: O God, make haste to help us.

All: Glory to the holy and undivided Trinity, one God:
as it was in the beginning, is now, and will be forever. Amen.
Alleluia.

The Alleluia is omitted throughout Lent.

PHOS HILARON

O gracious Light,
    pure brightness of the everliving God in heaven,
        O Jesus Christ, holy and blessed!

Now as we come to the setting of the sun,
    and our eyes behold the vesper light,
        we sing your praises, O God:
        Holy and Undivided Trinity.

You are worthy at all times to be praised by happy voices,
    O Word of God, O Giver of Life,
        and to be glorified through all the worlds.

The Psalms of the Day

The St. Helena schedule of Psalm readings or one of the Prayer Book schedules may be used. See pp. 547 and 550 for instructions. The following antiphons may be used with the Psalms. The antiphons for Sunday through Friday begin on page 64.

Saturday Vespers

Antiphons for Psalms

Ordinary Time:

Other antiphons are appointed according to the Saint or Season.

Your Name, O God, is everlasting; *
your renown endures from age to age.

or

Give thanks to the God of heaven, *
whose mercy endures forever.

Advent:

Behold, the Messiah will come, the One who will save the earth; *
happy are those who are prepared to meet God, Alleluia.

For Christmas, see p. 118.

From Ash Wednesday through the Week of Lent III:

Run the great race of faith and take hold of eternal life, *
for to this you were called.

From Vespers of Lent IV until Maundy Thursday:

You strengthen me more and more; *
you enfold and comfort me.

For the Triduum of Holy Week, see p. 150.

For Easter season, see p. 177.

After the psalm(s) is said:

Glory to the holy and undivided Trinity, one God, *
as it was in the beginning, is now and will be forever. Amen.

The antiphon is repeated.

THE LESSONS

Vespers continues with the First Lesson, followed by the canticle below or as appointed.

Saturday Vespers Canticle

Antiphon

> You, O God, saw everything that you had made, *
> and behold, it was very good.

BENEDICTUS ES
(SONG OF THE THREE YOUNG MEN, 29:3-4)

> Glory to you, O God of our forebears; *
> you are worthy of praise, glory to you.

> Glory to you for the radiance of your holy Name; *
> we will praise you and highly exalt you for ever.

> Glory to you in the splendor of your temple; *
> on the throne of your majesty, glory to you.

> Glory to you, seated between the cherubim; *
> we will praise you and highly exalt you for ever.

> Glory to you, beholding the depths; *
> in the high vault of heaven, glory to you.

> Glory to you, holy and undivided Trinity; *
> we will praise you and highly exalt you for ever.

The antiphon is repeated.

Advent:

REVELATION 22:12-17

> "Behold, I am coming soon," says Jesus,*
> "and bringing my reward with me.

> I am the Alpha and the Omega, the first and the last,*
> the beginning and the end.

> I, Jesus, have sent my angel to you*
> with this testimony for all the churches:

> I am the root and the offspring of David;*
> I am the bright morning star."

"Come," say the Spirit and the Bride;*
   "Come!" let each hearer reply.

Come forward, you who are thirsty;*
   let those who desire take the water of life as a gift.

For Christmas, see p. 118.

Lent:

ISAIAH 63:11-16

Remember the days of old,*
   of Moses, God's servant:

Where are you, O God,*
   who brought out of the Nile the shepherds of your flock?

Where are you who endowed them with your Holy Spirit,*
   who by the right hand of Moses set to work with such glorious power?

Who divided the waters before them*
   to win for yourself ever lasting renown?

Who made them walk through the depths of the Red Sea,*
   as easily as a horse through the desert?

Look down from heaven, O God;*
   look down from your holy and glorious dwelling.

Where is your ardor, your might,*
   the yearning of your inmost heart?

Do not withhold your compassion from us,*
   for you are our Savior.

Though Abraham does not own us,*
   Israel does not acknowledge us,

you yourself, O God, are our Savior:*
   our Redeemer is your ancient Name.

For Easter, see p. 178.

Other canticles are appointed according to the Saint or Season.

Vespers continues with the Second Lesson, followed by the hymn below, or as appointed.

Saturday Vespers Hymn

Ordinary Time:

> O Trinity of blessed light,
> O Unity of graceful might,
> although the fiery sun departs,
> shine forth your love into our hearts.
>
> To you our morning song of praise,
> to you our evening prayer we raise;
> your glory daily we adore
> and supplicate for evermore.
>
> O God, who made all things to be,
> redeemer of humanity,
> sustainer, advocate and friend,
> to you be glory without end. Amen.

Seasonal Hymns for Vespers

The following hymns are appropriate throughout the week of their respective seasons.

Advent:

> Creator of the stars of night,
> creation's everlasting light,
> Jesus, Redeemer, save us all,
> and hear your people when we call.
>
> For, grieving over ancient ill
> that haunts our world with evil still,
> you brought the healing balm of grace
> to save the wounded human race.
>
> The son of Mary, you were born
> into a world with conflict torn;
> you came as Bridegroom to your Bride:
> the holy church, for which you died.
>
> Jesus, your name is throned above,
> your ever-glorious name of Love.
> In hope we glorify your reign,
> await your coming once again.

To God, who was before all days,
and is, and is to be always,
laud, honor, praise and glory be,
this Advent and eternally. Amen.

For Christmas, see p. 118.

Epiphany Season:

When all the world before you lay,
you rested on the seventh day;
your holy voice proclaimed it blest
and named it for the Sabbath rest.

Jesus, who death by death subdued
and on the cross our life renewed,
on Saturday his Sabbath kept,
as in the heart of earth he slept.

And we while here on earth do dwell
have our six days to labor well,
to shun all evil, seek the best,
until we reach our Sabbath rest.

Then that great Sunday shall ensue
when heaven and earth are made anew;
our flesh from sin will then be free
and put on immortality.

O God, who made all things to be,
redeemer of humanity,
sustainer, advocate and friend,
to you be glory without end. Amen.

Ash Wednesday Through the Week of Lent III:

The glory of these forty days
we celebrate with songs of praise;
for Christ, through whom all things were made,
for us has fasted and has prayed.

Alone and fasting, Moses saw
the loving God who gave the law;
Queen Esther, fasting, won the grace
to bring back favor to her race.

So Daniel, strong in mystic sight,
was rescued from the lions' might;
and John, the Bridegroom's friend, became
the herald of Messiah's name.

To strengthen mind and heart and hand,
God, grant that we may understand
the ways that you would have us fast,
and bless our souls with joy at last.

O holy God, blest One in Three,
through fasting, prayer and ministry,
we dedicate these forty days
and with creation sing your praise. Amen.

From Vespers of Lent IV through Holy Week:

This hymn is sung in its entirety during Holy Week. At other times marked verses may be omitted.

The royal banners forward move;
the cross shows forth the saving love
of Jesus who shared human breath
and gave his life to conquer death.

From the deep wound in Jesus' side,
by cruel lance torn open wide,
both blood and water flowing free
have washed away iniquity.

Fulfilled is all the psalmists told
in true prophetic songs of old;
to all the nations they made plain
that from a tree our God would reign.

O tree of beauty, tree of light,
O cross with Jesus' blood made bright,
wood chosen and designed to bear
the holy limbs suspended there.

Upon your arms so widely flung,
the weight of this world's ransom hung,
the price of all our wrongs to pay
and spoil the spoiler of the prey.

O cross, our one reliance, hail!
Through him, who died on you, avail
to give to sinners glad release,
to saints enjoyment of your peace.

To you, all holy Three in One,
let worthy homage now be done
by all whom through the cross you free
to live with you eternally. Amen.

For Easter season, see p. 173.

Vespers continues with the Magnificat, found on p. 84.

Sunday Vespers

Antiphons for psalms

Ordinary Time:

Ever since the world began, your throne has been established; *
you are from everlasting.

or

Praise for your mighty acts, O God; *
praise for your excellent greatness.

Other antiphons are appointed according to the Saint or Season.

After the psalm(s) is said:

Glory to the holy and undivided Trinity, one God, *
as it was in the beginning, is now and will be forever. Amen.

The antiphon is repeated.

Vespers continues with the First Lesson, followed by the canticle below or as appointed.

Sunday Vespers Canticle   COLOSSIANS 1:15-20

Christ is the image of the invisible God*
and has the primacy over all created things.

In Christ everything in heaven and on earth was created,*
not only things visible, but also the invisible orders:

thrones sovereignties,*
   authorities, and powers.

The whole universe has been created through Christ and for Christ.*
   And Christ exists before everything,
   in whom all things are held together.

Christ is moreover, the head of the body, the church.*
   Christ is its origin, the first to return from the dead,
   to be in all things alone supreme.

For in Christ the complete being of God,*
   by God's own choice, came to dwell.

Through Christ, God chose to reconcile the whole universe into one,*
   making peace through the shedding of blood upon the cross;

to reconcile all things, whether on earth or in heaven,*
   through Christ alone.

Vespers continues with the Second Lesson, followed by the hymn below, or as appointed.

Sunday Vespers Hymn

Ordinary Time:

Over the chaos of the empty waters,
hovered the Spirit, bringing forth creation;
so from the empty tomb the Second Adam
issued triumphant.

By the same Spirit we, regenerated
into the body of our risen Savior,
seek, through the power of the new creation,
life everlasting.

Maker of all things, Jesus Christ our Savior,
and Holy Spirit, Trinity eternal,
to you be glory, in both earth and heaven,
throughout the ages. Amen.

Other hymns for Vespers are according to the Saint or Season.
For seasonal hymns, see Saturday Vespers.

Vespers continues with the Magnificat, found on p. 84.

Monday Vespers

Antiphons for psalms

Ordinary Time:

> Put your trust in God and do good; *
> dwell in the land and feed on its riches.

or

> You are my stronghold, O God, and my haven, *
> my rock in whom I put my trust.

Other antiphons are appointed according to the Saint or Season.

Advent:

> I will wait upon my God and Savior, *
> and I will look for the One who draws near, Alleluia

For Christmas, see p. 118.

Ash Wednesday through the Week of Lent III:

> Use the present opportunity to the full, for these are evil days; *
> try to understand what the will of God is.

From Vespers of Lent IV until Maundy Thursday:

> In God I trust and will not be afraid, *
> for what can flesh do to me?

For Easter season, see p. 177.

After the psalm(s) is said:

> Glory to the holy and undivided Trinity, one God, *
> as it was in the beginning, is now and will be forever. Amen.

The antiphon is repeated.

Vespers continues with the First Lesson, followed by the canticle below or as appointed.

Monday Vespers Canticle

I CHRONICLES 29:10-13

Blessed are you, O God, O God of Israel, the Holy One,*
    from everlasting and to everlasting.

Yours, O God, are the greatness and the power,*
    the glory, the majesty, and the splendor.

For all that is in the heavens and on the earth is yours;*
    yours, O God, is the dominion, and you are exalted as head above all.

Both riches and honor from you proceed,*
    and over all that is you have dominion.

In your hand are power and strength;*
    fame and courage are likewise yours to give to all.

And now, our God, we give you thanks,*
    And praise the glory of your Name.

Advent:

ISAIAH 40:1-5

Comfort, O comfort my people, says your God.*
    Speak tenderly to Jerusalem.

A voice cries out: In the wilderness*
    prepare the way of the Holy One;
    make straight in the desert a highway for our God.

Every valley shall be lifted up,*
    and every mountain and hill made low.

The uneven ground shall become level,*
    and the rough places a plain.

Then the glory of the Holy One shall be revealed,
and all people shall see it together,*
    for the mouth of the Holy One has spoken.

For Christmas, see p. 118.

Lent:

SIRACH 42:15-19

By the word of God all works are made,*
  and all creation obeys God's will.

The sun in its brilliance looks down on every thing,*
  so the glory of God fills all creation.

Even to the angels has not been given*
  the power to tell the full story of God's marvels,

which the Almighty has established*
  so that the universe may stand firm in God's glory.

God fathoms the abyss and the hearts of people*
  and is versed in their intricate secrets.

For God possesses all knowledge*
  and observes the signs of all time.

God discloses the past and the future*
  and uncovers the traces of the world's mysteries.

For Easter season, see p. 178.

Vespers continues with the Second Lesson, followed by the hymn below, or as appointed.

Monday Vespers Hymn

Ordinary Time:

Creator of all time and space,
you made the earth our dwelling place,
the land and sea and firmament
defined by your divine intent.

Above terrestrial waters you
collect and send the rain and dew,
which temper heat with welcome showers
to nurture field and grain and flowers.

Upon our thirsty souls bestow
your gift of grace in endless flow,
so that we do not faint or fall
but grow in strength to heed your call.

Let faith discover heavenly light,
so shall its ray direct us right
in paths of loving service here
that in your will we persevere.

O God, who made all things to be,
redeemer of humanity,
sustainer, advocate and friend,
to you be glory without end. Amen.

Other hymns for Vespers are according to the Saint or Season.
For seasonal hymns, see Saturday Vepsers.

Vespers continues with the Magnificat, found on p. 84.

Tuesday Vespers

Antiphons for psalms

Ordinary Time:
> For you, O God, have proved us; *
> you have tried us as silver is tried.

or

> Lead me in your truth and teach me; *
> O God of my salvation.

Advent:
> Behold, the Savior will come, the Savior of the whole earth, *
> who will take away the yoke of our captivity, Alleluia.

For Christmas, see p. 118.

Ash Wednesday through the Week of Lent III:
> Be on your guard, stand firm in the faith, act bravely; *
> do every thing with love.

From Vespers of Lent IV until Maundy Thursday:
> God is on my side to help me; *
> I will triumph over those who hate me.

For Easter season, see p. 177.

After the psalm(s) is said:

Glory to the holy and undivided Trinity, one God, *
as it was in the beginning, is now and will be forever. Amen.

The antiphon is repeated.

Vespers continues with the First Lesson, followed by the canticle below or as appointed.

Tuesday Vespers Canticle   Tobit 13:1-6

Blessed be God, who lives for ever,*
the whose reign endures throughout all ages.

Declare God's praise before the nations,*
you who are the children of Israel;

For if God has scattered you among them,*
there too God has shown power and greatness.

Extol God before all the living;*
the Holy One is our God for ever.

Though you may suffer for your iniquities,*
God will take pity on you.

God will gather you from every nation,*
wherever you have been scattered.

If you return to God with all your heart and all your soul,*
always behaving honestly,

then God will return to you*
and be hidden from you no longer.

Advent:

Song of Songs 2:8-13

The voice of my beloved!
Look, he comes, leaping upon the mountains,*
bounding over the hills.

Make haste, my beloved; come, like a gazelle,*
or a young stag upon the mountain of spices!

70   VESPERS

My beloved speaks and says to me:
"Arise, my love, my fair one, and come away."*
   Make haste, my beloved!

For Christmas, see p. 118.

Lent:

HOSEA 6:1-3

Come, let us return to God,*
   who has torn us and will heal us.

God has struck us and will bind up our wounds;*
   after two days revive us,

On the third day restore us,*
   that in God's presence we may live.

Let us humble ourselves; let us strive to know God,*
   whose justice dawns like morning light,
   and its dawning is as sure as the sunrise.

It will come to us like a shower,*
   like spring rains that water the earth.

For Easter season, see p. 178.

Vespers continues with the Second Lesson, followed by the hymn below, or as appointed.

Tuesday Vespers Hymn

During the Seasons of Epiphany and Pentecost (Ordinary Time):
   Earth's mighty Maker, your command
   raised from the sea the solid land,
   and set to ocean's rage a bound,
   to make secure the fertile ground,

   So that the soil might herbage yield
   and blossoms fair to deck the field,
   and golden fruit and harvest bear,
   and pleasant food for all prepare.

Let every soul your law obey,
and keep from every evil way,
that we may seek with eager will
our Savior's precepts to fulfill:

To love with heart and mind and soul
you, whom both heaven and earth extol;
and, as we strive your will to do,
to love you in our neighbor too.

O God, who made all things to be,
redeemer of humanity,
sustainer, advocate and friend,
to you be glory without end. Amen.

Other hymns for Vespers are according to the Saint or Season.
For seasonal hymns, see Saturday Vespers.

Vespers continues with the Magnificat, found on p. 84.

Wednesday Vespers

Antiphons for psalms

Ordinary Time:

You will not abandon your people, O God, *
nor will you forsake your own.

or

Be my strong rock, O God, a castle to keep me safe; *
you are my crag and my stronghold.

Advent:

Behold, the Messiah will come, the One who will save the earth; *
happy are those who are prepared to meet God, Alleluia.

For Christmas, see p. 118.

From Ash Wednesday through the Week of Lent III:

Run the great race of faith and take hold of eternal life, *
for to this you were called.

From Vespers of Lent IV until Maundy Thursday:
> You strengthen me more and more; *
>> you enfold and com fort me.

For Easter season, see p. 177.

Other antiphons are appointed according to the Saint or Season.

After the psalm (s) is said:
> Glory to the holy and undivided Trinity, one God, *
>> as it was in the beginning, is now and will be forever. Amen.

The antiphon is repeated.

Vespers continues with the First Lesson, followed by the canticle below or as appointed.

Wednesday Vespers Canticle   JUDITH 16:13-16

> O God, you are great, you are glorious,*
>> wonderfully strong, unconquerable.

> May your whole creation serve you,*
>> for you spoke and things came into being.

> You sent your breath and they were put together,*
>> and no one can resist your voice.

> Should mountains topple to mingle with the waves,
> should rocks melt like wax before your face,*
>> to those who fear you, you would still be merciful.

> A sweet-smelling sacrifice is a little thing indeed,*
>> but whoever fears God is great for ever.

Advent:

REVELATION 22:12-17

> "Behold, I am coming soon," says Jesus,*
>> "and bringing my reward with me.

> I am the Alpha and the Omega, the first and the last,*
>> the beginning and the end.

> I, Jesus, have sent my angel to you*
>> with this testimony for all the churches:

I am the root and the offspring of David;*
  I am the bright morning star."

"Come," say the Spirit and the Bride;*
  "Come!" let each hearer reply.

Come forward, you who are thirsty;*
  let those who desire take the water of life as a gift.

For Christmas, see p. 118.

Lent:

Isaiah 63:11-16

Remember the days of old,*
  of Moses, God's servant:

Where are you, O God,*
  who brought out of the Nile the shepherds of your flock?

Where are you who endowed them with your Holy Spirit,*
  who by the right hand of Moses set to work with such glorious power?

Who divided the waters before them*
  to win for yourself ever lasting renown?

Who made them walk through the depths of the Red Sea,*
  as easily as a horse through the desert?

Look down from heaven, O God;*
  look down from your holy and glorious dwelling.

Where is your ardor, your might,*
  the yearning of your inmost heart?

Do not withhold your compassion from us,*
  for you are our Savior.

Though Abraham does not own us,*
  Israel does not acknowledge us,

you yourself, O God, are our Savior:*
  our Redeemer is your ancient Name.

For Easter season, see p. 179.

Vespers continues with the Second Lesson, followed by the hymn below, or as appointed.

Wednesday Vespers Hymn

Ordinary Time:

> Almighty God, your will supreme,
> made ocean's womb with life to teem;
> each kind adapting to its need
> the means to breathe and move and feed;
>
> Appointing fishes in the sea
> and birds in open air to be,
> that beast and fish and bird might find
> the proper dwelling for its kind.
>
> Grant that your servants by the tide
> of blood and water purified,
> may not in guilt your love betray,
> nor lose your life of endless day;
>
> But in that wellspring here reborn,
> may we in hope await the morn
> when, by your grace our service done,
> we rise triumphant with the Sun.
>
> O God, who made all things to be,
> redeemer of humanity,
> sustainer, advocate and friend,
> to you be glory without end. Amen.

Other hymns for Vespers are according to the Saint or Season.
For seasonal hymns, see Saturday Vespers.

Vespers continues with the Magnificat, found on p. 84.

Thursday Vespers

Antiphons for psalms

Ordinary Time:

> Who can declare your mighty acts, O God, *
> or show forth all your praise?

or

> Sing praises to our God, sing praises, *
> and speak of all God's marvelous works.

Advent:
I will wait upon my God and Savior, *
and I will look for the One who draws near, Alleluia

For Christmas, see p. 118.

From Ash Wednesday through the Week of Lent III:
Use the present opportunity to the full, for these are evil days; *
try to understand what the will of God is.

From Vespers of Lent IV until Maundy Thursday:
In God I trust and will not be afraid, *
for what can flesh do to me?

For Maundy Thursday, see p. 150.

For Easter season, see p. 177.

After the psalm(s) is said:
Glory to the holy and undivided Trinity, one God, *
as it was in the beginning, is now and will be forever. Amen.

The antiphon is repeated.

Vespers continues with the First Lesson, followed by the canticle below or as appointed.

Thursday Vespers Canticle   JEREMIAH 31:10-14

Hear the word of God,*
and proclaim it to the coasts afar off, saying

"The One who scattered Israel will gather them again;*
and watch over them as a shepherd watches the flock."

For God has ransomed Jacob;*
and has redeemed them from the hands of the enemy.

They will come and shout for joy upon the heights of Zion,*
and be radiant because of the goodness of God.

Because of the grain and the wine and the oil,*
  because of the increase of their flocks and their herds,

their life will be like a watered garden,*
  and they will not languish any more.

Maidens will rejoice in the dance;*
  young men and old will disport themselves.

I will turn their mourning into gladness,*
  and satisfy my people with my goodness.

Advent:

ISAIAH 40:1-5

Comfort, O comfort my people, says your God.*
  Speak tenderly to Jerusalem.

A voice cries out: In the wilderness*
  prepare the way of the Holy One;
  make straight in the desert a highway for our God.

Every valley shall be lifted up,*
  and every mountain and hill made low.

The uneven ground shall become level,*
  and the rough places a plain.

Then the glory of the Holy One shall be revealed,
  and all people shall see it together,*
  for the mouth of the Holy One has spoken.

For Christmas, see p. 118.

Lent:

SIRACH 42:15-19

By the word of God all works are made,*
  and all creation obeys God's will.

The sun in its brilliance looks down on everything,*
  so the glory of God fills all creation.

Even to the angels has not been given*
  the power to tell the full story of God's marvels,

which the Almighty has established*
  so that the universe may stand firm in God's glory.

God fathoms the abyss and the hearts of people*
   and is versed in their intricate secrets.

For God possesses all knowledge*
   and observes the signs of all time.

God discloses the past and the future*
   and uncovers the traces of the world's mysteries.

For Easter season, see p. 178.

Vespers continues with the Second Lesson, followed by the hymn below, or as appointed.

Thursday Vespers Hymn

Ordinary Time:

O God, your hand has spread the sky
and all its shining stars on high,
and, painting it with fiery light,
made it so splendid and so bright.

You, when the fourth day had begun,
caused earth to circle round the sun,
and gave the moon its ordered change,
the stars their brilliance and their range.

You then divided night from day
that each may have its proper sway;
you gathered them in monthly rounds
to give to time determined bounds.

To you, creation's God, we pray
our lives to order day by day,
that joy and sorrow, good and ill,
may all be used to do your will.

O God, who made all things to be,
redeemer of humanity,
sustainer, advocate and friend,
to you be glory without end. Amen.

Other hymns for Vespers are according to the Saint or Season.
For seasonal hymns, see Saturday Vespers.

Vespers continues with the Magnificat, found on p. 84.

Friday Vespers

Antiphons for psalms

Ordinary Time:

You are our Savior, our God, *
and the Rock of our salvation.

or

Where can I go from your Spirit? *
Where can I flee from your presence?

Advent:

Behold, the Savior will come, the Savior of the whole earth, *
who will take away the yoke of our captivity, Alleluia.

For Christmas, see p. 118.

From Ash Wednesday through the Third Week of Lent:

Be on your guard, stand firm in the faith, act bravely; *
do every thing with love.

From Vespers of Lent IV through Thursday of Lent V:

God is on my side to help me; *
I will triumph over those who hate me.

For Good Friday, see p. 153.

For Easter season, see p. 177.

Other antiphons are appointed according to the Saint or Season.

After the psalm(s) is said:

Glory to the holy and undivided Trinity, one God, *
as it was in the beginning, is now and will be forever. Amen.

The antiphon is repeated.

Vespers continues with the First Lesson, followed by the canticle below or as appointed.

Friday Vespers Canticle

PRAYER OF AZARIAH 1:3-12

Blessed are you, O God of our forebears;*
  your name is worthy of praise and glorious for ever.

You are just in all your deeds and true in all your works;*
  straight are your paths, and all your judgments are righteous.

For we sinned and broke your law in rebellion against you;*
  we did not do what you commanded us for our good.

In all the hardships that have come to us,*
  your love has been steadfast.

Accept our pledge of faithfulness,*
  for no shame will come to those who put their trust in you.

Now we will follow you with our whole heart and fear you;*
  we seek your presence. Do not put us to shame,

but deal with us in your compassion,*
  and in the greatness of your mercy.

Advent:

SONG OF SONGS 2:8-13

The voice of my beloved!
  Look, he comes, leaping upon the mountains,*
    bounding over the hills.

  Make haste, my beloved; come, like a gazelle,*
    or a young stag upon the mountain of spices!

My beloved speaks and says to me:
  "Arise, my love, my fair one, and come away."*
    Make haste, my beloved!

For Christmas, see p. 118.

HOSEA 6:13

Come, let us return to God,*
  who has torn us and will heal us.

God has struck us and will bind up our wounds;*
  after two days revive us,

On the third day restore us,*
  that in God's presence we may live.

Let us humble ourselves; let us strive to know God,*
  whose justice dawns like morning light,
  and its dawning is as sure as the sunrise.

It will come to us like a shower,*
  like spring rains that water the earth.

For Easter season, see p. 178.

Vespers continues with the Second Lesson, followed by the hymn below, or as appointed.

Friday Vespers Hymn

Ordinary Time:

Divine Creator, from your throne
you order all things, God alone;
by your decree the teeming earth
to life of every kind gave birth.

The varied forms that fill the land,
instinct with life at your command,
have been entrusted to our care
that all this bounteous earth may share.

Forgive us, then, as we confess
our flawed response, our selfishness;
lest, overcome by greed, we lose
the way that you would have us choose.

In heaven your endless joys bestow,
and grant your gift of grace below;
from chains of strife our souls release,
make fast the gentle bonds of peace.

O God, who made all things to be,
redeemer of humanity,
sustainer, advocate and friend
to you be glory without end. Amen.

Other hymns for Vespers are according to the Saint or Season.
For seasonl hymns, see Saturday Vespers.

Vespers continues with the Magnificat, below.

Antiphons during Ordinary Time:

Sunday: *As appointed in the Proper.*

Monday: My spirit rejoices, O God my Savior,*
             to proclaim your greatness.

Tuesday: All generations will call me blessed,*
             for you have looked with favor on your lowly servant.

Wednesday: Almighty One, you did great things for me,*
             and holy is your Name.

Thursday: O God, you have lifted up the lowly *
             and filled the hungry with good things.

Friday: Show mercy, O God, on those who fear you *
             in every generation.

Saturday: *As appointed in the Proper.*

Other antiphons are appointed according to the Saint or Season.

Advent:

Monday and Thursday
> Behold, now comes the fullness of time, *
> at which God sent forth the Savior into the world, Alleluia.

Tuesday and Friday
> Lift up your eyes, O Jerusalem, and see the power of the Holy One. *
> Behold, the Savior comes to loose you from your chains, Alleluia.

Wednesday
> Behold, the glory of God will be revealed, *
> and all people will see it, Alleluia.

For Christmas, see p. 119.

From Ash Wednesday through the Third Week of Lent:

Monday and Thursday
>You must be made new in mind and spirit,
>and put on the new nature of God's creating, *
>   which shows itself in a just and devout life.

Tuesday and Friday
>Forgetting what is behind, and reaching out for that which lies ahead, *
>   press toward the goal to win the prize in Christ Jesus.

Wednesday
>Stand firm and immovable, and work for God always, *
>   since you know that in God your labor cannot be lost.

From Vespers of Lent IV until Maundy Thursday:

Monday and Thursday
>I am the light of the world; *
>   my followers shall not wander in the dark, but shall have the light of life.

Tuesday and Friday
>While you have light, trust to the light, *
>   and so become children of light.

Wednesday
>Those who live by the truth come to the light, *
>   so that it may be clearly seen that God is in all they do.

For the Triduum of Holy Week, see p. 148.

For Easter season, see p. 181.
(On Saturdays the antiphon on the Magnificat is in the Proper of the Sunday following.)

MAGNIFICAT

My soul proclaims your greatness, O God;
   my spirit rejoices in you, my Savior, *
     for you have looked with favor on your lowly servant.

   From this day all generations will call me blessed; *
    you, the Almighty, have done great things for me,
    and holy is your Name.

   You have mercy on those who fear you *
    from generation to generation.

   You, O God, have shown strength with your arm, *
    and scattered the proud in their conceit,

   Casting down the mighty from their thrones *
    and lifting up the lowly.

   You have filled the hungry with good things *
    and sent the rich away empty.

   You have come to the help of your servant Israel, *
    for you have remembered your promise of mercy,

   The promise made to our forebears, *
    to Abraham, Sarah and their children for ever.

   Glory to the holy and undivided Trinity, one God, *
    as it was in the beginning, is now and will be forever. Amen.

The antiphon is repeated.

VESPERS CLOSING PRAYERS

Officiant:	Kyrie eleison,		Lord, have mercy,
Response:	Christe eleison,	*or*	Christ, have mercy,
All:	Kyrie eleison.		Lord, have mercy.

All recite together:
   Our Father in heaven,
    hallowed be your Name,
    your kingdom come,
    your will be done,
      on earth as in heaven.

Give us today our daily bread.

Forgive us our sins
   as we forgive those who sin against us.

Save us from the time of trial,
   and deliver us from evil.

SUFFRAGES

The Suffrages are recited on all Saturdays and Sundays and on all major feasts.

A

   v. Show us your mercy, O God,
   r. and grant us your salvation.

   v. Clothe your ministers with righteousness;
   r. let your people sing with joy.

   v. Give peace, O God, in all the world,
   r. for only in you can we live in safety.

   v. O God, keep this nation under your care,
   r. and guide us in the way of justice and truth.

   v. Let your way be known upon earth,
   r. your saving health among all nations.

   v. Let not the needy, O God, be forgotten,
   r. nor the hope of the poor be taken away.

   v. Create in us clean hearts, O God,
   r. and sustain us with your Holy Spirit.

or

B

   That this evening may be holy, good and peaceful,
     We entreat you, O God.

   That your holy angels may lead us in paths of peace and goodwill,
     We entreat you, O God.

   That we may be pardoned and forgiven for our sins and offenses,
     We entreat you, O God.

   That there may be peace to your Church and to the whole world,
     We entreat you, O God.

That we may depart this life in your faith and fear, and not be condemned before the great judgment seat of Christ,
We entreat you, O God.

That we may be bound together by your Holy Spirit in the communion of [_____ and] all your saints, entrusting one another and all our life to Christ,
We entreat you, O God.

VESPERS COLLECTS

The collect at Vespers is the Collect of the Day, one of those below, or some other suitable collect. On major feasts, the collect for the feast is always used.

A Collect for Sundays:

Almighty God, our Savior Jesus Christ triumphed over the powers of death and prepared a place for us in the new Jerusalem: Grant that we, who have this day given thanks for the Resurrection, may praise you in that City of which Christ is the light; and where you live and reign for ever and ever. *Amen.*

A Collect for Fridays:

O Jesus Christ, by your death you took away the sting of death: Grant to us your servants so to follow in faith where you have led the way, that at the last we may fall asleep peacefully in you and wake up in your likeness; for your tender mercies' sake. *Amen.*

A Collect for Saturdays:

O God, the source of eternal light: Shed forth your unending day upon us who watch for you, that our lips may praise you, our lives may bless you, and our worship on the morrow give you glory; through Jesus Christ our Savior. *Amen.*

A Collect for Peace:

Most holy God, the source of all good desires, all right judgments, and all just works: Give to us your servants that peace which the world cannot give, so that our minds may be fixed on the doing of your will, and that we, being delivered from the fear of all enemies, may live in peace and quietness; through the mercies of Christ Jesus our Savior. *Amen.*

A Collect for the Presence of Christ:

O Jesus, stay with us, for evening is at hand and the day is past; be our companion in the way, kindle our hearts, and awaken hope, that we may know you as you are revealed in Scripture and the breaking of bread. Grant this for the sake of your love. *Amen.*

A Collect for Trust:

Most loving God, whose will it is for us to give thanks for all things, to fear nothing but the loss of you, and to cast our care on you who care for us: Preserve us from faithless fears and worldly anxieties, that no clouds of this mortal life may hide from us the light of that love which is immortal, and which you have manifested to us in Jesus Christ; who lives and reigns with you in the unity of the Holy Spirit, one God, now and for ever. *Amen.*

Other Collects:

O holy God, whom the whole heavens adore: Let the whole earth also worship you, all nations obey you, all tongues confess and bless you, and men and women everywhere love you and serve you in peace; through Jesus Christ our Savior. *Amen.*

O God, you manifest in your servants the signs of your presence: Send forth upon us the Spirit of love, that in companionship with one another your abounding grace may increase among us; through Jesus Christ our Savior. *Amen.*

Almighty God, you have given us grace at this time with one accord to make our common supplication to you; and you have promised that when two or three are gathered together in the name of Jesus, you will be in the midst of them: Fulfill now, O God, our desires and petitions as may be best for us; granting us in this world knowledge of your truth, and in the age to come life everlasting. *Amen.*

Sun of Righteousness, so gloriously risen: Shine in our hearts as we celebrate our redemption, that we may see the way to our eternal home; where you live and reign, one holy and undivided Trinity, now and for ever. *Amen.*

Officiant: Let us bless our God.
Response: To God be thanks for ever.

Vespers concludes with one of the following:
Officiant:

The grace of our Savior Jesus Christ, and the love of God, and the communion of the Holy Spirit, be with us all evermore. *Amen.*

May the God of hope fill us with all joy and peace in believing through the power of the Holy Spirit. *Amen.*

Glory to God, whose power working in us can do infinitely more than we can ask or imagine. Glory to God from generation to generation in the church, and in Christ Jesus for ever and ever. *Amen.*

COMPLINE

Officiant: May God Almighty grant us a peaceful night and a perfect end.
Response: Amen.

Officiant: Our help is in the name of the Holy One.
Response: The maker of heaven and earth.

Officiant: Let us confess our sins to God.

A brief period of silence follows.

CONFESSION

Both the Confession and the Absolution are said by all.

1. I confess to God Almighty, before the whole company of heaven and you,
    that I have sinned in thought, word, deed, and omission, by my own fault.
    Therefore, I pray God Almighty to have mercy on me, forgive me all my
    sins, and bring me to everlasting life.

    The almighty and merciful God grant us pardon, absolution, and remis-
    sion of all our sins. *Amen.*

or

2. I confess to Almighty God, to blessed Mary, and to all the saints in heaven
    and on earth, that I have sinned in thought, word, deed, and omission, by
    my own fault. Therefore I now ask blessed Mary, all the saints, and espe-
    cially you who are gathered here, to pray for me to our God.

    The almighty and merciful God grant us pardon, absolution, and remis-
    sion of all our sins. *Amen.*

or

3. Almighty God, we have sinned against you, through our own fault, in
    thought, and word, and deed, and in what we have left undone. For the
    sake of our Savior Jesus Christ, forgive us all our offenses, and grant that
    we may serve you in newness of life, to the glory of your Name. *Amen.*

    May the Almighty God grant us forgiveness of all our sins, and the grace
    and comfort of the Holy Spirit. *Amen.*

HYMN

To you before the close of day,
Creator of the world, we pray
that in your mercy you will be
our guardian and security.

By you forgiven, may we bestow
your pardoning love on friend and foe;
and with the world, ourselves and you,
before we sleep, your peace renew.

To you our souls we now commend,
that to our bodies you may send
sleep that will us more vigorous make
to serve you, God, when we awake.

Creator, grant that this be done
through Jesus, your Beloved One,
who, with the Spirit and with you,
shall live and reign all ages through. Amen.

Alternative hymn for Compline:

O Christ, you are the dawn and day
before whom darkest night gives way,
illuminating all our sight,
the source of faith and light of light.

To you, O blessed One, we pray,
defend us at the close of day;
may all our rest be found in you,
and peace be with us all night through.

O Christ, remember us, we cry,
who now as mortals live and die;
you, our souls' keeper and our friend,
be present with us to the end.

Creator, grant that this be done
through Jesus, your Beloved One,
who, with the Spirit and with you,
shall live and reign all ages through. Amen.

THE PSALM OF THE DAY

Sunday
Psalm 134, page 527

Monday and Thursday
Psalm 4, page 371

Tuesday and Friday
Psalm 31, page 398

Wednesday and Saturday
Psalm 91, page 474

At the end of the Psalm is said:

Glory to the holy and undivided Trinity, one God *
   as it was in the beginning, is now and will be forever. Amen.

COMPLINE LESSONS

Sunday   HEBREWS 13:20-21

Reader: May the God of peace, who brought again from the dead our
              Savior Jesus, the great shepherd of the sheep, by the blood of the
              eternal covenant, equip you with everything good that you may
              do God's will, working in you that which is pleasing in God's
              sight, through Jesus Christ; to whom be glory for ever and ever.

Response: Thanks be to God.

Monday and Thursday   MATTHEW 11:28-30

Reader: Come to me, all who labor and are heavy-laden, and I will give
              you rest. Take my yoke upon you, and learn from me; for I am
              gentle and lowly in heart, and you will find rest for your souls.
              For my yoke is easy, and my burden is light.

Response: Thanks be to God.

Tuesday and Friday   1 Peter 5:8-9

Reader: Be sober, be watchful. Your adversary the devil prowls around like a
              roaring lion, seeking someone to devour. Resist, firm in your faith.

Response: *Thanks be to God.*

Wednesday and Saturday   Jeremiah 14:9, 22

Reader: You, Christ, are in the midst of us, and we are called by your
              Name: do not forsake us, O God.

Response: Thanks be to God.

*On occasion a reading from a life of the saints or about a feast day to follow may be read
instead of a lesson above. Such a reading may end with:*

   v.   We praise you, O God, for all your saints.
   r.   And give thanks for their witness.

or
   v.   We praise you, O God, for the witness of the church.
   r.   And give thanks for its ministry.

Compline Respond

Officiant: Into your hands, O God, I commend my spirit.
              (*Eastertide*: Alleluia, alleluia)

Response: For you have redeemed me, O God of truth.
              (*Eastertide*: Alleluia, alleluia)

Compline Closing Prayers

Officiant:	Kyrie eleison,		Lord, have mercy,
Response:	Christe eleison,	*or*	Christ, have mercy,
All:	Kyrie eleison.		Lord, have mercy.

All recite together:

Our Father in heaven,
hallowed be your Name,
your kingdom come,
your will be done,
on earth as in heaven.

Give us today our daily bread.

Forgive us our sins
as we forgive those who sin against us.

Save us from the time of trial,
and deliver us from evil.

COMPLINE COLLECTS

The Officiant recites one of the following:

Visit this place, O God, and drive far from it all snares of the enemy; let your holy angels dwell with us to preserve us in peace; and let your blessing be upon us always; through Jesus Christ our Savior. *Amen.*

Be our light in the darkness, O God, and in your great mercy defend us from all perils and dangers of this night; for the love of our Savior Jesus Christ. *Amen.*

Be present, O merciful God, and protect us through the hours of this night, so that we who are wearied by the changes and chances of this life may rest in your eternal changelessness; through Jesus Christ our Savior. *Amen.*

Look down, O God, from your heavenly throne, and illumine this night with your celestial brightness; that by night as by day your people may glorify your holy Name; through Jesus Christ our Savior. *Amen.*

Keep watch, dear God, with those who work, or watch, or weep this night, and give your angels charge over those who sleep. Tend the sick, O Christ; give rest to the weary, bless the dying, soothe the suffering, pity the afflicted, shield the joyous; and all for your love's sake. *Amen.*

O God, the life of all who live, the light of the faithful, the strength of those who labor, and the repose of the dead: We thank you for the blessings of the day that is past, and humbly ask for your protection through the coming night. Bring us in safety to the morning hours; through the One who died and rose again for us, our Savior Jesus Christ. *Amen.*

O God, your unfailing providence sustains the world we live in and the life we live: Watch over those, both night and day, who work while others sleep, and grant that we may never forget that our common life depends upon each other's toil; through Jesus Christ our Savior. *Amen.*

Saturday:

We give you thanks, O God, for revealing Jesus Christ to us by the light of the Resurrection: Grant that as we sing your glory at the close of this day, our joy may abound in the morning as we celebrate the Paschal mystery; through our Savior Jesus Christ. *Amen.*

NUNC DIMITTIS

Antiphon

Guide us waking, O God, and guard us sleeping, * that awake we may watch with Christ, and asleep we may rest in peace. (*Eastertide*: Alleluia.)

O God, you now have set your servant free *
 to go in peace as you have promised;

For these eyes of mine have seen the Savior, *
 whom you have prepared for all the world to see:

A Light to enlighten the nations, *
 and the glory of your people Israel.

Glory to the holy and undivided Trinity, one God, *
 as it was in the beginning, is now and will be forever. Amen.

The antiphon is repeated.

A brief period of silence follows.

Compline closes with the following:
Officiant: May the divine help remain with us always.
Response: And with those who are absent from us.

The Season of Advent

The First Sunday of Advent

First Vespers (Saturday evening)

Antiphon on psalms for preceding Saturday Vespers

Come, everyone who thirsts, come to the waters; *
seek the One who wills to be found.

The antiphon on the Magnificat is below, as appointed for Year A, B, or C.

Antiphon on New Testament canticles

Year A

Keep awake, for you do not know *
on what day your Savior is to come.

Year B

Evening or midnight, cockcrow or early dawn, *
if the Savior comes suddenly, you must not be a sleep.

Year C

Then they will see the Promised One *
coming in a cloud with great power and glory.

Collect

Almighty God, give us grace to cast away the works of darkness, and put
on the armor of light, now in the time of this mortal life, in which Jesus
Christ came to visit us in great humility; that in the last day, when Christ
shall come again in glorious majesty to judge both the living and the dead,
we may rise to the life immortal; through the One who lives and reigns
with you and the Holy Spirit, one God, now and for ever. *Amen.*

Matins

Antiphon on Psalter

> In that day the mountains will drop down new wine, *
> and the hills will flow with milk and honey.

Diurnum

Antiphon on Psalter

> Behold, there comes a mighty prophet, *
> who alone renews Jerusalem.

Lesson and Respond   ROMANS 13:11

> It is time for you to wake out of sleep, for deliverance is nearer to us now
> than it was when we first believed.

Response: Thanks be to God.

> *v.* Come and save us, O God of hosts.
> *r.* Show the light of your countenance, and we shall be saved.

The Office continues with the Closing Prayers in the Ordinary of Diurnum, p. 55.

Second Vespers

Antiphon on Psalter

> Be joyful, O daughter of Zion, *
> and exceedingly glad, O daughter of Jerusalem.

All else as in First Vespers, above.

The Second Sunday of Advent

Antiphon on New Testament canticles

Year A

> Prove your repentance by the fruit it bears, and do not presume to say yourselves: *
> We have Abraham for our father.

Year B

> John the Baptist appeared in the wilderness, *
> proclaiming a baptism of repentance for the forgiveness of sins.

Year C

> Clear a path, prepare a highway for our Savior, *
> and all creation shall see the salvation of God.

Collect

> Merciful God, who sent your messengers the prophets to preach repentance and prepare the way for our salvation: Give us grace to heed their warnings and forsake our sins, that we may greet with joy the coming of Jesus Christ our Redeemer; who lives and reigns with you and the Holy Spirit, one God, now and for ever. *Amen.*

Matins

Antiphon on Psalter

> John was dressed in a rough coat of camel's hair, *
> and he fed on locusts and wild honey.

Diurnum

Antiphon on Psalter

> Elijah has already come, *
> and they have worked their will up on him.

Lesson and Respond   2 Peter 3:9

> It is not that God is slow in fulfilling the promise, as some suppose, but that God is very patient with you, because it is not Love's will for any to be lost, but for all to come to repentance.

Response: Thanks be to God.

    v. Come and save us, O God of hosts.

    r. Show the light of your countenance, and we shall be saved.

The Office continues with the Closing Prayers in the Ordinary of Diurnum, p .55.

Vespers

Antiphon on Psalter

    The one who comes after me is mightier than I, *
        the one whose sandals I am not worthy to remove.

THE THIRD SUNDAY OF ADVENT

Antiphon on New Testament canticles

Year A

    Go and tell John what you hear and see: *
        the blind recover their sight, the dead are raised to life;
        the poor are hearing the Good News.

Year B

    There appeared a man sent from God, whose name was John; *
        he came as a witness to the light.

Year C

    There is one to come who is mightier than I, *
        and who will baptize you with the Holy Spirit.

Collect

    Stir up your power, O Holy One, and with great might come among us;
    and, because we are sorely hindered by our sins, let your bountiful grace
    and mercy speedily help and deliver us; through Jesus Christ our Savior, to
    whom with you and the Holy Spirit be honor and glory, now and for ever.
    Amen.

Matins

Antiphon on Psalter

All the prophets and the Law foretold things to come until John appeared, *
and John is the destined Elijah, if you will but accept it.

Diurnum

Antiphon on Psalter

The Spirit of God is upon me, *
and has sent me to preach the Good News to the poor.

Lesson and Respond   2 Peter 3:9

The One who is to come is near; have no anxiety, but in everything make
your requests known to God in prayer and petition, with thanksgiving.

Response: Thanks be to God.

v. Come and save us, O God of hosts.
r. Show the light of your countenance, and we shall be saved.

The Office continues with the Closing Prayers in the Ordinary of Diurnum, p. 55.

Vespers

Antiphon on Psalter

He is far more than a prophet. *
Never has there appeared on earth a mother's son greater than
John the Baptist.

THE GREAT O ANTIPHONS

To be used with the Magnificat on the following days

December 16

O Wisdom, you came out of the mouth of the Most High, *
and reach to the earth's farthest bounds, mightily and sweetly ordering
all things: come and teach us the way of prudence.

December 17

O Adonai, and leader of the house of Israel, *
you appeared in the bush to Moses in a flame of fire, and gave him the
law on Sinai: come and redeem us with an outstretched arm.

December 18

O Root of Jesse, you stand for an ensign of the people; *
before you, the rulers will shut their mouths; and for you the nations
will seek: come and deliver us, and do not tarry.

December 19

O Key of David, and Scepter of the house of Israel, *
you open and no one can close, and you close and no one can open:
come and bring the prisoners out of the prison, those who sit in darkness
and the shadow of death.

December 20

O Day spring, Brightness of the light everlasting, *
and Sun of Righteousness: come and enlighten those who sit in darkness
and the shadow of death.

December 21

O Ruler of nations, and their desire, *
the Cornerstone, uniting both in one: come and save humankind, whom
you formed of clay.

December 22

O Emmanuel, our Sovereign and lawgiver, *
the desire of all nations and their salvation: come and save us, O Christ
our God.

December 23

O Virgin of virgins, how shall this be? *
For neither before you was there any seen like you, nor shall there be
after. Daughters of Jerusalem, why do you marvel at me? The thing
which you behold is a divine mystery.

THE FOURTH SUNDAY OF ADVENT

If this Sunday falls on December 23, the Office is of Advent IV with the exception of the antiphon on the Benedictus. See p. 30.

If this Sunday falls on December 24, Matins and Diurnum are as on Christmas Eve, p. 103, except the collect, which is of Advent IV below. Vespers is I Vespers of Christmas, p. 108.

Collect

Purify our conscience, Almighty God, by your daily visitation, that at the coming of Jesus Christ, we may be found to be mansions prepared for Love: we pray this in the name of the One who became incarnate for our sake, and who lives and reigns with you in the unity of the Holy Spirit, one God, for ever and ever. *Amen.*

Matins

Antiphon on Psalter

The Holy Spirit will come upon you, Mary; *
fear not, you shall bear in your womb the Holy Child of God.

Antiphon on Benedictus, unless it is December 23 (See p. 30)

Year A

Do not be afraid to take Mary home with you as your wife. *
It is by the power of the Holy Spirit that she has conceived this child.

Year B

The angel Gabriel was sent from God to a town in Galilee called Nazareth, *
to a maiden whose name was Mary.

Year C

How happy is she who has had faith *
that God's promise would be fulfilled!

Antiphon on Benedictus on December 23

Behold, all things are fulfilled *
which were spoken by the angel to Mary, Alleluia.

Diurnum

Antiphon on Psalter

> From Zion comes the One who is to reign over all; *
> the one whose name shall be called Emmanuel.

Lesson and Respond HEBREWS 10:7,10

> In the scroll of the book it is written of me: "See, God, I have come to do
> your will, O God." And it is by God's will that we have been sanctified
> through the offering of the body of Jesus Christ once for all.

Response: Thanks be to God.

> *v.* Come and save us, O God of hosts.
> *r.* Show the light of your countenance, and we shall be saved.

The Office continues with the Closing Prayers in the Ordinary of Diurnum, p. 55.

Vespers

Antiphon on Psalter

> Come, O Jesus, in peace; visit us with your salvation, *
> that we may rejoice before you with a perfect heart.

The Season of Christmas

December 24, commonly called Christmas Eve

Matins

Invitatory: Alleluia, our Savior is at hand:
Response: O come, let us worship, alleluia.

Antiphon on Psalter

O Judah and Jerusalem, be not dismayed. *
   Tomorrow go forth and the Savior will be with you, alleluia.

The hymn as in Advent, p. 6.

Antiphon on Benedictus

The Savior of the world shall arise as the sun *
   and shall come down in to the maiden's womb as the showers up
   on the grass, Alleluia.

Collect

O God, you come into our darkness to shine with the brightness of the
one true Light: Grant that we, who have known the mystery of that Light
on earth, may also enjoy the Light of Christ perfectly in heaven; through
the One who lives and reigns with you and the Holy Spirit, one God, in
glory everlasting. *Amen.*

Diurnum

Antiphon on Psalter

Tomorrow the iniquity of the earth will be blotted out, *
   and the Savior of the world will reign over us.

The Good News is about the Holy Child of God who, having taken human nature, was a descendant of David.

Response: Thanks be to God.

> *v.* You shall know this day your Savior will come,
> *r.* And in the morning you shall see the glory of God.

The Office continues with the Closing Prayers in the Ordinary of Diurnum, p. 55.

Christmastide begins on December 24 with I Vespers of Christmas and ends after Diurnum on January 5.

Matins

Invitatory: Alleluia, unto us a child is born:
Response: O come, let us worship, alleluia.

Antiphon on Psalter

The Word was made flesh and dwelt among us, *
and we beheld the glory of God, alleluia.

Canticle   ISAIAH 9:2-7

The people who walked in darkness have seen a great light; *
those who lived in a land of deep darkness,
upon them has light shined.

You have increased their joy; *
they rejoice before you as with joy at the harvest.

For you have shattered the yoke of their burden *
and removed the rod that lay across their shoulders.

For to us a child is born, *
to us a child is given.

The government rests upon the shoulders *
of the one whose name will be called *
Wonderful Counselor, Mighty God,
Everlasting One, the Holy One of Peace.

Of the increase of divine authority and of peace, *
    there shall be no end.

Upon the throne of David and over Israel *
    shall be established justice and righteousness,

From this time onward and for evermore; *
    the zeal of the Mighty One will do this.

Hymn at Matins

> From lands that see the sun arise,
> to earth's remotest boundaries,
> we celebrate the Savior's birth,
> who brought redemption to our earth.
>
> The Christ, who made all things to be,
> was born in great humility,
> that, liberating flesh by flesh,
> creation thus might live afresh.
>
> The crib and straw the baby bore,
> the cattle he did not abhor;
> our frail humanity sufficed
> the child of Mary, Jesus Christ.
>
> The heavenly chorus filled the sky;
> the angels sang to God on high,
> and to the shepherds, watching lone,
> they made creation's Shepherd known.
>
> O Jesus, to your name we raise
> our grateful hymn of love and praise;
> to our Creator homage bring,
> as by the Spirit here we sing. Amen.

Antiphon on Benedictus

While all things were in quiet silence, and that night was in the midst
of its swift course, *
    your almighty Word, O God, leaped down out of
    your royal throne, Alleluia.

The Benedictus will be found in the Ordinary of Matins, p. 31.

Collect

On ferias following Christmas Day and until the Second Sunday after Christmas, the following collect is used.

Almighty God, you have poured upon us the new light of your Incarnate Word: Grant that this light, enkindled in our hearts, may shine forth in our lives; through Jesus Christ our Savior, who lives and reigns with you, in the unity of the Holy Spirit, one God, now and for ever. *Amen.*

Diurnum

Antiphon on Psalter

All the ends of the world have seen *
the salvation of our God, Alleluia.

Lesson and Respond

Hebrews 1:1-3

Long ago God spoke to our ancestors in many and various ways by the prophets, but in these last days God has spoken to us by Christ, the only-begotten One, whom God appointed heir of all things, through whom God also created the worlds. Christ is the reflection of God's glory and the exact imprint of God's very being, and all things are sustained by the powerful word of Christ.

Response: Thanks be to God.

v. The Word was made flesh, alleluia, alleluia.
r. And dwelt among us, alleluia, alleluia.

The Office continues with the Closing Prayers in the Ordinary of Diurnum, p. 55.

Vespers

Antiphons on Psalter

Unto the godly there rises up light in the darkness; *
God is merciful, loving, and righteous.

Canticle at Vespers 1 JOHN 4:7-11

Beloved, let us love one another, *
for love is of God.

Whoever does not love, does not know God,*
for God is Love.

In this the love of God was revealed among us,*
that God sent the Incarnate Word into the world,
so that we might live through Jesus Christ.

In this is love, not that we loved God, but that God loved us*
and sent the Incarnate Word, that sins might be forgiven.

Beloved, since God loved us so much,*
we ought also to love one another.

For if we love one another, God abides in us,*
and God's love will be perfected in us.

Hymn at Vespers

Jesus, Love's sole-begotten One,
with God before time was begun,
divine Word from eternity:
through you all that is came to be.

Although by prophets long foretold,
who through the Spirit could behold
salvation's plan, all but a few
were unprepared to welcome you.

No room was found in house or home
when Mary's blessed hour had come,
yet angels did your birth proclaim
and shepherds to your cradle came.

And we, who by your precious blood
from sin redeemed, are marked for God,
on this the day that saw your birth,
sing the new song of ransomed earth.

O Jesus, to your name we raise
our grateful hymn of love and praise;
to our Creator homage bring,
as by the Spirit here we sing. Amen.

Antiphon on Magnificat

> Today the Christ is born; today has a savior appeared;
> today on earth angels are singing, archangels rejoicing. *
>> Today the righteous exult and say: Glory to God in the highest, Alleluia.

The Magnificat will be found in the Ordinary of Vespers, p. 84.

First Vespers of Christmas

Antiphons on Psalter

> The God of Peace is highly exalted, *
> for whose countenance all the earth longs.

or

> The Sovereign of Peace is highly exalted, *
> exceeding all the rulers of the whole earth.

or

> The days were completed for Mary, *
> that she should bring forth her firstborn son.

or

> Know that the reign of God is near; *
> truly I say to you, it will not tarry.

or

> Lift up your heads, *
> for behold, your redemption draws near.

The hymn is in the Ordinary of Christmas, p. 118.

Collect

> Almighty God, you have given your only-begotten One to take on our
> nature, and to be born this day of blessed Mary: Grant that we, who have
> been born again and made your children by adoption and grace, may daily
> be renewed by your Holy Spirit; through our Savior Jesus Christ, to whom
> with you and the same Spirit be honor and glory, now and for ever. *Amen.*

Antiphon on Magnificat at Vespers

When the sun has risen in the heavens, you shall see the Most Holy One,
proceeding from the Godhead, *
    as a bridegroom out of his chamber.

CHRISTMAS DAY: THE NATIVITY OF JESUS CHRIST

Matins

Invitatory: Alleluia, unto us a child is born:
Response: O come, let us worship, alleluia.

Antiphon on the Invitatory

Alleluia, unto us a Child is born: *
    O come, let us worship, Alleluia.

Antiphons for psalms

Whom did you behold, O shepherds? Tell us, declare to us the tidings,
on earth who has appeared: *
    We saw the newborn infant, and the choir of angels,
    praising God together, Alleluia, Alleluia.

or

She who labored has borne the Monarch whose name is everlasting;
she has the joy of a mother who was chosen by God: *
    before her none has been seen like her, nor will there be after, Alleluia.

or

The angel said to the shepherds: Behold, I bring you joyful tidings; *
    for to you is born this day the world's Redeemer, alleluia.

or

There was with the angel a multitude of the heavenly host,
praising God and saying, *
    Glory to God in the highest, and peace to all people on earth, Alleluia.

or

Unto us this day a Child is born, a Child is given, *
    whose name shall be the mighty God, Alleluia, alleluia.

The canticle is the Te Deum, p. 213.

The hymn and antiphon on the Benedictus are in the Ordinary of Christmas, pp. 118.

The collect is on p. 108.

Diurnum

All as in the Ordinary of Christmas, p. 117.

The Office continues with the Closing Prayers in the Ordinary of Diurnum, p. 55.

Vespers of Christmas Day

The antiphons on the psalms are as at Matins, p. 109.

The canticle is the Benedicite, p. 120.

The hymn and antiphon on the Magnificat are in the Ordinary of Christmas, pp. 118.

The collect is on p. 108.

THE FIRST SUNDAY AFTER CHRISTMAS

If Christmas Day falls on a Sunday, this Sunday is not observed.

All as in the Ordinary of Christmas except:

Matins

The canticle is the Te Deum, p. 213.

Collect

Almighty God, you have poured upon us the new light of your Incarnate Word: Grant that this light, enkindled in our hearts, may shine forth in our lives; through Jesus Christ our Savior, who lives and reigns with you, in the unity of the Holy Spirit, one God, now and for ever. *Amen.*

This collect is also used on ferias falling during the week that follows.

Diurnum

Lesson and Respond   GALATIANS 4:4-5

In the fullness of time, God sent forth the Incarnate One, born of a woman, born under the Law, to deliver from the Law those who were subject to it, so that we might receive our status as adopted heirs.

Response: Thanks be to God.

  v. The Word was made flesh, alleluia, alleluia.
  r. And dwelt among us, alleluia, alleluia.

The Office continues with the Closing Prayers in the Ordinary of Diurnum, p. 55.

Vespers

All as in the Ordinary of Christmas, pp. 118-119, except the canticle, which is the Dignus es, p. 220.

If the preceding Saturday is a feast day, the antiphon on the Magnificat is for that feast; if it is a feria, the antiphon is that in the Ordinary of Christmas, p. 119.

JANUARY 1: THE HOLY NAME OF JESUS

Matins

The antiphons on the psalms are as on Christmas Day, p. 109.
The canticle is the Te Deum, p. 213.

Hymn at Matins

> A maiden, blest by God and mild,
> conceived by grace a firstborn child;
> yet she, as earthly bride unknown,
> could call that newborn babe her own.
>
> From Mary's chaste and holy womb
> into the world has Jesus come,
> and God, on that young woman's breast,
> was nurtured and took human rest.
>
> Jesus shall all dominion hold,
> as Gabriel's message had foretold;
> ordained before the world's design
> to be both human and divine.
>
> To him the angel gave the name
> of Jesus, Savior, for he came
> to shepherd home through Jordan's wave
> the wand'ring flock he died to save.

O Jesus, to your name we raise
our grateful hymn of love and praise;
to our Creator homage bring,
as by the Spirit here we sing. Amen.

Antiphon on Benedictus

You shall call his name Jesus *
   for there is no other name given among mortals by which
   we must be saved, Alleluia.

Collect

Eternal God, you gave to your Incarnate One the Holy Name of Jesus to
be the sign of our salvation: Plant in every heart, we pray, the love of Jesus
Christ who is the Savior of the world; who lives and reigns with you and
the Holy Spirit, one God, in glory everlasting. *Amen.*

Diurnum

Antiphon on psalms

From the rising of the sun even to its going down, *
   may God's name be praised, alleluia.

Lesson and Respond   ROMANS 1:5
Through Jesus we received grace and apostleship, so that this name will be
known among all nations.

Response: Thanks be to God.

   v. Blessed be the Holy Name of God, alleluia, alleluia.
   r. From this time forth for evermore, alleluia, alleluia.

The Office continues with the Closing Prayers in the Ordinary of Diurnum, p. 55.

Vespers

The antiphons on the psalms are as on Christmas Day, p. 109.

The Second Sunday after Christmas

If January 6 falls on a Sunday, this Sunday is not observed.
All as in the Ordinary of Christmas, pp.115-119, except as below.

Matins

The canticle is the Te Deum, p. 213.

Antiphon on Benedictus

Joseph, being warned by a dream, withdrew to the region of Galilee. *
There he settled in a town called Nazareth.

Collect

O God, who wonderfully created, and yet more wonderfully restored, the
dignity of human nature: Grant that we may share the divine life of Jesus
Christ, the One who in humility shared our humanity; and who lives and
reigns with you in the unity of the Holy Spirit, one God, now and for
ever. *Amen.*

This collect is also used on ferias during the week that follows until Vespers of Epiphany.

Dirunum

Lesson and Respond   EPHESIANS 1:4

God chose us in Christ before the world began, to be holy and blameless
in God's sight, to be full of love.

Response: Thanks be to God.

  v. The Word was made flesh, alleluia, alleluia.
  r. And dwelt among us, alleluia, alleluia.

The Office continues with the Closing Prayers in the Ordinary of Diurnum, p. 55.

Vespers

The hymn is in the Ordinary of Christmas, p. 118.

Antiphon on Magnificat

As Jesus grew up, he advanced in wisdom *
and in favor with God and with people.

THE ORDINARY OF CHRISTMAS

Christmastide begins on December 24 with Vespers of Christmas and ends after Diurnum on January 5

MATINS

Invitatory: Alleluia, unto us a child is born:
Response: O come, let us worship, alleluia.

Antiphon on Psalter

The Word was made flesh and dwelt among us, *
and we beheld the glory of God, alleluia.

Canticle

ISAIAH 9:2-7

The people who walked in darkness have seen a great light; *
those who lived in a land of deep darkness,
upon them has light shined.

You have increased their joy; *
they rejoice before you as with joy at the harvest.

For you have shattered the yoke of their burden *
and removed the rod that lay across their shoulders.

For to us a child is born, *
to us a child is given.

The government rests upon the shoulders *
of the one whose name will be called *
Wonderful Counselor, Mighty God,
Everlasting One, the Holy One of Peace.

Of the increase of divine authority and of peace, *
there shall be no end.

Upon the throne of David and over Israel *
    shall be established justice and righteousness,

From this time onward and for evermore; *
    the zeal of the Mighty One will do this.

Hymn at Matins

From lands that see the sun arise,
to earth's remotest boundaries,
we celebrate the Savior's birth,
who brought redemption to our earth.

The Christ, who made all things to be,
was born in great humility,
that, liberating flesh by flesh,
creation thus might live afresh.

The crib and straw the baby bore,
the cattle he did not abhor;
our frail humanity sufficed
the child of Mary, Jesus Christ.

The heavenly chorus filled the sky;
the angels sang to God on high,
and to the shepherds, watching lone,
they made creation's Shepherd known.

O Jesus, to your name we raise
our grateful hymn of love and praise;
to our Creator homage bring,
as by the Spirit here we sing. Amen.

Antiphon on Benedictus

While all things were in quiet silence, and that night was in the midst
of its swift course, *
    your almighty Word, O God, leaped down out of your royal throne,
    Alleluia.

The Benedictus will be found in the Ordinary of Matins, p. 31.

Collect

On ferias(open days) following Christmas Day and until the Second Sunday after Christmas, the following collect is used.

Almighty God, you have poured upon us the new light of your Incarnate Word: Grant that this light, enkindled in our hearts, may shine forth in our lives; through Jesus Christ our Savior, who lives and reigns with you, in the unity of the Holy Spirit, one God, now and for ever. *Amen.*

DIURNUM

Antiphon on Psalter

All the ends of the world have seen *
    the salvation of our God, Alleluia.

Lesson and Respond   HEBREWS 1:1-3

Long ago God spoke to our ancestors in many and various ways by the prophets, but in these last days God has spoken to us by Christ, the only-begotten One, whom God appointed heir of all things, through whom God also created the worlds. Christ is the reflection of God's glory and the exact imprint of God's very being, and all things are sustained by the powerful word of Christ.

Response: Thanks be to God.

    v. The Word was made flesh, alleluia, alleluia.
    r. And dwelt among us, alleluia, alleluia.

The Office continues with the Closing Prayers in the Ordinary of Diurnum, p. 55.

VESPERS

Antiphon on Psalter

Unto the godly there rises up light in the darkness;*
God is merciful, loving, and righteous.

Canticle at Vespers   1 JOHN 4:7-11

Beloved, let us love one another,*
for love is of God.

Whoever does not love, does not know God,*
for God is Love.

In this the love of God was revealed among us,*
that God sent the Incarnate Word into the world,
so that we might live through Jesus Christ.

In this is love, not that we loved God, but that God loved us*
and sent the Incarnate Word, that sins might be forgiven.

Beloved, since God loved us so much,*
we ought also to love one another.

For if we love one another, God abides in us,*
and God's love will be perfected in us.

Hymn at Vespers

Jesus, Love's sole-begotten One,
with God before time was begun,
divine Word from eternity:
through you all that is came to be.

Although by prophets long foretold,
who through the Spirit could behold
salvation's plan, all but a few
were unprepared to welcome you.

No room was found in house or home
when Mary's blessed hour had come,
yet angels did your birth proclaim
and shepherds to your cradle came.

And we, who by your precious blood
from sin redeemed, are marked for God,
on this the day that saw your birth,
sing the new song of ransomed earth.

O Jesus, to your name we raise
our grateful hymn of love and praise;
to our Creator homage bring,
as by the Spirit here we sing. Amen.

Antiphon on Magnificat

Today the Christ is born; today has a savior appeared;
today on earth angels are singing, archangels rejoicing. *
' Today the righteous exult and say: Glory to God in the highest, Alleluia.

The Magnificat will be found in the Ordinary of Vespers, p. 84.

On some feast days in Christmas and other seasons the following canticle is sung as appointed.

(SONG OF THE THREE YOUNG MEN, 35-65)

Glorify God; sing praise and give honor for ever.

All you works of God in the high vault of heaven: *
    You angels and all powers of God,

Sun and moon and stars of the sky, *
    Every shower of rain and fall of dew,

Winter and summer, frost and cold *
    Ice and sleet, nights and days,

O shining light and enfolding dark, *
    Storm clouds and thunderbolts:

Glorify God; sing praise and give honor for ever.

Let the earth glorify the God: *
    All mountains and hills and all that grows on the earth,

O springs of water, seas and streams, *
    O whales and all that move in the waters,

All birds of the air and beasts of the wild, *
    And all you flocks and herds:

Glorify God; sing praise and give honor for ever.

O men and women everywhere, *
    All people of God,

O priests and servants of God, *
    O spirits and souls of the righteous,

All you that are holy and humble of hearts. *
    Let us glorify the holy and undivided Trinity:

Glorify God; sing praise and give honor for ever.

The Season of Epiphany

January 6: The Day of Epiphany

Antiphons on Psalter

> Before the morning star begotten and God from everlasting, *
> our Savior is made manifest to the world today, alleluia.

or

> Your light has come, O Jerusalem, *
> and the glory of God has risen up on you, Alleluia.

or

> All nations shall come to your light, *
> and their rulers to the brightness of your rising, Alleluia.

or

> When they had opened their treasures, the Magi presented to the Child *
> gold, frankincense, and myrrh, Alleluia.

or

> Like a flame of fire that star glitters yonder, revealing God,
> the Most Mighty One. *
> At the sight of it, the sages offered gifts to the Holy Child, Alleluia.

Collect

> O God, by the leading of a star you manifested your Holy Child to the
> peoples of the earth: Lead us, who know you now by faith, to your presence,
> where we may see your glory face to face; through Jesus Christ our Savior,
> who lives and reigns with you and the Holy Spirit, one God, now and for
> ever. *Amen.*

*This collect is also used on ferias (open days) between January 6 and the Feast of the Baptism of
Christ (First Sunday after the Epiphany).*

Matins

Invitatory: Alleluia, God is shown forth in glory:
Response: O come, let us worship, alleluia.

Antiphon on the Invitatory

Alleluia, God is shown forth in glory: *
  O come, let us worship, Alleluia.

The canticle is the Te Deum, p. 213.

Hymn at Matins

O more than mighty cities known,
dear Bethlehem, in you alone
the Savior of the world was born
of Mary, that first Christmas morn.

And from a star that far outshone
the radiant beauty of the sun,
glad tidings spread from sea to sea
of God in our humanity.

The sages came to greet the child
with Joseph and with Mary, mild;
they offered gifts in reverence
of gold and myrrh and frankincense.

The gold and incense are a sign
of rule both royal and divine;
the bitter, spicy dust of myrrh
foreshadows death and sepulcher.

To you, O Christ, all glory be
for your divine Epiphany;
to our Creator praise we bring
as by the Spirit here we sing. Amen.

Antiphon on Benedictus

Today the Church is joined to her heavenly Bridegroom; for in Jordan, Christ has washed away her sins; *

the Magi hasten to the wedding, and the guests are regaled with water made wine, Alleluia.

Diurnum

Antiphon on Psalter

O Christ, Light from Light, you have appeared, *
and to you the sages have presented their gifts, Alleluia.

Lesson and Respond   Isaiah 58:8

Your light will break forth like the dawn; your righteousness will go before you, and the glory of God will be your rear guard.

Response: Thanks be to God.

v. All they from Sheba shall come, alleluia, alleluia.
r. They shall bring gold and incense, alleluia, alleluia.

The Office continues with the Closing Prayers in the Ordinary of Diurnum, p. 55.

Vespers

The canticle at Vespers it is the Benedicite, p. 120.

Hymn at Vespers

Why, impious Herod, vainly fear
that Mary's firstborn child is here
to seize your realm, to have you slain?
Christ will not claim your worldly reign.

The Magi went to greet the birth
of Jesus, Savior of the earth;
called on by light, toward Light they pressed,
and, by their gifts, their God confessed.

The sinless one, to set us free,
took our complete humanity.
The Lamb of God, born to redeem,
deigned to be washed in Jordan's stream.

At Cana, Jesus gave a sign:
the water reddened into wine,
that nature, now made new, might show
God's heavenly power to us below.

To you, O Christ, all glory be
for your divine Epiphany;
to our Creator praise we bring
as by the Spirit here we sing. Amen.

Antiphon on Magnificat

To day we celebrate three miracles: today the sages followed the star; *
today at the wedding, water was made wine; today at Jordan,
Jesus was baptized for our salvation, Alleluia.

THE FIRST SUNDAY AFTER THE EPIPHANY: THE BAPTISM OF CHRIST

Antiphons on Psalter

Jesus came from Nazareth in Galilee *
and was baptized by John in the Jordan.

or

Jesus saw the heavens torn open *
and the Spirit, like a dove, descending upon him.

or

A voice spoke from heaven, *
You are my Child, my Beloved, on you my favor rests.

or

Christ was innocent of sin, *
and yet for our sake was made one with the sinfulness of all.

or

Behold, there is the Lamb of God, *
the One who takes away the sin of the world.

Collect

O God in heaven, who at the baptism in the River Jordan proclaimed Jesus your Beloved One and anointed him with the Holy Spirit: Grant that all who are baptized into the name of Jesus may keep the covenant they have made, and boldly confess Jesus Christ as Savior; who with you and the Holy Spirit lives and reigns, one God, in glory everlasting. *Amen.*

Matins

Invitatory: Christ was baptized for us in Jordan:
Response: O come, let us worship.

The canticle is the Te Deum, p. 213.

Hymn at Matins

From wilderness to Jordan came
the great forerunner to proclaim
repentance that must now begin
to cleanse the people of their sin.

The Baptist, dressed in camel hair,
cried, Be baptized, repent, prepare;
and, lest the ax hew down the tree,
be cleansed from your iniquity!

The Spirit came down as a dove
to rest on Jesus with God's love,
and from the heavens a voice was heard:
"Pay heed to my Beloved's word."

All glory, Christ, to you we pay
for your Epiphany today;
to our Creator tribute bring,
as by the Spirit here we sing. Amen.

Antiphon on Benedictus

> The cup that I drink, you shall drink, *
> and the baptism I am baptized with shall be your baptism.

Diurnum

Antiphon on Psalter

> God anointed Jesus of Nazareth *
> with the Holy Spirit and with power.

Lesson and Respond   ISAIAH 42:1

> Here is my servant whom I uphold, my chosen one in whom my soul
> delights and with whom I am well pleased.

Response: Thanks be to God.

> *v.* Christ came down from heaven for our salvation.
> *r.* Jesus bore our sins in his own body on the tree.

The Office continues with the Closing Prayers in the Ordinary of Diurnum, p. 55.

Vespers

The canticle at I Vespers is the Dignus es, p.220; at II Vespers it is the Benedicite, p. 120.

Hymn at I and II Vespers

> Wonder of wonders, that the Judge eternal
> came not to act from righteous indignation,
> but that we all might know divine redemption
>   through Christ our Savior.
>
> Full reparation for our disobedience
> was offered by God in our human nature
> when, in his dying, Jesus seemed forsaken
>   by God in heaven.
>
> God was in Jesus the world reconciling
> divine to human and, in Jesus' baptism,
> giving the sign of reconciliation
>   to all who follow.

So may we worship God forever blessed,
Maker, Redeemer, and the Holy Spirit:
to you be glory in both earth and heaven
throughout the ages. Amen.

Antiphon on Magnificat at Vespers

Christ loved the church and suffered death for it, *
to consecrate it, cleansing it by water and word.

THE SECOND SUNDAY AFTER EPIPHANY

Antiphon on New Testament canticles

Year A

The disciples went and saw where Jesus was staying *
and spent the rest of the day with him.

Year B

Philip told Nathanael, We have met the one spoken of by Moses
and the prophets; *
it is Jesus, son of Joseph, from Nazareth.

Year C

Jesus was revealed in glory *
and the disciples believed in him.

Collect

Almighty God, you gave our Savior Jesus Christ to be the light of the
world: Grant that your people, illumined by your word and sacraments,
may shine with the radiance of heavenly glory, that Christ may be known,
worshiped, and obeyed to the ends of the earth; through Jesus Christ our
Redeemer, who with you and the Holy Spirit lives and reigns, one God,
now and for ever. *Amen.*

The Third Sunday after Epiphany

Antiphon on New Testament canticles

Year A

Then Jesus saw two other brothers mending their nets,
and he called them. *
> And they left the boat and their father and followed him.

Year B

The time is fulfilled; the reign of God has come near. *
> Repent, and believe the gospel.

Year C

When Jesus had read from the scroll of the prophet Isaiah, *
> he said, To day this scripture has been fulfilled in your hearing.

Collect

Give us grace, O God, to answer readily the call of our Savior Jesus Christ
and proclaim to all people the good news of salvation, that we and the
whole world may perceive the glory of Christ's marvelous works; who lives
and reigns with you and the Holy Spirit, one God, for ever and ever.
Amen

The Fourth Sunday after Epiphany

Antiphon on New Testament canticles

Year A

Blessed are the peace-makers, *
> for they will be called children of God.

Year B

The people were astounded at Jesus' teaching, *
> for he taught them as one having authority, and not as the scribes.

Year C

Then Jesus said to them, *
> Today this scripture has been fulfilled in your hearing.

Collect

Almighty and everlasting God, you govern all things both in heaven and on earth: Mercifully hear the supplications of your people, and in our time grant us your peace; through Jesus Christ our Savior, who lives and reigns with you and the Holy Spirit, one God, for ever and ever. *Amen.*

THE FIFTH SUNDAY AFTER EPIPHANY

Antiphon on New Testament canticles

Year A

Let your light shine before others, *
　that they may give glory to God in heaven.

Year B

Jesus went all through Galilee, *
　proclaiming the message and casting out demons.

Year C

Simon fell at Jesus' feet and said, *
　Go away from me, Lord, sinner that I am.

Collect

Set us free, O God, from the bondage of our sins, and give us the liberty of that abundant life which you have made known to us in our Savior Jesus Christ; who lives and reigns with you and the Holy Spirit, one God, now and for ever. *Amen.*

THE SIXTH SUNDAY AFTER EPIPHANY

Antiphon on New Testament canticles

Year A

It is better for you to lose one part of yourself, *
　than for your whole body to go into hell.

Year B

The leper who was healed went out and began to proclaim it freely, *
　and people came to Jesus from every quarter.

Year C

> When you are persecuted rejoice in that day and leap for joy; *
> for surely your reward is great in heaven.

Collect

> O God, the strength of all who put their trust in you: Mercifully accept
> our prayers; and because in our weakness we can do nothing good without
> you, give us the help of your grace, that in keeping your commandments,
> we may please you both in will and deed; through Jesus Christ our Savior,
> who lives and reigns with you and the Holy Spirit, one God, now and for
> ever. *Amen.*

The Seventh Sunday after Epiphany

Antiphon on New Testament canticles

Year A

> Love your enemies and pray for those who persecute you, *
> so that you may be children of God.

Year B

> Since the Chosen One has authority on earth to forgive sins, *
> stand up, take your mat, and go home.

Year C

> Love your enemies and do good, and you will be children of the
> Most High, *
> for God is also kind to the ungrateful and wicked.

Collect

> O God, you have taught us that without love whatever we do is worth
> nothing: Send your Holy Spirit and pour into our hearts your greatest gift,
> which is love, the true bond of peace and of all virtue, without which
> whoever lives is accounted dead before you. Grant this for the sake of
> Jesus Christ, who lives and reigns with you and the Holy Spirit, one God,
> now and for ever. *Amen.*

THE EIGHTH SUNDAY AFTER EPIPHANY

Antiphon on New Testament canticles

Year A

No one can serve two masters; *
you cannot serve God and money.

Year B

The day will come when the Bridegroom is taken away from them, *
and on that day they will fast.

Year C

A good person out of the good treasure of the heart produces good; *
and the evil person out of evil treasure produces evil.

Collect

Most loving God, whose will it is for us to give thanks for all things, to fear nothing but the loss of you, and to cast our care on you who care for us: Preserve us from faithless fears and worldly anxieties, that no clouds of this mortal life may hide from us the light of that love which is immortal, and which you have manifested to us in Jesus Christ; who lives and reigns with you in the unity of the Holy Spirit, one God, now and for ever. *Amen.*

THE LAST SUNDAY AFTER EPIPHANY

Antiphon on New Testament canticles

Year A

Christ Jesus, the reflection of the Creator's splendor,
and the image of the Creator's being, *
shone in radiant glory on a mountain, Alleluia.

Year B

A voice called from the cloud, This is my Child, my Beloved, *
on whom my favor rests; hear and listen, Alleluia.

Year C

At the sound of the voice the disciples fell on their faces in terror. *
Jesus came and touched them, saying, Stand up, do not be afraid,
Alleluia.

Collect

O God, who before the Passion revealed Jesus in glory upon the holy mountain: Grant to us that we, beholding by faith that radiant countenance, may be strengthened to bear our cross, and be changed with Jesus from glory to glory; through our Savior and Redeemer, who lives and reigns with you and the Holy Spirit, one God, for ever and ever. *Amen.*

THE SUNDAYS AND SPECIAL WEEKDAYS IN LENT

THE TUESDAY BEFORE ASH WEDNESDAY: ALSO CALLED SHROVE TUESDAY

Hymn at Vespers

Alleluia, song of gladness,
    hymn of endless joy and praise.
Alleluia is the worship
    that celestial voices raise
and, delighting in God's glory,
    sing in heaven's courts always.

Alleluia, blessed Salem,
    home of all our hopes on high.
Alleluia, sing the angels;
    Alleluia, saints reply;
but we, for a time on this earth,
    chant a simpler melody.

Alleluias we now forfeit
    in this holy time of Lent.
Alleluias we relinquish
    as we for our sins repent,
trusting always in God's mercy
    and in Love omnipotent.

Blessed Trinity of Glory,
    hear your people as we pray.
Grant that we may know the Easter
    of the Truth, the Life, the Way,
chanting endless alleluias
    in the realms of endless day. Amen.

Antiphon on Magnificat

> We are invited in the name of the church *
> to the observance of a holy and consecrated Lent.

Alleluias are added to the final versicle and respond at Vespers.

Cantor:	Let us bless our God, Alleluia, Alleluia.
Response:	To God be thanks for ever, Alleluia, Alleluia.

ASH WEDNESDAY

Matins

Invitatory:	Our God is full of compassion and mercy:
Response:	O come, let us worship.

Antiphon on Psalter

> When you fast, do not look gloomy like the hypocrites, *
> who want others to see that they are fasting.

Canticle at Matins

The canticle for Ash Wednesday is in the Ordinary of Matins, p. 17.

Hymn at Matins

The hymn for Ash Wednesday is in the Ordinary of Matins, p. 6.

Antiphon on Benedictus

> The fast that God requires is to loose the fetters of injustice *
> and to set free those who have been crushed.

The Benedictus will be found in the Ordinary of Matins, p. 31.

Collect

Almighty and everlasting God, you hate nothing you have made and for-give the sins of all who are penitent: Create and make in us new and con-trite hearts, that we, worthily lamenting our sins and acknowledging our wretchedness, may obtain of you, the God of all mercy, perfect remission and forgiveness; through Jesus Christ our Savior, who lives and reigns with you and the Holy Spirit, one God, for ever and ever. *Amen.*

This collect is also used on the Thursday, Friday, and Saturday following Ash Wednesday when they are ferias.

Diurnum

Diurnum for Ash Wednesday is in the Ordinary Diurnum, beginning on p.37

Vespers

Antiphon on Psalter

When you fast, anoint your head and wash your face, *
so that people may not see you are fasting.

Canticle at Vespers

The canticle for Ash Wednesday is in the Ordinary of Vespers, p. 60.

Hymn at Vespers

The hymn for Ash Wednesday is in the Ordinary of Vespers, p. 62.

Antiphon on Magnificat

The fast that God requires is sharing your food with the hungry *
and not turning your back on your own.

The First Sunday in Lent

Antiphon on New Testament canticles

Year A

> Jesus was led away by the Spirit in to the wilderness, *
> to be tempted by the devil.

Year B

> Jesus was among the wild beasts, *
> and the angels waited on him.

Year C

> When Jesus had come to the end of all the devil's temptations, *
> the devil departed, awaiting an opportune time.

Collect

> Almighty God, whose Beloved One was led out by the Spirit to be tempt-
> ed by Satan: Come quickly to help us, who are assaulted by many tempta-
> tions, and as you know the weakness of each of us, let each one find you
> mighty to save; through Jesus Christ our Redeemer, who lives and reigns
> with you and the Holy Spirit, one God, now and for ever. *Amen.*

Matins

Antiphon on Psalter

> We cannot live by bread alone; *
> we live on every word that comes from the mouth of God.

Canticle

The canticle for Sundays in Lent is in the Ordinary of Sunday, p. 4.

Hymn

The hymn for Lent I is in the Ordinary of Matins, p. 6.

Diurnum

Antiphon on Psalter

> For you, O God, have proved us; *
> you have tried us as silver is tried.

Lesson and Respond   JAMES 1:12

Blessed is the one who perseveres when trials come. Such a person is of proven worth, and will win the prize of life: the crown that has been promised to all who love God.

Response: Thanks be to God.

v. Be not far away, O God, for you are my strength;
r. Hasten to help me.

The Office continues with the Closing Prayers in the Ordinary of Diurnum, p. 55.

Vespers

Antiphon on Psalter

Jesus said, *
    You shall do homage and give worship to God alone.

Canticle

The canticle for Sundays in Lent is in the Ordinary of Sunday, p. 60.

Hymn

The hymn for Lent I is in the Ordinary of Sunday, p. 62.

The Winter Ember Days are traditionally kept on the Wednesday, Friday, and Saturday after Lent I. See Common 11, p. 251.

THE SECOND SUNDAY IN LENT

Antiphon on New Testament canticles

Year A
    God so loved the world that God sent Jesus, the only begotten One, *
        that whoever believes will not perish, but will have eternal life.

Year B
    Any one who wishes to be a follower of mine must leave self behind, *
        take up the cross and come with me.

Year C

> O Jerusalem, Jerusalem, how often have I longed to gather your children, *
> as a hen gathers her brood under her wings.

Collect

> O God, whose glory it is always to have mercy: Be gracious to all who
> have gone astray from your ways, and bring them again with penitent
> hearts and steadfast faith to embrace and hold fast the unchangeable truth
> of your Word, Jesus Christ; who with you and the Holy Spirit lives and
> reigns, one God, for ever and ever. *Amen.*

Matins

Antiphon on Psalter

> You must regard yourselves as dead to sin and alive to God, *
> in union with Christ Jesus.

Canticle

The canticle for Sundays in Lent is in the Ordinary of Sunday, p. 4.

Hymn

The hymn for Lent II is in the Ordinary of Sunday, p. 6.

Diurnum

Antiphon on Psalter

> Nothing in all creation *
> can separate us from the love of God in Christ Jesus.

Lesson and Respond PHILIPPIANS 3:20

> Our citizenship is in heaven, and it is from there that we are expecting
> our Savior, Jesus Christ.

Response: Thanks be to God.

> *v.* Be not far away, O God, for you are my strength;
> *r.* Hasten to help me.

The Office continues with the Closing Prayers in the Ordinary of Diurnum, p. 55.

Antiphon on Psalter

> God makes the dead live and summons things that are not yet in existence, *
> as if they already were.

Canticle

The canticle for Sundays in Lent is in the Ordinary of Sunday, p. 60.

Hymn

The hymn for Lent II is in the Ordinary of Sunday, p. 62.

Antiphon on New Testament canticles

Year A

> The time is already here when those who are real worshipers *
> will worship God in spirit and in truth.

Year B

> Destroy this temple, and in three days I will raise it again. *
> Jesus was speaking of the temple of his body.

Year C

> Leave the fig tree one more year while I dig round it and tend it: *
> it may bear fruit next year; if not, then you can cut it down.

Collect

> Almighty God, you know that we have no power in ourselves to help our-
> selves: Keep us both outwardly in our bodies and inwardly in our souls,
> that we may be defended from all adversities which may happen to the
> body, and from all evil thoughts which may assault and hurt the soul;
> through our Savior Jesus Christ, who lives and reigns with you and the
> Holy Spirit, one God, for ever and ever. *Amen.*

The Third Sunday in Lent

Matins

Antiphon on Psalter

> Who is there to rescue me out of this body doomed to death? *
> God alone, through Jesus Christ our Redeemer.

Canticle

The canticle for Sundays in Lent is in the Ordinary of Sunday, p. 4.

Hymn

The hymn for Lent III is in the Ordinary of Sunday, p. 6.

Diurnum

Antiphon on Psalter

> Do not spurn correction from God, *
> for such discipline is given to all whom God loves.

Lesson and Respond   Romans 5:3-4

> Let us rejoice in our sufferings, knowing that suffering produces
> endurance, and endurance produces character, and character produces
> hope, and hope does not disappoint us, because God's love has been
> poured into our hearts.

Response: Thanks be to God.

> *v.* Be not far away, O God, for you are my strength;
> *r.* Hasten to help me.

The Office continues with the Closing Prayers in the Ordinary of Diurnum, p. 55.

Vespers

Antiphon on Psalter

> God is faithful and will not let you be tested beyond your strength, *
> but will provide the way for you to endure.

Canticle

The canticle for Sundays in Lent is in the Ordinary of Sunday, p. 60.

Hymn

The hymn for Lent III is in the Ordinary of Sunday, p. 62.

THE FOURTH SUNDAY IN LENT

Begin using materials for Lent from Vespers of Lent IV to Maundy Thursday.

Antiphon on New Testament canticles

Year A
>Jesus said, While I am in the world, *
>   I am the light of the world.

Year B
>Where are we to buy bread to feed these people? *
>   But Jesus himself knew what he meant to do.

Year C
>Let us have a feast to celebrate this day, *
>   for this son of mine was dead and has come back to life.

Collect
>Gracious God, whose blessed One, Jesus Christ, came down from heaven
>to be the true bread which gives life to the world: Evermore give us this
>bread, that Christ may live in us and we in Christ; who lives and reigns
>with you and the Holy Spirit, one God, now and for ever. *Amen.*

Matins

Antiphon on Psalter
>We are all children of light, children of day; *
>   we do not belong to night or darkness.

Canticle

The canticle for Sundays in Lent is as in the Ordinary of Sunday, p. 4.
Hymn

The hymn for Lent IV is as in the Ordinary of Sunday, p. 8.

Diurnum

Antiphon on Psalter

> God gave us grain from heaven, so we ate the bread of angels. *
> God provided for us food enough.

Lesson and Respond   1 CORINTHIANS 11:24

> Our Savior Jesus, on the night of his arrest, took bread and, after giving
> thanks to God, broke it and said, This is my body, which is for you.

Response: *Thanks be to God.*
> v. Be not far away, O God, for you are my strength;
> r. Hasten to help me.

The Office continues with the Closing Prayers in the Ordinary of Diurnum, p. 55.

Vespers

Antiphon on Psalter

> Come and gather for God's great supper. *
> Happy are they who are invited to the supper of the Lamb.

Canticle

The canticle for Sundays in Lent is as in the Ordinary of Sunday, p. 60.

Hymn

The hymn for Lent IV is in the Ordinary of Sunday, p. 63.

The Fifth Sunday in Lent

Antiphon on New Testament canticles

Year A

> Anyone who believes in me, even though they die, will live, *
>> and whoever lives and believes in me will never die.

Year B

> A grain of wheat remains a solitary grain unless it falls into the ground and dies, *
>> but if it dies, it bears a rich harvest.

Year C

> The stone which the builders rejected has become the main cornerstone. *
>> This is God's doing.

Collect

> Almighty God, you alone can bring into order the unruly wills and affections of sinners: Grant your people grace to love what you command and to desire what you promise; that among the swift and varied changes of the world, our hearts may surely there be fixed where true joys are to be found; through Jesus Christ our Savior, who lives and reigns with you and the Holy Spirit, one God, for ever and ever. *Amen.*

Matins

Antiphon on Psalter

> We despised him; we held him of no account, *
>> a thing from which people turn away their eyes.

Canticle

The canticle for Sundays in Lent is as in the Ordinary of Sunday, p. 4.

Hymn

The hymn for Lent V is in the Ordinary of Sunday, p. 8.

Diurnum

Antiphon on Psalter

> Though I walk through the valley of the shadow of death, *
> I shall fear no evil, for you are with me.

Lesson and Respond   Philippians 3:8-9

> I regard everything as loss because of the surpassing value of knowing
> Christ Jesus. I have suffered the loss of all things, and I regard them as
> rubbish, in order that I may gain Christ and be found in Christ.

Response: Thanks be to God.

> *v.* Be not far away, O God, for you are my strength;
> *r.* Hasten to help me.

The Office continues with the Closing Prayers in the Ordinary of Diurnum, p. 55.

Vespers

Antiphon on Psalter at Vespers

> In my own flesh I fill up what is lacking in the sufferings of Christ, *
> for the sake of Christ's Body, the Church.

Canticle

The canticle for Sundays in Lent is as in the Ordinary of Sunday, p. 60.

Hymn

The hymn for Lent V is in the Ordinary Sunday, p. 63.

Vespers of Saturday before Palm Sunday

Antiphon on Psalter

> Christ was innocent of sin, and yet for our sake *
> was made one with the sinfulness of all.

The canticle and the hymn are as in the Ordinary of Vespers, p. 60, 63. Note that the hymn is to be used in its entirety.

The antiphon on the Magnificat is as on Palm Sunday, p. 146 below.

The Collect for Palm Sunday

Almighty and everliving God, in your tender love for humanity you sent Jesus, to take our nature upon him and to suffer death upon the cross, giving us an example of great humility: Mercifully grant that we too may walk in the way of the cross and share in the resurrection; through the one who is our Savior and Redeemer and who lives and reigns with you and the Holy Spirit, one God, for ever and ever. *Amen.*

THE SUNDAY OF THE PASSION, ALSO CALLED PALM SUNDAY

Matins

Invitatory: Christ is reigning from the tree:
Response: O come, let us worship.

Antiphon on Psalter

Remember how I stood before you, pleading on their behalf, *
    to avert your wrath from them.

The Matins canticle for Palm Sunday will be found in the Ordinary of Matins, p. 4.

The Matins hymn for Palm Sunday will be found in the Ordinary of Matins p. 8. Note that all verses of the hymn are to be used.

Antiphon on Benedictus

The great body of pilgrims, hearing that Jesus was on the way
to Jerusalem, *
    took palm branches and went out to meet him, shouting,
    Hosanna, hosanna!

The collect for Palm Sunday is on this page, above.

Diurnum

Antiphon on Psalter

> This is my comfort in my trouble: *
> that your promise gives me life.

Lesson and Respond Hebrews 5:8

> Although Jesus was divine, he learned obedience through suffering, and
> having been made perfect, became the source of eternal salvation for all.

Response: Thanks be to God.

> *v.* Cast your burden upon God; God will sustain you.
> *r.* The Holy One will never let the righteous stumble.

The Office continues with the Closing Prayers in the Ordinary of Diurnum, p. 55.

Vespers

Antiphon on Psalter

> O Jerusalem, Jerusalem, how often have I longed to gather your children, *
> as a hen gathers her brood under her wings.

The Vespers canticle for Palm Sunday will be found in the Ordinary of Vespers, p. 60.

*The Vespers hymn for Palm Sunday will be found in the Ordinary of Vespers, p. 63. Note that all
verses of the hymn are to be used.*

Antiphon on Magnificat on Palm Sunday and evening before

> When Jesus came in sight of Jerusalem, he wept over it and said, *
> If only you had known, on this great day, the way that leads to peace.

MONDAY IN HOLY WEEK

Antiphon on Benedictus

> Mary of Bethany anointed the feet of Jesus and wiped them with her hair; *
> she was foreseeing the day of his burial.

Collect

Almighty God, whose Beloved One went not up to joy before suffering pain, and entered not into glory before being crucified: Mercifully grant that we, walking in the way of the cross, may find it none other than the way of life and peace; through Jesus Christ our Savior, who lives and reigns with you and the Holy Spirit, one God, for ever and ever. *Amen.*

Antiphon on Magnificat

You have the poor among you always, *
    but you will not always have me.

TUESDAY IN HOLY WEEK

Antiphon on Benedictus

Whoever believes in me, believes in God who sent me; *
    and whoever sees me, sees the one who sent me.

Collect

O God, by the passion of your blessed One you made an instrument of shameful death to be for us the means of life: Grant us so to glory in the cross of Christ, that we may faithfully endure shame and loss for the sake of our Savior Jesus Christ; who lives and reigns with you and the Holy Spirit, one God, for ever and ever. *Amen.*

Antiphon on Magnificat

I tell you this: one of you will betray me, *
    one who is eating with me.

WEDNESDAY IN HOLY WEEK

Antiphon on Benedictus

In two days the Passover will come *
    and Jesus will be handed over to be crucified.

Collect

Almighty God, whose Beloved One was whipped and spit upon: Give us grace to accept the sufferings of the present time, confident of the glory that shall be revealed; through Jesus Christ our Savior, who lives and reigns with you and the Holy Spirit, one God, for ever and ever. *Amen.*

Antiphon on Magnificat

Jesus said to Judas, Do quickly what you have to do. *
As soon as Judas had received the bread, he went out; it was night.

MAUNDY THURSDAY

Matins

The opening versicles and responds and the Venite with the invitatory antiphon are omitted. The Office begins with the following antiphons and the pslams. The Gloria is always omitted.

Antiphons on Psalter

You are justified, O God, when you speak, *
and upright in your judgment.

or

In the day of my trouble I sought after God; *
my hands were stretched out by night and did not tire.

or

When I called, O God, you answered me; *
you increased my strength within me.

Respond, to follow the reading from the Hebrew Scriptures

v. O my vineyard, did I not plant you? I fenced you and gathered out the stones.
r. O my people, what have I done to you? Tell me how I have wearied you.

v. I have built a watchtower in the middle and hewn out a winepress.
r. O my people, what have I done to you? Tell me how I have wearied you.

Respond, to follow the reading from the New Testament

    v. Judas Iscariot went to the chief priests and said,
      What will you give me to betray Jesus to you?
    r. They weighed out to him thirty silver pieces.

    v. The traitor gave them this sign: The one I kiss is your man; seize him.
    r. They weighed out to him thirty silver pieces.

Antiphon on Benedictus

Jesus laid aside his garments, and taking a towel, *
    he poured water into a basin and began to wash the disciples' feet.

After the antiphon is repeated the following is recited at once:
Christ, for our sake, in obedience accepted death.

Collect

Almighty God, whose dear One, on the night before being crucified, instituted the Sacrament of the Body and Blood: Mercifully grant that we may receive it thankfully in remembrance of Jesus Christ our Savior, who in these holy mysteries gives us a pledge of eternal life; and now lives and reigns with you and the Holy Spirit, one God, for ever and ever. *Amen.*

Nothing further is added.

Diurnum

The opening versicles and responds and the hymn are omitted. The Office opens with the antiphon below and the Psalter appointed for Thursday (Ordinary of Diurnum, p. 48). The Gloria is always omitted.

Antiphon on Psalter

I give you a new commandment: Love one another; *
    as I have loved you, so you are to love one another.

The Office closes with the Ending as above in Matins.

Vespers

The opening versicles and responds and the Phos hilaron are omitted. The Office begins with the following antiphons and the psalms. The Gloria is always omitted.

Antiphon for Psalm(s)

Righteousness and justice are the foundations of your throne; *
love and truth go before your face.

or

I will keep my love for David for ever, *
and my covenant will stand firm for all time.

or

How long will you hide yourself, O God; *
how long will your anger burn like fire?

Respond, to follow the reading from the Hebrew Scriptures
v. My heart is ready to break with grief; stop here and stay awake with me.
r. They will come out as against a bandit, with swords and cudgels.

v. The hour is come: the Anointed One is betrayed to sinners.
r. They will come out as against a bandit, with swords and cudgels.

Respond, to follow the reading from the New Testament
v. Upon the Mount of Olives he prayed: Abba, if it be possible, let this cup pass me by.
r. The spirit is willing, but the flesh is weak.

v. Wake up now, and pray that you may be spared the test.
r. The spirit is willing, but the flesh is weak.

Antiphon on Magnificat

Who is greater, the one who sits at table or the one who serves? *
Yet here am I among you as a servant.

The Office closes with the Ending as at Matins, p. 149, above.

Compline

This form for Compline is used each day during the Triduum (Maundy Thursday, Good Friday, Holy Saturday). The Gloria is always omitted.

The Office begins with a period of silence followed by the Confession and Absolution.

The hymn is omitted.

The Psalter follows, as appointed for the day and week in the Ordinary of Compline.

The Lesson is omitted.

The Nunc dimittis is recited at once without antiphon.

The Office closes with the Ending as at Matins, p. 149.

GOOD FRIDAY

Matins

The opening versicles and responds and the Venite with the invitatory antiphon are omitted. The Office begins with the following antiphons and the psalms. The Gloria is always omitted.

Antiphons for the Psalm(s)

They pierce my hands and my feet; they divide my garments among them; *
they cast lots for my clothing.

or

Those who hate you take secret counsel against your people *
and plot against those whom you protect.

or

God takes pleasure in the people *
and adorns the poor with victory.

    v. He had no beauty, no majesty to draw our eyes, no grace to make us delight in him.

    r. He was pierced for our transgressions, and by his scourging we are healed.

    v. On himself he bore our sufferings; our torments he endured.

    r. He was pierced for our transgressions, and by his scourging we are healed.

Respond, to follow the reading from the New Testament

    v. All my friends have forsaken me; those who laid wait have prevailed against me.

    r. They have smitten me with blows; they gave me vinegar to drink.

    v. One whom I love has betrayed me; they have cast me out among the wicked.

    r. They have smitten me with blows; they gave me vinegar to drink.

Antiphon on Benedictus

Jesus, carrying his own cross, went out to Golgotha, *
where they crucified him.

After the antiphon is repeated the following is recited at once:
Christ, for our sake, in obedience accepted death, even death on a cross.

Collect

Almighty God, we pray you graciously to behold this your family, for whom our Savior Jesus Christ was willing to be betrayed and given into the hands of sinners, and to suffer death upon the cross; who now lives and reigns with you and the Holy Spirit, one God, for ever and ever. *Amen.*

Nothing further is added.

Diurnum

The opening versicles and responds and the hymn are omitted. The Office opens with the antiphon below and the Psalter appointed for Friday (Ordinary of Diurnum, p. 51). The Gloria is always omitted.

Antiphon on Psalter

> Pilate wrote an inscription to be fastened to the cross; *
> it read: Jesus of Nazareth, King of the Jews.

The Office closes with the Ending at Matins, above.

Vespers

The opening versicles and responds and the Phos hilaron are omitted. The Office begins with the following antiphons and the psalms. The Gloria is always omitted.

Antiphons for the Psalm(s)

> You trace my journeys and my resting places; *
> if I make the grave my bed, you are there also.

or

> You, O God, redeem our life from the grave, *
> and crown us with mercy and loving-kindness.

or

> You, O God, remember that we are but dust; *
> your merciful goodness endures for ever on those who fear you.

Respond, to follow the reading from the Hebrew Scriptures

> *v.* At noon darkness fell over the whole land and lasted till mid-afternoon,
> when Jesus cried, Eli, Eli, lama sabachthani?
> *r.* Jesus again gave a loud cry and breathed his last.

> *v.* Jesus said, Abba, into your hands I commit my spirit.
> *r.* Jesus again gave a loud cry and breathed his last.

Respond, to follow the reading from the New Testament

> *v.* The curtain of the temple was torn in two from top to bottom.
> *r.* There was an earthquake, the rocks split, and the graves opened.

> *v.* Many of God's saints were raised from sleep, coming out of their graves
> after Jesus' resurrection.
> *r.* There was an earthquake, the rocks split, and the graves opened.

Antiphon on Magnificat

>One of the soldiers stabbed Jesus' side with a lance, *
>and at once there was a flow of blood and water.

The Office closes with the Ending as at Matins, p. 152.

Compline

The form of Compline is as on Maundy Thursday, p. 151, with the Ending for Good Friday as on p. 152.

HOLY SATURDAY

Matins

The opening versicles and responds and the Venite with the invitatory antiphon are omitted. The Office begins with the following antiphons and the psalms. The Gloria is always omitted.

Antiphons for the Psalm(s)

>Do not hide your face from me, or I shall be like those who go down to the pit. *
>Let me hear of your loving-kindness in the morning.

or

>Truly, salvation is very near to those who fear God, *
>that God's glory may dwell in the land.

or

>Be still, then, and know that I am God; *
>I will be exalted among the nations.

Respond, to follow the reading from the Hebrew Scriptures

>v. He was afflicted; he submitted to be struck down and did not open his mouth.
>
>r. He was put to death for the people's transgressions.
>
>v. He was cut off from the world of the living and assigned a grave with the wicked.
>
>r. He was put to death for the people's transgressions.

    v. The chief priests and the Pharisees came in a body to Pilate and asked
       for the grave to be made secure.
    r. They sealed the stone and left the guard in charge.

    v. Pilate said, Go and make it as secure as you can.
    r. They sealed the stone and left the guard in charge.

Antiphon on Benedictus

Joseph took the body of Jesus, wrapped it in a clean linen cloth, *
    and laid it in his own unused tomb.

After the antiphon the following is recited at once:

Christ, for our sake, in obedience accepted death, even death on a cross,
and therefore was raised to the heights and given the name above all
names.

Collect

O God, Creator of heaven and earth: Grant that, as the crucified body of
Jesus was laid in the tomb and rested on this holy sabbath, so we may
await the coming of the third day, and rise with Christ to newness of life;
who now lives and reigns with you and the Holy Spirit, one God, for ever
and ever. *Amen.*

Nothing further is added.

Diurnum

*The opening versicles and responds and the hymn are omitted. The Office opens with the
antiphon below and the Psalter appointed for Saturday (Ordinary of Diurnum, p. 53).
The Gloria is always omitted.*

Antiphon on Psalter

Mary of Magdala was there, and the other Mary, *
    sitting opposite the grave.

The Office closes with the Ending as at Matins, above.

Vespers

The opening versicles and responds and the Phos hilaron are omitted. The Office begins with the following antiphons and the psalms. The Gloria is always omitted.

Antiphons for the Psalm(s)

My very bones will say, O God, who is like you? *
You deliver the poor from those who are too strong for them.

or

Give me justice, O my God. *
Do not let them triumph over me.

or

God gives the people justice *
and shows compassion to all.

Respond, to follow the reading from the Hebrew Scriptures

v. I am counted among those who go down to the pit.
r. I have become like those with no strength left.

v. Lost among the dead, like the slain who lie in the grave.
r. I have become like those with no strength left.

Respond, to follow the reading from the New Testament

v. Behold how the righteous perish, and no one lays it to heart.
r. They are taken from the presence of evil and shall enter into peace.

v. The upright are oppressed and condemned, and no one is distressed.
r. They are taken from the presence of evil and shall enter into peace.

Antiphon on Magnificat

At the place where he had been crucified, there was a garden *
and in the garden, a new tomb where they laid Jesus.

The Office closes with the Ending as at Matins, p. 155.

Compline

The form of Compline is as on Maundy Thursday, p. 151, with the Ending for Holy Saturday on p. 155.

THE PROPER OF EASTER

THE SUNDAY OF THE RESURRECTION: ALSO CALLED EASTER DAY

Matins

Matins, as below, is ordinarily included in the Easter Vigil.

The invitatory antiphon and Venite are omitted, and the Office begins as follows:

Antiphon on Psalter

> Alleluia, Alleluia, Alleluia.

Then follows Psalm 150, p. 542.

The lessons, canticle and hymn are omitted.

Antiphon on Benedictus

> And very early in the morning, the first day of the week, *
>   they went to the sepulcher at the rising of the sun, alleluia.

Collect

> Almighty God, who through your only-begotten One, Jesus Christ,
> overcame death and opened for us the gate of everlasting life: Grant that
> we, who celebrate with joy this day of resurrection may be raised from the
> death of sin by your life-giving Spirit; through Jesus Christ our Savior,
> who lives and reigns with you and the Holy Spirit, one God, now and for
> ever. *Amen.*

*The festal Benedicamus, below, is used at Matins and Vespers throughout Easter Week and at
Sunday Matins and Saturday and Sunday Vespers throughout Eastertide.*

Cantor:	Let us bless our God, Alleluia, Alleluia.
Response:	To God be thanks for ever, Alleluia, Alleluia.

Diurnum

Antiphon on Psalter

Alleluia, Alleluia, Alleluia.

Lesson and Respond   MATTHEW 28:5-6

At the tomb the angel said to the women, Do not be afraid; I know that you are looking for Jesus who was crucified. He is not here, for he has been raised, as he said. Come, see the place where he lay.

Response: Thanks be to God.

v. Christ is risen from the grave, alleluia, alleluia.
r. And has appeared to Mary of Magdala, alleluia, alleluia.

This Lesson and Respond are also used daily throughout Easter Week.

The Office continues with the Closing Prayers in the Ordinary of Diurnum, p. 55.

Vespers

Antiphons on Psalter

Go and take word to the disciples that they are to leave for Galilee; *
    they will see me there, Alleluia.

or

Mary of Magdala went to the disciples with her news: *
    I have seen the Lord, Alleluia.

or

Jesus took bread and said the blessing; he broke the bread and
offered it to them. *
    Then their eyes were opened and they recognized him, Alleluia.

or

Jesus asked, Why do questionings arise in your minds? *
    Look at my hands and feet; it is I myself, Alleluia.

or

When he saw the net full of fishes, *
    the disciple whom Jesus loved said to Peter, It is the Lord, Alleluia.

The canticle is the Benedicite, p. 120.

158   THE PROPER OF EASTER

Antiphon on Magnificat

> The angel said to the women, Fear nothing: you are looking for
> Jesus of Nazareth. *
> > He has been raised from the dead, Alleluia.

During Easter week, the canticle at Matins is the Te deum, p. 213 at Vespers it is the canticle appointed for that day of the week in the Ordinary of Easter, pp. 178-179.

MONDAY IN EASTER WEEK

Antiphon on Benedictus

> Suddenly Jesus appeared to the women and gave them his greeting, *
> > and they came up and clasped his feet, Alleluia.

Collect

> Grant, we pray, almighty God, that we who celebrate with awe the Paschal
> feast may be found worthy to attain to everlasting joys; through Jesus
> Christ our Savior, who lives and reigns with you and the Holy Spirit, one
> God, now and for ever. *Amen.*

Antiphon on Magnificat

> Go and take word to the disciples that they are to leave for Galilee; *
> > they will see me there, Alleluia.

TUESDAY IN EASTER WEEK

Antiphon on Benedictus

> Mary saw Jesus standing there, but did not recognize him. *
> > Jesus called her by name; Mary turned to him and said, Rabboni! Alleluia.

O God, who by the glorious resurrection of Jesus Christ destroyed death, and brought life and immortality to light: Grant that we, who now share in the resurrection, may abide in Christ's presence, and rejoice in the hope of eternal glory; through Jesus Christ our Savior, to whom with you and the Holy Spirit, be dominion and praise for ever and ever. *Amen.*

Antiphon on Magnificat

Mary of Magdala went to the disciples with her news: *
I have seen the Lord, Alleluia.

WEDNESDAY IN EASTER WEEK

Antiphon on Benedictus

Jesus came up and walked a long with them; *
their hearts were on fire as he opened the scriptures to them, Alleluia.

Collect

O God, whose blessed One was made known to the disciples in the breaking of bread: Open the eyes of our faith, that we may behold the redeeming work of Christ; who lives and reigns with you in the unity of the Holy Spirit, one God, now and for ever. *Amen.*

Antiphon on Magnificat

Jesus took bread and said the blessing; he broke the bread and offered it to them.*
Then their eyes were opened and they recognized him, Alleluia.

THURSDAY IN EASTER WEEK

Antiphon on Benedictus

Jesus was there standing among them.*
They were startled and terrified, but he reassured them, Alleluia.

Collect

Almighty and everlasting God, who in the Paschal mystery established the new covenant of reconciliation: Grant that all who have been reborn into the community of Christ's body, may show forth in their lives what they profess by their faith; through Jesus Christ our Savior, who lives and reigns with you and the Holy Spirit, one God, for ever and ever. *Amen.*

Antiphon on Magnificat

Jesus asked, Why do questionings arise in your minds?*
  Look at my hands and feet; it is I myself, Alleluia.

FRIDAY IN EASTER WEEK

Antiphon on Benedictus

Jesus stood on the shore and called out to the disciples:*
  Cast your net to starboard and you will make a catch, Alleluia.

Collect

Almighty God, who gave Jesus to die for our sins and to rise for our justification; Give us grace so to put away the leaven of malice and wickedness, that we may always serve you in holiness and truth; through Jesus Christ our Redeemer, who lives and reigns with you and the Holy Spirit, one God, now and for ever. *Amen.*

Antiphon on Magnificat

When he saw the net full of fishes,*
  the disciple whom Jesus loved said to Peter, It is the Lord, Alleluia.

SATURDAY IN EASTER WEEK

Antiphon on Benedictus

Jesus said to the disciples, Go forth to every part of the world *
  and proclaim the gospel to the whole creation, Alleluia.

We thank you, O God, that you have delivered us from the dominion of sin and death, and brought us into the reign of Jesus Christ; by whose death we have been recalled to life, and by whose love we are raised to eternal joys; and who with you and the Holy Spirit lives and reigns, one God, now and for ever. *Amen.*

Antiphon on Magnificat

Jesus said to the disciples, Peace be with you.*
As God in heaven has sent me, so send I you, Alleluia.

THE SECOND SUNDAY OF EASTER

Matins

Antiphon on Benedictus

Jesus said to Thomas, Reach your finger here; see my hands.*
Reach your hand here and put it into my side, Alleluia.

Collect

Almighty and everlasting God, who in the Paschal mystery established the new covenant of reconciliation: Grant that all who have been reborn into the community of Christ's body, may show forth in their lives what they profess by their faith; through Jesus Christ our Redeemer, who lives and reigns with you and the Holy Spirit, one God, for ever and ever. *Amen.*

Diurnum

Antiphon on Psalter

Alleluia, Alleluia, Alleluia.

Lesson and Respond   1 PETER 1:8-9

You have not seen God, yet you love God, and trusting in Jesus whom you do not now see, you are transported with a joy too great for words, while you reap the harvest of your faith, that is, salvation for your souls.

Response: Thanks be to God.

v. Jesus has triumphed over death, alleluia, alleluia. *

r. And reigns with God in glory, alleluia, alleluia.

The Office continues with the Closing Prayers in the Ordinary of Diurnum, p. 55.

Vespers

Antiphon on Magnificat

Because you have seen me, Thomas, you have found faith.*

Happy are they who never saw me and yet have found faith, Alleluia.

THE THIRD SUNDAY OF EASTER

Antiphon on New Testament Canticles

Year A

Jesus took bread and said the blessing; he broke the bread and offered it to them. *

Then their eyes were opened and they recognized him, Alleluia.

Year B

Jesus asked, Why do questionings arise in your minds? *

Look at my hands and feet; it is I myself, Alleluia.

Year C

When he saw the net full of fishes, *

the disciple whom Jesus loved said to Peter, It is the Lord, Alleluia.

Collect

O God, whose blessed One was made known to the disciples in the breaking of bread: Open the eyes of our faith, that we may behold the redeeming work of Christ; who lives and reigns with you in the unity of the Holy Spirit, one God, now and for ever. *Amen.*

Antiphon on Psalter

> Alleluia, Alleluia, Alleluia.

Lesson and Respond   ACTS 10:41

> God allowed Jesus to appear, not to the whole people, but to witnesses
> whom God had chosen, to us who ate and drank with him after his rising
> from the dead.

Response: Thanks be to God.

> *v.* Christ has triumphed over death, alleluia, alleluia. *
> *r.* And reigns with God in glory, alleluia, alleluia.

The Office continues with the Closing Prayers in the Ordinary of Diurnum, p. 55.

THE FOURTH SUNDAY OF EASTER

At Vespers of the preceding Saturday, Hymn E in the Ordinary of Eastertide, p. 180, is used.

Antiphon on New Testament Canticles

Year A

> Faithful shepherds call their own sheep by name and lead them out.*
> Sheep follow because they know their shepherd's voice, Alleluia.

Year B

> Jesus said, I am the good shepherd;*
> I lay down my life for the sheep, Alleluia.

Year C

> Jesus said, My own sheep listen to my voice; I know them and they
> follow me.*
> I give them eternal life, Alleluia.

Collect

O beloved Jesus, you are the good shepherd of your people: Grant that when we hear your voice we may know you who call us each by name and follow where you lead; this we pray in the name of the holy and undivided Trinity, one God, for ever and ever. *Amen.*

Matins

Hymn B in Ordinary of Eastertide, p. 173.

Diurnum

Antiphon on Psalter

Alleluia, Alleluia, Alleluia.

Lesson and Respond   REVELATION 7:17

The Lamb who is at the heart of the throne will be their shepherd and will guide them to the springs of the water of life.

Response: Thanks be to God.

   v. Christ has triumphed over death, alleluia, alleluia. *
   r. And reigns with God in glory, alleluia, alleluia.

The Office continues with the Closing Prayers in the Ordinary of Diurnum, p. 55.

THE FIFTH SUNDAY OF EASTER

Antiphon on New Testament Canticles

Year A

If I go and prepare a place for you, I shall come again and receive you to myself,*

   so that where I am you may be also, Alleluia.

Year B

> They who have received my commandments and obey them, are the ones who love me;*
>> they also are loved by God in heaven, and I will love them and disclose myself to them, Alleluia.

Year C

> I give you a new commandment: Love one another;*
>> as I have loved you, so you are to love one another, Alleluia.

Collect

> Almighty God, whom truly to know is everlasting life: Grant us so perfectly to know Jesus Christ to be the way, the truth, and the life, that we may steadfastly follow in the way that leads to eternal life; through the One who is our Savior and Redeemer, and who lives and reigns with you in the unity of the Holy Spirit, one God, for ever and ever. *Amen.*

Diurnum

Antiphon on Psalter

> Alleluia, Alleluia, Alleluia.

Lesson and Respond   1 PETER 2:9

> You are a chosen people, a royal priesthood, a holy nation, a people belonging to God, that you may declare the praises of the one who called you out of darkness into a wonderful light.

Response: Thanks be to God.

> *v.* Christ has triumphed over death, alleluia, alleluia. *
> r. And reigns with God in glory, alleluia, alleluia.

The Office continues with the Closing Prayers in the Ordinary of Diurnum, p. 55.

The Sixth Sunday of Easter

Antiphons on New Testament Canticles

Year A

No branch can bear fruit by itself,*
but only if it remains united with the vine, Alleluia.

Year B

If you heed my commands you will dwell in my love,*
as I have heeded God's commands and dwell in God's love, Alleluia.

Year C

They who love me will heed what I say,*
and God in heaven will love them,
and we will come and make our dwelling with them, Alleluia.

Collect

O God, you have prepared for those who love you such good things as surpass our understanding: Pour into our hearts such love toward you, that we, loving you in all things and above all things, may obtain your promises, which exceed all that we can desire; through Jesus Christ our Redeemer, who lives and reigns with you and the Holy Spirit, one God, forever and ever. *Amen.*

Diurnum

Antiphon on Psalter

Alleluia, Alleluia, Alleluia.

Lesson and Respond   1 JOHN 4:16

We have come to know and believe the love which God has for us. God is love; they who dwell in love are dwelling in God, and God in them.

Response: Thanks be to God.

v. Christ has triumphed over death, alleluia, alleluia.*
r. And reigns with God in glory, alleluia, alleluia.

The Office continues with the Closing Prayers in the Ordinary of Diurnum, p. 55.

ASCENSION DAY

Antiphons on Psalter

> Jesus led the disciples out as far as Bethany,*
> and blessed them with uplifted hands, Alleluia.

or

> As they watched, Jesus was lifted up,*
> and a cloud removed him from their sight, Alleluia.

or

> As they were gazing intently into the sky,*
> all at once there stood beside them two people in white, Alleluia.

or

> People of Galilee, why stand there looking up into the sky?*
> This Jesus, who has been taken away from you up to heaven,
> will come in the same way as you have seen him go, Alleluia.

or

> They returned to Jerusalem with great joy,*
> and spent all their time in the temple praising God, Alleluia.

Collect

> Grant, we pray, almighty God, that as we believe your only-begotten One
> to have ascended into heaven, so we may also in heart and mind there
> ascend and with Christ continually dwell; who lives and reigns with you
> and the Holy Spirit, one God, for ever and ever. *Amen.*

Matins

Invitatory: Alleluia, Christ our God has ascended to heaven:
Response: O come, let us worship, alleluia.

This invitatory antiphon is used daily until the Day of Pentecost.
The canticle is the Te Deum, p. 213.
The hymn is Hymn C in the Ordinary of Eastertide, p. 174.

Antiphon on Benedictus

> Jesus said, I am going to send you what God has promised,*
> but stay where you are until you have been clothed
> with power from on high, Alleluia.

Diurnum

Antiphon on Psalter

When Jesus ascended on high, captivity itself was made captive;*
gifts were given to the saints for the work of ministry, Alleluia.

Lesson and Respond   ACTS 1:1-2

In the first part of my work, Theophilus, I wrote all that Jesus did and
taught from the beginning until the day when, after giving instructions
through the Holy Spirit to the apostles whom he had chosen, he was taken
up to heaven.

Response: Thanks be to God.

   v. Christ ascended into heaven, alleluia, alleluia.
   r. And reigns with God in glory, alleluia, alleluia.

The Office continues with the Closing Prayers in the Ordinary of Diurnum, p. 55.

Vespers

Hymn F in the Ordinary of Eastertide, p. 180.

Antiphon on Magnificat

O Mighty One of glory and God of Hosts,
today in triumph you ascended above all heavens;*
   leave us not orphans, but send to us the promise of God,
   even the Spirit of truth, Alleluia.

THE SEVENTH SUNDAY OF EASTER

Antiphon on New Testament Canticles

Year A

O God, glorify me in your own presence*
   with the glory which I had with you before the world began, Alleluia.

Year B

Holy God, protect by the power of your name those whom you have given me,*

that they may be one, as we are one, Alleluia.

Year C

May they all be one; as you, O God, are in me, and I in you,*

so also may they be in us, Alleluia.

Collect

O God, the Mighty One of glory, you have exalted Jesus Christ with great triumph to your dominion in heaven: Do not leave us comfortless, but send your Holy Spirit to strengthen us, and bring us to that place where our Savior Christ has gone before; who lives and reigns with you and the Holy Spirit, one God, in glory everlasting. *Amen.*

Diurnum

Antiphon on Psalter

Alleluia, Alleluia, Alleluia.

Lesson and Respond   Acts 1:8

You will receive power when the Holy Spirit comes upon you, and you will bear witness for me in Jerusalem, and all Judea and Samaria, and to the ends of the earth.

Response: Thanks be to God.

v. Christ is ascended into heaven, alleluia, alleluia.

r. And reigns with God in glory, alleluia, alleluia.

The Office continues with the Closing Prayers in the Ordinary of Diurnum, p. 55.

THE ORDINARY OF EASTER

Eastertide begins with the Easter Vigil and ends after Compline on the Day of Pentecost.
The Easter canticles are used on the days appointed until Pentecost, including Easter Week.
There are special propers appointed for Easter Week, beginning on p. 157.

MATINS

This invitatory antiphon is used daily until Ascension Day.

Invitatory: Alleluia, Christ is risen indeed:
Response: O come, let us worship, alleluia.

Antiphon on Psalter

Alleluia, alleluia, alleluia.

Canticles

The canticles below are used on the days appointed until Pentecost.

Monday and Thursday   EZEKIEL 36:24-28

I will take you out of the nations *
   and gather you from every land,
   and bring you to your own soil.

I will sprinkle clean water over you,
   and you shall be clean from all that defiles you; *
   I will cleanse you from the taint of all your idols.

I will give you a new heart *
   and put a new spirit within you;

I will take the heart of stone from your body *
   and give you a heart of flesh.

I will put my spirit into you
and make you conform to my statutes; *
you shall keep my laws and live by them.

You shall live in the land which I gave to your ancestors; *
you shall be my people,
and I will be your God.

Tuesday and Friday   PHILIPPIANS 4:47, 19-20

Rejoice in God always, *
and again I say, rejoice.

Let your gentleness be known to everyone: *
God is near.

Worry about nothing, *
but in everything, by prayer and with thanksgiving,
let your requests be made known to God;

Then the peace of God, which surpasses all understanding, *
will guard your hearts and your minds in Christ Jesus.

God will fully satisfy every need of yours, *
according to the glorious riches in Christ Jesus.

To God be honor and praise and blessing *
for ever and ever.

Wednesday and Saturday   ISAIAH 66:10-14

Rejoice with Jerusalem and be glad; *
all you who love Zion, rejoice, rejoice.

All you who mourn over the holy city, *
drink deeply with delight,
as from a mother's comforting breast.

For thus says God: *
I will extend peace to you like a river,
the wealth of nations like an overflowing stream.

You shall nurse and be carried on God's arm, *
and you shall nestle in God's lap.

As a mother comforts a child, so will I comfort you; *
   you shall be comforted in Jerusalem.

You shall see, and your heart shall rejoice; *
   you shall flourish like the grass of the field.

Hymns

A: From Easter Day through the week of Easter III:

> The light of radiant dawn streams out
> and praise fills heaven all about;
> earth echoes the exultant shout
> and groaning hell is put to rout.
>
> The risen Christ in glory bright
> has banished death's eternal night,
> and having harrowed hell with might
> brings forth the sleeping saints to light.
>
> We pray you, Christ, with glory crowned,
> let this our paschal joy resound;
> for we, who once by death were bound,
> through you have life and freedom found.
>
> To you, O risen Christ, once more,
> our joyous alleluias soar,
> whom with the Spirit we adore
> and the Creator evermore. Amen.

B: From Easter IV until Ascension Day:

> Entombed behind the stone of late,
> securely sealed, where soldiers wait,
> now shining in triumphant state,
> Christ rises victor from death's gate.
>
> Hell's chains are loosed and demons fled;
> captivity is captive led;
> the angel, crowned with light, has said:
> The Christ is risen from the dead.

We pray you, Christ, with glory crowned,
let this our paschal joy resound;
for we, who once by death were bound,
through you have life and freedom found.

To you, O risen Christ, once more,
our joyous alleluias soar,
whom with the Spirit we adore
and the Creator evermore. Amen.

C: From Ascension Day until Pentecost:

Jesus, Redemption from above,
for whom we long with reverent love,
born as a mortal, you began
to consummate creation's plan.

How great a love was yours to take
our human woes for humans' sake,
and pangs and cruel death to bear,
to ransom us from death's despair.

To you the power of hell gave way
when you called forth its captive prey;
and having won us for your own,
you have ascended to God's throne.

Let love and mercy lead you still
to raise us, conquering all our ill,
into your presence, there to be
in bliss throughout eternity.

All praise from every heart and tongue,
to you, ascended Christ, be sung,
whom, with the Spirit evermore
and the Creator, we adore. Amen.

Antiphon on Benedictus

For Sundays in Easter, see the Proper of Easter, p. 157.
The Benedictus will be found in the Ordinary of Matins, p. 31.

From the week of Easter II until Ascension Day:

Monday and Thursday

    God raised Jesus to life on the third day. *
        Jesus then appeared, not to the whole people,
        but to witnesses whom God had chosen, alleluia.

Tuesday and Friday

    Christ who died and was raised from the dead *
        is at God's right hand and pleads our cause, alleluia.

Wednesday

    It was Mary Magdalene, Joanna, Mary the mother of James,
    and the other women with them *
        who told the apostles of Jesus' resurrection, alleluia.

Saturday

    Rejoice and be glad, O Mary, alleluia; *
        for Christ is risen indeed, alleluia.

From the Friday after Ascension Day through the week of Easter VII:

Monday and Thursday

    Jesus said, If I do not go, your Advocate will not come; *
        but if I go, I will send the Spirit to you, alleluia.

Tuesday and Friday

    After giving instructions through the Holy Spirit to the apostles, *
        Jesus was taken up into heaven, alleluia.

Wednesday and Saturday

    You will receive power when the Holy Spirit comes upon you, *
        and you will be my witnesses, alleluia.

DIURNUM

Diurnum during Easter Week is as on Easter Day, p. 158.

Beginning with the week of Easter II:

Monday and Thursday
Antiphon on Psalter

    Alleluia, Alleluia, Alleluia.

Lesson and Respond from the week of Easter II until Ascension Day

ROMANS 6:9-10

    Christ being raised from the dead will never die again; death no longer has dominion. The death that Christ died was death to sin, once for all, but the life Christ lives, is life to God.

Response: Thanks be to God.

    v. Christ is risen from the dead, alleluia, alleluia.
    r. Who for our sake hung upon the tree, alleluia, alleluia.

The Office continues with the Closing Prayers in the Ordinary of Diurnum, p. 55.

Tuesday and Friday
Antiphon on Psalter

    Alleluia, Alleluia, Alleluia.

Lesson and Respond from the week of Easter II until Ascension Day

1 CORINTHIANS 15:20-22

    Christ has been raised from the dead, the first fruits of those who have fallen asleep. For since by a human being came death, by a human being has come also the resurrection of the dead. For as in Adam all die, so also in Christ shall all be made alive. Alleluia.

Response: Thanks be to God.

    v. Christ is risen from the dead, alleluia, alleluia.
    r. And has walked with the disciples on the road, alleluia, alleluia.

The Office continues with the Closing Prayers in the Ordinary of Diurnum, p. 55.

Wednesday and Saturday

Antiphon on Psalter

Alleluia, Alleluia, Alleluia.

Lesson and Respond from the week of Easter II until Ascension Day

COLOSSIANS 3:1-2

Since you have been raised up in company with Christ, set your heart on what pertains to higher realms where Christ is seated at God's right hand. Be intent on things above rather than on things of earth.

Response: Thanks be to God.

v. Then the disciples were glad, alleluia, alleluia.

r. When they saw the risen Christ, alleluia, alleluia.

The Office continues with the Closing Prayers in the Ordinary of Diurnum, p. 55.

Lesson and Respond from Friday after Ascension Day through week of Easter VII

ACTS 1:14

After Jesus ascended into heaven, the disciples, with the women, were constantly devoting themselves to prayer.

Response: Thanks be to God.

v. Christ has ascended into heaven, alleluia, alleluia.

r. And reigns with God in glory, alleluia, alleluia.

The Office continues with the Closing Prayers in the Ordinary of Diurnum, p. 55.

VESPERS

Antiphon on Psalter

Alleluia, alleluia, alleluia.

Canticles

Monday and Thursday EXODUS 15:1-18

Alleluia, I will sing to you, O God, for you are lofty and uplifted;*
  the chariots of Pharaoh and his army you have hurled into the sea.

The fathomless deep has overwhelmed them;*
  they sank into the depths like a stone, Alleluia.

Your right hand, O God, is glorious in might;*
  your right hand, O God, has overthrown the enemy, Alleluia.

Who can be compared with you, O God, among the gods?*
  Who is like you, glorious in holiness,
  awesome in renown, and worker of wonders?

With your constant love you led the people you redeemed;*
  with your might you brought them in safety
  to your holy dwelling, Alleluia.

You will bring them and plant them*
  on the mount of your possession:

the resting place you have made for yourself, O God,*
  the sanctuary, O God, that your hand has established.

God shall reign*
  for ever and ever, Alleluia.

Tuesday and Friday REVELATION 19:1-6

I heard the loud voice of a great multitude in heaven,*
  saying, "Alleluia, Alleluia!

Salvation and glory and power to our God,*
  whose judgments are true and just, Alleluia, Alleluia!"

The twenty-four elders and the four living creatures*
  fell down and worshiped God who is seated on the throne,
  saying, "Amen, Alleluia!"

From the throne came a voice saying, "Praise our God, all you servants,*
  and all who fear God, small and great."

Then I heard what seemed to be the cry of a great multitude,*
  like the sound of many waters, like the sound of mighty thunder-peals.

And the voices cried out, "Alleluia! Our God, the Almighty One,*
  reigns for ever, Alleluia, Alleluia!"

Alleluia, Alleluia.*
  See what love has been given to us,

that we should be called children of God;*
  for indeed so we are. Alleluia.

The world does not recognize us,*
  for the world has not recognized God.

Beloved, we are God's children now;*
  what we later will be has yet to be revealed.

What we do know is this:*
  when all things come to light, we will be like God,

for we will truly see God as God truly is: Alleluia.*
  All who have such hope in God purify themselves,

just as Christ is pure.*
  Alleluia, Alleluia.

Hymns

D: From Easter Day through the week of Easter III:

Now Christ our Passover we praise,
the Lamb who blesses all our days,
who for our freedom paid the price,
a full and perfect sacrifice.

Our people fled through parted sea
from Pharaoh's ruthless tyranny,
protected on that paschal night
from the destroying angel's might.

O Christ, you died the world to save,
and now are risen from the grave;
your captive people are set free
to share your endless victory.

To you, O risen Christ, we sing,
our alleluias echoing,
whom with the Spirit we adore
and the Creator evermore. Amen.

E: From Vespers of Saturday before Easter IV until eve of Ascension Day:
The Lamb's high feast that has no end
in festal garments we attend;
the Red Sea crossed, its terror past,
to you, O Christ, we sing at last.

Upon the altar of the cross
your body has redeemed our loss;
sustained now with your flesh and blood,
our life is hid with you in God.

Arisen from the dread abyss,
in triumph you return to bliss.
Hell's tyrant is subdued and chained,
and paradise for us regained.

To you, O risen Christ, we sing,
our alleluias echoing,
whom with the Spirit we adore
and the Creator evermore. Amen.

F: From the eve of Ascension Day until the eve of Pentecost:
Eternal Christ, let praises ring!
Salvation through your blood we sing;
by you the death of death was wrought
and grace to human life was brought.

Ascended to the throne of might
and seated at the Maker's right,
all power, Jesus, is your own
that here on earth you had not known.

To you the whole creation now
must in its ordered nature bow:
all things on earth, in sky and sea,
and to the farthest galaxy.

With awe the angels contemplate
the wondrous change in human state;
though flesh has sinned, flesh purged the stains,
and in that flesh our God now reigns.

All praise from every heart and tongue
to you, ascended Christ, be sung,
whom, with the Spirit evermore
and the Creator, we adore. Amen.

Antiphon on Magnificat

For Sundays in Easter, see the Proper of Easter, p. 159 ff.

The Magnificat will be found in the Ordinary of Vespers, p. 84.

From the week of Easter II to Ascension Day:

Monday and Thursday

God, who raised Christ Jesus from the dead, *
will also give new life to your mortal bodies through the indwelling
Spirit, Alleluia.

Tuesday and Friday

God who raised Jesus to life will with Jesus raise us, too, *
and bring us in to the holy presence, Alleluia.

Wednesday

You have come to trust in God through Jesus who was raised from
the dead and given glory, *
and so your faith and hope are fixed on God, Alleluia.

The antiphon on the Magnificat for Saturday is of the Sunday following.

From the Friday after Ascension Day through the week of Easter VII:

Monday and Thursday

All who are moved by the Spirit of God *
are children of God and can cry, Abba! Alleluia.

Tuesday and Friday

In Christ Jesus the life-giving law of the Spirit *
has set you free from the law of sin and death, Alleluia.

Wednesday

Make fast with bonds of peace the unity the Spirit gives.*
There is one Body and one Spirit, Alleluia.

The antiphon on the Magnificat on Saturday is of the Sunday following.

Eastertide ends after Compline on the Day of Pentecost.

THE DAY OF PENTECOST AND THE SEASON FOLLOWING

THE DAY OF PENTECOST

All as in Ordinary Time except as follows:

Antiphons on Psalter

While the day of Pentecost was running its course, *
the disciples were all together in one place, Alleluia.

or

Suddenly there came from the sky a noise like that of a strong
driving wind, *
which filled the whole house where they were sitting, Alleluia.

or

There appeared to them tongues like flames of fire, *
dispersed among them and resting on each one, Alleluia

or

They were all filled with the Holy Spirit, and began to talk in other
tongues, *
as the Spirit gave them the power of utterance, Alleluia.

or

The Spirit of God has filled the whole world, *
Alleluia, Alleluia, Alleluia.

Collect

Almighty God, on this day you opened the way of eternal life to all peoples
and nations by the promised gift of your Holy Spirit: Shed abroad this gift
throughout the world by the preaching of the gospel, that it may reach to
the ends of the earth; through Jesus Christ our Savior, who lives and reigns
with you in the unity of the Holy Spirit, one God, for ever and ever. *Amen.*

Matins

Invitatory: Alleluia, the Spirit of God renews the face of the earth:
Response: O come, let us worship, alleluia.

The canticle is the Te Deum, p. 213.

Hymn at Matins

Blest joys for mighty wonders wrought:
the yearly round once more has brought
the season when the Spirit came
on the disciples as in flame.

In many languages they praised;
the gathering people stood amazed;
and whom the Counselor divine
inspired, they mocked as full of wine.

But what the prophets once foresaw
was now received in wondering awe:
on those who served in Jesus' name,
the Spirit came in wind and flame.

O Holy Spirit, through our hearts
show forth the love your grace imparts;
from sin and strife grant us release,
and in our time, we pray, give peace.

O Holy Paraclete, to you
be praise and honor as is due,
whom with our Maker we adore,
and Jesus Christ, for evermore. Amen.

Antiphon on Benedictus

Receive the Holy Spirit. *
If you forgive anyone's sins, they stand forgiven, Alleluia.

Diurnum

Antiphon on Psalter

The Holy Spirit, whom God will send in my name, *
will teach you everything, Alleluia.

Lesson and Respond   1 Corinthians 12:6-7

There are many forms of work, but all of them, in all people, are the work of the same God. To each is given the manifestation of the Spirit for the common good.

Response: Thanks be to God.

    v. The Holy Spirit, the Counselor, alleluia, alleluia. *
    r. Will be with you for ever, alleluia, alleluia.

The Office continues with the Closing Prayers in the Ordinary of Diurnum, p. 55.

Vespers

The canticle at Vespers is the Benedicite, p. 120.

Hymn at Vespers

> O come, Creator Spirit, come,
> and make within our souls your home.
> Come with your grace and heavenly aid,
> and fill the hearts which you have made.
>
> To you, the gift of God most high,
> to you, the Counselor, we cry:
> enflame our souls with holy fire,
> and warm us with divine desire.
>
> Drive far away our unseen foe.
> your sevenfold gift to us bestow;
> your wisdom to our minds impart,
> and shed your light in every heart.
>
> Flood our dull senses with your light:
> in mutual love our hearts unite;
> your power the whole creation fills:
> make strong our weak, uncertain wills.
>
> So make our great Creator known,
> teach us th'eternal Christ to own,
> while we, with all the saints above,
> acknowledge you the bond of love.

To you, O Holy Spirit, blest,
all praise and honor be addressed,
whom with our Maker we adore,
and Jesus Christ, for evermore. Amen.

Antiphon on Magnificat at Vespers

I will ask God, who will give you another to be your advocate, *
who will be with you for ever, the Spirit of Truth, Alleluia.

or

Today is the fiftieth day: today the Spirit came in fire; today God
bestowed manifold graces upon the disciples, *
and sent them through the world
to preach the Gospel: believe and be baptized, Alleluia.

*For ferias (open days) occurring in the week of Pentecost, use the Ordinary of the Office with the
collect from the numbered Propers below, p. 194ff.*

THE FIRST BOOK OF COMMON PRAYER

This feast is appropriately observed in the week following the Day of Pentecost.

All as in Common 9, p. 244, except as below.

Collect

Almighty and everliving God, you endowed your servant Thomas Cranmer
with rare and enduring gifts in language and liturgy and enabled him with
others to present to your people the prayers of the Church in their own
tongue: We give you thanks for this legacy, and pray that it may continue
to transform and enrich the Church, so that it may offer worship to your
greater glory; through the Word made flesh, who lives and reigns with you
and the Holy Spirit, one God, now and for ever. *Amen.*

Antiphon on Benedictus

Blessed Savior, you have caused all holy scriptures to be written for
our learning; *
may we hear them, read, mark, learn and inwardly digest them
and ever hold fast the blessed hope of everlasting life.

Antiphon on Magnificat

Grant to us your people that we may love what you command and
desire what you promise *
    that our hearts may surely there be fixed where true joys are to be found.

THE EMBER DAYS

The Ember Days are traditionally kept on Wednesday, Friday and Saturday after the Day of Pentecost.

The Office is Common 11, p. 251.

TRINITY SUNDAY: THE FIRST SUNDAY AFTER PENTECOST

Antiphons on Psalter

Praise and unending glory to the Creator, and the Word,
and the Holy Spirit, *
    three Persons in one God, Alleluia.

or

The Creator spoke the Word, and there was light, *
    and the Spirit moved over the face of the waters.

or

The Living Word was conceived by the power of the Holy Spirit *
    and was sent for our salvation.

or

Go and make all nations my disciples, *
    baptizing them in the Name of the Trinity, one God in three Persons.

or

Of whom are all things, through whom are all things,
in whom are all things: *
    to God be glory for ever.

Collect

Almighty and everlasting God, you have given to us your servants grace, by the confession of a true faith, to acknowledge the glory of the eternal Trinity, and to worship the Unity: Keep us steadfast in this faith and worship, and bring us at last to see you in your one and eternal glory, for you live and reign, one God in three Persons, for ever and ever. *Amen.*

Matins

Invitatory: God is one: Source of all being, Incarnate Word and Holy Spirit:
Response: O come, let us worship.

The canticle is the Te Deum, p. 213.

Hymn at Matins

> Be present, Holy Trinity,
> one splendor and one deity,
> the source on whom all things depend,
> divine beginning without end.
>
> The hosts of interstellar space
> adore and sing your wondrous grace;
> the whole creation joins to bless
> your everlasting holiness.
>
> And we, your people, humbly pay
> all homage to your name today;
> we join with the celestial throng
> to honor you in sacred song.
>
> All laud to our Creator be,
> to Jesus Christ eternally,
> and to the Spirit equal praise
> from joyful hearts we ever raise. Amen.

Antiphon on Benedictus

Blessed be the holy Creator and governor of all things, the holy and undivided Trinity, *
> both now and to endless ages of ages.

Diurnum

Antiphon on Psalter

The grace of our Savior Jesus Christ, and the love of God, *
and the communion of the Holy Spirit, be with you all.

Lesson and Respond   ROMANS 11:33

O the depth of the riches and wisdom and knowledge in God! How
unsearchable are God's judgments, how untraceable God's ways!

Response: Thanks be to God.

v. Blest are you, O Holy One, in the firmament of heaven.
r. You are to be praised and glorified for ever.

The Office continues with the Closing Prayers in the Ordinary of Diurnum, p. 55.

Vespers

The canticle at Vespers is the Benedicite, p. 120.

Hymn at Vespers

O great Creator, merciful and faithful;
O Jesus, Savior, humble and most loving;
O Holy Spirit, advocate, sustainer;
    Godhead eternal.

The whole creation serves you in its being;
let all your creatures laud and magnify you;
we also laud you, Trinity most holy:
    hear us, we pray you.

Trinity blessed, Unity most steadfast,
true God most holy, goodness beyond measure,
light of the angels, help of the forsaken,
    hope of all nations.

In the one Spirit we are called to worship
God our Creator, Savior, Sanctifier:
to you be glory in both earth and heaven
    throughout the ages. Amen.

Antiphon on Magnificat at Vespers

> Let praise and glory resound from all creation *
> to the Mighty God, and the Incarnate One, and the Holy Spirit.

For ferias (open days) occurring in the week of Trinity Sunday, the Ordinary of the Office with the collect from the numbered Propers below, p. 194 ff, is used.

THE FEAST OF THE HOLY EUCHARIST

On the Thursday after Trinity Sunday: also called Corpus Christi

Lessons:	I VESPERS	Exodus 12:21-28	Mark 14:12-26
	MATINS	Genesis 14:13-20	Hebrews 4:14--5:10
	II VESPERS	Exodus 16:4, 14-21	John 6:27-40

Antiphons on Psalter

> Christ, the Anointed One, a priest for ever after the order of Melchizedek, *
> offered bread and wine.

or

> The gracious and merciful God provides bread and wine for the faithful: *
> the body and blood of Christ.

or

> I will lift up the cup of salvation, *
> and offer the sacrifice of thanksgiving.

or

> May the children of the church be like olive branches *
> around the table of the Holy One.

or

> The One who makes peace in the church's borders is the Holy One, *
> who fills us with the finest of the wheat.

Collect

O Jesus Christ, in a wonderful Sacrament you have left us a memorial of your passion: Grant us so to venerate the sacred mysteries of your body and blood, that we may ever perceive within ourselves the fruit of your redemption; who with the Creator and the Holy Spirit live and reign, one God, for ever and ever. *Amen.*

Matins

Invitatory: Jesus said, My flesh is food indeed, and my blood is drink indeed:
Response: O come, let us worship.

The canticle is the Te Deum, p. 213.

Hymn at Matins

Now my tongue, the mystery telling,
    sing the glorious body's worth,
and the blood, all price excelling,
    which the Savior of the earth
in a woman's womb once dwelling,
    shed for all of human birth.

Given for us, and condescending
    to be born for us below,
Jesus, loving and befriending,
    taught us truth we longed to know,
till that life with wondrous ending
    closed in agony and woe.

Word-made-flesh, your word is making
    living bread your flesh to be;
with your blood, the wine is slaking
    all our thirst eternally;
faith, not sense, is now awaking
    to proclaim this mystery.

Now in hymns and joy confessing,
    let us praise the Trinity:
to the Word, our love addressing,
    to the Spirit, glory be,
to our Maker, we sing blessing
    now and in eternity. Amen.

Antiphon on Benedictus

I am that living bread which has come down from heaven; *
anyone who eats this bread shall live for ever, Alleluia.

Diurnum

Antiphon on Psalter

Wisdom has built her house; she has mingled her wine *
and furnished her table.

Lesson and Respond   1 CORINTHIANS 11:23-24

I received what I also handed on to you, that Jesus on the night when he
was betrayed took a loaf of bread, and when he had given thanks, he broke
it and said, "This is my body that is for you. Do this in remembrance of me."

Response: Thanks be to God.

v.   The bread which I give is my flesh, alleluia, alleluia.
r.   I give it for the life of the world, alleluia, alleluia.

The Office continues with the Closing Prayers in the Ordinary of Diurnum, p. 55.

Vespers

The canticle at Vespers is the Benedicite, p. 120.

> That last night, at supper lying
> > with the twelve, his chosen band,
> Jesus, with the law complying,
> > keeps the feast its rites demand;
> then, more precious food supplying,
> > gives himself with his own hand.
>
> Therefore we before God bending,
> > this great sacrament revere;
> types and shadows have their ending,
> > for the newer rite is here;
> faith, our outward sense befriending,
> > makes our inward vision clear.
>
> Now in hymns and joy confessing,
> > let us praise the Trinity:
> to the Word, our love addressing,
> > to the Spirit, glory be,
> to our Maker, we sing blessing
> > now and in eternity. Amen.

Antiphon on Magnificat at Vespers

To show kindness to your people, O God, you give them that sweetest bread from heaven, *
> you fill the hungry with good things and send the rich and
> scornful away empty, Alleluia.

or

O sacred banquet, in which Jesus is received, the memory of his passion is renewed, *
> the soul is filled with grace, and a pledge of future glory is bestowed,
> Alleluia.

After Pentecost

After Pentecost (Ordinary Time), the lessons at Matins and Vespers, the antiphon on the New Testament canticles for Saturday Vespers and Sunday Matins and Vespers, and the collects are taken from the numbered propers below. All the rest is from the Ordinary of the Office.

Each Sunday after Pentecost uses the Proper of the date to which it comes nearest, whether before or after. In the weeks of Pentecost and of Trinity Sunday the festal propers, including the collect, are used only on the Sunday; the numbered Proper is used on ferias(open days) through the following week. Since Propers 1 and 2 can fall only on Pentecost or Trinity Sunday, antiphons on New Testament canticles are not provided for those propers. For an explanation of the use of Years A, B, and C, see the editors' introduction.

PROPER 1   The Sunday closest to May 11

Collect

> Remember, O God, what you have wrought in us and not what we deserve; and as you have called us to your service, make us worthy of our calling; through Jesus Christ our Savior, who lives and reigns with you and the Holy Spirit, one God, now and for ever. *Amen.*

PROPER 2   The Sunday closest to May 18

Collect

> Almighty and merciful God, in your goodness keep us, we pray, from all things that may hurt us, that we, being ready both in mind and body, may accomplish with free hearts those things which belong to your purpose; through Jesus Christ our Savior, who lives and reigns with you and the Holy Spirit, one God, for ever and ever. *Amen.*

PROPER 3   The Sunday closest to May 25

Antiphon on New Testament Canticles

Year A

> No servant can be the slave of two masters; *
> you cannot serve God and money.

Year B

> The time will come when the bridegroom will be taken away from them, *
> and in that day they will fast.

Year C

> The good person out of the good treasure of the heart produces good, *
> for it is out of the abundance of the heart that the mouth speaks.

Collect

Grant, O God, that the course of this world may be peaceably governed by your providence; and that your Church may joyfully serve you in confidence and serenity; through Jesus Christ our Savior, who lives and reigns with you and the Holy Spirit, one God, now and for ever. *Amen.*

PROPER 4   The Sunday closest to June 1

Antiphon on New Testament Canticles

Year A

Everyone who hears these words of mine and acts upon them *
  is like one who had the sense to build a house on rock.

Year B

The sabbath was made for humankind, not humankind for the Sabbath; *
  so God's Chosen One reigns even over the Sabbath.

Year C

It is not for me to have you under my roof; *
  but say the word and my servant will be cured.

Collect

O God, your never-failing providence sets in order all things both in heaven and earth: Put away from us, we entreat you, all hurtful things, and give us those things which are profitable for us; through Jesus Christ our Savior, who lives and reigns with you and the Holy Spirit, one God, for ever and ever. *Amen.*

PROPER 5   The Sunday closest to June 8

Antiphon on New Testament Canticles

Year A

Jesus said, It is not the healthy that need a doctor, but the sick; *
  I did not come to call virtuous people, but sinners.

Year B

Jesus said, Whoever does the will of God *
  is my brother, my sister, my mother.

A great prophet has risen among us, they said. *
God has looked with favor on the people.

Collect

O God, from whom all good proceeds: Grant that by your inspiration we
may think those things that are right, and by your merciful guidance may
do them; through Jesus Christ our Savior, who lives and reigns with you
and the Holy Spirit, one God, now and for ever. *Amen.*

PROPER 6   The Sunday closest to June 15

Antiphon on New Testament Canticles

Year A

The crop is heavy, but the laborers are few; *
you must therefore beg the owner to send laborers to harvest the crop.

Year B

With many such parables Jesus would give them his message, *
so far as they were able to receive it.

Year C

Her great love proves that her many sins have been forgiven; *
where little has been forgiven, little love is shown.

Collect

Keep, O Holy One, your household the Church in your steadfast faith and
love; that through your grace we may proclaim your truth with boldness
and administer your justice with compassion; for the sake of our Savior
Jesus Christ, who lives and reigns with you and the Holy Spirit, one God,
for ever and ever. *Amen.*

PROPER 7   The Sunday closest to June 22

Antiphon on New Testament Canticles

Year A

Even the hairs of your head have all been counted; *
so have no fear, you are worth more than any number of sparrows.

Year B

> Jesus said to them, Why are you such cowards? *
> Have you no faith even now?

Year C

> Anyone who wishes to be a follower of mine must leave self behind, *
> take up the cross and come with me.

Collect

> O God, may we have perpetual love and reverence for your holy name, for
> you never fail to help and govern those whom you have set upon the sure
> foundation of your loving-kindness ; through Jesus Christ our Savior, who
> lives and reigns with you and the Holy Spirit, one God, for ever and ever.
> *Amen.*

PROPER 8   The Sunday closest to June 29

Antiphon on New Testament Canticles

Year A

> Anyone who gives so much as a cup of cold water to one of these little ones *
> will not go unrewarded.

Year B

> Jesus said, Get up, my child; and immediately the girl got up, *
> and he told them to give her something to eat.

Year C

> No one who sets hand to the plow and then keeps looking back *
> is fit for the reign of God.

Collect

> Almighty God, you have built your Church upon the foundation of the
> apostles and prophets, Jesus Christ being the chief cornerstone: Grant us
> so to be joined together in unity of spirit by their teaching, that we may
> be made a holy temple acceptable to you; through Jesus Christ our Savior,
> who lives and reigns with you and the Holy Spirit, one God, for ever and
> ever. *Amen.*

The Sunday closest to July 6

Antiphon on New Testament Canticles

Year A

> Take my yoke upon you and learn from me; *
> for I am gentle and humble in heart, and you will find rest for your souls.

Year B

> Prophets are not without honor, *
> except in their home town, and among their own kin,
> and in their own house.

Year C

> The crop is heavy, but the laborers are scarce; *
> you must therefore beg the owner to send laborers to harvest the crop.

Collect

> O God, you have taught us to keep all your commandments by loving you
> and our neighbor: Grant us the grace of your Holy Spirit, that we may be
> devoted to you with our whole heart, and united to one another with pure
> affection; through Jesus Christ our Savior, who lives and reigns with you
> and the Holy Spirit, one God, for ever and ever. *Amen.*

PROPER 10 The Sunday closest to July 13

Antiphon on New Testament Canticles

Year A

> Whoever hears the word of God and understands it *
> is one who bears much fruit.

Year B

> The disciples set out and called publicly for repentance, *
> and many sick people they anointed and cured.

Year C

> Love God with all your heart, with all your soul, with all your strength,
> and with all your mind; *
> and your neighbor as yourself.

Collect

O God, mercifully receive the prayers of your people who call upon you, and grant that they may know and understand what things they ought to do, and also may have grace and power faithfully to accomplish them; through Jesus Christ our Savior, who lives and reigns with you and the Holy Spirit, one God, now and for ever. *Amen.*

PROPER 11   The Sunday closest to July 20

Antiphon on New Testament Canticles

Year A

The righteous will shine as brightly as the sun *
   in the reign of God.

Year B

Jesus' heart went out to the people, because they were like sheep without a shepherd, *
   and he had much to teach them.

Year C

The part that Mary has chosen is best, *
   and it shall not be taken away from her.

Collect

Almighty God, the fountain of all wisdom, you know our necessities before we ask and our ignorance in asking: Have compassion on our weakness; and mercifully give us those things which for our unworthiness we dare not, and for our blindness we cannot ask; through the worthiness of Jesus Christ our Savior, who lives and reigns with you and the Holy Spirit, one God, now and for ever. *Amen.*

PROPER 12   The Sunday closest to July 27

Antiphon on New Testament Canticles

Year A

The reign of heaven is like yeast, which a woman took *
   and mixed with half a hundredweight of flour till it was all leavened.

Year B

> Jesus, coming to the disciples on the turbulent sea, said, *
> Take heart! It is I; do not be afraid.

Year C

> Ask and you will receive, seek and you will find, *
> knock and the door will be opened.

Collect

O God, the protector of all who trust in you, without whom nothing is strong, nothing is holy: Increase and multiply upon us your mercy; that, with you as our ruler and guide, we may so pass through things temporal, that we lose not the things eternal; through Jesus Christ our Savior, who lives and reigns with you and the Holy Spirit, one God, now and for ever. *Amen.*

PROPER 13   The Sunday closest to August 3

Antiphon on New Testament Canticles

Year A

> When Jesus came ashore and saw a great crowd, *
> his heart went out to them, and he fed them all.

Year B

> I am the bread of life; whoever comes to me shall never be hungry, *
> and whoever believes in me shall never be thirsty.

Year C

> Be on your guard against greed of every kind, *
> for wealth does not give us life.

Collect

Let your continual mercy, O God, cleanse and defend your Church; and, because it cannot continue in safety without your help, protect and govern it always by your goodness; through Jesus Christ our Savior, who lives and reigns with you and the Holy Spirit, one God, for ever and ever. *Amen.*

PROPER 14 The Sunday closest to August 10

Antiphon on New Testament Canticles

Year A

> Jesus climbed into the boat and the wind dropped; *
> they fell at his feet, exclaiming, Truly you are the Anointed One of God.

Year B

> All that God gives me will come to me, *
> and they that come to me I will never turn away.

Year C

> Provide for yourselves a never-failing treasure in heaven, *
> where no thief can get near it, no moth destroy it.

Collect

> Grant to us, O God, we pray, the spirit to think and do always those
> things that are right, that we, who cannot exist without you, may by you
> be enabled to live according to your will; through Jesus Christ our Savior,
> who lives and reigns with you and the Holy Spirit, one God, now and for
> ever. *Amen.*

PROPER 15 The Sunday closest to August 17

Antiphon on New Testament Canticles

Year A

> Jesus replied, Woman, what faith you have! Be it as you wish. *
> From that moment her daughter was healed.

Year B

> They who eat my flesh and drink my blood *
> dwell continually in me and I dwell in them.

Year C

> I have a baptism to undergo *
> and how hampered I am until the ordeal is over.

Collect

Almighty God, you have given your Incarnate One to be for us a sacrifice for sin, and also an example of godly life: Give us grace to receive thankfully the fruits of Jesus' redeeming work, and to follow daily in the blessed steps of that most holy life; this we pray in the name of the Trinity, one God, in glory everlasting. *Amen.*

PROPER 16 The Sunday closest to August 24

Antiphon on New Testament Canticles

Year A

Simon Peter answered, You are the Messiah, *
the Holy One of God.

Year B

The Spirit alone gives life, the flesh is of no avail; *
the words which I have spoken to you are both spirit and life.

Year C

Some who are now last will be first; *
and some who are first will be last.

Collect

Grant, O merciful God, that your Church, being gathered together in unity by your Holy Spirit, may show forth your power among all peoples, to the glory of your name; through Jesus Christ our Savior, who lives and reigns with you and the Holy Spirit, one God, now and for ever. *Amen.*

PROPER 17 The Sunday closest to August 31

Antiphon on New Testament Canticles

Year A

Those who would save their lives will lose them, *
and those who lose their lives for my sake, will find their true selves.

Year B

Jesus rebuked those who put aside the commandments of God *
in order to maintain human tradition.

Year C

Those who exalt themselves will be humbled; *
and those who humble themselves will be exalted.

Collect

God of all power and might, the author and giver of all good things: Graft in our hearts the love of your name; increase in us true religion; nourish us with all goodness; and bring forth in us the fruit of good works; through Jesus Christ our Savior, who lives and reigns with you and the Holy Spirit, one God, now and for ever. *Amen.*

PROPER 18   The Sunday closest to September 7

Antiphon on New Testament Canticles

Year A

If two of you agree on earth about any request, *
that request will be granted by my God in heaven.

Year B

The people said, All Jesus does he does well; *
he even makes the deaf hear and the mute speak.

Year C

Would any of you think of building a tower *
without first calculating the cost?

Collect

Grant us, O God, to trust in you with all our heart; for as you always resist the proud who confide in their own strength, so you never forsake those who make their boast in your mercy; through Jesus Christ our Savior, who lives and reigns with you and the Holy Spirit, one God, now and for ever. *Amen.*

PROPER 19   The Sunday closest to September 14

Antiphon on New Testament Canticles

Year A

Peter asked, How often am I to forgive, if they go on wronging me? *
Jesus replied, I do not say seven times; I say seventy times seven.

> If anyone is ashamed of me and mine in this wicked and godless age, *
> I will be ashamed of them when I come in glory.

Year C

> The good shepherd goes after the missing sheep until it is found, *
> then brings it home with jubilation.

Collect

> O God, because without you we are not able to please you: Mercifully
> grant that your Holy Spirit may in all things direct and rule our hearts;
> through Jesus Christ our Savior, who lives and reigns with you and the
> Holy Spirit, one God, for ever and ever. *Amen.*

THE EMBER DAYS

The Ember Days are traditionally kept on Wednesday, Friday and Saturday after September 14.

The Office is Common 11, p. 251.

PROPER 20   The Sunday closest to September 21

Antiphon on New Testament Canticles

Year A

> Call the laborers and give them their pay, *
> beginning with those who came last and ending with the first.

Year B

> Those who want to be first, *
> must make themselves last of all and servants of all.

Year C

> No servant can be the slave of two masters; *
> you can not serve God and money.

Collect

Grant us, O God, not to be anxious about earthly things, but to love things heavenly; and even now, while we are placed among things that are passing away, to hold fast to those that shall endure; through Jesus Christ our Savior, who lives and reigns with you and the Holy Spirit, one God, now and for ever. *Amen.*

PROPER 21　　　　The Sunday closest to September 28

Antiphon on New Testament Canticles

Year A

The son who said, I will not, but afterwards did the task, *
is the one who did his father's will.

Year B

No one who does a work of divine power in my name *
will be able the next moment to speak evil of me.

Year C

If they do not listen to Moses and the prophets, *
they will pay no heed even if someone should rise from the dead.

Collect

O God, you declare your mighty power chiefly in showing mercy and pity: Grant us the fullness of your grace, that we, running to obtain your promises, may become partakers of your heavenly treasure; through Jesus Christ our Savior, who lives and reigns with you and the Holy Spirit, one God, now and for ever. *Amen.*

PROPER 22　　　　The Sunday closest to October 5

Antiphon on New Testament Canticles

Year A

The stone which the builders rejected has become the main cornerstone, *
and this is God's doing.

Year B

What God has joined together, *
let no one separate.

Year C

> When you have carried out all your orders, you should say, *
> we have only done our duty.

Collect

> Almighty and everlasting God, you are always more ready to hear than
> we to pray, and to give more than we either desire or deserve: Pour upon
> us the abundance of your mercy, forgiving us those things of which our
> conscience is afraid, and giving us those good things for which we are not
> worthy to ask, except through the merits and mediation of Jesus Christ
> our Savior; who lives and reigns with you and the Holy Spirit, one God,
> now and for ever. *Amen.*

PROPER 23   The Sunday closest to October 12

Antiphon on New Testament Canticles

Year A

> The servants went out in to the streets and collected all they could find; *
> so the wedding hall was filled with guests.

Year B

> Jesus said, Go, sell everything you have and give to the poor, *
> and you will have riches in heaven.

Year C

> Were not all ten cleansed? The other nine, where are they? *
> Would none give praise to God except this Samaritan?

Collect

> O God, we pray that your grace may always precede and follow us, that
> we may continually be given to good works; through Jesus Christ our
> Savior, who lives and reigns with you and the Holy Spirit, one God, now
> and for ever. *Amen.*

PROPER 24   The Sunday closest to October 19

Antiphon on New Testament Canticles

Year A

Pay Caesar what is due to Caesar, *
and pay God what is due to God.

Year B

The cup that I drink, you shall drink, *
and the baptism I am baptized with shall be your baptism.

Year C

God will vindicate all those who call day and night *
and will listen patiently to them.

Collect

Almighty and everlasting God, in Christ you have revealed your glory among the nations: Preserve the works of your mercy, that your Church throughout the world may persevere with steadfast faith in the confession of your name; through Jesus Christ our Savior, who lives and reigns with you and the Holy Spirit, one God, for ever and ever. *Amen.*

PROPER 25   The Sunday closest to October 26

Antiphon on New Testament Canticles

Year A

Love God: this is the first and greatest commandment. *
The second is like it: love your neighbor as yourself.

Year B

Blind Bartimaeus shouted, Son of David, Jesus, have pity on me! *
Jesus replied, Go, your faith has cured you.

Year C

It was the penitent tax collector, not the Pharisee, *
who went home acquitted of his sins.

Collect

Almighty and everlasting God, increase in us the gifts of faith, hope, and charity; and, that we may obtain what you promise, make us love what you command; through Jesus Christ our Savior, who lives and reigns with you and the Holy Spirit, one God, now and for ever. *Amen.*

PROPER 26 The Sunday closest to November 2

Antiphon on New Testament Canticles

Year A

Those who exalt themselves will be humbled; *
  and those who humble themselves will be exalted.

Year B

Love God: this is the first and greatest commandment. *
  The second is like it: love your neighbor as yourself.

Year C

Jesus looked up and said, Zacchaeus, be quick and come down; *
  I must come and stay with you today.

Collect

Almighty and merciful God, it is only by your gift that your faithful people offer you true and laudable service: Grant that we may run without stumbling to obtain your heavenly promises; through Jesus Christ our Savior, who lives and reigns with you and the Holy Spirit, one God, for ever and ever. *Amen.*

PROPER 27 The Sunday closest to November 9

Antiphon on New Testament Canticles

Year A

When the bridegroom arrived, those that were ready went in with him to the wedding; *
  and then the door was shut.

Year B

This poor widow has given more than any of the others; *
  for she has given all that she had to live on.

Year C

    God is not God of the dead but of the living; *
        for in God all are alive.

Collect

    O God, who sent Jesus into the world to destroy the powers of evil and
    make us children of God and heirs of eternal life: Grant that, having this
    hope, we may grow in holiness of life; and that, when Christ comes with
    power and great majesty, we may share in the glory of all the redeemed;
    this we pray in the name of the Trinity, one God, in glory everlasting..
    Amen.

PROPER 28   The Sunday closest to November 16

Antiphon on New Testament Canticles

Year A

    After a long time, the owner returned *
        and settled accounts with the servants.

Year B

    Imposters will come, claiming to be messiahs or prophets. *
        Be on your guard; I have forewarned you.

Year C

    Take care that you are not misled. *
        For many will come, claiming my Name.

Collect

    Blessed God, who caused all holy scriptures to be written for our learning:
    Grant us so to hear them, read, mark, learn, and inwardly digest them,
    that we may embrace and ever hold fast the blessed hope of everlasting life
    which you have given us in our Savior Jesus Christ; who lives and reigns
    with you and the Holy Spirit, one God, now and for ever. *Amen.*

PROPER 29   The Sunday closest to November 23

The Feast of Christ in Majesty: The Last Sunday in Pentecost

Antiphons on Psalter

Christ shall be called the Peaceful One, *
whose reign shall be established for ever, Alleluia.

or

The reign of Christ is an everlasting reign *
and all dominions shall serve and obey God, Alleluia.

or

Here is the one named the Branch, who will be enthroned and will govern, *
and will speak peace to all, Alleluia.

or

God has given Christ dominion and power and glory, *
that all peoples, nations, and languages should serve the Savior, Alleluia.

or

Christ shall be great even to the ends of the earth, *
and all shall know everlasting peace, Alleluia.

Collect

O everlasting God, whose will it is to restore all things in Jesus Christ, the
One who reigns in majesty: Mercifully grant that the peoples of the earth,
divided and enslaved by sin, may be freed and brought together under
Christ's most gracious rule; who lives and reigns with you and the Holy
Spirit, one God, now and for ever. *Amen.*

Matins

Invitatory: Alleluia, Christ is our peace, who ever reigns on high:
Response: O come, let us worship, alleluia.

The canticle is the Te Deum, p. 213.

Hymn at Matins

> Christ is enthroned at God's right hand,
> creation's homage to command;
> may we our grateful voices raise
> to sing the reign of love in praise.
>
> Christ has not won an empire here
> by devastation, force or fear,
> but on the cross, by love alone,
> draws all who love to be God's own.
>
> May every nation, tribe and race
> respond to love's divine embrace,
> Christ's true authority acclaim,
> and join in worship of that Name.
>
> All thanks to you, eternal Christ,
> who for our world was sacrificed,
> whom with the Most High we adore,
> and Holy Spirit evermore. Amen.

Antiphon on Benedictus

> My dominion does not belong to this world. *
> My authority comes from elsewhere, Alleluia.

Diurnum

Antiphon on Psalter

> Let us praise the Christ of God, the Holy One of Peace, *
> whose love is everlasting, Alleluia.

Lesson and Respond   COLOSSIANS 1:11-14

> May you be made strong with all the strength that comes from God's
> glorious power, and may you be prepared to endure everything with
> patience, while joyfully giving thanks to the one who has enabled you to
> share in the inheritance of the saints in the light. You have been rescued
> from the power of darkness and transferred into the dominion of the
> Holy One, in whom you have redemption, the forgiveness of sins.

Response: Thanks be to God.

v. Jesus said, Full authority has been committed to me, alleluia, alleluia.
r. Go forth and make all nations my disciples, alleluia, alleluia.

Vespers

The canticle at Vespers is the Benedicite, p. 120.

Hymn at Vespers

To you, who made all worlds to be,
all time and all eternity,
O Christ, we dedicate our days
and this day fill with grateful praise.

Our universe is in your hand,
the planet earth, its seas and land;
you, Christ, who fashioned starry space,
brought to our world your saving grace.

O Jesus, guard us and subdue
all rebel thoughts that banish you,
and bring before your loving sway
all those who wander from your way.

Our dearest advocate and friend,
help us awaken and attend,
that we, in our time, may increase
your law of love, your reign of peace.

All thanks to you, eternal Christ,
who for our world was sacrificed,
whom with the Most High we adore,
and Holy Spirit evermore. Amen.

Antiphon on Magnificat at Vespers

Christ will come in glory, with all the holy angels, *
and will reign in glorious majesty, Alleluia.

or

Blessed be Christ who comes to reign in the name of God: *
Peace in heaven, and glory in the highest, Alleluia.

The Common of Saints

Common 1

Presentation *(February 2)*, Annunciation *(March 25)*, Visitation *(May 31)*, and all feasts of Mary

For the collect, see the Proper of Saints.

Matins

Invitatory: (*in Eastertide*, Alleluia.) The Word was made flesh and dwelt among us:

Response: O come, let us worship. (*in Eastertide*, Alleluia.)

Antiphon on Psalter

God has been gracious to you, Mary; you will conceive and bear a child *
who shall be given the name Jesus. (ET Alleluia.)

Canticle at Matins   Te Deum

We praise you, O God; *
  we acclaim you as the Holy One:

All creation worships you, *
  Sovereign eternal.

To you all angels, all the powers of heaven, *
  cherubim and seraphim, sing in endless praise.

Holy, holy, holy One, God of power and might, *
  and earth are full of your glory.

The glorious company of apostles praise you; *
  the noble gathering of prophets praise you;

The white-robed choir of martyrs praise you; *
　　throughout the world the holy church acclaims you:

God of infinite majesty,
your true and only Word, worthy of all worship, *
　　the Holy Spirit, advocate and guide.

❖　　　❖　　　❖

You, Christ, reign in glory, *
　　you are the eternal Word of God.

When you came among us to set us free, *
　　you chose to be born of a woman.

You overcame the sting of death *
　　and opened heaven to all believers.

You are seated at God's right hand in glory; *
　　we believe that you will come and be our judge.

❖　　　❖　　　❖

Come then, Christ, and help your people, *
　　bought with the price of your own blood;

And bring us with your saints *
　　to glory everlasting.

Hymn at Matins

O glorious maid exalted far
beyond the light of radiant star,
by your Creator you were given
grace to conceive the Word from heaven.

As second Eve, you brought to birth
the second Adam, who on earth
the powers of evil overthrew;
in Jesus we are born anew.

Through you, the gate of heavenly grace,
was born the Savior of our race.
Christians, rejoice! for through a maid
our life eternal is conveyed.

O Jesus, to your name we raise
our grateful hymn of love and praise;
to our Creator homage bring,
as by the Spirit here we sing. Amen.

Antiphon on Benedictus

How happy is she who has had faith *
that God's promise would be fulfilled! (*in Eastertide*, Alleluia.)

Diurnum

Antiphon on Psalter

Mary said, I am God's servant; *
as you have spoken, so be it. (*in Eastertide*, Alleluia.)

Lesson and Respond   Isaiah 7:14

Therefore God will give you this sign: the young woman shall conceive,
and bear a child, who shall be named Emmanuel.

Response: Thanks be to God.

  v. Hail Mary, full of grace, God is with you.
  (*in Eastertide*, Alleluia, alleluia.)
  r. Blest are you among women, and blest is the fruit of your womb.
  (*in Eastertide*, Alleluia, alleluia.)

The Office continues with the Closing Prayers in the Ordinary of Diurnum, p. 55.

Vespers

Antiphon on Psalter

The Holy Spirit will come upon you, and the power of the Most High
will overshadow you; *
  therefore the child to be born will be called the Holy One of God.
  (*in Eastertide*, Alleluia.)

Canticle at Vespers TRADITIONAL MARIAN ANTIPHON WITH TEXT FROM
LUKE 1:26-31 AND OTHER SOURCES

The Archangel Gabriel appeared and spoke to Mary:*
  Hail, hail, most favored one, blest and chosen by God.

The Holy Spirit shall overshadow you,*
grace shall be given you;*
  you shall bear a son, and you shall name him Jesus.

Thus was she called to bear the Christ Child;*
  likewise are we also called
  to bring forth God's light into the world.

May Mary be to us a model of servanthood,*
  and show us Jesus, the blessed fruit of her womb.

O gentle, O tender,*
  O gracious Mother of Jesus.

Hymn at Vespers

Mary, fairest mortal,
whom God chose as portal
for the Incarnation,
we give veneration.

You, Ave receiving,
Gabriel's word believing,
turned to peace and gladness
Eva's name of sadness.

Mother's care displaying,
bless your child in praying,
who, when born our brother,
chose you for his mother.

Maiden all excelling,
gentle past our telling,
you we join in raising
to your child our praising.

Creator eternal,
Spirit all supernal,
with the Word, we bless you,
Three in One confess you. Amen.

Wonderfully has God, the Mighty One dealt with me *
and blest is the name of the Holy One. (*in Eastertide*, Alleluia.)

or

From this day forth, O Mary, *
all generations will call you blessed. (*in Eastertide*, Alleluia.)

COMMON 2

APOSTLES AND EVANGELISTS

Matins

Invitatory: (*in Eastertide*, Alleluia.) Christ, the cornerstone, has built the
church upon apostles and prophets:

Response: O come, let us worship. (*in Eastertide*, Alleluia.)

Antiphon on Psalter

I give you a new commandment: love one another; *
as I have loved you, so you are to love one another. (ET Alleluia.)

Canticle at Matins   TE DEUM

We praise you, O God; *
we acclaim you as the Holy One:

All creation worships you, *
Sovereign eternal.

To you all angels, all the powers of heaven, *
cherubim and seraphim, sing in endless praise.

Holy, holy, holy One, God of power and might, *
heaven and earth are full of your glory.

The glorious company of apostles praise you; *
the noble gathering of prophets praise you;

The white-robed choir of martyrs praise you; *
throughout the world the holy church acclaims you:

God of infinite majesty,
your true and only Word, worthy of all worship, *
   the Holy Spirit, advocate and guide.

❖   ❖   ❖

You, Christ, reign in glory, *
   you are the eternal Word of God.

When you came among us to set us free, *
   you chose to be born of a woman.

You overcame the sting of death *
   and opened heaven to all believers.

You are seated at God's right hand in glory; *
   we believe that you will come and be our judge.

❖   ❖   ❖

Come then, Christ, and help your people, *
   bought with the price of your own blood;

And bring us with your saints *
   to glory everlasting.

Hymn at Matins

Except in Eastertide

> Christ is made the sure foundation,
>   and the head and cornerstone;
> chosen in God's love, and precious,
>   binding all the church in one;
> holy Zion's help for ever,
>   and its confidence alone.
>
> Foursquare is that heavenly city,
>   three on each side are its gates;
> twelve in all, and every portal
>   one apostle designates,
> in new Israel, a founder
>   of a tribe Christ recreates.

Bright with pearl glows every portal,
    open to all hearts in prayer;
and by virtue of Christ's passion
    faithful souls may enter there,
who for Jesus' name in this world
    suffered agony and care.

Glory be to our Creator,
    to the Word all glory be,
laud and honor to the Spirit,
    God the Holy Trinity;
consubstantial, coeternal,
    now, and through eternity. Amen.

Hymn in Eastertide

In this our paschal joy, we raise
our hymn of gratitude and praise
that Jesus, from the tomb set free,
is known in glorious victory.

On Easter morn the angel gave
the women tidings at the grave:
Soon you may your dear Jesus see
as risen Christ in Galilee.

This summons, when to them conveyed,
th'eleven joyfully obeyed,
that they might once again behold
their friend and leader as of old.

O Jesus, risen Christ, we raise
our joyful hymns of love and praise;
to our Creator homage bring,
as by the Spirit here we sing. Amen.

Diurnum

Antiphon on Psalter

As God has sent me into the world, *
    so have I sent them into the world. (*in Eastertide*, Alleluia.)

Lesson and Respond   EPHESIANS 2:19-20

You are no longer strangers or foreign visitors; you are citizens like all the saints, and part of God's household. You are part of a building that has the apostles and prophets for its foundation, and Christ for its main cornerstone.

Response: Thanks be to God.

v. Their voice has gone out into all lands. (ET Alleluia, alleluia.)
r. And their message to the earth's farthest bounds. (ET Alleluia, alleluia.)

The Office continues with the Closing Prayers in the Ordinary of Diurnum, p. 55.

Vespers

Antiphon on Psalter

There is no greater love than this: *
to lay down your life for your friends. (*in Eastertide*, Alleluia.)

Canticle at Vespers   DIGNUS ES (REVELATION 4:11; 5:9-10; 13)

Splendor and honor and royal power*
   are yours by right, O God most high,

for you created everything that is,*
   and by your will they were created and have their being;

and yours by right, O Lamb that was slain,*
   for with your blood you have redeemed for God,

from every family, language, people and nation,*
   a royal priesthood to serve our God.

And so, to the One who sits upon the throne*
   and to Christ the Lamb,

be worship and praise, dominion and splendor,*
   for ever and for evermore. Amen.

Hymn at Vespers
For Apostles, except in Eastertide

The gifts of Christ we sing today;
and those disciples of the Way
who kept the faith alive and strong,
we honor with our grateful song.

220   THE COMMON OF SAINTS

They followed the Anointed One;
they saw and shared all that was done:
the narrow road, the heavenly bread,
and saw Christ risen from the dead.

It was the yearning faith of saints,
unconquered hope that never faints,
and love of God that knows not shame,
that this world's evil overcame.

Redeemer, keep us in your love,
that with your glorious saints above,
your servants, too, may find a place
and reign forever through your grace.

All laud to you Creator, be,
and to your Word eternally;
both with the Holy Spirit one,
while everlasting ages run. Amen.

Hymn at Vespers

For Evangelists, except in Eastertide

This scribe and herald of God's words
today the church much joy affords,
as one of four who published wide
the treasures that in God abide.

Their pens to every age have taught
the mighty deeds God's Spirit wrought
of Christ, who in humanity,
has brought to us divinity.

Though all were by one Spirit swayed,
and one Christ all the four portrayed,
yet each, unique in mind and heart,
proclaimed that Christ with fitting art.

And now to God our thanks we pay
on this evangelist's own day,
for good news, bringing life afresh,
of God with us, the Word made flesh. Amen.

Hymn at Vespers

During Eastertide

> Th'apostles gathered Easter night
> behind the doors they locked in fright;
> yet Jesus in their midst appeared
> with "Peace" to banish all they feared.

> With joy they heard the good news borne
> by Magdalene that very morn:
> how Jesus from the tomb was free,
> and life had won the victory.

> They saw the wounded hands and side
> which to their Savior testified;
> their dread was calmed when Jesus ate
> to show his risen, human state.

> Th'apostles then, with hearts on fire
> with zeal and heavenly desire,
> learned how the scriptures were fulfilled
> when Christ's redeeming blood was spilled.

> We sing to you, O risen Christ,
> our true and perfect sacrifice;
> to our Creator homage bring,
> as by the Spirit here we sing. Amen.

COMMON 3

PROPHETIC WITNESSES

Matins

Invitatory: (*in Eastertide*, Alleluia.) Christ came to the powerless and oppressed:

Response: O come, let us worship. (Alleluia.)

Antiphon on Psalter

> Since there will never cease to be some in need on the earth, *
>   I therefore command you, open your hand to the poor and needy
>   neighbor in your land. (*in Eastertide*, Alleluia.)

To whom then will you compare me, *
    or who is my equal? says the Holy One.

Lift up your eyes on high and see: *
    I am great in strength, mighty in power.

Have you not known? Have you not heard? *
    I am the everlasting God, the Creator of the ends of the earth.

I do not faint or grow weary; my understanding is unsearchable. *
    I give power to the faint and strengthen the powerless.

Even youths will faint and be weary, and the young will fall exhausted,*
    but those who wait for me shall renew their strength;

They shall mount up with wings like eagles, *
    they shall run and not be weary,
    they shall walk and not faint.

Hymn at Matins

    O living God, we praise your name;
    pour out on us your gifts and grace;
    enlighten with your Spirit's flame
    the errors of our human race.

    Give hearts of peace and tongues of fire
    to preach your gospel, live your Way;
    and with the power of love, inspire
    prophetic witness for our day.

    We thank you, God, for those who give
    their lives for justice and for right;
    who speak for freedom, and who live
    to bring our evils to your light.

    To you, our great Creator, praise,
    and to your Word all glory be,
    and to the Spirit prayer we raise,
    one God through all eternity. Amen.

In Eastertide the doxology is

    To you, O risen Christ, be praise;
    to you, Creator, glory be;
    to you, O Spirit, hymns we raise;
    one God through all eternity.

Antiphon on Benedictus

Those who want to save their life will lose it, *
and those who lose their life for my sake will find it.

The Common Collect

Almighty God, you give to your servants boldness and courage to confront those with power and position in this world on behalf of the weak
and oppressed: Grant that we may always be ready to give a reason for the
hope that is in us, and bear witness to mercy, truth, and justice in the
name of our Savior Jesus Christ; who lives and reigns with you and the
Holy Spirit, one God, for ever and ever. *Amen.*

Diurnum

Antiphon on Psalter

Whoever follows me will have the light of life *
and will never walk in darkness. (*in Eastertide*, Alleluia.)

Lesson and Respond   LUKE 4:18-19

The Spirit of God is upon me, because I have been anointed to bring
good news to the poor. I have been sent to proclaim release to the captives
and recovery of sight to the blind, to let the oppressed go free, to proclaim the year of God's favor.

Response: Thanks be to God.

v. Let the righteous be glad and rejoice before God.
(*in Eastertide*, Alleluia, alleluia.)
r. Let them also be merry and joyful. (*in Eastertide*, Alleluia, alleluia.)

The Office continues with the Closing Prayers in the Ordinary of Diurnum, p. 55.

Vespers

Antiphon on Psalter

I have observed the misery of my people; I have heard their cry;
I know their sufferings. *
I will send you to bring my people into freedom.

I pray that, according to the riches of God's glory,*
    you may be strengthened in your inner being
    with power through the Holy Spirit.

May Christ dwell in your hearts through faith,*
    as you are rooted and grounded in love.

I pray that you may have the power to comprehend, with all the saints,*
    what is the breadth and length and height and depth
    of the love of God for us, and that you may know the love of Christ

that surpasses knowledge,*
    and be filled with all the fullness of God.

Hymn at Vespers

    See what a cloud of witnesses
    is there to light our way!
    They once, like us, knew doubt and fear
    but now eternal day.

    Let us, with fervent love like theirs,
    be faithful on our path;
    that good may triumph over sin
    and mercy over wrath.

    O Jesus, best of witnesses,
    we magnify your name;
    you showed us love's extremity
    upon the cross of shame.

    God, give us grace that our own lives
    may serve to honor you:
    our words be witness to your love,
    our actions just and true.

    Now let us sing our Maker's praise
    who made all worlds to be:
    you, with the Spirit and the Word,
    reign through eternity. Amen.

Anyone who wants to be a follower of mine must leave self behind, *
take up the cross every day, and follow me. *(in Eastertide,* Alleluia.)

COMMON 4

MARTYRS

Matins

Invitatory: (*in Eastertide,* Alleluia.) Christ calls the faithful to embrace the cross:
Response: O come, let us worship. (Alleluia.)

Antiphon on Psalter

Blest are those who are persecuted for righteousness' sake; *
theirs is the dominion of heaven. (Alleluia.)

Canticle at Matins   SIRACH 51:13,12

I give you thanks, O God, and praise you, my Savior; *
I give thanks to your name,

For you have been my helper *
and have delivered me from destruction.

In the face of my adversaries you have come to my aid; *
you have delivered me from the hand of those seeking my life,
from the many troubles I endured.

I thank you and praise you, and I bless the name of God, *
for you saved me from destruction
and rescued me in time of trouble.

Give thanks to God who is good, *
whose mercy endures for ever.

> They followed, martyrs of our God,
> the path that Jesus Christ has trod;
> both fear and death they overcame,
> to glory in a victor's name.
>
> True witnesses of love are they
> who lost their lives to win the way;
> their holy death brought peace and rest
> and life eternal with the blest.
>
> We therefore pray you, loving Christ,
> that as these martyrs sacrificed
> their lives and all they held most dear,
> that we, as they, may persevere.
>
> All praise to you, all-loving God,
> and to your sole-begotten Word,
> both with the Holy Spirit One
> while everlasting ages run. Amen.

In Eastertide the doxology is

> To you, O risen Christ, we raise
> our songs of gratitude and praise;
> to our Creator homage bring,
> as by the Spirit now we sing. Amen.

Antiphon on Benedictus

These are the ones who have come safely through the great ordeal; *
   they have washed their robes and made them white in the blood
   of the Lamb. (Alleluia.)

The Common Collect

Almighty God, by whose grace and power your holy martyrs triumphed over suffering and were faithful even to death: Grant us who now remember them in thanksgiving to be so faithful in our witness to you in this world that we may receive with them the crown of life; through Jesus Christ our Savior, who lives and reigns with you and the Holy Spirit, one God, now and for ever. *Amen.*

Diurnum

Antiphon on Psalter

> Blest are those who are invited *
> to the wedding supper of the Lamb. (Alleluia.)

Lesson and Respond   WISDOM 3:13

> The souls of the just are in the hand of God, and no torment shall touch
> them. They seemed, in the view of the foolish, to be dead; but they are in
> peace.

Response: Thanks be to God.

> *v.* Let the righteous be glad and rejoice before God. (Alleluia, alleluia.)
> *r.* Let them also be merry and joyful. (Alleluia, alleluia.)

The Office continues with the Closing Prayers in the Ordinary of Diurnum, p. 55.

Vespers

Antiphon on Psalter

> See how they are accounted among the children of God *
> and their lot is with the saints. (ET Alleluia.)

Canticle at Vespers   ISAIAH 51:6-8

> Lift up your eyes to the heavens, and look at the earth beneath;*
> for the heavens will vanish like smoke,
>
> the earth will wear out like a garment,*
> but my salvation will be forever,
> and my deliverance will never end.
>
> All you who know righteousness,*
> you people who have my teaching in your hearts,
>
> do not fear the reproach of others,*
> and do not be dismayed when they revile you.
>
> For the moth will eat them up like a garment,*
> and the worm will eat them like wool;
>
> but my deliverance will be for ever,*
> and my salvation to all generations.

Blessed city, heavenly Salem,
    vision dear of peace and love,
you, of living stones assembled,
    are the joy of heaven above;
and, with angel choirs encircled,
    as a bride to earth you move.

Many a blow of pain or sorrow
    polished well those stones elect,
in their places now established
    by the heavenly Architect,
who has willed that they the beauty
    of that city should perfect.

All that dedicated city,
    dearly loved by God on high,
in exultant jubilation
    pours perpetual melody;
God the Three in One adoring
    in glad hymns eternally.

Praise to God, our great Creator,
    honor to the Spirit blest;
praise to Jesus, our Redeemer,
    triune God made manifest;
who, to all the saints adoring,
    grants the joy of heavenly rest. Amen.

Antiphon on Magnificat

Be glad and rejoice, for your reward is great in heaven; *
    in the same way they persecuted the prophets before you. (Alleluia.)

Common 5

Doctors of the Church

Matins

Invitatory: (*in Eastertide*, Alleluia.) The Spirit of wisdom guides into all truth:
Response: O come, let us worship. (Alleluia.)

Antiphon on Psalter

Oh, how I love your Law; *
it is my meditation all the day. (Alleluia.)

Canticle at Matins   Wisdom 7:14, 25-28

Wisdom is an unfailing treasure for mortals; *
those who find wisdom gain friendship with God.

Wisdom is a breath of the power of God, *
a pure emanation of the glory of the Almighty.

Wisdom is a reflection of the eternal light,
untarnished mirror of God's active power, *
the image of God's goodness.

In each generation Wisdom passes into holy souls,
making them friends of God and prophets; *
for God loves the one who lives with Wisdom.

Hymn at Matins

O Doctors, God-lit stars, you make the heavens shine;
you are the salt of earth, the seasoning divine,
preserving faithful souls, lest they be led astray,
and all unknowing lose their way.

By you the truth preserved from error still remains,
and so the holy faith its purity retains;
through you God takes delight rich treasure to unfold,
that wisdom may to us be told.

Like tranquil streams, where flow the living waters clear,
you make Christ's fields abound with nourishment and cheer;
you first give milk to babes, then solid food to eat;
the diverse needs of souls you treat.

O Christ, eternal Truth, in you do we rejoice,
though now our outward ears may not perceive your voice;
still in your Doctors' words, your teachings we discern,
and thus of you our spirits learn. Amen.

Antiphon on Benedictus

The fear of the Holy One is wisdom, *
and to depart from evil is understanding. (Alleluia.)

The Common Collect

O God, by your Holy Spirit you give to some the word of wisdom, to others the word of knowledge, and to others the word of faith: We praise your name for the gifts of grace manifested in your servants, and we pray that your Church may never be destitute of such gifts; through Jesus Christ our Savior, who lives and reigns with you and the Holy Spirit, one God, for ever and ever. *Amen.*

Diurnum

Antiphon on Psalter

Make me understand the way of your commandments, *
that I may meditate on your marvelous works. (Alleluia.)

Lesson and Respond   WISDOM 10:10

Wisdom guided the just in direct ways, showed them the realm of God, and gave them knowledge of holy things; wisdom prospered them in their labors and made abundant the fruit of their works.

Response: Thanks be to God.

    v. God will direct the wise as they ponder holy mysteries;
    (ET Alleluia, alleluia.)

    r. Their delight is in the law of the Holy One. (ET Alleluia, alleluia.)

The Office continues with the Closing Prayers in the Ordinary of Diurnum, p. 55.

Vespers

Antiphon on Psalter

> With my lips will I recite *
> all the judgments of your mouth. (Alleluia.)

Canticle at Vespers   PROVERBS 4:10-13

> Hear, my child, hear and accept my words this day,*
> that the years of your life may be many.

> I have taught you the way of wisdom.*
> I have led you in the paths of uprightness.

> When you walk, your step will not be hampered,*
> and if you run, you will not stumble.

> Keep hold of instruction; do not let it go;*
> guard wisdom, for it is your life.

Hymn at Vespers

> Hail to the Doctors of the Church, whose witness
> all faithful people celebrate and honor,
> who with the guidance of the Holy Spirit,
>   studied the scriptures.

> From the rich treasure of that holy writing
> they drew out for us things both new and ancient;
> Christ's sacred doctrine clearly they expounded
>   for our instruction.

> We now, with gladness chanting in thanksgiving
> our joyful hymn for Doctors wise and holy,
> ask that we also in our lives and teaching
>   show forth true wisdom.

> To God be honor, praise and adoration,
> who over all things reigns in heavenly glory,
> earth's fruitful grandeur ruling and directing,
>   One in three Persons. Amen.

Antiphon on Magnificat

O blessed [N,] wise and holy teacher, light of God's people,
lover of the gospel, *
   join with us in prayer to the Holy One. (Alleluia.)

At [N], insert appropriate name as below:

Ambrose	Bernard	John Chrysostom
Anselm	Catherine	John of Damascus
Athanasius	Ephrem	Leo
Augustine	Gregory	Teresa
Basil	Hilary	Thomas Aquinas
Bede	Jerome	

COMMON 6

MISSIONARIES

Matins

Invitatory: (*in Eastertide*, Alleluia.) Christ has proclaimed the gospel in all lands:

Response: O come, let us worship. (Alleluia.)

Antiphon on Psalter

I determined that while I was with you *
   I would speak of nothing but Jesus Christ,
   the One who was crucified. (Alleluia.)

Canticle at Matins   ISAIAH 52:7-12

How beautiful upon the mountains *
   are the feet of the messenger who announces peace:

The one who brings good news,
who announces salvation, *
   who says to Zion, "Your God reigns."

Listen! Your sentinels lift up their voices,
together they sing for joy, *
   for in plain sight they see the return of God to Zion.

Break forth together into singing; *
    the people have been comforted;
    Jerusalem has been redeemed.

The Mighty One has shown strength before the eyes of all the nations, *
    and all the earth shall see the salvation of God.

Hymn at Matins

> We, in grateful, holy measure,
> sing of those who spread the treasure
> in the sacred gospel shrined;
> blessed tidings of salvation,
> peace on earth their proclamation,
>   love of God to humankind.
>
> Forth they fared, their home forsaking,
> arduous journey undertaking
>   leading others where they trod;
> by their holy deeds and preaching,
> love of Christ to all outreaching,
>   helped them hear the Word of God.
>
> O that we, your truth confessing,
> and your holy word possessing,
>   Jesus, may your love requite;
> and to you our voices raising,
> you with all the ransomed praising,
>   in your worship now delight.
>
> Holy Author of creation,
> you we praise in adoration
>   with the Spirit, guide and friend;
> so with Christ in love united
> that by all you must be cited
>   Three in One, world without end. Amen.

Antiphon on Benedictus

> God has made them a light to the nations, *
> that salvation might reach to the ends of the earth. (Alleluia.)

The Common Collect

> Almighty God, whose will it is to be glorified in your saints, and who raised up your servants to be lights in the world: Shine, we pray, in our hearts, that we also in our generation may show forth your praise, who calls us out of darkness into your marvelous light; through Jesus Christ our Savior, who lives and reigns with you and the Holy Spirit, one God, now and for ever. *Amen.*

Diurnum

Antiphon on Psalter

> I will tell of your decrees before rulers, *
> and will not be ashamed. (Alleluia.)

Lesson and Respond   Ephesians 3:8

> To me, the least of all believers, was given the grace to preach to all nations the infinite riches of Christ.

Response: Thanks be to God.

> *v.* Their voice has gone out into all lands. (Alleluia, alleluia.)
> *r.* And their message to the earth's farthest bounds. (Alleluia, alleluia.)

The Office continues with the Closing Prayers in the Ordinary of Diurnum, p. 55.

Vespers

Antiphon on Psalter

> Christ came to bring the good news of peace: *
> peace to you who were far away. (Alleluia.)

Canticle at Vespers   Ephesians 4:17; 14-16

Let us lead a life worthy of the calling*
  to which we have been called.

Make every effort to maintain the unity of the Spirit*
  in the bond of peace.

There is one body and one Spirit,*
  just as we were called to the one hope of our calling.

There is one Word, one faith, one baptism,*
  one Creator and God of all,
  who is above all, and through all, and in all.

Each of us was given grace*
  according to the measure of Christ's gift.

Let us no longer be children,*
  tossed about by every wind of doctrine,
  but speaking the truth in love,

let us grow up in every way*
  into the one who is the head, into Christ.

Hymn at Vespers

Hail to the heralds of the Word, whose witness
all faithful people celebrate and honor,
who, in the power of the Holy Spirit,
    furthered God's message.

Naught could deter them, when a holy calling
urged them to travel into distant places;
they, in true witness of God's liberation,
    proclaimed the gospel.

Glory and honor, praise and adoration,
be to our God who, sitting in the highest,
governs and orders all the whole creation,
    Trinity blessed. Amen.

Antiphon on Magnificat

How beautiful upon the mountains *
  are the feet of those who bring good tidings, who publish peace. (Alleluia.)

COMMON 7

MONASTICS AND OTHER RELIGIOUS

Matins

Invitatory: (*in Eastertide*, Alleluia.) Christ came to do God's will:
Response: O come, let us worship. (Alleluia.)

Antiphon on Psalter

Those who hope in God shall renew their strength; *
    they will soar as with eagles' wings. (Alleluia.)

Canticle at Matins   EPHESIANS 1:3-8

Blessed be God, *
    who has blessed us in Christ with every spiritual blessing.

We were chosen in Christ before the foundation of the world, *
    chosen to be holy and blameless in love.

Through Jesus Christ, God destined us for adoption as children, *
    according to the good pleasure of the divine will.

Praise to God for that glorious grace *
    so freely bestowed on us in the Beloved.

In the Beloved we have redemption through the blood of the cross; *
    we have the forgiveness of our sins
    through the riches of God's grace so freely given to us.

Hymn at Matins

Jesus, our way and heavenly end,
our highest truth and nearest friend,
you with unending joys endue
your saints who gave their lives to you.

They valued all delights of earth
for your true glory, their true worth,
and loved with humblest reverence those
you sent to them, both friends and foes.

With single-hearted zeal they sought
the prize which your obedience brought;
for mind and spirit they preferred
your living bread, your holy word.

This saint [These saints] whose life [lives] we praise today
with gladness took the narrow way,
resisted evil, chose the best,
and God's great love made manifest.

All praise to our Creator be,
and to the Word eternally,
both with the Holy Spirit one,
while everlasting ages run. Amen.

In Eastertide the doxology is

To you, O risen Christ, we raise
our hymns of gratitude and praise;
to our Creator homage bring,
as by the Spirit here we sing. Amen.

Antiphon on Benedictus

Blest are those who hunger and thirst for righteousness, *
  for they shall be satisfied. (Alleluia.)

The Common Collect

O Jesus Christ, you became poor for our sake, that we might be made rich through your poverty: Guide and sanctify, we pray, those whom you call to follow you under the vows of poverty, chastity, and obedience; that by their prayer and service your Church may be enriched and your name be glorified; for you reign with the Creator and the Holy Spirit, one God, now and for ever. *Amen.*

Diurnum

Antiphon on Psalter

Happy are they who walk in the way of God's law, *
  who seek God with all their hearts. (Alleluia.)

Lesson and Respond PHILIPPIANS 3:8-9

I have come to rate all as loss in the light of the surpassing knowledge of my Savior Jesus Christ. Thus I have forfeited everything; I have accounted all else rubbish so that Christ may be my wealth.

Response: Thanks be to God.

v. Happy are they who dwell in your house. (Alleluia, alleluia.)
r. They will always be praising you. (Alleluia, alleluia.)

The Office continues with the Closing Prayers in the Ordinary of Diurnum, p. 55.

Vespers

Antiphon on Psalter

Those who seek after God shall lack nothing that is good, *
    for those who fear God have no want. (Alleluia.)

Canticle at Vespers

JOHN OF THE CROSS:
FROM "SONG OF THE SOUL THAT IS GLAD TO KNOW GOD BY FAITH"

How well I know that fountain's rushing flow,*
    although by night, its deathless spring is hidden.

Even so full well I guess from whence its sources flow,*
    though it be night. Its origin (since it has none) none knows:

but that all origin from it arose,*
    although by night.

The eternal source hides in the Living Bread,*
    that we with life eternal may be fed,

though it be night. Here to all creatures it is crying, hark!*
    that they should drink their fill though in the dark,

for it is night. This living fount which is to me so dear,*
    within the bread of life I see it clear,
    though it be night.

THE COMMON OF SAINTS   239

Hymn at Vespers

> Hail the confessors of our God, whose witness
> all faithful people celebrate and honor,
> who, by religious vow, to prayer and service
> > gave themselves wholly.

> Filled with all virtues, steadfast, true and humble,
> helping each other, loving God in all things,
> led by the Spirit, they were true disciples
> > while in this body.

> So, let us honor this [these] devout religious,
> who now in union with the saints in heaven
> join[s] in the choir of endless alleluias
> > for all creation.

> Maker of all things, God of our redemption,
> Spirit of wisdom, and of all compassion,
> to you be glory, praise and adoration,
> > God in Three Persons. Amen.

Antiphon on Magnificat

> I have been crucified with Christ; the life I now live is not my life, *
> but the life which Christ lives in me. (Alleluia.)

COMMON 8

TEACHERS

Matins

Invitatory: (Alleluia.) Christ speaks the truth to every age:
Response: O come, let us worship. (Alleluia.)

Antiphon on Psalter

> When you turn to the right or to the left,
> your ears shall hear a word behind you; *
> > you shall hear your Teacher saying,
> > "This is the way; walk in it." (Alleluia.)

If you accept my words and treasure my commandments, *
  and make your ear attentive to wisdom;

If you incline your heart to truth, *
  and you indeed cry out for insight,
  raising your voice for understanding;

If you seek wisdom like silver *
  and search for it as for hidden treasures,

Then you will understand the fear of the Holy One *
  and find the knowledge of God.

For God gives wisdom, *
  and from God's mouth come knowledge and discernment.

Hymn at Matins

Shepherd Divine, you deign to share
with human pastors your own care
of all the sheep: the faith to teach,
the hurt to soothe, the lost to reach.

Today the church its homage pays:
commemorates with fitting praise
a saintly teacher who was given
part of the flock to lead to heaven.

This teacher worked with zeal to feed
the hungry mind and spirit's need;
to guide and strengthen those who erred
and bring to all Christ's saving Word.

To you, Creator, glory be,
and to your Word, eternally;
to you, the Spirit, equal praise
from joyful hearts we ever raise. Amen.

In Eastertide the doxology is

To you, O risen Christ, we raise
our hymns of gratitude and praise;
to our Creator worship bring
as by the Spirit here we sing. Amen.

Antiphon on Benedictus

> The gospel of Christ will be proclaimed throughout the earth *
> as a testimony to the nations. (Alleluia.)

The Common Collect

> Almighty God, you gave to your servants special gifts of grace to under-
> stand and teach the truth as it is in Christ Jesus: Grant that by this teach-
> ing we may know you, the one true God, and Jesus Christ whom you have
> sent; who lives and reigns with you and the Holy Spirit, one God, now
> and for ever. *Amen.*

Diurnum

Antiphon on Psalter

> Instruct me, O Mighty One, in your statutes; *
> with my lips I proclaim all the goodness that comes from you. (Alleluia.)

Lesson and Respond   Isaiah 59:21

> This is my covenant, says the Holy One: My spirit that is upon you, and
> my words that I have put in your mouth shall not depart out of your
> mouth, or out of the mouths of your children, or out of the mouths of
> your children's children, says the Holy One, from now on and for ever.

Response: Thanks be to God.

> *v.* The mouths of the righteous speak of wisdom. (Alleluia, alleluia.)
> *r.* And their tongues speak what is right. (Alleluia, alleluia.)

The Office continues with the Closing Prayers in the Ordinary of Diurnum, p. 55.

Vespers

Antiphon on Psalter

> Though you be given the bread of adversity and the water of affliction, *
> with your own eyes you shall see your Teacher, who will be hidden
> from you no longer. (Alleluia.)

God is exalted in power; who can be a teacher like God?*
  Surely God is great, unsearchable is the number of God's years.

God draws up the drops of water, distills the mist in rain,*
  which the skies pour down and drop upon the earth abundantly.

God scatters the lightning and covers the roots of the sea.*
  God cares for all people, giving food in abundance.

God speaks wondrously in creation*
  and does great things that we cannot comprehend.

How great is God*
  beyond our understanding!

Hymn at Vespers

Hail to the teacher of the faith, whose witness
all faithful people celebrate and honor,
who, by the power of the Holy Spirit,
    doctrine expounded.

Not in the wisdom of the worldly sages,
but by the folly of Christ's saving passion,
this godly teacher, by the Spirit's power
    opened the scriptures.

We now, with gladness chanting in thanksgiving
this joyous tribute to a life so fruitful,
ask that, enlightened, we may now and ever
    seek holy wisdom.

To God be honor, praise and adoration,
who over all things reigns in heavenly glory,
all of creation ruling and directing,
    One in three Persons. Amen.

Antiphon on Magnificat

The wise shall shine brightly like the splendor of the firmament, *
  and those who lead many to righteousness shall be like stars for ever.
  (Alleluia.)

COMMON 9

PASTORS

Matins

Invitatory: (*in Eastertide,* Alleluia.) Christ ever feeds the flock:
Response: O come, let us worship. (Alleluia.)

Antiphon on Psalter

God has given me a well-trained tongue, *
   that I might know how to speak to the weary
   a word that will rouse them. (Alleluia.)

Canticle at Matins

DEUTERONOMY 10:14, 17-21

To God belongs the heaven of heavens, *
   the earth with all that is in it.

For our God is God of gods, mighty and awesome, *
   who is not partial and takes no bribe;

Who executes justice for the orphan and widow; *
   who loves the strangers, providing them food and clothing.

You also shall love the stranger, *
   for you were strangers in the land of Egypt.

You shall fear God, and God alone you shall worship; *
   this is the God to whom you shall hold fast
   and by whose name you shall swear.

God, your own God, is your praise, *
   who has done for you these great and awesome things
   that your own eyes have seen.

Hymn at Matins

Shepherd Divine, you deign to share
with human pastors your own care
of all the sheep: the faith to teach,
the hurt to soothe, the lost to reach.

Today the church its homage pays:
commemorates with fitting praise
these saintly pastors who were given
part of the flock to lead to heaven.

No robber, who some other way
attacked the fold to steal and prey;
through Christ, the Door, these pastors came
to tend the sheep in Jesus' name.

Creator, let our prayers be heard
through Jesus, your eternal Word;
whom with the Spirit we adore
one only God for evermore. Amen.

In Eastertide the doxology is

To you, O risen Christ, we raise
our hymns of gratitude and praise;
to our Creator worship bring
as by the Spirit here we sing. Amen.

Antiphon on Benedictus

I will give you shepherds after my own heart *
who will feed you with knowledge and understanding. (Alleluia.)

The Common Collect

Heavenly God, Shepherd of your people, we thank you for your servants,
who were faithful in the care and nurture of your flock; and we pray that,
following the example and teaching of their holy lives, we may by your
grace grow into the stature of the fullness of our Savior Jesus Christ; who
lives and reigns with you and the Holy Spirit, one God, for ever and ever.
Amen.

Diurnum

Antiphon on Psalter

Let those who fear you turn to me *
and also those who know your decrees. (Alleluia.)

Lesson and Respond JOHN 10:14-15

I am the Good Shepherd. I know my own and my own know me, and I lay down my life for the sheep.

Response: Thanks be to God.

v. Give me understanding, that I may learn your commandments. (Alleluia, alleluia.)

r. Fulfill your promise to your servant. (Alleluia, alleluia.)

The Office continues with the Closing Prayers in the Ordinary of Diurnum, p. 55.

Vespers

Antiphon on Psalter

I may have the gift of inspired preaching, *
but if I have not love, I am nothing. (Alleluia.)

Canticle at Vespers COLOSSIANS 3:13; 12-16

Christ has been raised and is seated at the right hand of God;*
therefore set your mind on things that are above,

not on things that are on earth, for you have died,*
and your life is hid with Christ in God.

As God's chosen ones, holy and beloved,*
clothe yourselves with compassion and kindness.

Bear with one another, and as God has forgiven you,*
so you also must forgive.

Let the word of Christ dwell in you richly,*
and with gratitude in your hearts,
sing psalms, hymns, and spiritual songs to God.

Above all, clothe yourselves with love,*
which binds everything together in perfect harmony.

Hymn at Vespers

Hail to the pastors of the flock, whose witness
all faithful people celebrate and honor,
who, by the power of the Holy Spirit,
served in God's pastures.

Leaders, sustainers of God's holy people,
humble in all things after Christ's example,
with deep compassion did these faithful pastors
    carry their sorrows.

We now with gladness chanting in thanksgiving
this joyful tribute to a life so holy
ask that we, also, may in prayerful service
    show forth God's mercy.

Glory and honor, praise and adoration,
be to our God who, merciful and mighty,
governs and orders all the worlds and heavens,
    Trinity blessed. Amen.

Antiphon on Magnificat

> Christ has given us the ministry of reconciliation; *
> we come therefore as ambassadors of Christ. (Alleluia.)

COMMON 10

CONFESSORS

Matins

Invitatory: (*in Eastertide,* Alleluia.) O holy God, your service is perfect freedom:
Response: O come, let us worship. (Alleluia.)

Antiphon on Psalter

> Wisdom guided the righteous in straight paths *
> and showed them the dominion of God. (Alleluia.)

Canticle at Matins   ISAIAH 11:1-9

> The spirit of God will rest on you, *
> the spirit of wisdom and understanding,
>
> The spirit of counsel and strength, *
> the spirit of knowledge and reverence for God.

You will delight in the fear of God; *
    not by appearance shall you judge,
    nor by hearsay shall you decide,

But with righteousness you shall judge the poor, *
    and decide with equity for the meek of the earth.

The wolf shall live with the lamb, *
    the leopard shall lie down with the kid,

The calf and the lion and the fatling together, *
    and a little child shall lead them.

Nothing will hurt or destroy on all my holy mountain; *
    for the earth will be full of the knowledge of God
    as the waters cover the sea.

Hymn at Matins

Christ, our redeemer and our heart's fulfillment,
joyful we praise the splendor of your glory
which shines upon us from your blessed servant[s]
    whom now we honor.

Total your giving, and love's revelation
opened the hearts of those who longed to answer,
true in response, in witness, and in service,
    love and obedience.

Now let us celebrate the love that joins us,
blest in the grace of sharing our salvation,
bound with your saints in giving and receiving,
    each to the other.

This is the love that draws us and unites us:
love of our Maker in the love of Jesus,
love of the Spirit, One in Three eternal.
    Praise to your glory! Amen.

Antiphon on Benedictus

Anything you did for one of these, however humble, *
    you did it for me. (Alleluia.)

The Common Collect

Almighty God, by your Holy Spirit you have made us one with your saints in heaven and on earth: Grant that in our earthly pilgrimage we may always be supported by this community of love and prayer, and know ourselves to be surrounded by their witness to your power and mercy. We ask this for the sake of Jesus Christ, in whom all our intercessions are acceptable through the Spirit, and who lives and reigns for ever and ever. *Amen.*

Diurnum

Antiphon on Psalter

Your word is a lantern to my feet, *
    and a light upon my path. (Alleluia.)

Lesson and Respond   Acts 20:24

I do not count my life of any value to myself, if only I may finish my course and the ministry that I received from Jesus Christ, to testify to the good news of God's grace.

Response: Thanks be to God.

    v. I have chosen the way of faithfulness. (Alleluia, alleluia.)
    r. I have set your judgments before me. (Alleluia, alleluia.)

The Office continues with the Closing Prayers in the Ordinary of Diurnum, p. 55.

Vespers

Antiphon on Psalter

A servant does not rank above a master, *
    so a servant should be content to share the master's lot. (Alleluia.)

Canticle at Vespers   Hildegard of Bingen (Song 7: O Happy Soul)

O happy soul,
whose body has risen from the earth which you wander,*
    which you tread on during your sojourn in this world.

Made to be the very mirror of Divinity,*
    you have been crowned with divine imagination and intelligence.

The Holy Spirit looks upon you*
and discovers its very own dwelling place.

Made to be the very mirror of Divinity,*
you have been crowned with divine imagination and intelligence.

Hymn at Vespers

Christ's noble servants, we would sing your greatness:
how you wrought wonders in your faith so steadfast.
Earth in your honor now unites with heaven's
endless rejoicings.

You, too, were mortal, like all men and women,
and yet you served God with such humble valor
that now, immortal, you in endless glory
with Christ are reigning.

Thus will our hymns, your charity declaring,
praise God's own goodness for your prayerful service.
May we, encouraged by your true example,
also bear witness.

Glory and honor, praise and adoration,
be to our God who, merciful and mighty,
governs and orders all the worlds and heavens,
Trinity blessed. Amen.

Antiphon on Magnificat

In the heavenly realm the blessed have their dwelling place, *
and their rest for ever. (Alleluia.)

Common 11

Ember Days

The Ember Days are traditionally observed four times a year, on the Wednesday, Friday and Saturday following
   1)   the Third Sunday of Advent
   2)   the First Sunday in Lent
   3)   the Day of Pentecost
   4)   Holy Cross Day (September 14)

All as in the weekday Office of the occurring season except as below.

Matins

On all three days

Invitatory:	Christ, the cornerstone, has built the church upon apostles and prophets:
Response:	O come, let us worship.

Antiphon on Psalter

Wednesday
   They shall be ministers in my sanctuary; *
      they shall attend my people and serve them.

Friday
   Proclaim the message; be persistent; *
      convince, rebuke, and encourage;
      have utmost patience in teaching.

Saturday
   See how they are accounted among the children of God *
      and their lot is with the saints.

The following lessons shall be used on the three Ember Days following Holy Cross Day (September 14) and may be used at other times.

Lessons

Wednesday

MATINS	Ezekiel 3:16-21	2 Timothy 3:1-6, 4:5
VESPERS	Jeremiah 42:1-6	Matthew 28:16-20

Friday

MATINS   Isaiah 6:1-8   2 Timothy 2:19-26

VESPERS   Deuteronomy 18:15-22   Luke 10:1-11

Saturday

MATINS   Ecclesiasticus 39:1-11   Romans 13:7-14

Canticle at Matins   1 CORINTHIANS 1:17-23 AND GALATIANS 2:19-20

On all three days

> Christ sent me to proclaim the gospel, *
> so that the cross of Christ might not be emptied of its power.
>
> For the message of the cross is foolishness to those who are perishing. *
> but to us who are being saved, it is the power of God.
>
> Some demand signs, and some desire wisdom, *
> but we proclaim the message of Christ crucified,
> a stumbling block to some and foolishness to others.
>
> I have been crucified with Christ; *
> it is no longer I who live,
> but it is Christ who lives in me;
>
> And the life I now live in the flesh, *
> I live by faith in Christ Jesus.

Hymn at Matins

On all three days

> Christ is made the sure foundation,
> and the head and cornerstone;
> chosen in God's love, and precious,
> binding all the church in one;
> holy Zion's help for ever,
> and its confidence alone.
>
> Foursquare is that heavenly city,
> three on each side are its gates;
> twelve in all, and every portal
> one apostle designates,
> in new Israel, a founder
> of a tribe Christ recreates.

252   THE COMMON OF SAINTS

Bright with pearl glows every portal,
     open to all hearts in prayer;
and by virtue of Christ's passion
     faithful souls may enter there,
who for Jesus' name in this world
     suffered agony and care.

Glory be to our Creator,
     to the Word all glory be,
laud and honor to the Spirit,
     God the Holy Trinity;
consubstantial, coeternal,
     now, and through eternity. Amen.

Antiphon on Benedictus

Wednesday

Look around you, look at the fields; *
     already they are white, ready for harvest.

Friday

When Jesus saw the crowds, he had compassion on them, *
     because they were harassed and dejected,
     like sheep without a shepherd.

Saturday

Anyone who wants to be a follower of mine must leave self behind, *
     take up the cross every day and follow me.

Collect

Wednesday

(For those to be ordained)

Almighty God, the giver of all good gifts, in your divine providence you have appointed various orders in your Church: Give your grace, we humbly pray, to all who are called to any office and ministry for your people; and so fill them with the truth of your doctrine and clothe them with holiness of life, that they may faithfully serve before you, to the glory of your great name and for the benefit of your holy Church; through Jesus Christ our Savior, who lives and reigns with you, in the unity of the Holy Spirit, one God, now and for ever. *Amen.*

Friday

(For the choice of fit persons for the ministry)

O God, you led your holy apostles to ordain ministers in every place: Grant that your Church, under the guidance of the Holy Spirit, may choose suitable persons for the ministry of word and sacrament, and may uphold them in their work for the extension of your realm; through the One who is the Shepherd and Bishop of our souls, Jesus Christ our Savior, who lives and reigns with you and the Holy Spirit, one God, for ever and ever. *Amen.*

Saturday

(For all Christians in their vocation)

Almighty and everlasting God, by whose Spirit the whole body of your faithful people is governed and sanctified: Receive our supplications and prayers, which we offer before you for all members of your holy Church; that in their vocation and ministry they may truly and devoutly serve you; through our Savior Jesus Christ, who lives and reigns with you, in the unity of the Holy Spirit, one God, now and for ever. *Amen.*

Diurnum

Antiphon on Psalter (all three days)

As God has sent me into the world, *
so have I sent them into the world.

Lesson and Respond (all three days)   EPHESIANS 2:19-20

You are no longer strangers or foreign visitors; you are citizens like all the saints, and part of God's household. You are part of a building that has the apostles and prophets for its foundation, and Christ for its main cornerstone.

Response: Thanks be to God.

  v. Their voice has gone out into all lands.
  r. And their message to the earth's farthest bounds.

The Office continues with the Closing Prayers in the Ordinary of Diurnum, p. 55.

Vespers

On Wednesday and Friday
Vespers on Saturday is the regularly appointed Office.

Antiphon on Psalter

Wednesday

Happy are those who walk in the way of God's law, *
who seek God with all their hearts.

Friday

Those who seek after God shall lack nothing that is good, *
for those who fear God have no want.

Canticle at Vespers   EPHESIANS 3:16-19
Wednesday and Friday

I pray that, according to the riches of God's glory,*
you may be strengthened in your inner being
with power through the Holy Spirit.

May Christ dwell in your hearts through faith,*
as you are rooted and grounded in love.

I pray that you may have the power to comprehend, with all the saints,*
what is the breadth and length and height and depth of the love
of God for us,

and that you may know the love of Christ that surpasses knowledge,*
and be filled with all the fullness of God.

Hymn at Vespers

We, in grateful, holy measure
sing of those who spread the treasure,
in the sacred word enshrined;
blessed tidings of salvation,
peace on earth their proclamation,
love of God to humankind.

O that we, your truth confessing,
and your holy word possessing,
    Jesus, may your love requite;
and to you our voices raising,
you with all the ransomed praising,
    in your worship now delight.

Holy Author of creation,
you we praise in adoration
    with the Spirit, guide and friend;
so with Christ in love united
that by all you must be cited
    Three in One, world without end. Amen.

Antiphon on Magnificat

Wednesday

The reaper is bringing in the grain for eternal life, *
    and thus sower and reaper rejoice together.

Friday

The harvest is rich but the laborers are few, *
    so ask the God of abundance to send laborers in to the harvest.

During Advent, the Great O antiphons on the Magnificat (p. 99ff) take precedence over those above.
The antiphon on the Magnificat on Saturdays is of the Sunday following.

COMMON 12

ROGATION DAYS

The Rogation Days are traditionally observed on the Monday, Tuesday, and Wednesday before Ascension Day.

The Psalter is as in the regularly appointed Office.

Matins

On all three days

Invitatory: Alleluia, the Spirit of God renews the face of the earth:

Response: O come, let us worship, alleluia

Monday: For fruitful seasons

> You shall eat the fruit of your labor; *
>> blessings and prosperity shall be yours, alleluia.

Tuesday: For commerce and industry

> Potters sit at their work and turn the wheel with their feet; *
>> they rely on their hands and are skillful in their own work, alleluia.

Wednesday: For stewardship of creation

> God beheld the whole of creation *
>> and saw that it was very good, alleluia.

Canticle at Matins   OSH

All three days

> Alleluia, praise to you, O bountiful God, *
>> for all you have so graciously given.
>
> You fashioned heavens of unreachable mystery: *
>> galaxies, stars, and velvet dark.
>
> You created atoms and molecules,
> and smaller particles of existence *
>> beyond our comprehension.
>
> You created the earth with all its abundance; *
>> you give us the seedtime and harvest.
>
> You give us richness of life, *
>> creation spread horizon to horizon.
>
> Praise to you, O God, for this wondrous universe; *
>> for all your gifts, we offer thanks and glory, alleluia.

Hymn at Matins and at Vespers

> God of Almighty changeless energy, creation's secret source,
> holding all things in perfect rhythmic dance.
>
> The heavens tell the glory of your work: day moving on to day,
> and night to night proclaims its ordered sway.
>
> Within our changing swiftly passing lives, unite all hearts
>> with yours,
> that praising, we may enter heaven's courts.

All honor and praise to you, O heavenly God,
the source of all that is:
all light, all love, all joy: thanks be to God. Amen.

Antiphon on Benedictus

Monday

Creation waits with eager longing to be set free *
and to obtain the freedom of the glory of the children of God, alleluia.

Tuesday

Store up for yourselves treasures in heaven, *
for where your treasure is, there will your heart be also, alleluia.

Wednesday

To do good, to be rich in good works, to be generous and willing to share: *
this is the way to make sure of the only life that is life indeed, alleluia.

Collect

Monday

Almighty God, Creator of heaven and earth: We humbly pray that your
gracious providence may give and preserve to our use the harvest of land
and sea, and may prosper all who labor to gather it, that we, who are constantly receiving good things from your hand, may always give you thanks;
through Jesus Christ our Savior, who lives and reigns with you and the
Holy Spirit, one God, for ever and ever. *Amen.*

Tuesday

Almighty God, whose Beloved One in earthly life shared our toil and sanctified our labor: Be present with your people where they work; help those
who carry on the industries and commerce of this land to be responsive to
your will; and give to us all a pride in what we do and a just return for our
labor; through Jesus Christ our Savior, who lives and reigns with you, in
the unity of the Holy Spirit, one God, now and for ever. *Amen.*

Wednesday

O merciful Creator, your hand is open wide to satisfy the needs of every
living creature: Make us always thankful for your loving providence; and
grant that we, remembering the account that we must one day give, may
be faithful stewards of your good gifts; through Jesus Christ our Savior,
who with you and the Holy Spirit lives and reigns, one God, for ever and
ever. *Amen.*

Diurnum

Antiphon on Psalter (all three days)

> O God, how manifold are your works! *
> In wisdom you have made them all;
> the earth is full of your creatures, Alleluia.

Lesson and Respond (all three days) JAMES 1:17

> Every generous act of giving, with every perfect gift, is from above, coming down from the Creator of lights, with whom there is no variation or shadow due to change.

Response: Thanks be to God.

> v. You open your hand, and all are filled with good things, alleluia, alleluia.
> r. You give proper food in due season, alleluia, alleluia.

The Office continues with the Closing Prayers in the Ordinary of Diurnum, p. 55.

Vespers

Antiphon on Psalter

Monday
> The earth produces of itself, first the stalk, and then the ear, *
> then the full grain in the ear, Alleluia.

Tuesday
> Why spend money on that which is not bread, and your labor on
> that which does not satisfy? *
> God says, Listen to me, and eat what is good,
> and your soul will delight in the richest of fare, Alleluia.

Canticle at Vespers OSH

> O God our Creator,*
> you feed us from the fruit of the earth,
>
> freely giving food to sustain our lives*
> and those of future generations.
>
> We thank you for this gracious gift of love,*
> so abundantly shared.

We sing to you; we praise you; we give thanks to you;*
    we show our gratitude in acts of stewardship every day.

In living together in communion with one another,*
    with the earth and all creation,
    we celebrate the life you have given us,

generation after generation.*
    We sing to you; we praise you, O our God.

The hymn is as at Matins.

Antiphon on Magnificat

Monday
    When the crop is ready, the reaper loses no time, *
        but starts to reap, because the harvest has come, Alleluia.

Tuesday
    No one can be the slave of two masters; *
        you cannot serve both God and money, Alleluia.

COMMON 13

NATIONAL DAYS

Matins

Invitatory: The Spirit of wisdom guides into all truth:
Response: O come, let us worship.

Antiphon on Psalter

    May God give strength to all people; *
        may God bless all people with peace.

The canticle is the Te Deum, found on p. 213.

Hymn at Matins

Christ is made the sure foundation,
    and the head and cornerstone;
chosen in God's love, and precious,
    binding all the church in one;
holy Zion's help for ever,
    and its confidence alone.

Bright with pearl glows every portal,
    open to all hearts in prayer;
and by virtue of Christ's passion
    faithful souls may enter there,
who for Jesus' name in this world
    suffered agony and care.

Glory be to our Creator,
    to the Word all glory be,
praise and honor to the Spirit,
    God the Holy Trinity;
consubstantial, coeternal,
    now, and through eternity. Amen.

Antiphon on Benedictus

Christ is our peace, whose flesh has broken down the walls of hostility, *
    creating one new humanity.

Collect

O loving God, you have made the peoples of the earth for your glory, to
serve you in freedom and in peace: Give to all nations a zeal for justice and
the strength of forbearance, that we may use the gifts you have given us in
accordance with your gracious will; through Jesus Christ our Savior, who
lives and reigns with you and the Holy Spirit, one God, for ever and ever.
Amen.

Diurnum

Antiphon on Psalter

Great peace have they who love your law; *
    nothing can make them stumble.

The effect of righteousness will be peace, and the result of righteousness, quietness and trust forever. My people will abide in a peaceful habitation, in secure dwellings, and in quiet resting places.

Response: Thanks be to God.

> *v.* Bring me to your holy hill and to your dwelling,
> *r.* That I may go to your altar, O God.

The Office continues with the Closing Prayers in the Ordinary of Diurnum, p. 55.

Vespers

Antiphon on Psalter

Love your enemies and pray for your persecutors; *
only so can you truly be children of God.

Hymn at Vespers

> Blessed city, heavenly Salem,
> vision dear of peace and love,
> you, of living stones assembled,
> are the joy of heaven above;
> and, with angel choirs encircled,
> as a bride to earth you move.
>
> All that dedicated city,
> dearly loved by God on high,
> in exultant jubilation
> pours perpetual melody;
> God the Three in One adoring
> in glad hymns eternally.
>
> Praise to God our great Creator,
> honor to the Spirit blest;
> praise to Jesus, our Redeemer,
> triune God made manifest;
> who to all the saints adoring,
> grants the joy of heavenly rest. Amen.

Antiphon on Magnificat

> They shall beat their swords into plowshares,
>> and their spears into pruning hooks. *
>> Nation shall not lift up sword against nation,
>> neither shall they learn war any more.

COMMON 14

HARVEST THANKSGIVING

Matins

Invitatory: The holy God's bounty fills the earth:
Response: O come, let us worship.

Antiphon on Psalter

> I will offer a sacrifice of thanksgiving *
>> and call upon the name of God.

The canticle is the Te Deum, p. 213.

Hymn at Matins and at Vespers

> God of Almighty changeless energy, creation's secret source,
> holding all things in perfect rhythmic dance,
> the heavens tell the glory of your work: day moving on to day,
> and night to night proclaims its ordered sway.

> Within our changing swiftly passing lives, unite all hearts
>> with yours,
> that praising, we may enter heaven's courts.
> All honor and praise to you, O heavenly God, the source of
>> all that is:
> all light, all love, all joy: thanks be to God. Amen.

Antiphon on Benedictus

> God has given you a good land, where you may eat bread without scarcity; *
> you shall bless your God for what has been given to you.

Collect

Almighty and gracious God, we give you thanks for the fruits of the earth in their season and for the labors of those who harvest them: Help us, we pray, to be faithful stewards of your great bounty, for the provision of our necessities and the relief of all who are in need, to the glory of your name; through Jesus Christ our Savior, who lives and reigns with you and the Holy Spirit, one God, now and for ever. *Amen.*

Diurnum

Antiphon on Psalter

O God, how manifold are your works! *
   In wisdom you have made them all; the earth is full of your creatures.

Lesson and Respond   JAMES 1:17

Every generous act of giving, with every perfect gift, is from above, coming down from the Creator of lights, with whom there is no variation or shadow due to change.

Response: Thanks be to God.

   v. You open your hand, and we are filled with good things;
   r. You give us our food in due season.

The Office continues with the Closing Prayers in the Ordinary of Diurnum, p. 55.

Vespers

Antiphon on Psalter

You are our God and we are the people of your pasture, *
   and the sheep of your hand.

Canticle at Vespers   OSH

O God our Creator,*
   you feed us from the fruit of the earth,

freely giving food to sustain our lives*
   and those of future generations.

We thank you for this gracious gift of love,*
 so abundantly shared.

We sing to you; we praise you; we give thanks to you;*
 we show our gratitude in acts of stewardship every day.

In living together in communion with one another,*
 with the earth and all creation,
 we celebrate the life you have given us,

generation after generation.*
 We sing to you; we praise you, O our God.

The hymn is as at Matins.

Antiphon on Magnificat

Blessed be God who has lifted up the lowly, *
 and filled the hungry with good things.

COMMON 15

DEPARTED

This Office is always said in the plural, even when offered for an individual, except for the collect.
All is as in the Ordinary of the Office, except as below.
The Gloria is always omitted, with the "Rest eternal" said instead.
Other lessons suitable to the occasion may be substituted for those appointed.

Matins

The opening versicles are omitted.
The Office begins with the invitatory antiphon below, followed by the Venite.

Invitatory: The Holy One is the source of all life:
Response: O come, let us worship.

Antiphon on Psalter

I believe that I shall see the goodness of God *
 in the land of the living.

In place of the Gloria shall be recited throughout the Office:
Rest eternal grant to them, O God, *
and let light perpetual shine upon them.

First Lesson   Ezekiel 37:1-14

Respond, in place of the canticle
    v. I know that my Redeemer lives,
    r. I will see God with my own eyes.

    v. How my heart yearns within me!
    r. I will see God with my own eyes.

    v. Rest eternal grant to them, O God,
    r. And let light perpetual shine upon them.

Second Lesson   1 Corinthians 15:35-49

Respond, in place of the hymn
    v. Set your troubled hearts at rest. Trust God always; trust also in me
    r. There are many dwelling places in the house of God.

    v. I am going there on purpose to prepare a place for you;
    r. There are many dwelling places in the house of God.

    v. Rest eternal grant to them, O God,
    r. And let light perpetual shine upon them.

Antiphon on Benedictus

    I am the resurrection and the life, says Jesus. *
        Those who have faith in me, even though they die, they shall come to life.

In place of the Gloria:

    Rest eternal grant to them, O God, *
        and let light perpetual shine upon them.

The Office continues with the Closing Prayers in the Ordinary of Matins, p. 32, but with the collect and Ending below. The Benedicamus is omitted.

The Common Collect

O God, whose mercies cannot be numbered: Accept our prayers on behalf of your servants and grant them an entrance into the land of light and joy, in the company of your saints; through Jesus Christ our Savior, who lives and reigns with you and the Holy Spirit, one God, now and for ever. *Amen.*

Collect for an individual

If the Office is said for an individual, as for example, a departed sister or a loved one, the collect below is used, with the name of the individual inserted where appropriate.

O God, who by the glorious resurrection of Jesus destroyed death and brought life and immortality to light: Grant that your servant N., being raised to life everlasting, may know the strength of Christ's presence, and rejoice in Christ's eternal glory; who with you and the Holy Spirit lives and reigns, one God, for ever and ever. *Amen.*

The Ending

Officiant:	Rest eternal grant to them, O God.
Response:	And let light perpetual shine upon them.
Officiant:	May they rest in peace.
Response:	Amen.

Diurnum

The opening versicles and the hymn are omitted.
The Office begins with the Psalter and its antiphon.

Antiphon on Psalter

You have rescued my soul from death and my feet from stumbling, *
 that I may walk before God in the light of the living.

In place of the Gloria:

Rest eternal grant to them, O God, *
 and let light perpetual shine upon them.

Lesson and Respond ROMANS 8:38-39

I am convinced that neither death, nor life, nor angels, nor rulers, nor things present, nor things to come, nor powers, nor height, nor depth, nor anything else in all creation, will be able to separate us from the love of God in Christ Jesus our Savior.

Response: Thanks be to God.

   v. Again a little while, and you will see me,
   r. Because I am going to my God and your God.

After a short pause, the Office continues with the Closing Prayers in the Ordinary of Diurnum, p. 55.

After the collect, the Ending is as below. The Benedicamus is omitted.

The Ending

Officiant: Rest eternal grant to them, O God.
Response: And let light perpetual shine upon them.

Officiant: May they rest in peace.
Response: Amen.

Vespers

The opening versicles are omitted.
The Office begins with the Phos hilaron, p. 57.

Antiphon on Psalter

Have no fear, little flock; *
   for God has chosen to give you the joys of heaven.

In place of the Gloria:

Rest eternal grant to them, O God, *
   and let light perpetual shine upon them.

First Lesson 2 SAMUEL 12:15B-23

Respond, in place of the canticle

   v. Though I walk through the valley of the shadow of death,
     I shall fear no evil;
   r. I will dwell in the house of God for ever.

v. Surely your goodness and mercy shall follow me all the days of my life.
r. I will dwell in the house of God for ever.

v. Rest eternal grant to them, O God,
r. And let light perpetual shine upon them.

Second Lesson 1 THESSALONIANS 5:1-11

Respond, in place of the hymn
v. You, O God, raised Lazarus already corrupting from the grave.
r. Grant them mercy, O God, and everlasting peace.

v. You are the resurrection and the life;
r. Grant them mercy, O God, and everlasting peace.

v. Rest eternal grant to them, O God,
r. And let light perpetual shine upon them.

Antiphon on Magnificat

Jesus said, All that God gives me will come to me, *
and no one who comes to me will I ever turn away.

In place of the Gloria:
Rest eternal grant to them, O God, *
and let light perpetual shine upon them.

The Office continues with the Closing Prayers in the Ordinary of Vespers, p. 84

After the collect, the Ending is as below. The Benedicamus is omitted.

The Ending

Officiant:	Rest eternal grant to them, O God.
Response:	And let light perpetual shine upon them.
Officiant:	May they rest in peace.
Response:	Amen.

Compline

The opening versicles are omitted.

The Office begins, after a period of silence, with the Confession and Absolution as in the Ordinary of Compline, p. 89.

The hymn is omitted.

After the Psalms of the Day are recited, the lesson is omitted, unless an appropriate passage from one of the spiritual writers is read.

Respond

> *v.* Into your hands, O God, I commend my spirit;
> *r.* For you have redeemed me, O God of truth.
>
> *v.* Rest eternal grant to them, O God,
> *r.* And let light perpetual shine upon them.

After a short pause, the Office continues with the Closing Prayers in the Ordinary of Compline, p. 92, using the collect below.

Collect

Look down, we pray, O merciful God, upon the souls of all your servants for whom we humbly pray, that they may be counted worthy to enter into everlasting rest; through Jesus Christ our Savior and Redeemer, who lives and reigns with you and the Holy Spirit, one God, for ever and ever. *Amen.*

The Nunc dimittis with its usual antiphon (p. 94) follows.
In place of the Gloria:

> Rest eternal grant to them, O God, *
>   and let light perpetual shine upon them.

Compline closes with the Ending as below.

The Ending

Officiant:	Rest eternal grant to them, O God.
Response:	And let light perpetual shine upon them.
Officiant:	May they rest in peace.
Response:	Amen.

The Collects for Saints' Days and Major Holy Days

Major saints days and holy days from the Book of Common Prayer, together with additional observances celebrated as major holy days by the Order of Saint Helena, may be celebrated fully with prescribed readings as indicated. The other observances (lesser feasts) may be celebrated more simply by including the collect as one of the prayers in the regular daily office. If desired, other material from the Common indicated for a particular day may also be included in the regular daily office.

November 30   **ANDREW**
Apostle

Common 2, p. 217. For readings, see p.612.

Collect

O Jesus Christ, you gave such grace to your apostle Andrew that he readily obeyed your call and brought his brother with him: Give us, and all those who hear your call, grace to follow you without delay, and to bring those near to us into your gracious presence; who with the Creator and the Holy Spirit lives and reigns, one God, now and for ever. *Amen.*

December 1   **NICHOLAS FERRAR**
Deacon, 1637

Common 10, p. 247

Collect

O God, make us worthy of your perfect love; that, with your deacon Nicholas Ferrar and his household, we may rule ourselves according to your word, and serve you with our whole heart; through Jesus Christ our Savior, who lives and reigns with you and the Holy Spirit, one God, for ever and ever. *Amen.*

December 2   CHANNING MOORE WILLIAMS
                    Missionary Bishop in China and Japan, 1910

Common 6, p. 233

Collect

Almighty and everlasting God, we thank you for your servant Channing
Moore Williams, whom you called to preach the gospel to the people in
China and Japan. Raise up in this and every land evangelists and heralds of
your reign, that your Church may proclaim the unsearchable riches of our
Savior Jesus Christ; who lives and reigns with you and the Holy Spirit, one
God, for ever and ever. *Amen.*

December 4   JOHN OF DAMASCUS
                    Priest, c. 760

Common 5, p. 230

Collect

Strengthen our minds and hearts, O God, in the mysteries of the true
faith, set forth with power by your servant John of Damascus; that we,
with him, confessing Jesus to be truly God and truly human, and singing
the praises of the risen Savior, may by the power of the resurrection attain
to eternal joy; through Jesus Christ our Redeemer, who lives and reigns
with you and the Holy Spirit, one God, now and for ever. *Amen.*

December 5   CLEMENT OF ALEXANDRIA
                    Priest, c. 210

Common 8, p. 240

Collect

O God of unsearchable wisdom, you gave your servant Clement grace to
understand and teach the truth as it is in Jesus Christ, the source of all
truth: Grant to your Church the same grace to discern your word wherever truth is found; through Jesus Christ our unfailing light, who lives and
reigns with you and the Holy Spirit, one God, for ever and ever. *Amen.*

December 6   **NICHOLAS**
Bishop of Myra, c. 342

Common 10, p. 247

Collect

Almighty God, in your love you gave your servant Nicholas of Myra a perpetual name for deeds of kindness both on land and sea: Grant, we pray, that your Church may never cease to work for the happiness of children, the safety of sailors, the relief of the poor, and the help of those tossed by tempests of doubt or grief; through Jesus Christ our Savior, who lives and reigns with you and the Holy Spirit, one God, for ever and ever. *Amen.*

December 7   **AMBROSE**
Bishop of Milan, 397

Common 5, p. 230

Collect

O God, you gave your servant Ambrose grace to proclaim with eloquence your righteousness in the great congregation, and to bear reproach without fear for the honor of your name: Mercifully grant to all bishops and pastors such excellence in preaching and faithfulness in ministering your word, that your people may be partakers with them of the glory that shall be revealed; through Jesus Christ our Savior, who lives and reigns with you and the Holy Spirit, one God, now and for ever. *Amen.*

December 14   **JOHN OF THE CROSS**
Carmelite Friar, Mystic, and Reformer, 1591

Common 7, p. 237

Collect

O Holy God, giver of all good gifts and source of all life and love, we bless you for your servant John of the Cross and praise you for his gifts of poetry and mystical insight. May we, too, follow his example in striving for holiness of life and standing firm against religious oppression. We ask this through our Savior Jesus Christ, who lives and reigns with you and the Holy Spirit, one God, for ever and ever. *Amen.*

December 21   **THOMAS**
Apostle

Common 2, p. 217. For readings, see p.612.

Collect

Everliving God, who strengthened your apostle Thomas with unshakeable
faith in the resurrection of Jesus: Grant us so perfectly and without doubt
to believe in Jesus Christ, our Redeemer and our God, that our faith may
never be found wanting in your sight; through the One who lives and
reigns with you and the Holy Spirit, one God, for ever and ever. *Amen.*

December 26   **STEPHEN**
Deacon and Martyr

Common 4, p. 226. For readings, see p. 612.

Collect

We give you thanks, O God of glory, for the example of the first martyr
Stephen, who looked up to heaven and prayed for his persecutors to our
Savior Jesus Christ, who stands at your right hand and who lives and
reigns with you and the Holy Spirit, one God, in glory everlasting. *Amen.*

December 27   **JOHN**
Apostle and Evangelist

Common 2, p. 217. For readings, see p.612.

Collect

Shed upon your Church, O God, the brightness of your light, that we,
being illumined by the teaching of your apostle and evangelist John, may
so walk in the light of your truth, that we may attain to the fullness of
eternal life; through Jesus Christ our Savior, who lives and reigns with you
and the Holy Spirit, one God, for ever and ever. *Amen.*

December 28   **THE HOLY INNOCENTS**

Common 4, p.226. For readings, see p, 612.

Collect

O God of compassion and mercy, we remember today the slaughter of the holy innocents of Bethlehem: Receive, we pray, into the arms of your mercy all those killed unjustly, and by your great might frustrate the powers of oppression and establish your rule of justice, love and peace; through Jesus Christ our Savior, who lives and reigns with you and the Holy Spirit, one God, for ever and ever. *Amen.*

December 29   **THOMAS BECKET**
                                  Archbishop of Canterbury and Martyr, 1170

Common 4, p. 226

Collect

O God, our strength and our salvation, you called your servant Thomas Becket to be a shepherd of your people and a defender of your Church: Keep your household from all evil and raise up among us faithful pastors and leaders who are wise in the ways of the Gospel; through Jesus Christ, the shepherd of our souls, who lives and reigns with you and the Holy Spirit, one God, for ever and ever. *Amen.*

January 9   **JULIA CHESTER EMERY**
                                  Founder Women's Auxiliary;
                                  Founder United Thank Offering, 1922

Common 3, p. 222

Collect

God of all creation, you call us in Christ to make disciples of all nations and to proclaim your mercy and love: We thank you for your servant Julia Chester Emery and for her vision, courage and untiring efforts to expand the contributions of women throughout the Church and for her work toward establishing the United Thank Offering; through Jesus Christ our light and our salvation, who lives and reigns with you and the Holy Spirit, one God, for ever and ever. *Amen.*

January 10   **WILLIAM LAUD**
Archbishop of Canterbury, 1645

Common 4, p. 226

Collect

Keep us, O God, constant in faith and zealous in witness, that, like your servant William Laud, we may live with tireless faith, die in your favor, and rest in your peace; for the sake of Jesus Christ our Savior, who lives and reigns with you and the Holy Spirit, one God, for ever and ever. *Amen.*

January 12   **AELRED**
Abbot of Rievaulx, 1167

Common 7, p. 237

Collect

Pour into our hearts, O God, the Holy Spirit's gift of love, that we, clasping each the other's hand, may share the joy of friendship, human and divine, and with your servant Aelred draw many to your community of love; through Jesus Christ the Righteous, who lives and reigns with you and the Holy Spirit, one God, for ever and ever. *Amen.*

January 13   **HILARY**
Bishop of Poitiers, 367

Common 5, p. 230

Collect

O Holy God, you raised up your servant Hilary to be a champion of the catholic faith: Keep us steadfast in that true faith which we professed at our baptism, so we may rejoice in having you as our God, and may abide in Christ, in the communion of the Holy Spirit: one God in Trinity of Persons, for ever and ever. *Amen.*

January 15   MARTIN LUTHER KING, JR.
              Civil Rights Leader, 1968

(May also be celebrated on April 4)

Common 3, p. 222

Collect

Almighty God, by the hand of Moses your servant you led your people out of slavery, and made them free at last: Grant that the Church, following the example of your prophet Martin Luther King, may resist oppression in the name of your love, and may secure for all your children the blessed liberty of the gospel of Jesus Christ; who lives and reigns with you and the Holy Spirit, one God, for ever and ever. *Amen.*

January 17   ANTONY
              Abbot in Egypt, 356

Common 7, p. 237

Collect

Almighty God, you called your servant Antony into the desert where you strengthened him to overcome many temptations and to live a holy and godly life: Give us grace, we pray, that with pure hearts and minds we too may follow you, the only God, wherever you may lead; this we ask in the name of the Holy and undivided Trinity. *Amen.*

January 18   CONFESSION OF PETER THE APOSTLE

Common 2, p. 217. For readings, see p. 612.

Collect

Almighty God, who inspired Simon Peter, first among the apostles, to confess Jesus as the Messiah: Keep your Church steadfast upon the rock of this faith, so that in unity and peace we may proclaim the living truth and follow the Savior Jesus Christ; who lives and reigns with you and the Holy Spirit, one God, for ever and ever. *Amen.*

January 19   **WULFSTAN**
                       Bishop of Worcester, 1095

Common 9, p. 244

Collect

Almighty God, your only-begotten One led captivity captive and gave gifts to your people: Multiply among us faithful pastors who, like your holy bishop Wulfstan, will give courage to those who are oppressed and held in bondage; and bring us all, we pray, into the true freedom of your dominion; through Jesus Christ our Savior, who lives and reigns with you and the Holy Spirit, one God, for ever and ever. *Amen.*

January 20   **FABIAN**
                       Bishop and Martyr of Rome, 250

Common 4, p. 226

Collect

O God, in your providence you singled out the holy martyr Fabian as worthy to be chief pastor of your people, and guided him so to strengthen your Church that it stood fast in the day of persecution: Grant that those whom you call to any ministry in the Church may in all humility be obedient to your call, and be enabled to carry out their tasks with diligence and faithfulness; through Jesus Christ our Savior, who lives and reigns with you and the Holy Spirit, one God, for ever and ever. *Amen.*

January 21   **AGNES**
                       Martyr at Rome, 304

Common 4, p. 226

Collect

O God of transcendent majesty, you have chosen what is weak in the world to confound the strong, that all may be brought to that love which came to perfection on the cross: Grant us so to honor your holy martyr Agnes, that in the face of the threats of the powerful we may share her courage and steadfast faith in you; through Jesus Christ, who lives and reigns with you and the Holy Spirit, one God in glory everlasting. *Amen.*

January 22   **VINCENT**
Deacon of Saragossa and Martyr, 304

Common 4, p. 226

Collect

God of boundless compassion, who made your holy deacon Vincent a
worthy partner in the sufferings of Christ: Strengthen us to endure all
adversity with invincible and steadfast faith, that our assurance of your saving
justice may vanquish all dangers that assault our bodies and all wounds
that would harm our souls; through Jesus Christ our Savior, who lives and
reigns with you and the Holy Spirit, one God, for ever and ever. *Amen.*

January 23   **PHILLIPS BROOKS**
Bishop of Massachusetts, 1893

Common 9, p. 244

Collect

O everlasting God, you revealed your truth to Phillips Brooks, and so
formed and molded his mind and heart that he was able to preach that
truth with grace and power: Grant, we pray, that all whom you call to
proclaim the gospel may steep themselves in your Word, and conform
their lives to your will; through Jesus Christ our Savior, who lives and
reigns with you and the Holy Spirit, one God, for ever and ever. *Amen.*

January 24   **FLORENCE LI TIM-OI**
First Woman Priest in the Anglican Communion, 1944

Common 9, p. 244

Collect

Gracious God, we thank you for calling Florence Li Tim-Oil, whose name
means much-beloved daughter, to be the first woman to exercise the office
of a priest in our Communion: By the grace of your Spirit inspire us to
follow her example, serving your people with patience and happiness all
our days, and witnessing in every circumstance to our Savior Jesus Christ;
who lives and reigns with you and the same Spirit, one God, for ever and
ever. *Amen.*

January 25   CONVERSION OF PAUL

Common 2, p. 217. For readings, see p. 612.

Collect

Almighty God, by the preaching of your servant Paul your caused the light of the gospel to shine throughout the world: May we who celebrate his wonderful conversion follow him in bearing witness to your truth, and remember that no persecutor is beyond the power of your call to new life; through Jesus Christ our Redeemer, who lives and reigns with you and the Holy Spirit, one God, now and for ever. *Amen.*

January 26   TIMOTHY AND TITUS
                                   Bishops, Companions of Saint Paul

Common 8, p. 240

Collect

Almighty God, you called Timothy and Titus to be evangelists and teachers, and made them strong to stand fast in adversity: Strengthen us to endure hardship, and to live godly and righteous lives in this present time, that with sure confidence we may look for our blessed hope, the glorious appearing of our great God and Savior Jesus Christ; who lives and reigns with you and the Holy Spirit, one God, now and for ever. *Amen.*

January 27   JOHN CHRYSOSTOM
                                   Bishop of Constantinople, 407

Common 5, p. 230

Collect

O God, you gave your servant John Chrysostom grace to proclaim with eloquence your righteousness in the great congregation, and to bear reproach without fear for the honor of your name: Mercifully grant to all bishops and pastors such excellence in preaching, and faithfulness in ministering your word, that your people may be partakers with them of the glory that shall be revealed; through Jesus Christ our Savior, who lives and reigns with you and the Holy Spirit, one God, for ever and ever. *Amen.*

January 28   **THOMAS AQUINAS**
Priest and Friar, 1274

Common 5, p. 230

Collect

O God, you blessed your servant Thomas Aquinas with singular gifts of wisdom and insight, that your people might love with their understanding what you give them to know by faith: Grant us the freedom to embrace your Church's teaching and the obedience to deepen its faith, that our knowledge may be perfected in worship and our faith may be fulfilled in love; through Jesus Christ our Redeemer, who lives and reigns with you and the Holy Spirit, one God, now and for ever. *Amen.*

February 1   **BRIGID [BRIDE]**
Abbess of Kildare, c. 523

Common 7, p. 237

Collect

Everliving God, we rejoice today in the witness of your servant Brigid of Kildare, who served as courageous leader and mentor, faithfully shepherding both men and women in her monastery and guiding them into holiness of life: Inspire us with life and light, and give us perseverance to serve you in our own day. This we ask in the name of the Holy and Undivided Trinity, one God, in glory everlasting. *Amen.*

February 2   **THE PRESENTATION OF JESUS CHRIST IN THE TEMPLE**
Common 1, p. 213. For readings, see pp.612-613

Collect

Almighty and everliving God, we humbly pray that, as your only-begotten Child was this day presented in the temple by Mary and Joseph, so may we be presented to you with pure and clean hearts by Jesus Christ our Savior, who lives and reigns with you and the Holy Spirit, one God, for ever and ever. *Amen.*

February 3   **ANSKAR**
Archbishop of Hamburg,
Missionary to Denmark and Sweden, 865

Common 6, p. 233

Collect

Almighty and everlasting God, you sent your servant Anskar as an apostle
to the people of Scandinavia, and enabled him to lay a firm foundation for
their conversion, though he did not see the results of his labors: Keep your
Church from discouragement in the day of small things, knowing that
when you have begun a good work you will bring it to a fruitful conclu-
sion; through Jesus Christ our Savior, who lives and reigns with you and
the Holy Spirit, one God, for ever and ever. *Amen.*

February 4   **CORNELIUS THE CENTURION**
Confessor (Acts 10)

Common 10, p. 247

Collect

O God, by your Spirit you called Cornelius the Centurion to be the first
Christian among the Gentiles: Grant to your Church such a ready will to
go where you send and to do what you command, that under your guidance it may welcome all who turn to you in love and faith, and proclaim
the gospel to all nations; through Jesus Christ our Savior, who lives and
reigns with you and the Holy Spirit, one God, for ever and ever. *Amen.*

February 5   **THE MARTYRS OF JAPAN**
1597

Common 4, p. 226

Collect

O Loving God, source of strength to all your saints, you brought the holy
martyrs of Japan through the suffering of the cross to the joys of eternal
life: Grant that we, encouraged by their example, may hold fast the faith
we profess, even to death itself; through Jesus Christ our Savior, who lives
and reigns with you and the Holy Spirit, one God, in glory everlasting.
Amen.

February 13   ABSALOM JONES
                   First African American Priest

Common 3, p. 222

Collect

> Set us free, O Holy God, from every bond of prejudice and fear; that, honoring the steadfast courage of your servant Absalom Jones, we may show forth in our lives the reconciling love and true freedom of the children of God, which you have given us in our Savior Jesus Christ; who lives and reigns with you and the Holy Spirit, one God, in glory everlasting. *Amen.*

February 14   CYRIL AND METHODIUS
                   Monk and Bishop, Missionaries to the Slavs, 869, 885

Common 6, p. 233

Collect

> Almighty and everliving God, by the power of the Holy Spirit you moved your servants Cyril and his brother Methodius to bring the light of the gospel to a hostile and divided people: Overcome all bitterness and strife among us by the love of Christ, and make us one united family under the banner of the Holy One of Peace; who lives and reigns with you and the Holy Spirit, one God, for ever and ever. *Amen.*

February 15   THOMAS BRAY
                   Priest and Missionary; Social Activist
                   Founder SPCK and SPG, 1730

Common 3, p. 222

Collect

> O God of compassion, you opened the eyes of your servant Thomas Bray to see the needs of the church in the New World, and led him to found societies to meet those needs: Make the Church in this and every land diligent at all times to propagate the gospel among those who have not received it, and to promote the spread of Christian knowledge; through Jesus Christ our Savior, who lives and reigns with you and the Holy Spirit, one God, for ever and ever. *Amen.*

February 17   **JANANI LUWUM**
Archbishop of Uganda, and Martyr, 1977

Common 4, p. 226

Collect

O Loving Jesus, you are the Good Shepherd who laid down your life for
the sheep: We give you thanks for your faithful shepherd, Janani Luwum,
who after his Savior's example gave up his life for the people of Uganda.
Grant us to be so inspired by his witness that we make no peace with
oppression, but live as those who are sealed with the cross of Christ; who
died and rose again, and now lives and reigns with the Creator and the
Holy Spirit, one God, in glory everlasting. *Amen.*

February 18   **MARTIN LUTHER**
Reformer, 1546

Common 3, p. 222

Collect

O God, our refuge and our fortress; you gave your servant Martin Luther
grace and courage to speak fearlessly against the abuse and corruption in
the Church of his day: Give us also the strength and wisdom to work for
the renewal of the Church in our day, that we may boldly proclaim the
fullness of your grace which you have made known in Jesus Christ our
Savior; who lives and reigns with you and the Holy Spirit, one God, now
and for ever. *Amen.*

February 23   **POLYCARP**
Bishop and Martyr of Smyrna, 156

Common 4, p. 226

Collect

O God, the maker of heaven and earth, you gave your venerable servant,
the holy and gentle Polycarp, boldness to confess Jesus as Savior and
Redeemer, and steadfastness to die for his faith: Give us grace, following
his example, to share the cup of Christ and rise to eternal life; through
Jesus Christ our Savior, who lives and reigns with you and the Holy Spirit,
one God, in glory everlasting. *Amen.*

February 24   **MATTHIAS**
Apostle

Common 2, p. 217. For readings, see p. 613.

Collect

Almighty God, who in the place of Judas chose your faithful servant
Matthias to be numbered among the Twelve: Grant that your Church,
being delivered from false apostles, may always be guided and governed by
faithful and true pastors; through Jesus Christ our Savior, who lives and
reigns with you and the Holy Spirit, one God, for ever and ever. *Amen.*

February 27   **GEORGE HERBERT**
Priest and Poet, 1633

Common 9, p. 244

Collect

Our God and King, you called your servant George Herbert from the
pursuit of worldly honors to be a pastor of souls, a poet and a priest in
your temple: Give us grace, we pray, joyfully to perform the tasks you give
us to do, knowing that nothing is menial or common that is done for your
sake; through Jesus Christ our Savior, who lives and reigns with you and
the Holy Spirit, one God, in glory everlasting. *Amen.*

March 1   **DAVID**
Bishop of Menevia, Wales, c. 544

Common 6, p. 233

Collect

Almighty God, you called your servant David to be a faithful and wise
steward of your mysteries for the people of Wales: Mercifully grant that
we may follow his example in his zeal for spreading the gospel, and heed
his words to remember the little things; through Jesus Christ our Savior,
who lives and reigns with you and the Holy Spirit, one God, in glory
everlasting. *Amen.*

March 2   **CHAD**
Bishop of Lichfield, 672

Common 9, p. 244

Collect

> Almighty God, for the peace of the Church your servant Chad relinquished cheerfully the honors that had been thrust upon him, only to be rewarded with equal responsibility: Keep us, we pray, from thinking of ourselves more highly than we ought to think, and ready at all times to step aside for others, that the cause of Christ may be advanced; through the One who lives and reigns with you and the Holy Spirit, one God, now and for ever. *Amen.*

March 3   **JOHN AND CHARLES WESLEY**
Priests and hymnodists, 1791, 1788

Common 9, p. 244

Collect

> O God, you inspired your servants John and Charles Wesley with passion for the sanctification of souls, and endowed them with eloquence in speech and song: Kindle in your Church, we pray, such fervor, that those whose faith has cooled may be renewed in their love for you, and those who have not known your redeeming grace may turn and be saved; through Jesus Christ our Savior, who lives and reigns with you and the Holy Spirit, one God, for ever and ever. *Amen.*

March 7   **PERPETUA AND HER COMPANIONS**
Martyrs at Carthage, 202

Common 4, p. 226

Collect

> O God, the Sovereign of all saints, you strengthened your servants Perpetua and Felicitas and their companions to stand fast for the love of Christ: May we also, following their example, encourage one another to remain faithful in times of suffering and trial; for the sake of our Savior Jesus Christ, who lives and reigns with you and the Holy Spirit, one God, now and for ever. *Amen*

March 9   **GREGORY OF NYSSA**
Bishop of Nyssa, c. 394

Common 5, p. 230

Collect

Almighty God, you have revealed to your Church your eternal Being of glorious majesty and perfect love as one God in Trinity of Persons: Give us grace that, like your bishop Gregory of Nyssa, we may continue steadfast in the confession of this faith and constant in our worship of the Holy and Undivided Trinity, one God; who lives and reigns now and for ever. *Amen.*

March 12   **GREGORY THE GREAT**
Bishop of Rome, 604

Common 5, p. 230

Collect

Almighty and merciful God, you raised up Gregory of Rome to be a servant of the servants of God and gave him grace to be a wise and holy pastor committed to the spread of the Church and the enrichment of its liturgy and music: May we also be faithful to your call and praise you in song, word, and deed to our life's end; in the name of the holy and undivided Trinity. *Amen.*

March 17   **PATRICK**
Bishop and Missionary to Ireland, 461

Common 6, p. 233

Collect

Almighty God, in your providence you chose your servant Patrick to bring the Christian faith to those who once had enslaved him: Encourage us by his example, that we may know your power made perfect in our weakness, and delight in serving others for the sake of the one who became servant of all, our Savior Jesus Christ; who lives and reigns with you and the Holy Spirit, one God, for ever and ever. *Amen.*

March 18   **CYRIL OF JERUSALEM**
Bishop of Jerusalem, 386

Common 8, p. 240

Collect

Strengthen, O God, the bishops of your Church in their special calling to
be teachers and ministers of the sacraments; so that they, like your servant
Cyril of Jerusalem, may effectively instruct your people in Christian faith
and practice; and that we, taught by them, may enter more fully into the
celebration of the Paschal mystery, through Jesus Christ our Savior, who
lives and reigns with you and the Holy Spirit, one God, for ever and ever.
Amen.

March 19   **JOSEPH**

All as in the Ordinary of the Office. For readings, see p. 613.

Collect

O God, who from the family of your servant David raised up Joseph to
be the earthly father of your Incarnate One and the spouse of his mother:
Give us grace to imitate his uprightness of life and his obedience to your
commands; through Jesus Christ our Savior, who lives and reigns with you
and the Holy Spirit, one God, for ever and ever. *Amen.*

March 20   **CUTHBERT**
Monk and Bishop of Lindisfarne, 687

Common 7, p. 237

Collect

Almighty God, you called your servant Cuthbert from being a shepherd
of sheep to become a shepherd in your Church as missionary bishop:
Mercifully grant that we may follow him in the way of prayer and service,
and like him seek those who have erred and strayed from your ways and
lead them back to you; in the name of Jesus the Good Shepherd, who lives
and reigns with you and the Holy Spirit, one God, now and for ever.
Amen.

| March 21 | **THOMAS KEN** |
| | *Bishop of Bath and Wells, Hymnodist, 1711* |

Common 10, p. 247

Collect

> Almighty God, you gave your servant Thomas Ken grace and courage to bear witness to the truth before those in power: Give us strength also, that following his example as a faithful pastor, we may constantly defend what is right, boldly reprove what is evil, and patiently suffer for the truth's sake; through Jesus Christ our Savior, who lives and reigns with you and the Holy Spirit, one God, for ever and ever. *Amen.*

| March 22 | **JAMES DEKOVEN** |
| | *Priest, 1879* |

Common 9, p. 244

Collect

> Almighty and everlasting God, the source and perfection of all virtues, you inspired your servant James DeKoven to do what is right and to preach what is true: Grant that all ministers and stewards of your mysteries may impart to your people, by word and example, the knowledge of your grace; through Jesus Christ our Savior, who lives and reigns with you and the Holy Spirit, one God, for ever and ever. *Amen.*

| March 23 | **GREGORY THE ILLUMINATOR** |
| | *Bishop and Missionary of Armenia, c. 332* |

Common 6, p. 233

Collect

> Almighty God, whose will it is to be glorified in your saints, and who raised up your servant Gregory the Illuminator to be a light in the world, and to preach the gospel to the people of Armenia: Shine, we pray, in our hearts, that we also in our generation may show forth your praise, who called us out of darkness into your marvelous light; through Jesus Christ our Savior, who lives and reigns with you and the Holy Spirit, one God, for ever and ever. *Amen.*

March 25   THE ANNUNCIATION TO MARY

Common 1, p. 213. For readings, see p. 613.

Collect

> Pour your grace into our hearts, O God, that we who have known the
> incarnation of your only-begotten One Jesus Christ, announced by an
> angel to Mary, may by the cross and passion be brought to the glory of
> the resurrection; this we pray in the name of Jesus Christ, who lives and
> reigns with you in the unity of the Holy Spirit, one God, now and for
> ever. *Amen.*

March 27   CHARLES HENRY BRENT
                   Bishop of the Philippines; and of Western New York, 1929

Common 6, p. 233

Collect

> Holy God in heaven, whose Beloved One prayed that we all might be one:
> Deliver us from arrogance and prejudice, and give us wisdom and forbear-
> ance, that, following your servant Charles Henry Brent, we may be united
> in one family with all who confess the name of Jesus Christ; who lives and
> reigns with you and the Holy Spirit, one God, now and for ever. *Amen.*

March 29   JOHN KEBLE
                   Priest and Poet, 1866

Common 9, p. 244

Collect

> Grant, O God, that in all times of testing we may know your presence and
> obey your will; that following the example of your servant John Keble, we
> may accomplish with integrity and courage what we are given to do, and
> endure what we are given to bear; through Jesus Christ our Savior, who
> lives and reigns with you and the Holy Spirit, one God, for ever and ever.
> *Amen.*

March 31

JOHN DONNE
Priest and Poet, 1631

Common 10, p. 247

Collect

Merciful God, you gave your servant John Donne power in sermon and song to preach the forgiveness of sin and celebrate the glory of redemption; may we, like him, strive to relate the freedom and demands of the gospel to the concerns of all peoples; through the One who shared our human life that we might share the divine life and who lives and reigns with you and the Holy Spirit, one God, now and for ever. *Amen.*

April 1

FREDERICK DENISON MAURICE
Priest and Ecumenist, 1872

Common 3, p. 222

Collect

Almighty God, you restored our human nature to heavenly glory through the perfect obedience of our Savior Jesus Christ: Keep alive in your Church, we pray, a passion for justice and truth; that, like your servant Frederick Denison Maurice, we may maintain a vision of a reconciling Church, and work and pray for the triumph of the reign of Christ; who lives and reigns with you and the Holy Spirit, one God, now and for ever. *Amen*

April 2

JAMES LLOYD BRECK
*Priest, Founder of Nashotah House and
SeaburyWestern Seminaries, 1876*

Common 6, p. 233

Collect

Teach your Church, O God, we pray, to value and support pioneering and courageous missionaries, whom you call, as you called your servant James Lloyd Breck, to preach and teach, and plant your Church on new frontiers; through Jesus Christ our Savior, who lives and reigns with you and the Holy Spirit, one God, for ever and ever. *Amen.*

| April 3 | RICHARD |
| | *Bishop of Chichester, 1253* |

Common 9, p. 244

Collect

We thank you, O God, for all the benefits you have given us in Jesus Christ, our most merciful redeemer, friend and brother, who for us bore pains and insults; and we pray that following the example of your saintly bishop Richard of Chichester, we may see Christ more clearly, love Christ more dearly, and follow Christ more nearly; who lives and reigns with you and the Holy Spirit, one God, now and for ever. *Amen.*

| April 4 | MARTIN LUTHER KING, JR. |

See January 15

| April 8 | WILLIAM AUGUSTUS MUHLENBERG |
| | *Priest, 1877* |

Common 9, p. 244

Collect

Do not let your Church close its eyes, O God, to the plight of the poor and neglected, the homeless and destitute, the old and the sick, the lonely and those who have no one to care for them. Give us the vision and compassion with which you so richly endowed your servant William Augustus Muhlenberg, that we may labor tirelessly to heal those who are broken in body or spirit, and to turn their sorrow into joy; through Jesus Christ our Savior, who lives and reigns with you and the Holy Spirit, one God, for ever and ever. *Amen.*

April 9   **DIETRICH BONHOEFFER**
Pastor and Theologian, Martyr, 1945

Common 9, p. 244

Collect

Gracious God, the Beyond in the midst of our life, you gave grace to your servant Dietrich Bonhoeffer to know and to teach the truth as it is in Jesus Christ, and to bear the cost of discipleship: Grant that we, strengthened by his teaching and example, may receive your word and embrace its call with an undivided heart; through Jesus Christ our Savior, who lives and reigns with you and the Holy Spirit, one God, for ever and ever. *Amen.*

April 10   **WILLIAM LAW**
Priest, 1761

Common 9, p. 244

Collect

O God, you gave your servant William Law the grace to commit himself wholly to Christian living: Give us grace so to follow his example of simplicity, devotion, and charity that we may grow ever stronger in our faith; through the One who calls us brothers and sisters, our Savior Jesus Christ, who lives and reigns with you and the Holy Spirit, one God, now and for ever. *Amen.*

April 11   **GEORGE AUGUSTUS SELWYN**
Bishop of New Zealand, and Bishop of Lichfield, 1878

Common 6, p. 233

Collect

Almighty and everlasting God, we thank you for your servant George Augustus Selwyn, whom you called to preach the gospel to the people of New Zealand and Melanesia, and to lay a firm foundation for the growth of your Church in many nations. Raise up in this and every land evangelists and heralds of your reign, that your Church may proclaim the unsearchable riches of our Savior Jesus Christ; who lives and reigns with you and the Holy Spirit, one God, now and for ever. *Amen.*

| April 19 | **ALPHEGE** |
| | *Archbishop of Canterbury, and Martyr, 1012* |

Common 4, p. 226

Collect

O loving God, your martyr bishop Alphege of Canterbury suffered violent death when he refused to permit a ransom to be extorted from his people: Grant that all pastors of your flock may pattern themselves on the Good Shepherd, whose life was freely laid down for the sheep; and who with you and the Holy Spirit lives and reigns, one God, for ever and ever. *Amen.*

| April 21 | **ANSELM** |
| | *Archbishop of Canterbury, 1109* |

Common 5, p. 230

Collect

Almighty God, you raised up your servant Anselm to teach the Church of his day to understand its faith in your eternal Being, perfect justice, and saving mercy: Provide your Church in every age with devout and learned theologians and teachers, that we may be able to give a reason for the hope that is in us; through Jesus Christ our Savior, who lives and reigns with you and the Holy Spirit, one God, for ever and ever. *Amen.*

| April 25 | **MARK** |
| | *Evangelist* |

Common 2, p. 217. For readings, see p. 613.

Collect

Almighty God, by the hand of Mark the evangelist you have given to your Church the gospel of Jesus, the Word of God: We thank you for this witness, and pray that we may be firmly grounded in its truth; through Jesus Christ our Savior, who lives and reigns with you and the Holy Spirit, one God, for ever and ever. *Amen.*

April 29   **CATHERINE OF SIENA**
Monastic and Doctor, 1380

Common 5, p. 230

Collect

> Everlasting God, you kindled such holy love in the heart of your servant
> Catherine that she devoted her life to the poor and the sick and to the
> peace and unity of your Church: Grant us strength to meditate upon the
> passion of Jesus, that we may work according to the image of that compas-
> sion until we rejoice in the revelation of the divine glory; who in one God
> lives and reigns in Trinity of Persons and Unity of Being. *Amen.*

May 1   **PHILIP AND JAMES**
Apostles

Common 2, p. 217. For readings. see p. 613.

Collect

> Almighty God, who gave to your apostles Philip and James grace and
> strength to bear witness to the truth: Grant that we, being mindful of
> their victory of faith, may glorify in life and death the name of our Savior
> Jesus Christ; who lives and reigns with you and the Holy Spirit, one God,
> now and for ever. *Amen.*

May 2   **ATHANASIUS**
Bishop of Alexandria, 373

Common 5, p. 230

Collect

> O God, by the grace of your wisdom your blessed servant Athanasius
> stood fast against all error and false compromise in defense of the true
> divinity of our Savior Jesus Christ: Stir our hearts to ponder your word,
> and grant us never to lost heart in our proclamation of your saving mystery;
> through Jesus Christ our Redeemer, who lives and reigns with you and
> the Holy Spirit, one God, now and for ever. *Amen.*

May 3   THE FINDING OF THE CROSS

Lessons: **MATINS**   Exodus 14:13-18   Colossians 2:8-15
                     VESPERS   Exodus 15:23-27   Luke 14:27-33

Matins

All as in the Ordinary of Matins, except as noted.

Invitatory: Alleluia, Christ is reigning from the Tree:
Response: O come, let us worship, alleluia.

Antiphon on Psalter

> The cross is sheer folly to those on their way to ruin, *
>> but to us who are on the way to salvation, it is the power of God,
>> alleluia.

The canticle is the Te deum, p. 213.

Hymn at Matins

> Faithful cross, above all other,
> one and only noble tree,
> none in foliage, none in blossom,
> none in fruit your peer may be;
> sweetest wood and nails together
> bearing sweetest majesty.

> Bend your boughs, O tree of glory,
> your relaxing sinews bend;
> for awhile the ancient rigor
> that your birth bestowed, suspend,
> and the body of our Savior
> on your bosom gently tend.

> You alone were counted worthy
> this world's ransom to sustain,
> with the sacred blood anointed
> of the Lamb for sinners slain,
> that a shipwrecked race forever
> might a port of refuge gain.

Glory be to our Creator;
praise for our salvation won
through the Savior, in the Spirit,
ever Three and ever One;
who with joy fills all creation
while eternal ages run. Amen.

Antiphon on Benedictus

You alone excel in stature all the cedars of Lebanon, for on you
the life of the world was hanged, *

on you was Christ victorious, and death over death for ever triumphed,
Alleluia.

Collect

Almighty God, whose Beloved One for our sake willingly endured the
agony and shame of the cross: Remove from us all cowardice of heart and
give us courage to take up our cross and bear it patiently in godly service;
through Jesus Christ our Savior, who lives and reigns with you and the
Holy Spirit, one God, for ever and ever. *Amen.*

Diurnum

Antiphon on Psalter

Anyone who does not carry the cross and come with me *
cannot be a disciple of mine, Alleluia.

Lesson and Respond   GALATIANS 6:14

God forbid that I should boast of anything but the cross of Jesus Christ,
through which the world is crucified to me and I to the world.

Response: Thanks be to God.

v. This sign of the cross will be in heaven, alleluia, alleluia.
r. When God comes in judgment, alleluia, alleluia.

The Office continues with the Closing Prayers in the Ordinary of Diurnum, p. 55.

All as in the Ordinary of Vespers, except as noted.

Antiphon on Psalter

> I have been crucified with Christ; the life I now live is not my life, *
> but the life which Christ lives in me, Alleluia.

The canticle is the Dignus es, p. 220.

Hymn at Vespers

> O tree of beauty, tree of light,
> O cross with Jesus' blood made bright,
> wood chosen and designed to bear
> the holy limbs suspended there.
>
> Upon your arms so widely flung,
> the weight of this world's ransom hung,
> the price of all our wrongs to pay
> and spoil the spoiler of the prey.
>
> O cross, our one reliance, hail!
> Through him, who died on you, avail
> to give to sinners glad release,
> to saints enjoyment of your peace.
>
> To you, all holy Three in One,
> let worthy homage now be done
> by all whom through the cross you free
> to live with you eternally. Amen.

Antiphon on Magnificat

> O cross, surpassing all the stars in splendor, world renowned, holier than
> all things, you alone were counted worthy to uphold the world's ransom. *
>
> Sweet the wood, sweet the iron, bearing so sweet a burden; we have here
> assembled to celebrate your praises, Alleluia.

| May 4 | MONNICA |
| | *Mother of Augustine of Hippo, 387* |

Common 10, p. 247

Collect

O God, through spiritual discipline you strengthened your servant Monnica to persevere in offering her love and prayers and tears for the conversion of her husband and of Augustine their son: Deepen our devotion, we pray, and use us in accordance with your will to bring others, even our own family, to acknowledge Jesus Christ as Savior and Redeemer; who with you and the Holy Spirit lives and reigns, one God, for ever and ever. *Amen.*

| May 8 | JULIAN OF NORWICH |
| | Anchoress, c. 1417 |

Common 7, p. 237, except

Matins

Invitatory:	Alleluia, the high might of the Trinity our father,
	the deep wisdom of the Trinity our mother,
	the great love of the Trinity our savior:
Response:	O come, let us worship, alleluia.

Antiphon on Psalter

Before God made us, God loved us, *
and when we were made, we loved God, alleluia.

Canticle at Matins ADAPTED FROM JULIAN OF NORWICH (TRANS CLIFTON WOLTERS)

It is I who am the strength and goodness of fatherhood,

I who am the wisdom of motherhood, *
I who am light and grace and blessed love.

It is I who am Trinity, I who am Unity, *
I who am the sovereign goodness of everything.

It is I who enable you to love, *
I who enable you to long.

It is I, the eternal satisfaction *
of every true desire.

God is nearer to us than our own soul, *
for God is the ground in whom our soul stands, alleluia.

Collect

O God, in your compassion you granted to the Lady Julian many revelations of your nurturing and sustaining love: Move our hearts, like hers, to seek you above all things, for in giving us yourself, you give us all; through Jesus Christ our Savior, who lives and reigns with you and the Holy Spirit, one God, for ever and ever. *Amen.*

Diurnum

Antiphon on Psalter

Our soul sits in God in very rest, and our soul stands in God in very strength, *

and our soul is kindly rooted in God in endless love, Alleluia.

Lesson and Respond FROM THE SHOWINGS OF JULIAN

God is really our mother as God is our father. God showed this throughout, and particularly when was said that sweet word, "It is I who am the strength and goodness of fatherhood; I who am the wisdom of motherhood; I who am light and grace and blessed love; I who am Trinity; I who am Unity; I who am the sovereign goodness of every single thing; I who enable you to love; I who enable you to long. It is I, the eternal satisfaction of every genuine desire.

Response: Thanks be to God.

v. What joy and bliss and endless pleasing to me, alleluia, alleluia.
r. That ever I suffered passion for you, alleluia, alleluia.

The Office continues with the Closing Prayers in the Ordinary of Diurnum, p. 55.

Vespers

Antiphon on Psalter

> Sin is cause of all this pain, but all shall be well and all shall be well *
> and all manner of thing shall be well, Alleluia.

Antiphon on Magnificat

> Let be all your love, my dear worthy child, attend to me. *
> I am enough for you; take joy in your Savior and your salvation, Alleluia.

May 9	GREGORY OF NAZIANZUS
	Bishop of Constantinople, 389

Common 5, p. 230

Collect

> Almighty God, you have revealed to your Church your eternal Being of
> glorious majesty and perfect love as one God in Trinity of Persons: Give
> us grace that, like your bishop Gregory of Nazianzus, we may continue
> steadfast in the confession of this faith and constant in our worship of you,
> one only God, in glory everlasting. *Amen.*

May 14	PACHOMIUS
	Monastic, 346

Common 7, p. 237

Collect

> Almighty God, we give you thanks for the witness and ministry of your
> servant Pachomius, and for his vision in establishing monasteries for both
> men and women in the desert of Egypt: May we, like him, remain faithful
> to you in the desert times of our lives and seek you always. This we pray in
> the name of our Savior Jesus Christ, who lives and reigns with you and the
> Holy Spirit, one God, for ever and ever. *Amen.*

May 19   **DUNSTAN**
                               Archbishop of Canterbury, 988

Common 9, p. 244

Collect

O God of truth and beauty, you richly endowed your bishop Dunstan with
skill in music and the working of metals, and with gifts of administration
and reforming zeal: Teach us, we pray, to see in you the source of all our
talents, and move us to offer them for the adornment of worship and the
advancement of true religion; through Jesus Christ our Savior, who lives and
reigns with you and the Holy Spirit, one God, now and for ever. *Amen.*

May 20   **ALCUIN**
                               Deacon, and Abbot of Tours, 804

Common 8, p. 240

Collect

Almighty God, in a rude and barbarous age you raised up your deacon
Alcuin to rekindle the light of learning: Illumine our minds, we pray, that
amid the uncertainties and confusions of our own time we may show forth
your eternal truth; through Jesus Christ our Savior, who lives and reigns
with you and the Holy Spirit, one God, for ever and ever. *Amen.*

May 24   **JACKSON KEMPER**
                               First Missionary Bishop in the United States, 1870

Common 6, p. 233

Collect

O God, in your providence Jackson Kemper was chosen first missionary
bishop in this land, and by his arduous labor and travel congregations were
established in scattered settlements of the West: Grant that the Church
may always be faithful to its mission and have the vision, courage, and
perseverance to make known to all people the Good News of Jesus Christ;
who with you and the Holy Spirit lives and reigns, one God, for ever and
ever. *Amen.*

| May 25 | **BEDE THE VENERABLE** |
| | *Priest, and Monk of Jarrow, 735* |

Common 5, p. 230

Collect

O God in heaven, you called your servant Bede, while still a child, to devote his life to your service in the disciplines of religion and scholarship: Grant that as he labored in the Spirit to bring the riches of your truth to his generation, so we, in our varied vocations, may strive to make you known in all the world; through Jesus Christ our Savior, who lives and reigns with you and the Holy Sprit, one God, for ever and ever. *Amen.*

| May 26 | **AUGUSTINE OF CANTERBURY** |
| | *First Archbishop of Canterbury, 605* |

Common 6, p. 233

Collect

O God, through Jesus Christ you called your apostles and sent them forth to preach the gospel to the nations: We bless your holy name for your servant Augustine, first Archbishop of Canterbury, who laid the foundations of your Church among the English people; and we pray that all whom you call and send may do your will, grow in your love, and see your glory; through Jesus Christ our Savior, who lives and reigns with you and the Holy Spirit, one God, for ever and ever. *Amen.*

| May 31 | **VISITATION OF MARY TO ELIZABETH** |

Common 1, p. 213. For readings, see p. 613.

Collect

Almighty God, who looked with favor on your servant Mary and called her to be the mother of your Chosen One: Nurture in us the humility and gentleness that found favor in your sight, that with her we may proclaim the greatness of your name and find the mercy you show to those who fear you; through Jesus Christ our Redeemer, who lives and reigns with you and the Holy Spirit, one God, now and forever. *Amen.*

June 1   **JUSTIN**
Martyr at Rome, c. 167

Common 4, p. 226

Collect

Almighty and everlasting God, you found your servant Justin wandering
from teacher to teacher, seeking the true God, and you revealed to him
the sublime wisdom of your eternal Word: Grant that all who seek you, or
a deeper knowledge of you, may find and be found by you, through Jesus
Christ our Savior, who lives and reigns with you and the Holy Spirit, one
God for ever and ever. *Amen.*

June 2   **THE MARTYRS OF LYONS**
Gaul, c. 177

Common 4, p. 226

Collect

Grant, O God, that we who keep the feast of the holy martyrs Blandina
and her companions may be rooted and grounded in love of you; and we
pray that we may endure the suffering of this life for the glory that shall be
revealed in us; through Jesus Christ our Redeemer, who lives and reigns
with you and the Holy Spirit, one God, now and for ever. *Amen.*

June 3   **THE MARTYRS OF UGANDA**
1886

Common 4, p. 226

Collect

O God, by your providence the blood of the martyrs is the seed of the
Church: Grant that we who remember before you the blessed martyrs of
Uganda may, like them, be steadfast in our faith in Jesus Christ, to whom
they gave obedience, even to death, and by their sacrifice brought forth a
plentiful harvest; through Jesus Christ our Savior, who lives and reigns
with you and the Holy Spirit, one God, for ever and ever. *Amen.*

June 5	BONIFACE
	Archbishop of Mainz, Missionary to Germany,
	and Martyr, 754

Common 4, p. 226

Collect

Almighty God, you called your faithful servant Boniface to be a witness and martyr in Germany, and by his labor and suffering you raised up a people for your own possession: Pour out your Holy Spirit upon your Church in every land, that by the service and sacrifice of many your holy name may be glorified and your kingdom enlarged; through Jesus Christ our Savior, who lives and reigns with you and the Holy Spirit, one God, for ever and ever. *Amen.*

| June 9 | COLUMBA |
| | *Monk and Abbot of Iona, 597* |

Common 7, p. 237

Collect

O God, by the preaching of your blessed servant Columba you caused the light of the gospel to shine in Ireland and Scotland: Grant, we pray, that, remembering his life as pilgrim and monastic, we may show our thankfulness to you by following the example of his faithfulness; through Jesus Christ our Savior, who lives and reigns with you and the Holy Spirit, one God, for ever and ever. *Amen.*

| June 10 | EPHREM OF EDESSA |
| | *Deacon, 373* |

Common 5, p. 230

Collect

Pour out on us, O God, that same spirit by which your deacon Ephrem rejoiced to proclaim in sacred song the mysteries of faith; and so gladden our hearts that we, like him, may be devoted to you alone; through Jesus Christ our Redeemer, who lives and reigns with you and the Holy Spirit, one God, now and for ever. *Amen.*

| June 11 | **BARNABAS** |
| | *Apostle* |

Common 2, p. 217. For readings, see p. 614.

Collect

Grant, O God, that we may follow the example of your faithful servant
Barnabas, who, seeking not his own renown but the wellbeing of your
Church, gave generously of his life and substance for the relief of the poor
and the spread of the Gospel; through Jesus Christ our Savior, who lives
and reigns with you and the Holy Spirit, one God, for ever and ever.
Amen.

| June 12 | **ENMEGAHBOWH** |
| | *Native American Priest and Missionary, 1902* |

Common 6, p. 233

Collect

God, you led your pilgrim people of old with fire and cloud: Grant that
the ministers of your Church, following the example of blessed
Enmegabowh, may stand before your holy people, leading them with fiery
zeal and gentle humility. This we ask through Jesus the Christ, who lives
and reigns with you in the unity of the Holy Spirit, one God, for ever and
ever. *Amen.*

| June 14 | **BASIL THE GREAT** |
| | *Bishop of Caesarea, 379* |

Common 5, p. 230

Collect

Almighty God, you have revealed to your Church your eternal Being of
glorious majesty and perfect love as one God in Trinity of Persons: Give us
grace that, like your bishop Basil of Caesarea, we may continue steadfast in
the confession of this faith, and constant in our worship of you; one God,
in glory everlasting. *Amen.*

June 15   **EVELYN UNDERHILL**
Teacher and Mystic, 1941

Common 8, p. 240

Collect

> O God, Origin, Sustainer, and End of all your creatures: Grant that your Church, taught by your servant Evelyn Underhill, guarded evermore by your power, and guided by your Spirit into the light of truth, may continually offer to you all glory and thanksgiving and attain with your saints the blessed hope of everlasting life, which you have promised by our Savior Jesus Christ; who lives and reigns with you and the Holy Spirit, one God, now and for ever. *Amen.*

June 16   **JOSEPH BUTLER**
Bishop of Durham, 1752

Common 8, p. 240

Collect

> O Eternal God, we thank you for your servant Joseph Butler who devoted his life to you as pastor and teacher: May we follow his example of reasoned defense of the faith born out of profound learning and deep piety, and use our minds and hearts in your service; this we pray in the name of the One who is source of all wisdom, our Savior Jesus Christ, who lives and reigns with you and the Holy Spirit, one God, now and for ever. *Amen.*

June 17   **MINISTERING ANGELS**

All as in the Ordinary of the Office

Collect

> O God, we give you thanks for the ministries of angels and mortals: Open our eyes that we may perceive those whom you send to us, and give us willing hearts to serve all to whom we are sent; we ask this in the name of the Trinity, origin of all that is, seen and unseen, one God in glory everlasting. *Amen.*

June 18   BERNARD MIZE
                             Catechist and Martyr in Rhodesia, 1896

Common 4, p. 226

Collect

Almighty and everlasting God, who kindled the flame of your love in the heart of your holy martyr Bernard Mize: Grant to us your humble servants a like faith and power of love, that we who rejoice in his triumph may profit by his example; through Jesus Christ our Savior, who lives and reigns with you and the Holy Spirit, one God, for ever and ever. *Amen.*

June 22   ALBAN
                             First Martyr of Britain, c. 304

Common 4, p. 226

Collect

Almighty God, you conferred on your holy martyr Alban such love for the mercy of Christ that he gave his life to save a hunted Christian: Grant us, after his example, to be so faithful in our confession of your gospel that we may shelter those who flee from persecution, and bear the reproaches which threaten their lives; though Jesus Christ our Savior, who lives and reigns with you and the Holy Spirit, one God, for ever and ever. *Amen.*

June 24   THE NATIVITY OF JOHN THE BAPTIST

Common 3, p. 222. For readings, see p. 614.

Collect

Almighty God, by whose providence your servant John the Baptist was wonderfully born to be in life and death the forerunner of our Savior Jesus Christ: Give us grace to repent according to his preaching, and following his example, constantly to speak the truth, boldly rebuke vice, and patiently suffer for the truth's sake; through Jesus Christ our Savior, who lives and reigns with you and the Holy Spirit, one God, now and for ever. *Amen.*

June 28   **IRENAEUS**
Bishop of Lyons, c. 202

Common 9, p. 244

Collect

> Almighty God, you upheld your servant Irenaeus with strength to maintain
> the truth against all false doctrine: Keep us, we pray, steadfast in our faith,
> that in constancy and peace we may walk in the way that leads to eternal
> life; through Jesus Christ our Savior, who lives and reigns with you and
> the Holy Spirit, one God, for ever and ever. *Amen.*

June 29   **PETER AND PAUL**

Common 2, p. 217. For readings, see p. 614.

Collect

> Almighty God, whose blessed apostles Peter and Paul glorified you by
> their martyrdom: Grant that your Church, instructed by their teaching and
> example, and knit together in unity by your Spirit, may ever stand firm
> upon the one foundation, which is Jesus Christ our Savior; who lives and
> reigns with you and the Holy Spirit, one God, for ever and ever. *Amen.*

July 4   **INDEPENDENCE DAY, USA**

Common 13, p. 260. For readings, see p. 614.

Collect

> O God Almighty, in whose name the founders of this country won liberty
> for themselves and for us, and lit the torch of freedom for nations then
> unborn: Grant that we and all the people of this and every land may have
> grace to maintain our liberties in righteousness and peace; through Jesus
> Christ our Savior, who lives and reigns with you and the Holy Spirit, one
> God, for ever and ever. *Amen.*

July 11   **BENEDICT**
Abbot of Monte Cassino, c. 540

Common 7, p. 237

Collect

Almighty and everlasting God, your precepts are the wisdom of a loving parent: Give us grace, following the teaching and example of your servant Benedict, to walk with loving and willing hearts in the school of God's service; let your ears be open to our prayers; and prosper with your blessing the work of our hands; through Jesus Christ our Savior, who lives and reigns with you and the Holy Spirit, one God, for ever and ever. *Amen.*

July 17   **WILLIAM WHITE**
Bishop of Pennsylvania, 1836

Common 9, p. 244

Collect

O God, in a time of turmoil and confusion you raised up your servant William White, and endowed him with wisdom, patience and a reconciling temper, that he might lead your Church into ways of stability and peace: Hear our prayer and give us wise and faithful leaders, that through their ministry your people may be blessed and your will be done; through Jesus Christ our Savior, who lives and reigns with you and the Holy Spirit, one God, for ever and ever. *Amen.*

July 19   **MACRINA**
Monastic, Theologian, and Teacher, 379

Common 7, p. 237

Collect

O God of Wisdom, you called your servant Macrina to counsel and challenge her brothers Gregory, Basil, and Peter, bishops in the Church, that they might become leading defenders of the Christian faith: Grant that we, following her example, may always seek the way of truth and wisdom, and engage the spiritual and theological issues of our time; through Jesus Christ our Savior, who lives and reigns with you and the Holy Spirit, one God, for ever and ever. *Amen.*

July 20   **ELIZABETH CADY STANTON**
                 AMELIA BLOOMER
                 SOJOURNER TRUTH
                 HARRIET ROSS TUBMAN
                 Liberators and Prophets, 1902, 1894, 1883, 1913

Common 3, p. 222

Collect

O God, whose Spirit guides us into all truth and makes us free: Strengthen and sustain us as you did your servants Elizabeth, Amelia, Sojourner, and Harriet. Give us vision and courage to stand against oppression and injustice, and all that works against the glorious liberty to which you call all your children; through Jesus Christ our Savior, who lives and reigns with you and the Holy Spirit, one God, for ever and ever. *Amen.*

July 22   **MARY MADGALENE**

Common 10, p. 247, except the hymns as noted below. For readings, see p. 614.

Collect

O Jesus Christ, we thank you for Mary Magdalene who was restored to health of body and of mind, and called by you to be the first witness of your resurrection: Mercifully grant that by your grace we may be healed from all our infirmities and serve you with unswerving loyalty to our life's end; in the name of the Holy and Undivided Trinity. *Amen.*

Hymn at Matins

> Out of the night where hope had died,
> to tomb once sealed, now gaping wide,
> the Magdalene made haste, to mourn
> and bring her spices through the dawn.
>
> She gazed in disbelief and pain
> where Jesus in his death had lain,
> until the radiant angel said:
> Seek not the living with the dead.
>
> Soon trusting love cast out her fears;
> she rose and brushed away her tears.
> As first apostle, Mary ran
> to tell God's resurrection plan.

Jesus is risen! Mary cries,
Lift up your hearts and dry your eyes,
Jesus is risen—come and see—
and goes before to Galilee.
All glory be to God above,
for Mary's apostolic love,
all praise to God whom we adore
for ever and for evermore. Amen.

Hymn at Vespers

Most loving God, receive our praise
on Magdalene's great day of days,
this faithful woman, by your grace,
with the apostles holds a place.

When Jesus called, her demons fled;
restored, she followed where he led;
she gave herself and gave her gold,
receiving back a hundredfold.

When Jesus' hour had come, she stayed
beneath the cross, and grieving, prayed
that she might love him to the end:
her healer, teacher, and her friend.

Mary, when Easter morn began,
beheld the empty tomb, and ran
to bring the news. Rejoice! she cried,
the Christ is risen, who had died!

No death could that great love destroy;
her tears were turned from loss to joy.
All glory be to God alone
for such divine compassion shown. Amen.

July 24   THOMAS A KEMPIS
Priest, 1471

Common 7, p. 237

Collect

Holy God, you have nourished and strengthened your Church by the inspired writings of your servant Thomas a Kempis: Grant that we may learn from him to know what is necessary to be known, to love what is to be loved, to praise what highly pleases you, and always to seek to know and follow your will; through Jesus Christ our Savior, who lives and reigns with you and the Holy Spirit, one God, for ever and ever. *Amen.*

July 25   JAMES
Apostle

Common 2, p. 217. For readings, see p. 614.

Collect

O gracious God, we remember before you today your servant and apostle James, first among the Twelve to suffer martyrdom for the name of Jesus Christ; and we pray that you will pour out upon the leaders of your Church that spirit of self-denying service by which alone they may have true authority among your people; through Jesus Christ our Savior, who lives and reigns with you and the Holy Spirit, one God, now and for ever. *Amen.*

July 26   PARENTS OF MARY, MOTHER OF JESUS

Common 10, p. 247

Collect

Almighty God, we remember in thanksgiving this day the parents of Mary, the Mother of Jesus; and we pray that all humankind may be made one in the heavenly family of Christ Jesus our Savior; who lives and reigns with you and the Holy Spirit, one God, now and for ever. *Amen*

July 27   WILLIAM REED HUNTINGTON
Priest, 1909

Common 9, p. 244

Collect

> O God, we thank you for instilling in the heart of your servant William
> Reed Huntington a fervent love for your Church and its mission in the
> world; and we pray that, with unflagging faith in your promises, we may
> make known to all people your blessed gift of eternal life; through Jesus
> Christ our Savior, who lives and reigns with you and the Holy Spirit, one
> God, for ever and ever. *Amen.*

July 29   MARY AND MARTHA OF BETHANY
Confessors (John 11 and 12)

Common 10, p. 247

Matins

Antiphon on Psalter

> A woman named Martha made Jesus welcome in her house; *
> her sister Mary listened to his words.

Antiphon on Benedictus

> The part that Mary has chosen is best, *
> and it shall not be taken away from her.

Collect

> O welcoming God, Jesus Christ enjoyed rest and refreshment in the home
> of Mary and Martha of Bethany: Give us the will to love you, open our
> hearts to hear you, and strengthen our hands to serve you in others for
> Jesus' sake; who lives and reigns with you and the Holy Spirit, one God,
> now and for ever. *Amen.*

Vespers

Antiphon on Psalter

> Jesus loved Martha and her sister Mary, *
> and their brother Lazarus.

Antiphon on Magnificat

> There was a supper given in Jesus' honor, at which Martha served; *
> and Mary brought perfume and anointed Jesus' feet.

July 30	WILLIAM WILBERFORCE
	Confessor and Social reformer, 1833

Common 3, p. 222

Collect

O God of compassion and mercy, you made all peoples to be free: We
thank you for your servant William Wilberforce, who worked to further
the cause of those who have no helper and labored unceasingly for the
abolition of slavery: Grant us strength and courage to open our hands to
the needy and work faithfully for the liberation of all persons; through the
One who brought good news to the poor and set the captives free, our
Savior Jesus Christ, who lives and reigns with you and the Holy Spirit, one
God, now and for ever. *Amen.*

July 31	IGNATIUS OF LOYOLA
	Priest; Founder of the Society of Jesus, 1556

Common 7, p. 237

Collect

Almighty God, from whom all good things come: You called Ignatius of
Loyola to the service of your Divine Majesty and to find you in all things.
Strengthened by your companionship and inspired by his example, may we
labor without counting the cost and seek no reward other than knowing
that we do your will; through Jesus Christ our Savior, who lives and reigns
with you and the Holy Spirit, one God, for ever and ever. *Amen.*

August 1   **JOSEPH OF ARIMATHEA**
Confessor
(Matthew 27:57-60; Mark 15:43; Luke 23:50-53;
     John 19:38)

Common 10, p. 247

Matins

Antiphon on Psalter

> Joseph of Arimathaea was a member of the Sanhedrin *
> who had dissented from their policy and opposed the action they
> had taken.

Antiphon on Benedictus

> Joseph of Arimathaea bravely went to Pilate *
> and asked for the body of Jesus.

Collect

> Merciful God, whose servant Joseph of Arimathaea with reverence and
> godly fear prepared the body of our Savior for burial and laid it in his own
> tomb: Grant to us, your faithful people, grace and courage to love and
> serve Jesus with sincere devotion all the days of our life; in the name of the
> holy and undivided Trinity, one God, who lives and reigns for ever and
> ever. *Amen.*

Vespers

Antiphon on Psalter

> A man from Arimathea, Joseph by name, was a man of means, *
> and had himself become a disciple of Jesus.

Antiphon on Magnificat

> Joseph took the body of Jesus, wrapped it in a clean linen sheet, *
> and laid it in his own unused tomb.

August 6   THE TRANSFIGURATION OF JESUS

All in the Ordinary of the Office, except the hymns as noted below. For readings, see p. 614.

Collect

O God, who on the holy mount revealed to chosen witnesses your well-beloved Child, wonderfully transfigured, in raiment white and glistening: Mercifully grant that we, being delivered from the disquietude of this world, may by faith behold the Christ in beauty; who with you, O Creator, and you, O Holy Spirit, lives and reigns, one God, for ever and ever. *Amen.*

Hymn at Matins

> When to the faithful you appear,
> O Holy Jesus, strong and clear,
> away the clouds and darkness roll,
> and rapture overflows the soul.
>
> In countenance and raiment bright
> you manifest the Godhead's light;
> And for a sacred moment shine
> with love both human and divine.
>
> Upon the holy mount you show
> more glory than our minds can know;
> the fullness of your love imparts
> your presence to all faithful hearts.
>
> To you, transfigured Christ we raise
> our voices in resounding praise;
> to our Creator homage bring
> as by the Spirit here we sing. Amen.

Hymn at Vespers

> All you who seek for Jesus raise
> your eyes from earth and upward gaze;
> there you may see the wondrous sign
> of never-ending glory shine.
>
> Behold the Christ in gleaming rays,
> who never knows an end of days,
> exalted, infinite, sublime,
> beyond the bounds of space and time.

The three disciples knelt in awe
to see the Prophets and the Law
in Moses and Elijah speak
with Jesus on the cloudy peak.

To Christ the scriptures testify,
and that same witness from on high
God seals for those who would receive:
Hear my Beloved and believe.

To you, transfigured Christ we raise
our voices in resounding praise;
to our Creator homage bring
as by the Spirit here we sing. Amen.

August 7	**JOHN MASON NEAL**	
	Priest and Hymnodist, 1866	

Common 8, p. 240

Collect

Grant, O God, that in all times of our testing, we may know your presence and obey your will, that, after the example of John Mason Neal, we may with integrity and courage accomplish what you give us to do, and endure what you give us to bear; through Jesus Christ our Savior, who lives and reigns with you and the Holy Spirit, one God, now and for ever. *Amen.*

August 8	**DOMINIC**
	Priest and Friar, 1221

Common 7, p. 237

Collect

O God of the prophets, you opened the eyes of your servant Dominic to perceive a famine of hearing the word of God, and moved him, and those he drew about him, to satisfy that hunger with sound preaching and fervent devotion: Make your Church, O Christ, in this and every age, attentive to the hungers of the world, and quick to respond in love to those who are perishing; through Jesus Christ our Redeemer, who lives and reigns with you and the Holy Spirit, one God, for ever and ever. *Amen.*

| August 10 | **LAURENCE** |
| | *Deacon and Martyr at Rome, 258* |

Common 4, p. 226

Collect

Almighty God, you called your deacon Laurence to serve you with deeds of love and gave him the crown of martyrdom: Grant that we, following his example, may fulfill your commandments by defending and supporting the sick and the poor, and by loving you with all our hearts; through the love of Jesus Christ our Savior, who lives and reigns with you and the Holy Spirit, one God, for ever and ever. *Amen.*

| August 11 | **CLARE** |
| | *Abbess at Assisi, 1253* |

Common 7, p. 237

Collect

O Jesus, you became poor that through your poverty we may be rich: Deliver us from an inordinate love of this world, that inspired by the devotion of your servant Clare, we may serve you with singleness of heart, and attain to the riches of the age to come; through Jesus Christ our Savior, who lives and reigns with you and the Holy Spirit, one God, now and for ever. *Amen.*

| August 12 | **FLORENCE NIGHTINGALE** |
| | *Nurse and Social Reformer, 1910* |

Common 3, p. 222

Collect

Compassionate God, you alone have power over life and death, over health and sickness: Give power, wisdom, and gentleness to those who follow the lead of Florence Nightingale, that they, bearing with them your presence, may not only heal but bless, and shine as lanterns of hope in the darkest hours of pain and fear; through Jesus Christ, the healer of body and soul, who lives and reigns with you and the Holy Spirit, one God, for ever and ever. *Amen.*

August 13	**JEREMY TAYLOR**
	Bishop of Down, Connor, and Dromore, 1667

Common 8, p. 240

Collect

O God, whose days are without end, and whose mercies cannot be numbered: Make us, like your servant Jeremy Taylor, deeply aware of the shortness and uncertainty of human life; and let your Holy Spirit lead us in holiness and righteousness all our days; through Jesus Christ our Savior, who lives and reigns with you and the Holy Spirit, one God, now and for ever. *Amen.*

August 14	**JONATHAN MYRICK DANIELS**
	Seminarian and Witness for Civil Rights, and Martyr, 1965

Common 3, p. 222

Collect

O God of justice and compassion, you put down the proud and mighty from their place and lift up the poor and the afflicted: We give you thanks for your faithful witness Jonathan Myrick Daniels, who, in the midst of injustice and violence, risked and gave his life for another; and we pray that we, following his example, may make no peace with oppression; through Jesus Christ the just one, who lives and reigns with you and the Holy Spirit, one God, for ever and ever. *Amen.*

August 15	**MARY THE MOTHER OF JESUS**

Common 1, p. 213. For readings, see p. 615.

Collect

O God, you have taken to yourself Mary, mother of your incarnate Son: Grant that we, who have been redeemed by his blood, may share with her the glory of your eternal dominion; through Jesus Christ our Savior, who lives and reigns with you and the Holy Spirit, one God, now and for ever. *Amen.*

August 18   HELENA
                             Empress and Mother of Constantine the Great, c. 250-330;
                             Patron of the Order of St. Helena

All as in the Ordinary of the Office, except

Lessons: MATINS   Isaiah 61:1-4   Romans 12:10-21
                  II VESPERS   Isaiah 43:3-10   Luke 14:27-33

Antiphons for Psalm(s):

   After her conversion, Helena took to heart the sayings of Jesus *
      and her life was filled with love for God.

or

   Helena went about doing good in both word and deed; *
      she visited the sick and gave generously to the poor and the destitute.

or

   Helena prayed that she would find the cross *
      on which Jesus had been crucified.

or

   When she saw the cross in a well,
   Helena believed she had found the sacred wood; *
      touching it brought life and healing.

or

   Fruitful even in her old age,
   Helena built many shrines and churches to glorify God *
      and to mark the holy places of Jesus.

Collect

   O loving God, we thank you for your servant the Empress Helena, who
   was fervent and devout in her commitment to the gospel and gave generously of her time and wealth to help spread the message of Christ: Give us
   grace to seek the cross in our own lives, and having found it, to bear it
   faithfully in true devotion to you; through the grace and power of the
   Holy Trinity. *Amen.*

Matins

Invitatory: God is glorious in the saints:
Response: O come, let us worship.

The canticle is the Te Deum, p. 213.

Hymn at Matins

> When we survey the wondrous cross
> where Christ who reigns in glory died,
> our richest gains we count but loss,
> and pour contempt on all our pride.
>
> Forbid it, God, that we should boast,
> save in the holy cross of Christ:
> all those vain things that charm us most
> for love's sake now are sacrificed.
>
> Were the whole realm of nature mine,
> that were an offering far too small;
> love so amazing, so divine,
> demands my soul, my life, my all.
>
> To you, O Jesus Christ, be praise;
> to you, Creator, glory be;
> to you, O Spirit, hymns we raise:
> one God through all eternity. Amen.

Antiphon on Benedictus

> Helena, filled with love for God *
> sought to find the one true cross.

Diurnum

Antiphon on Psalter

> Anyone who does not carry the cross and come with me *
> cannot be a disciple of mine.

God forbid that I should boast of anything but the cross of our Savior Jesus Christ, through which the world has been crucified to me and I to the world.

Response: Thanks be to God.

v. Helena was a Christian and followed the teaching of Jesus;

r. She sought the cross of the crucified.

The Office continues with the Closing Prayers in the Ordinary of Diurnum, p. 55.

Vespers

The canticle at Vespers is the Benedicite, p. 120.

Hymn at Vespers

The Empress Helen, urged by grace,
came as a pilgrim to the place
where Jesus died upon the cross
and rose, redeeming human loss.

How could she find the holy rood
among the beams of aspen wood
with ancient nails and writing still
preserved beneath that gallows hill?

The true cross did itself declare
by power of Christ who suffered there:
the legend tells that by the tree
the sick arose, restored and free.

Saint Helena with thankful prayer
sent out the good news everywhere
that on Mount Calvary's holy ground
the cross where Jesus died was found!

All laud to you, Creator, be,
to you, O Christ, eternally;
to you, the Spirit, equal praise
from joyful hearts we ever raise. Amen.

Encouraged by her son the emperor Constantine,
Helena made a pilgrimage to the Holy Land *
   where she built many churches to the glory of God.

August 19   WILLIAM PORCHER DUBOSE
(date transferred)   *Priest and Theologian, 1918*
Common 8, p. 240

Collect

Almighty God, you gave to your servant William Porcher DuBose special
gifts of grace to understand the Scriptures and to teach the truth as it is in
Christ Jesus: Grant that by this teaching we may know you, the one true
God, and Jesus Christ whom you have sent; who lives and reigns with you
and the Holy Spirit, one God, now and for ever. *Amen.*

August 20   BERNARD
                              Abbot of Clairvaux, 1153
Common 5, p. 230

Collect

O God, by whose grace your servant Bernard of Clairvaux, kindled with
the flame of your love, became a burning and shining light in your
Church: Grant that we also may be aflame with the spirit of love and
discipline, and walk before you as children of light; through Jesus Christ
our Savior, who lives and reigns with you and the Holy Spirit, one God,
now and for ever. *Amen.*

August 24   **BARTHOLOMEW**
Apostle

Common 2, p. 217. For readings, see p. 615.

Collect

Almighty and everlasting God, you gave to your apostle Bartholomew
grace truly to believe and to preach your word: Grant that your Church
may love what he believed and preach what he taught; through Jesus
Christ our Savior, who lives and reigns with you and the Holy Spirit, one
God, for ever and ever. *Amen.*

August 25   **LOUIS IX**
King of France, 1270

Common 10, p. 247

Collect

O God, you called your servant Louis of France to an earthly throne that
he might advance your heavenly kingdom, and gave him zeal for your
Church and love for your people: Mercifully grant that we who commemorate him this day may be fruitful in good works and attain to the glorious
crown of your saints; through Jesus Christ our Savior, who lives and reigns
with you and the Holy Spirit, one God, for ever and ever. *Amen.*

August 27   **THOMAS GALLAUDET AND HENRY WINTER SYLE**
Ministers to the Deaf, 1902 and 1890

Common 9, p. 244

Collect

O loving God, whose will it is that everyone should come to you and be
saved: We bless your holy name for your servants Thomas Gallaudet and
Henry Winter Syle whose labors with and for those who are deaf we commemorate today, and we pray that you will continually move your Church
to respond in love to the needs of all people; through Jesus Christ, who
opened the ears of the deaf, and who lives and reigns with you and the
Holy Spirit, one God, now and for ever. *Amen.*

August 28	AUGUSTINE
	Bishop of Hippo, 430

Common 5, p. 230, except

Matins

Invitatory:	The Spirit of wisdom guides into all truth:
Response:	O come, let us worship.

Antiphon on Psalter

You have pierced my heart with the arrow of your love, *
and I have carried your words, transfixing my soul.

The canticle is the Te Deum, p. 213.

Hymn at Matins

All citizens of heaven, rejoice;
all earthly pilgrims, raise your voice:
to join in gladness as we pray
upon Augustine's feast today.

Take up and read, Augustine heard,
and was obedient to the word;
by penitence and faith set free,
he wrote of Love's great mystery.

Then let us with Augustine's prayers
unite our own, our needs and cares;
that we may know in our own time
the way of truth and peace sublime.

All laud to you, Creator, be,
and to your Word, eternally;
to you, the Spirit, equal praise
from joyful hearts we ever raise. Amen.

Antiphon on Benedictus

We praise you, O God, that we may love you, *
and we love you, that we may praise you.

Collect

O God, the light of the minds that know you, the life of the souls that love you, and the strength of the hearts that serve you: Help us, following the example of your servant Augustine of Hippo, so to know you that we may truly love you, and so to love you that we may fully serve you, whom to serve is perfect freedom; through Jesus Christ our Savior, who lives and reigns with you and the Holy Spirit, one God, for ever and ever. *Amen.*

Diurnum

Antiphon on Psalter

In your Word, O God, and in your only-begotten One, *
we have seen heaven and earth.

Lesson and Respond   HEBREWS 12:22-23

You have come to Mount Zion and to the city of the living God, the heavenly Jerusalem, and to innumerable angels in festal gathering, and to the assembly of the firstborn who are enrolled in heaven, and to God the judge of all.

Response: Thanks be to God.

v. In the midst of the congregation he opened his mouth,
r. And God filled him with the Spirit of wisdom.

The Office continues with the Closing Prayers in the Ordinary of Diurnum, p. 55.

Vespers

Antiphon on Psalter

I tasted you, O God, and I hunger and thirst; *
you touched me and I burn for your peace.

Holy Doctor, blest Augustine,
join our prayers as they ascend;
there you live with Christ in glory
and delight that has no end;
join our earthly alleluias;
be in Christ our guide and friend.

By your call and your own seeking
and your mother's fervent prayer,
you found Jesus, holy lover,
and that love you vowed to share;
bishop of Christ's flock, you led them
with a Christ-like love and care.

Glory to the God of heaven,
praise and honor, endless reign;
joining with the choir of angels,
let us sound the glad refrain;
may we be with blest Augustine
citizens of heaven's domain. Amen.

Antiphon on Magnificat

You have made us for yourself, O God, *
and our hearts are restless until they find their rest in you.

August 31   **AIDAN**
                 Monk and Bishop of Lindisfarne, 651

Common 7, p. 237

Collect

O loving God, you called your servant Aidan from Iona's cloister to
reestablish the Christian mission in northern England, and endowed him
with gentleness, simplicity and strength: Grant that we, following the
example of his great humility, may use the gifts you have given us for the
relief of human need and may persevere in commending the saving gospel
of our Redeemer Jesus Christ; who lives and reigns with you and the
Holy Spirit, one God, for ever and ever. *Amen.*

September 1   **DAVID PENDLETON OAKERHATER**
Deacon and Missionary to the Cheyenne, 1931

Common 6, p. 233

Collect

O God of unsearchable wisdom and infinite mercy, you chose a captive warrior, David Oakerhater, to be a missionary to his own people and to exercise the office of a deacon among them: Liberate us from bondage to self, and empower us for service to you and to the neighbors you have given us; through Jesus Christ, source of our salvation; who lives and reigns with you and the Holy Spirit, one God, for ever and ever. *Amen.*

September 2   **THE MARTYRS OF NEW GUINEA**
1942

Common 4, p. 226

Collect

Almighty God, we remember before you this day the blessed martyrs of New Guinea, who, following the example of Jesus Christ, laid down their lives for their friends; and we pray that we who honor their memory may imitate their loyalty and faith; through the same Jesus Christ, whose life was laid down for us all and who lives and reigns with you and the Holy Spirit, one God, for ever and ever. *Amen.*

September 4   **PAUL JONES**
Bishop and Peace Advocate, 1941

Common 3, p. 222

Collect

Merciful God, you sent Jesus to preach peace to those who were far off and to those who were near: Raise up in this and every land witnesses who, after the example of your servant Paul Jones, will stand firm in integrity of conscience and in proclaiming the gospel of the Holy One of Peace, our Savior Jesus Christ; who lives and reigns with you and the Holy Spirit, one God, for ever and ever. *Amen.*

September 8   NATIVITY OF MARY, THE MOTHER OF JESUS

Common 1, p. 213, except

Lessons: **MATINS**   Isaiah 28:15-18   Revelation 12:1-6
             VESPERS   Zechariah 8:1-8   Luke 2:41-52

Hymn at Matins and at Vespers

> Hail, O Mary, fairest woman,
> full of wisdom, full of grace;
> praise to you through whose obedience
> Jesus came to save our race.
>
> Flower of your people's lineage,
> by the love of God prepared
> to be mother of the Savior
> as the prophets had declared.
>
> Holy church today, blest Mary,
> celebrates your day of birth.
> Saints in heaven hymn your praises
> echoed by the saints on earth.
>
> Glory be to God, Creator,
> and to the Incarnate One;
> thanks and honor to the Spirit
> that in you love's will was done. Amen.

Collect

Eternal God, who revealed the mystery of your loving providence in the birth of Mary, the Mother of Jesus: Grant that we who now call her blest may be clothed with the light of your new creation and rejoice with her in the radiance of your glory; whom we adore as one God in Trinity of Persons and Unity of Being, now and for ever. *Amen.*

September 9   **CONSTANCE, SISTER OF CSM, AND HER COMPANIONS**
Commonly called "The Martyrs of Memphis", 1878

Common 10, p. 247

Collect

We give you thanks and praise, O God of compassion, for the heroic witness of Constance and her companions, who, in a time of plague and pestilence, were steadfast in their care for the sick and dying, and served them faithfully, even unto death: Inspire in us a like love and commitment to those in need, following the example of our Savior Jesus Christ, who with you and the Holy Spirit lives and reigns, one God, now and for ever. *Amen.*

September 10   **ALEXANDER CRUMMELL**
Priest, Missionary, and Educator, 1898
Founder of the Union of Black Episcopalians

Common 3, p. 222

Collect

Almighty and everlasting God, we thank you for your servant Alexander Crummell, who labored unfailingly in supporting the cause of black peoples in this country and in Liberia: Give us grace to follow his example of leadership, creativity, and perseverance, that we, too, may ever witness to the gospel of love and equality; through our Savior Jesus Christ, who lives and reigns with you and the Holy Spirit, one God, for ever and ever. *Amen.*

September 12   **JOHN HENRY HOBART**
Bishop of New York, 1830;
A Founder of General Theological Seminary

Common 9, p. 244

Collect

Revive your Church, O God of hosts, whenever it falls into complacency, by raising up devoted leaders like your servant John Henry Hobart whom we remember today; and grant that their faith and vigor of mind may awaken your people to your message and their mission; through Jesus Christ our Savior, who lives and reigns with you and the Holy Spirit, one God, now and for ever. *Amen.*

September 13   **CYPRIAN**
Bishop and Martyr of Carthage, 258

Common 4, p. 226

Collect

Almighty God, who gave to your servant Cyprian boldness to confess the name of our Savior Jesus Christ before the rulers of this world, and courage to die for this faith: Grant that we may always be ready to give a reason for the hope that is in us, and to suffer gladly for the sake of our Savior Jesus Christ; who lives and reigns with you and the Holy Spirit, one God, for ever and ever. *Amen.*

September 14   **EXALTATION OF THE HOLY CROSS**

For readings, see p. 615. All as in the Ordinary of the Office, except

Antiphons for the Psalm(s)

The cross is sheer folly to those on their way to ruin, *
but to those who are on the way to salvation, it is the power of God.

or

God forbid that I should boast of anything *
but the cross of Jesus Christ.

or

Through the cross the world is crucified to me *
and I am crucified to the world.

or

I have been crucified with Christ; the life I now live is not my life, *
but the life which Christ lives in me.

or

Christ died on the cross in weakness, but now lives by the power of God; *
and we who share that weak ness shall by the power of God
live with Christ.

Collect

> Almighty God, our Savior Jesus Christ was lifted high upon the cross to
> draw the whole world to you: Mercifully grant that we, who glory in the
> mystery of our redemption, may have grace to take up our cross and fol-
> low Jesus; who lives and reigns with you and the Holy Spirit, one God, in
> glory everlasting. *Amen.*

Matins

Invitatory: Christ is reigning from the tree:
Response: O come, let us worship.

The canticle is the Te Deum, p. 213.

Hymn at Matins

> Sing, my tongue, the glorious battle,
> sing the winning of the fray;
> now above the cross, the trophy,
> sound the high triumphal lay:
> tell how Jesus, our redeemer,
> through surrender won the day.
>
> Thirty years among us dwelling,
> his appointed time fulfilled;
> born for this, he met his passion,
> which he saw and freely willed;
> on the cross he was uplifted,
> where his lifeblood then was spilled.
>
> He endured the nails, the spitting,
> vinegar and spear and reed;
> from your holy body broken,
> blood and water forth proceed;
> earth and stars and sky and ocean
> by that flood from stain are freed.

Faithful cross, above all other,
one and only noble tree,
none in foliage, none in blossom,
none in fruit your peer may be;
sweetest wood and nails together
bearing sweetest majesty.

Bend your boughs, O tree of glory,
your relaxing sinews bend;
for awhile the ancient rigor
that your birth bestowed, suspend,
and the body of our Savior
on your bosom gently tend.

You alone were counted worthy
this world's ransom to sustain,
with the sacred blood anointed
of the Lamb for sinners slain,
that a shipwrecked race forever
might a port of refuge gain.

Glory be to our Creator;
praise for our salvation won
through the Savior, in the Spirit,
ever Three and ever One;
who with joy fills all creation
while eternal ages run. Amen.

Antiphon on Benedictus

Jesus said, I shall draw all people to myself *
when I am lifted up from the earth.

Diurnum

Antiphon on Psalter

> No one who does not carry the cross and come with me *
> can be a disciple of mine.

Lesson and Respond   COLOSSIANS 2:13-14

> God made us alive together with Christ, in that all our trespasses have
> been forgiven; the record that stood against us with its legal demands has
> been erased and set aside by being nailed to the cross.

Response: Thanks be to God.

> *v.* We adore you, O Christ, and we bless you.
> *r.* Because by your holy cross, you have redeemed the world.

The Office continues with the Closing Prayers in the Ordinary of Diurnum, p. 55.

Vespers

Hymn at Vespers

> The royal banners forward move;
> the cross shows forth the saving love
> of Jesus who shared human breath
> and gave his life to conquer death.
>
> From the deep wound in Jesus' side,
> by cruel lance torn open wide,
> both blood and water flowing free
> have washed away iniquity.
>
> Fulfilled is all the psalmists told
> in true prophetic songs of old;
> to all the nations they made plain
> that from a tree our God would reign.
>
> O tree of beauty, tree of light,
> O cross with Jesus' blood made bright,
> wood chosen and designed to bear
> the holy limbs suspended there.

Upon your arms so widely flung,
the weight of this world's ransom hung,
the price of all our wrongs to pay
and spoil the spoiler of the prey.

O cross, our one reliance, hail!
Through him, who died on you, avail
to give to sinners glad release,
to saints enjoyment of your peace.

To you, all holy Three in One,
let worthy homage now be done
by all whom through the cross you free
to live with you eternally. Amen.

September 16   **NINIAN**
Bishop in Galloway, c. 430

Common 6, p. 233

Collect

O God, by the preaching of your blest servant and bishop Ninian you caused the light of the gospel to shine in the land of Scotland: Grant, we pray, that having his life and labors in remembrance, we may show our thankfulness by following the example of his zeal and patience; through Jesus Christ our Savior, who lives and reigns with you and the Holy Spirit, one God, for ever and ever. *Amen.*

September 17   **HILDEGARD OF BINGEN**
Mystic, and Abbess of Bingen, 1179

Common 7, p. 237

Collect

God of all times and seasons: Give us grace that we, after the example of your servant Hildegard, may both know and make known the joy and jubilation of being part of your creation, and show forth your glory not only with our lips, but in our lives; through Jesus Christ our Savior, who lives and reigns with you and the Holy Spirit, one God, for ever and ever. *Amen.*

September 18   EDWARD BOUVERIE PUSEY
                  Priest, Leader of the Oxford Movement, 1882

Common 8, p. 240

Collect

Grant, O God, that in all time of our testing we may know your presence
and obey your will; that following the example of Edward Bouverie Pusey,
we may with integrity and courage accomplish what you give us to do, and
endure what you give us to bear; through Jesus Christ our Savior, who
lives and reigns with you and the Holy Spirit, one God, for ever and ever.
Amen.

September 19   THEODORE OF TARSUS
                  Archbishop of Canterbury, 690

Common 9, p. 244

Collect

Almighty God, you called your servant Theodore of Tarsus from Rome to
the See of Canterbury, and gave him gifts of grace and wisdom to establish
unity where there had been division, and order where there had been
chaos: Create in your Church, by the working of the Holy Spirit, such
unity and concord that it may proclaim, both by word and example, the
gospel of the Holy One of Peace, our Savior Jesus Christ; who lives and
reigns with you and the Holy Spirit, one God, for ever and ever. *Amen.*

September 20   JOHN COLERIDGE PATTESON
                  Bishop of Melanesia, and his Companions, Martyrs, 1871

Common 4, p. 226

Collect

Almighty God, you called your faithful servant John Coleridge Patteson
and his companions to be witnesses and martyrs in the islands of Melanesia,
and by their labors and sufferings raised up a people for your own possession: Pour out your Holy Spirit upon your Church in every land, that by
the service and sacrifice of many, your holy name may be glorified and
your realm enlarged; through Jesus Christ our Savior, who lives and reigns
with you and the Holy Spirit, one God, for ever and ever. *Amen.*

September 21   **MATTHEW**
                                    Apostle and Evangelist

Common 2, p. 217. For readings, see p. 615.

Collect

> We thank you, O God, for the witness of your apostle and evangelist
> Matthew to the gospel of Jesus Christ; and we pray that we may with
> ready wills and hearts obey the calling to follow the one who is our Savior
> and Redeemer; who lives and reigns with you and the Holy Spirit, one
> God, now and for ever. *Amen.*

September 22   **PHILANDER CHASE**
                                    Bishop of Ohio, and of Illinois, 1852

Common 9, p. 244

Collect

> O Jesus Christ, the pioneer and perfecter of our faith, we give you heart-
> felt thanks for the pioneering spirit of your servant Philander Chase, and
> for his zeal in opening new frontiers for the ministry of your Church:
> Grant us grace to minister in your name in every place, led by bold wit-
> nesses to your gospel of peace. We pray in the name of the holy and undi-
> vided Trinity, one God, now and for ever. *Amen.*

September 25   **SERGIUS**
                                    Abbot of Holy Trinity, Moscow, 1392

Common 7, p. 237

Collect

> O Most Holy God, you call us to turn away from worldly wealth and to
> follow you in love and obedience: Give us grace to follow the example of
> your servant Sergius of Moscow, whose gentleness of life and faithfulness
> to his native Russia inspired many to commit themselves to a deeper spiri-
> tual life in the midst of troubled times; through our Savior Jesus Christ,
> who lives and reigns with you and the Holy Spirit, one God, for ever and
> ever. *Amen.*

September 26   LANCELOT ANDREWES
Bishop of Winchester, 1626

Common 8, p. 240

Collect

> O God, by your grace your Church was enriched by the great learning and
> eloquent preaching of your servant Lancelot Andrewes, but even more by
> his example of biblical and liturgical prayer: Conform our lives, like his, to
> the image of Christ, that our hearts may love you, our minds serve you,
> and our lips proclaim the greatness of your mercy; through Jesus Christ
> our Savior, who lives and reigns with you and the Holy Spirit, one God,
> now and for ever. *Amen.*

September 29   MICHAEL AND ALL ANGELS

For readings, see p. 615. All as in the Ordinary of the Office, except

Antiphons for the Psalm(s)

> Michael shall appear, Michael the great captain, *
>   who stands guard over the faithful.

or

> Michael and the angels waged war upon the dragon. *
>   The dragon, whose name is Satan, was thrown down.

or

> An angel stood at the altar, holding a golden censer, *
>   and was given much incense to offer with the prayers of the saints.

or

> I heard the voice of countless angels round the throne: *
>   Worthy is the Lamb that was slain to receive honor and glory.

or

> Angels and archangels, thrones and dominions, principalities
> and powers, virtues of the heavens, *
>   O praise the God of heaven, Alleluia.

Collect

Everlasting God, you have ordained and constituted in a wonderful order the ministries of angels and mortals: Mercifully grant that, as your holy angels always serve and worship you in heaven, so by your appointment they may help and defend us here on earth; through Jesus Christ our Savior, who lives and reigns with you and the Holy Spirit, one God, for ever and ever. *Amen.*

Matins

Invitatory:	O holy God, your angels adore you: *
Response:	O come, let us worship, alleluia.

The canticle is the Te Deum, p. 213.

Hymn at Matins

Christ, the fair glory of the holy angels,
as you have made us and in life sustain us,
grant of your mercy strength that we may follow
    your way to heaven.

Send your archangel Michael to our succor;
peacemaker blessed, may he from us banish
striving and hatred, so that for the peaceful,
    all things may prosper.

Send your archangel Gabriel to help us;
may he keep from us all the wiles of evil;
herald of heaven, may he guard the temples
    where you are worshipped.

Send your archangel Raphael, the restorer
of the misguided ways of us who wander;
who at your bidding strengthens soul and body
    with your anointing.

So may we worship God forever blessed,
Maker, Redeemer, with the Holy Spirit:
to you be glory in both earth and heaven
    throughout the ages. Amen.

Antiphon on Benedictus

> You shall see heaven wide open, *
>> and God's angels ascending and descending upon the Promised One,
>> Alleluia.

Diurnum

Antiphon on Psalter

> God shall have the angels watch over you, *
>> to keep you in all your ways.

Lesson and Respond   REVELATION 22:16

> I, Jesus, have sent my angel to you with this testimony for the churches.
> I am the scion and offspring of David, the bright star of dawn.

Response: Thanks be to God.

> v. The smoke of the incense went up before God from the angel's hand,
> r. With the prayers of the saints.

The Office continues with the Closing Prayers in the Ordinary of Diurnum, p. 55.

Vespers

Hymn at Vespers

> Christ you are the cosmic splendor,
>> lighting each created thing;
> in the presence of the angels,
>> here your rightful praise we sing
> duly in united chorus,
>> that our homage we may bring.
>
> Thus we praise with veneration
>> all the myriads of the sky;
> chiefly Michael, great archangel,
>> armed with right and chivalry,
> who in primal holy combat
>> cast Abbadon from on high.

Michael and all holy angels
     in the power of God's grace,
fight the good fight by repelling
     all things evil, all things base;
grant us, Jesus, by your mercy,
     in your paradise a place.

          Glory be to God and honor;
     to our Savior, glory be;
and with them the Holy Spirit:
     ever One and ever Three;
who with joy fills all creation
     through time and eternity. Amen.

Antiphon on Magnificat

O prince most glorious, Michael the archangel, *
     keep us in remembrance here and everywhere; always entreat God
     for us, Alleluia.

September 30   **JEROME**
                                 Priest and Monk of Bethlehem, 420

Common 5, p. 230

Collect

O God of truth, your word is a lantern to our feet and a light upon our
path: We give you thanks for your servant Jerome, and those who, like
him, have labored to render the Holy Scriptures in the language of the
people; and we pray that your Holy Spirit will overshadow us as we read
the written word, and that Christ, the living Word, will transform us
according to your righteous will; through Jesus Christ our Savior, who
lives and reigns with you and the Holy Spirit, one God, now and for ever.
Amen.

| October 1 | REMIGIUS |
| | *Bishop of Rheims, c. 530* |

Common 8, p. 240

Collect

O God, by the teaching of your faithful servant and bishop Remigius you turned the nation of the Franks from idolatry to worship you, the true and living God, in the fullness of the Christian faith: Grant that we who glory in the name of Christ may show forth our faith in worthy deeds; through Jesus Christ our Savior, who lives and reigns with you and the Holy Spirit, one God, for ever and ever. *Amen.*

| October 4 | FRANCIS OF ASSISI |
| | *Friar, 1226* |

Common 7, p. 237

Collect

Most high, omnipotent, good God: Grant your people the grace to renounce gladly the vanities of this world; that, following the way of blessed Francis, we may for love of you delight in your whole creation with perfectness of joy; through Jesus Christ our Savior, who lives and reigns with you and the Holy Spirit, one God, for ever and ever. *Amen.*

| October 6 | WILLIAM TYNDALE |
| | *Priest, Translator, Martyr, 1536* |

Common 3, p. 222

Collect

Almighty God, you planted in the heart of your servant William Tyndale a consuming passion to bring the scriptures to people in their native language, endowed him with the gift of powerful and graceful expression, and with strength to persevere against all obstacles: Reveal to us your saving word, as we read and study the scriptures, and hear them calling us to repentance and newness of life; through Jesus Christ our Savior, who lives and reigns with you and the Holy Spirit, one God, for ever and ever. *Amen.*

October 9   **ROBERT GROSSETESTE**
Bishop of Lincoln and Theologian, 1253

Common 8, p. 240

Collect

> O heavenly God, you raised up your faithful servant Robert Grosseteste to be a bishop and prophetic leader in your Church and to feed your flock: Give abundantly to all pastors the gifts of your Holy Spirit, that they may speak out fearlessly against corruption, and minister in your household as true servants of Christ, and stewards of your divine mysteries; through Jesus Christ our Savior, who lives and reigns with you and the Holy Spirit, one God, for ever and ever. *Amen.*

October 11   **PHILIP THE DEACON**
Deacon and Evangelist (Acts 6:5, Acts 8:5-13 and 26-40)

Common 8, p. 240

Collect

> O Holy God, no one is excluded from your love, and your truth transforms the minds of all who seek you: As your servant Philip was led to embrace the fullness of your salvation and to bring the stranger to Baptism, so give us the grace to be heralds of the gospel, proclaiming your love to those who are strangers among us; through Jesus Christ our Savior, who lives and reigns with you and the Holy Spirit, one God, for ever and ever. *Amen.*

October 14   **SAMUEL ISAAC JOSEPH SCHERESCHEWSKY**
Bishop of Shanghai, 1906

Common 6, p. 233

Collect

> O God, in your providence you called Joseph Schereschewsky from his home in Eastern Europe to the ministry of the Church, and sent him as a missionary to China, upholding him in his infirmity, that he might translate the bible into languages of that land. Lead us, we pray, to commit our lives and talents to you, in the confidence that when you give your servants any work to do, you also supply the strength to do it; through Jesus Christ our Savior, who lives and reigns with you and the Holy Spirit, one God, for ever and ever. *Amen.*

October 15	TERESA OF AVILA
	Monastic, Mystic, and Reformer, 1582

Common 5, p. 230

Collect

O God, by your Holy Spirit you moved Teresa of Avila to manifest to your Church the way of perfection: Grant us, we pray, to be nourished by her excellent teaching, and kindle within us a keen and unquenchable longing for true holiness; through Jesus Christ, the joy of loving hearts, who with you and the Holy Spirit lives and reigns, one God, for ever and ever. *Amen*.

October 16	HUGH LATIMER AND NICHOLAS RIDLEY;
	AND THOMAS CRANMER
	Bishops and Martyrs, 1555; Archbishop of Canterbury, 1556

Common 3, p. 222

Collect

Keep us, O God, constant in faith and zealous in witness, that, like your servants Hugh Latimer, Nicholas Ridley and Thomas Cranmer, we may live in your fear, die in your favor, and rest in your peace; for the sake of Jesus Christ our Savior and Redeemer, who lives and reigns with you and the Holy Spirit, one God, for ever and ever. *Amen*.

October 17	THOMAS THOMPSON AND PHILIP QUAQUE
	Missionaries in Ghana, 1816

Common 6, p. 233

Collect

Almighty God, we praise you for your servants Thomas Thompson and Philip Quaque who served as missionaries to the peoples of Ghana, establishing schools and working to spread the gospel: Give us strength and courage to emulate their dedication in promoting Christian learning; through Jesus Christ our Redeemer, who with you and the Holy Spirit, lives and reigns in glory everlasting. *Amen*.

October 18	**LUKE**
	Evangelist

Common 2, p. 217. For readings, see p. 615.

Collect

> Almighty God, you inspired your servant Luke the physician to set forth in the gospel the love and healing power of Jesus: Graciously continue in your Church this love and power to heal, to the praise and glory of your name; through Christ our Savior and Redeemer, who lives and reigns with you, in the unity of the Holy Spirit, one God, now and for ever. *Amen.*

October 19	**HENRY MARTIN**
	Priest and Missionary to India and Persia, 1812

Common 6, p. 233

Collect

> O God of the nations, you gave your servant Henry Martyn a brilliant mind, a loving heart and a gift for languages, that he might translate the scriptures and other holy writings for the peoples of India and Persia: Inspire in us a love like his, eager to commit both life and talents to you in faithful service; through Jesus Christ our Savior, who lives and reigns with you and the Holy Spirit, one God, for ever and ever. *Amen.*

October 20	**IGNATIUS**
(date transferred)	*Bishop of Antioch and Martyr, c. 115*

Common 4, p. 226

Collect

> Almighty God, we praise your name for your bishop and martyr Ignatius of Antioch, who offered himself as grain to be ground, that he might be presented to you as the pure bread of sacrifice: Accept, we pray, the willing tribute of our lives and give us a share in the pure and spotless offering of Jesus, the Incarnate One; who lives and reigns with you and the Holy Spirit, one God, for ever and ever. *Amen.*

October 23   JAMES OF JERUSALEM
Apostle and Brother of Jesus

Common 2, p. 217. For readings, see p. 615.

Collect

Grant, O God, that, following the example of your servant James the Just, brother of our Savior, your Church may devote itself continually to prayer and the ministry of reconciliation; through Jesus Christ our Redeemer, who lives and reigns with you and the Holy Spirit, one God, now and for ever. *Amen.*

October 26   ALFRED THE GREAT
King of the West Saxons, 899

Common 8, p. 240

Collect

O Sovereign God, you brought your servant Alfred to a troubled throne that he might establish peace in a ravaged land and revive learning and the arts among his people: Awake in us also a keen desire to increase our understanding while we are in this world, and an eager longing to reach that endless life where all will be made clear; through Jesus Christ our Savior, who lives and reigns with you and the Holy Spirit, one God, for ever and ever. *Amen.*

October 28   SIMON AND JUDE
Apostles

Common 2, p. 217. For readings, see p. 616.

Collect

O God, we thank you for the glorious company of the apostles, and especially on this day for Simon and Jude; and we pray that, as they were faithful and zealous in their mission, so we may with ardent devotion make known the love and mercy of our Savior and Redeemer Jesus Christ; who lives and reigns with you and the Holy Spirit, one God, for ever and ever. *Amen.*

October 29   JAMES HANNINGTON
                    Bishop of Eastern Equatorial Africa,
                    and his Companions, Martyrs, 1885

Common 4, p. 226

Collect

Great is your compassion, O God, at the death of your saints, whom you always hold in the palm of your hand: We give you thanks for your martyrs James Hannington and his companions, who purchased with their blood a road into Uganda for the proclamation of the gospel; and we pray that we also may attain to the joy of all who love the appearing of our Savior Jesus Christ; who lives and reigns with you and the Holy Spirit, one God, for ever and ever. *Amen.*

November 1   ALL SAINTS DAY

For readings, see p. 616. All as in the Ordinary of the Office, except

Antiphons on the Psalm(s)

I looked and saw a vast throng which no one could count, *
    from every nation, standing in front of the throne and before the Lamb.

or

The twenty-four elders fall down before the One who sits on the throne *
    and worship God who lives for ever and ever.

or

Worthy is the Lamb, by whose own blood was purchased for God *
    those of every tribe and language, people and nation.

Collect

Almighty God, you have knit together all the redeemed in the mystical body of Christ: Give us grace to follow your saints in all holy living, that we may come to those inexpressible joys that you have prepared for those who truly love you; through Jesus Christ our Savior, who with you and the Holy Spirit lives and reigns, one God, in glory everlasting. *Amen.*

Matins

Invitatory: Alleluia, God is glorious in the saints:
Response: O come, let us worship, alleluia.

The canticle is the Te Deum, p. 213.

Hymn at Matins

> The praises that the blest ones know,
> the church now imitates below
> as here we hail in yearly song
> the joys that to the saints belong.
>
> They changed the vanities of earth
> for bliss of far-surpassing worth;
> their grateful hymns fill deepest space
> for all God's loving power and grace.
>
> On earth we cannot comprehend
> this glad fulfillment without end;
> we have no sense or words to sing
> the joy that endless life will bring.
>
> One instant of those glorious rays
> is better than earth's thousand days;
> the saints are bathed in holy light
> and made full welcome in God's sight.
>
> All laud to you, Creator, be,
> to you, O Christ, eternally;
> to you, the Spirit, equal praise
> from joyful hearts we ever raise. Amen.

Antiphon on Benedictus

The glorious company of apostles praise you; the noble gathering of
prophets praise you; the white-robed choir of martyrs praise you; *
  throughout the world the holy church acclaims you:
  O blessed Trinity, one only God.

Diurnum

Antiphon on Psalter

> The just live for ever; their reward is in God's keeping, *
> and the Most High cares for them.

Lesson and Respond   ECCLESIASTICUS 50:22

> Come then, praise the God of the universe, who everywhere works great
> wonders, who from our birth ennobles our life and deals with us in mercy.

Response: Thanks be to God.

> *v.* Let the righteous be glad and rejoice before God.
> *r.* Let them also be merry and joyful.

The Office continues with the Closing Prayers in the Ordinary of Diurnum, p. 55.

Vespers

Hymn at Vespers

> Were it possible to number
> all the saints whose lives were blest,
> we might comprehend the gladness
> of the everlasting rest,
> which, their time on earth completed,
> they in heaven have possessed.
>
> After facing doubts and shadows,
> both together and alone,
> we shall see God's brilliant splendor
> and shall know as we are known,
> fixing our enlightened vision
> on the radiance of the throne.
>
> There the holy ones in glory,
> crowned in joy and robed in light,
> put aside their mortal troubles
> and are peaceful in God's sight,
> singing praises to their maker,
> cosmic anthems of delight.

There for ever and for ever
alleluias may be heard,
for unending, for unbroken,
is the feast day of the Word;
every heart and every spirit
is with joyous blessing stirred.

Praise to God our great Creator,
honor to the Spirit blest,
praise to Jesus our redeemer:
triune God made manifest;
who, to all the saints adoring,
grants the joy of heavenly rest. Amen.

Antiphon on Magnificat

O angels and archangels, O patriarchs and prophets,
O apostles and martyrs, Holy confessors, and all saints: *
   may our prayers rise together like incense to the Holy One.

November 2   **ALL SOULS DAY**
                                 Commemoration of All the Departed

Common 15, p. 265

Collect

O Jesus Christ, you have destroyed death by death, giving life to those in
the tomb; O Sun of Righteousness, you are gloriously risen, giving light
to those who sat in darkness and the shadow of death: Grant to all the
departed that they may go from strength to strength and attain to the
peace that passes understanding and to the joys of life eternal. This we
pray in the name of our Creator, our Redeemer, and our Sustainer, the
holy and merciful God, who lives and reigns for ever and ever. *Amen.*

November 3   **Richard Hooker**
                    Priest and Theologian, 1600

Common 8, p. 240

Collect

O God of truth and peace, you raised up your servant Richard Hooker in a day of bitter controversy to defend with sound reasoning and great charity the catholic and reformed religion: Grant that we may maintain that middle way, not as a compromise for the sake of peace, but as a comprehension for the sake of truth; through Jesus Christ our Savior, who lives and reigns with you and the Holy Spirit, one God, for ever and ever. *Amen.*

November 5   **The Saints of the Hebrew Scriptures**
All as in the Ordinary of the Office, except

Matins

Invitatory: God is glorious in the saints:
Response: O come, let us worship.

Antiphon on Psalter

Our forebears were loyal to God; *
thanks to them their children are within the covenants.

The canticle is in the Ordinary of the week.

Antiphon on Benedictus

Abraham rejoiced that he would see my day; he saw it and was glad.*
But I tell you, before Abraham was, I am.

Collect

Almighty and everlasting God, in every age you have revealed your purpose to chosen witnesses, that all nations might be called to salvation: We give you thanks for the saints of the Hebrew scriptures whose faithfulness and testimony have led to the fulfillment of all your saving acts in Jesus Christ; who lives and reigns with you and the Holy Spirit, one God, for ever and ever. *Amen.*

Diurnum

Antiphon on Psalter

The just live for ever; their reward is in God's keeping, *
and the Most High cares for them.

Lesson and Respond   HEBREWS 11:13-14

All of these died in faith without having received the promises, but from a distance they saw and greeted them. They confessed that they were strangers and foreigners on the earth, for people who speak in this way make it clear that they are seeking a homeland.

Response: Thanks be to God.

v. Let the righteous be glad and rejoice before God.
r. Let them also be merry and joyful.

The Office continues with the Closing Prayers in the Ordinary of Diurnum, p. 55.

Vespers

Antiphon on Psalter

All these won fame in their own generation *
and were the pride of their times.

The canticle is in the Ordinary of the week.

> Were it possible to number
> all the saints whose lives were blest,
> we might comprehend the gladness
> of the everlasting rest,
> which, their time on earth completed,
> they in heaven have possessed.
>
> There for ever and for ever
> alleluias may be heard,
> for unending, for unbroken,
> is the feast day of the Word;
> every heart and every spirit
> is with joyous blessing stirred.
>
> Praise to God our great Creator,
> honor to the Spirit blest,
> praise to Jesus our redeemer:
> triune God made manifest;
> who, to all the saints adoring,
> grants the joy of heavenly rest. Amen.

Antiphon on Magnificat

> O bless God, all you chosen ones; *
> keep a day of rejoicing, and give thanks to God.

November 6   **WILLIAM TEMPLE**
Archbishop of Canterbury, 1944

Common 9, p. 244

Collect

> O God of light and love, you illumined your Church through the witness of your servant William Temple: Inspire us, we pray, by his teaching and example, that we may rejoice with courage, confidence, and faith in the Word made flesh, and may be led to establish that city which has justice for its foundation and love for its law; through Jesus Christ, the light of the world, who lives and reigns with you and the Holy Spirit, one God, now and for ever. *Amen.*

November 7   **WILLIBRORD**
Archbishop of Utrecht, Mission to Frisia, 739

Common 6, p. 233

Collect

O God, you call whom you will and send them where you choose: We thank you for sending your servant Willibrord to be an apostle to the Low Countries, to turn them from the worship of idols to serve you, the living God; and we entreat you to preserve us from the temptation to exchange the perfect freedom of your service for servitude to false gods and to idols of our own devising; through Jesus Christ our Savior, who lives and reigns with you and the Holy Spirit, one God, for ever and ever. *Amen.*

November 8   **FOUNDING OF THE ORDER OF SAINT HELENA**

All as in the Ordinary of the Office, except

Lessons:

	I VESPERS	Deuteronomy 7:6-8a	Mark 10:23-31
	MATINS	Isaiah 42:5-10a	John 15:4-8
	II VESPERS	Deuteronomy 30:15-21	Romans 12:1-10

Antiphons for the Psalm(s)

There can be no other foundation beyond that which is already laid; *
     I mean, that of Jesus Christ.

or

Anyone who wishes to be a follower of mine must leave self behind, *
     take up the cross and come with me.

or

They who dwell in me, as I dwell in them, bear much fruit; *
     for apart from me, you can do nothing.

or

As you have sent me into the world, I have sent them into the world; *
     for their sake I consecrate myself, that they too may be consecrated
     by truth.

or

O Holy One, protect by the power of your name those whom
you have given me, *
     that they may be one as we are one.

Collect

O gracious God, through whose Beloved One we are able to know ourselves also as beloved, we thank you for the nine women whose vision and
trust in you brought this community into being: Clothe us, who have
been called together by you, with the garments of compassion, kindness,
humility, gentleness, and patience; let the message of Christ in all its richness inform our lives, that true forgiveness, gratitude and love may grow
among us and show forth in our lives and service; through Jesus Christ
who has taken our humanity into your divinity and lives and reigns with
you and the Holy Spirit, one God, now and for ever. *Amen.*

Matins

Invitatory: Our God is infinitely more than we can comprehend:
Response: O come, let us worship.

The canticle is the Te Deum, p. 213.

Hymn at Matins

O God of new beginnings, bless
this day of anniversary;
on this day in your graciousness
you called forth our community.

Grace all our ministry and prayer,
redeem the acts in which we erred,
that each and all of us may share
in the proclaiming of your Word.

Help us remember thankfully
the sisters who have gone before,
who sought the truth that makes us free
to love and serve you more and more.

As we begin each day anew
with every blessing it may bring,
help us, O Christ, to find in you
our center and eternal spring.

To you all glory, Trinity,
all laud, O Holy Unity;
this festal day in joy we raise
our grateful hymns of love and praise. Amen.

Antiphon on Benedictus

You are a people claimed to be God's very own; *
to proclaim the triumphs of the One who has called you out of darkness
into God's marvelous light.

Diurnum

Antiphon on Psalter

They shall live under the shelter of my dwelling; *
I will become their God, and they shall become my people.

Lesson and Respond   DEUTERONOMY 27:9

Be silent, Israel, and listen; this day you have become a people belonging
to your God.

Response: Thanks be to God.

v. You have called us by name, O God; we are yours.
r. May we be conformed to your image day by day.

The Office continues with the Closing Prayers in the Ordinary of Diurnum, p. 55.

Vespers

The canticle at Vespers is the Benedicite, p. 120.

Hymn at Vespers

> Creator God, you called forth space
> with teeming worlds for love's increase,
> and named our earth to be the place
> to which you brought your own Love's peace.

> You chose a people for your own,
> through Sarah and through Abraham,
> who in their faith made your truth known:
> the saving power of I AM.

> You call us still to live your praise,
> from each beginning that we share,
> in joy and pain through all our days,
> in faithful lives, in work and prayer.

> And as we celebrate this year
> our founding and continuing grace,
> bless us in faith to persevere
> until we see you face to face.

> To you, O Jesus Christ, be praise;
> to you, Creator, glory be;
> to you, O Spirit, hymns we raise:
> one God through all eternity. Amen.

Antiphon on Magnificat at Vespers

> I implore you by God's mercy to offer your very selves, *
> a living sacrifice, dedicated and fit for God's acceptance,
> the worship offered by mind and heart.

| November 10 | **LEO THE GREAT** |
| | *Bishop of Rome, 461* |

Common 5, p. 230

Collect

> O God, grant that your Church, following the teaching of your servant Leo of Rome, may hold fast the great mystery of our redemption: May we adore the one Christ, truly God and truly human, neither divided from our human nature nor separate from your divine Being; through Jesus Christ our Savior, who lives and reigns with you and the Holy Spirit, one God, now and for ever. *Amen.*

| November 11 | **MARTIN** |
| | *Bishop of Tours, 397* |

Common 9, p. 244

Collect

> O God of hosts, you clothed your servant Martin the soldier with the spirit of sacrifice, and set him as a bishop in your Church to be a defender of the Christian faith: Give us also the spirit of loving sacrifice, that at the last we may be found clothed with righteousness in the dwellings of peace; through Jesus Christ our Savior, who lives and reigns with you and the Holy Spirit, one God, for ever and ever. *Amen.*

| November 12 | **CHARLES SIMEON** |
| | *Priest; Founder Church Missionary Society, 1836* |

Common 8, p. 240

Collect

> O loving God, we know that all things are ordered by your unerring wisdom and unbounded love: Grant us to see your hand in all things; that, following the example and teaching of your servant Charles Simeon, we may walk with Christ in all simplicity, and serve you with a quiet and contented mind; through Jesus Christ our Savior, who lives and reigns with you and the Holy Spirit, one God, for ever and ever. *Amen.*

November 14   Consecration of Samuel Seabury
First American Bishop, 1784

Common 9, p. 244, except

Matins

Invitatory:	Christ, the cornerstone, has built the church upon apostles and prophets:
Response:	O come, let us worship.

Antiphon on Psalter

Let your priests be clothed with righteousness; *
  let your faithful people sing with joy.

Hymn at Matins

Today the church in grateful song
remembers that succession strong
of bishops who to us were sent,
who feed by word and sacrament.

The bond of apostolic grace
calls all the faithful to embrace
the unity we have in Christ,
who for us all was sacrificed.

All laud to you, Creator be;
to you, O Christ, eternally;
to you, the Spirit, equal praise
from joyful hearts we ever raise. Amen.

Antiphon on Benedictus

Jesus' heart went out to the people,
because they were like sheep without a shepherd, *
  and he had much to teach them.

Collect

We give you thanks, O God, for your goodness in bestowing upon this Church the gift of the episcopate, which we celebrate in this remembrance of the consecration of Samuel Seabury, first bishop in the Episcopal Church; and we pray that, joined together in unity with our bishops, and nourished by your holy sacraments, we may proclaim the gospel of redemption with apostolic zeal; through Jesus Christ our Savior, who lives and reigns with you and the Holy Spirit, one God, now and for ever. *Amen.*

Diurnum

Antiphon on Psalter

The descendants of those who fear God will be faithful in the land; *
the generation of the upright shall be blest.

Lesson and Respond   EPHESIANS 4:11-12

These were the gifts of Christ: some to be apostles, some prophets, some evangelists, some pastors and teachers, to equip God's people for the work of ministry, to the building up of the body of Christ.

Response: Thanks be to God.

    v. I will clothe my priests with salvation;
    r. All faithful people will rejoice and sing.

The Office continues with the Closing Prayers in the Ordinary of Diurnum, p. 55.

Vespers

Antiphon on Psalter

Those who are planted in the house of the Holy One *
shall flourish in the courts of our God.

Hymn at Vespers

> Christ is made the sure foundation
>> and the head and cornerstone;
> chosen in God's love and precious,
>> binding all the church in one;
> holy Zion's help for ever
>> and its confidence alone.

> All that dedicated city,
>> dearly loved by God on high,
> in exultant jubilation
>> pours perpetual melody,
> God the One in Three adoring
>> in glad hymns eternally.

> To the church, in sad division,
>> come, O God of hosts, today;
> with your wonted loving-kindness ,
>> hear your people as they pray
> for a unity of vision
>> as in you we seek the way.

> Glory be to our Creator,
>> to the Word all glory be,
> praise and honor to the Spirit,
>> God, the Holy Trinity;
> consubstantial, coeternal,
>> now and through eternity. Amen.

Antiphon on Magnificat

The crop is heavy, but the laborers are scarce; *
   you must therefore beg the owner to send laborers to harvest the crop.

November 16   **MARGARET**
Queen of Scotland, 1093

Common 10, p. 247

Collect

O God, you called your servant Margaret to an earthly throne that she might advance your heavenly realm, and gave her zeal for your Church and love for your people: Mercifully grant that we who commemorate her this day may be fruitful in good works, and attain to the glorious crown of your saints; through Jesus Christ our Savior, who lives and reigns with you and the Holy Spirit, one God, for ever and ever. *Amen.*

November 17   **HUGH**
Bishop of Lincoln, 1200

Common 9, p. 244

Collect

Holy God, who endowed Hugh of Lincoln with strength to stand boldly before sovereigns and grace to walk humbly with his flock: May we follow him in fighting for the cause of the outcast and oppressed and, fearing nothing but the loss of you, stand firm for the sake of truth; through our Savior Jesus Christ who lives and reigns with you and the Holy Spirit, one God in glory everlasting. *Amen.*

November 18   **HILDA**
Abbess of Whitby, 680

Common 7, p. 237

Collect

O God of peace, by whose grace the abbess Hilda was endowed with gifts of justice, prudence, and strength to rule as a wise mother over the nuns and monks of her household, and to become a trusted and reconciling friend to leaders of the Church: Give us the grace to recognize and accept the varied gifts you bestow on men and women, that our common life may be enriched and your gracious will be done; through Jesus Christ our Savior, who lives and reigns with you and the Holy Spirit, one God, now and for ever. *Amen.*

November 19   **ELIZABETH**
Princess of Hungary, 1231

Common 10, p. 247

Collect

Almighty God, by your grace your servant Elizabeth of Hungary recognized and honored Jesus in the poor of this world: Grant that we, following her example, may with love and gladness serve those in any need or trouble; in the name and for the sake of Jesus Christ; who lives and reigns with you and the Holy Spirit, one God, for ever and ever. *Amen.*

November 20   **EDMUND**
King of East Anglia, Martyr, 870

Common 4, p. 226

Collect

O God of inexpressible mercy, you gave grace and fortitude to blessed Edmund the king of East Anglia to triumph over the invading enemy, by remaining steadfast in his faith and loyal to his people in spite of great adversity: Bestow on us your servants the shield of faith with which we can withstand the assaults of our ancient enemy; through Jesus Christ our Redeemer, who lives and reigns with you and the Holy Spirit, one God, now and for ever. *Amen.*

November 22   **CLIVE STAPLES LEWIS**
Theologian, Apologist, and Spiritual Writer, 1963

Common 8, p. 240

Collect

O God of searing truth and surpassing beauty, we give you thanks for C. S. Lewis, whose inspired imagination lights fires of faith in young and old alike: Surprise us also with your joy and draw us into that new and abundant life which is ours in Christ Jesus; who lives and reigns with you and the Holy Spirit, one God, now and for ever. *Amen.*

November 23   **CLEMENT**
                   Bishop of Rome, c. 100

Common 10, p. 247

Collect

>Almighty God, you chose your servant Clement of Rome to recall the
>Church in Corinth to obedience and stability: Grant that your Church
>may be grounded and settled in your truth by the indwelling of the Holy
>Spirit; reveal to it what is not yet known; fill up what is lacking; confirm
>what has already been revealed; and keep it blameless in your service;
>through Jesus Christ our Savior, who lives and reigns with you and the
>Holy Spirit, one God, for ever and ever. *Amen.*

November 25   **JAMES OTIS SARGENT HUNTINGTON**
                   Priest and Monastic, ·
                   Founder of the Order of the Holy Cross, 1935

Common 7, p. 237, except

Lessons: **MATINS**   Exodus 17:8-13   Ephesians 6:10-18
                VESPERS   Judges 7:2-9   Mark 10:17-31

Matins

Invitatory: Christ, who came to do God's will:
Response: O come, let us worship.

Antiphon on Psalter

>The cross is our all-sufficing treasure, *
>   and Christ's love our never-ending reward.

The canticle is the Te Deum, p. 213.

Antiphon on Benedictus

>We are to be continually praising God; *
>   we are practicing for the endless Alleluia of the heavenly courts.

Collect

O loving God, by your grace your servant James Huntington gathered a community dedicated to love and discipline and devotion to the holy cross of our Savior Jesus Christ: Send your blessing on all who proclaim Christ crucified, and move the hearts of many to look upon our redeemer and be saved; who with you and the Holy Spirit lives and reigns, one God, for ever and ever. *Amen.*

Diurnum

Antiphon on Psalter

We must rejoice in the Holy cross *
as the glory of the Christian name.

Lesson and Respond PHILIPPIANS 3:8-9

I have come to rate all as loss in the light of the surpassing knowledge of my Savior Jesus Christ, for whose sake I have forfeited everything; I have accounted all else rubbish so that Christ may be my wealth.

Response: Thanks be to God.

v. We adore you, O Christ, and we bless you;
r. By your holy cross you have redeemed the world.

The Office continues with the Closing Prayers in the Ordinary of Diurnum, p. 55.

Vespers

Antiphon on Psalter

Holiness is the brightness of divine love; *
love must act as light must shine and fire must burn.

Antiphon on Magnificat

Ask them to forgive me; tell them I forgive them. *
I want them to have joy; I will always intercede.

November 28　　　　　KAMEHAMEHA AND EMMA
　　　　　　　　　　King and Queen of Hawaii, 1864, 1885

Common 10, p. 247

Collect

O Sovereign God, who raised up Kamehameha and Emma to be rulers in Hawaii, and inspired and enabled them to be diligent in good works for the welfare of their people and the good of your Church: Receive our thanks for their witness to the gospel, and grant that we, with them, may attain to the crown of glory that never fades away; through Jesus Christ our Savior and Redeemer, who with you and the Holy Spirit lives and reigns, one God, for ever and ever. *Amen.*

The Psalter

Book One

First Day: Morning Prayer

Psalm 1

1 Happy are they who have not walked in the counsel of
        the wicked, *
    nor lingered in the way of sinners,
    nor sat in the seats of the scornful!

2 Their delight is in the law of the Holy One, *
    and they meditate on that law day and night.

3 They are like trees planted by streams of water,
    bearing fruit in due season, with leaves that do not wither; *
    everything they do shall prosper.

4 It is not so with the wicked; *
    they are like chaff which the wind blows away.

5 Therefore the wicked shall not stand upright when
        judgment comes *
    nor the sinner in the council of the righteous;

6 For the Holy One knows the way of the righteous, *
    but the way of the wicked is doomed.

Psalm 2

1 Why are the nations in an uproar; *
    why do the peoples mutter empty threats?

2 Why do the mighty of the earth rise up in revolt
    and the rulers plot together, *
        against God and against God's Anointed?

3 "Let us break their yoke," they say; *
    "let us cast off their bonds from us."

4 You whose throne is in heaven are laughing; *
    you have them in derision.

5 Then you speak to them in your wrath, *
    and your rage fills them with terror.

6 "I myself have set my monarch *
    upon my holy hill of Zion."

7 Let me announce the decree of God, *
    who has said to me, "You are my Son;
    this day have I begotten you.

8 Ask of me, and I will give you the nations for
        your inheritance *
    and the ends of the earth for your possession.

9 You shall crush them with an iron rod *
    and shatter them like a piece of pottery."

10 And now, you monarchs, be wise; *
    be warned, you rulers of the earth.

11 Submit to God with fear, *
    and with trembling bow before the Most High,

12 Lest God be angry and you perish, *
    for divine wrath is quickly kindled.

13 Happy are they all *
    who take refuge in God!

PSALM 3

1 O God, how many adversaries I have; *
    how many there are who rise up against me!

2 How many there are who say of me, *
    there is no help for me in my God.

3 But you, O God, are a shield about me; *
    you are my glory, the one who lifts up my head.

4 I call aloud to you, O God, *
    and you answer me from your holy hill.

5 I lie down and go to sleep; *
    I wake again, because you sustain me.

6 I do not fear the multitudes of people *
   who set themselves against me all around.

7 Rise up, O God; set me free, O my God; *
   surely, you will strike all my enemies across the face;
   you will break the teeth of the wicked.

8 Deliverance belongs to you, O Most High. *
   Your blessing be upon your people!

PSALM 4

1 Answer me when I call, O God, defender of my cause; *
   you set me free when I am hard-pressed;
   have mercy on me and hear my prayer.

2 "You mortals, how long will you dishonor my glory; *
   how long will you worship dumb idols
   and run after false gods?"

3 Know that God does wonders for the faithful; *
   when I call, God will hear me.

4 Tremble, then, and do not sin; *
   speak to your heart in silence upon your bed.

5 Offer the appointed sacrifices, *
   and put your trust in the Most High.

6 Many are saying,
   "Oh, that we might see better times!" *
   Lift up the light of your countenance upon us, O God.

7 You have put gladness in my heart, *
   more than when grain and wine and oil increase.

8 I lie down in peace; at once I fall asleep; *
   for only you, God, make me dwell in safety.

PSALM 5

1 Give ear to my words, O God; *
   consider my meditation.

2 Hearken to my cry for help, my Sovereign and my God, *
   for I make my prayer to you.

3 In the morning you hear my voice; *
   early in the morning I make my appeal and watch for you.

4 For you are not a God who takes pleasure in wickedness, *
    and evil cannot dwell with you.

5 Braggarts cannot stand in your sight; *
    you hate all those who work wickedness.

6 You destroy those who speak lies; *
    the bloodthirsty and deceitful, O God, you abhor.

7 But as for me, through the greatness of your mercy
        I will go into your house; *
    I will bow down toward your holy temple in awe of you.

8 Lead me, O God, in your righteousness,
    because of those who lie in wait for me; *
    make your way straight before me,

9 For there is no truth in their mouth; *
    there is destruction in their heart;

10 Their throat is an open grave; *
    they flatter with their tongue.

11 Declare them guilty, O God; *
    let them fall, because of their schemes.

12 Because of their many transgressions, cast them out, *
    for they have rebelled against you.

13 But all who take refuge in you will be glad; *
    they will sing out their joy for ever.

14 You will shelter them, *
    so that those who love your Name may exult in you.

15 For you, O God, will bless the righteous; *
    you will defend them with your favor as with a shield.

First Day: Evening Prayer

Psalm 6

1 O God, do not rebuke me in your anger; *
    do not punish me in your wrath.

2 Have pity on me, O God, for I am weak; *
    heal me, for my bones are racked.

3 My spirit shakes with terror; *
    how long, O God, how long?

4 Turn, O God, and deliver me; *
   save me for your mercy's sake.

5 For in death no one remembers you, *
   and who will give you thanks in the grave?

6 I grow weary because of my groaning; *
   every night I drench my bed
   and flood my couch with tears.

7 My eyes are wasted with grief *
   and worn away because of all my enemies.

8 Depart from me, all evildoers, *
   for God has heard the sound of my weeping.

9 God has heard my supplication; *
   God accepts my prayer.

10 All my enemies shall be confounded and quake with fear; *
   they shall turn back and suddenly be put to shame.

Psalm 7

1 O Most High, I take refuge in you; *
   save and deliver me from all who pursue me;

2 Lest like a lion they tear me in pieces *
   and snatch me away with none to deliver me.

3 O my God, if I have done these things: *
   if there is any wickedness in my hands,

4 If I have repaid my friend with evil *
   or plundered anyone who without cause is my enemy,

5 Then let my enemy pursue and overtake me, *
   trample my life into the ground
   and lay my honor in the dust.

6 Stand up, O God, in your wrath; *
   rise up against the fury of my enemies.

7 Awake, O my God, decree justice; *
   let the assembly of the peoples gather round you.

8 Be seated on your lofty throne, O Most High; *
   O God, judge the nations.

9 Give judgment for me according to my
    righteousness, O God, *
  and according to my innocence, O Most High.

10 Let the malice of the wicked come to an end,
  but establish the righteous, *
    for you test the mind and heart, O righteous God.

11 God is my shield and defense, *
  the savior of the true in heart.

12 God is a righteous judge, *
  who sits in judgment every day.

13 If they will not repent, God will whet a sword, *
  bend a bow and make it ready.

14 God has prepared the weapons of death *
  and has made arrows shafts of fire.

15 Look at those who are in labor with wickedness, *
  who conceive evil, and give birth to a lie.

16 They dig a pit and make it deep *
  and fall into the hole that they have made.

17 Their malice turns back upon their own head; *
  their violence falls on their own scalp.

18 I will bear witness that God is righteous; *
  I will praise the Name of the Most High.

PSALM 8

1 O God, our Governor, *
  how exalted is your Name in all the world!

2 Out of the mouths of infants and children, *
  your majesty is praised above the heavens.

3 You have set up a stronghold against your adversaries, *
  to quell the enemy and the avenger.

4 When I consider your heavens, the work of your fingers, *
  the moon and the stars you have set in their courses,

5 What are we that you should be mindful of us, *
  mere mortals that you should seek us out?

6 You have made us but little lower than the angels; *
  you adorn us with glory and honor;

7 You give us mastery over the works of your hands; *
   you put all things under our feet:

8 All sheep and oxen, *
   even the wild beasts of the field,

9 The birds of the air, the fish of the sea, *
   and whatsoever walks in the paths of the sea.

10 O God, our Governor, *
   how exalted is your Name in all the world!

Second Day: Morning Prayer

PSALM 9

1 I will give thanks to you, O God, with my whole heart; *
   I will tell of all your marvelous works.

2 I will be glad and rejoice in you; *
   I will sing to your Name, O Most High.

3 When my enemies are driven back, *
   they will stumble and perish at your presence.

4 For you have maintained my right and my cause; *
   you sit upon your throne judging right.

5 You have rebuked the ungodly and destroyed the wicked; *
   you have blotted out their name for ever and ever.

6 As for the enemy, they are finished, in perpetual ruin, *
   their cities plowed under, the memory of them perished;

7 But you, O God, are enthroned for ever; *
   you have set up your throne for judgment.

8 You rule the world with righteousness *
   and judge the peoples with equity.

9 You will be a refuge for the oppressed, *
   a refuge in time of trouble.

10 Those who know your Name will put their trust in you, *
   for you never forsake those who seek you, O God.

11 Sing praise to the Holy One who dwells in Zion; *
   proclaim to the peoples the things God has done.

12 The Avenger of blood will remember them *
   and will not forget the cry of the afflicted.

13 Have pity on me, O God; *
    see the misery I suffer from those who hate me,
    O you who lift me up from the gate of death,

14 So that I may tell of all your praises
    and rejoice in your salvation *
    in the gates of the city of Zion.

15 The ungodly have fallen into the pit they dug, *
    and in the snare they set is their own foot caught.

16 You are known, O God, by your acts of justice; *
    the wicked are trapped in the works of their own hands.

17 The wicked shall be given over to the grave *
    and also all the peoples that forget God.

18 For the needy shall not always be forgotten, *
    and the hope of the poor shall not perish for ever.

19 Rise up, O God; let not the ungodly have the upper hand; *
    let them be judged before you.

20 Put fear upon them, O God; *
    let the ungodly know they are but mortal.

PSALM 10

1 Why do you stand so far off, O God, *
    and hide yourself in time of trouble?

2 The wicked arrogantly persecute the poor, *
    but they are trapped in the schemes they have devised.

3 The wicked boast of their heart's desire; *
    the covetous curse and revile God.

4 The wicked are so proud that they care not for God; *
    their only thought is, "God does not matter."

5 Their ways are devious at all times;
    your judgments are far above out of their sight; *
    they defy all their enemies.

6 They say in their heart, "I shall not be shaken; *
    no harm shall happen to me ever."

7 Their mouth is full of cursing, deceit, and oppression; *
    under their tongue are mischief and wrong.

8 They lurk in ambush in public squares,
    and in secret places they murder the innocent; *
        they spy out the helpless.

9 They lie in wait, like a lion in a covert;
    they lie in wait to seize upon the lowly; *
        they seize the lowly and drag them away in their net.

10 The innocent are broken and humbled before them; *
    the helpless fall before their power.

11 They say in their heart, "God has forgotten; *
    God has looked away and will never notice."

12 Rise up, O Holy One;
    lift up your hand, O God; *
        do not forget the afflicted.

13 Why should the wicked revile God; *
    why should they say in their heart, "You do not care"?

14 Surely, you behold trouble and misery; *
    you see it and take it into your own hand.

15 The helpless commit themselves to you, *
    for you are the helper of orphans.

16 Break the power of the wicked and evil; *
    search out their wickedness until you find none.

17 God is sovereign for ever and ever; *
    the ungodly shall perish from the land.

18 God will hear the desire of the humble; *
    you will strengthen their heart and your ears shall hear,

19 To give justice to the orphan and oppressed, *
    so that mere mortals may strike terror no more.

PSALM 11

1 In God have I taken refuge; *
    how then can you say to me,
        "Fly away like a bird to the hilltop,

2 For see how the wicked bend the bow
    and fit their arrows to the string, *
        to shoot from ambush at the true of heart.

3 When the foundations are being destroyed, *
    what can the righteous do?"

4 You, O God, are in your holy temple; *
    your throne is in heaven.

5 Your eyes behold the inhabited world; *
    your piercing eye weighs our worth.

6 You weigh the righteous as well as the wicked, *
    but those who delight in violence you abhor.

7 Upon the wicked you shall rain coals of fire
      and burning sulfur; *
    a scorching wind shall be their lot.

8 For you are righteous;
    you delight in righteous deeds, *
    and the just shall see your face.

Second Day: Evening Prayer

PSALM 12

1 Help me, O God, for there is no godly one left; *
    the faithful have vanished from among us.

2 They all speak falsely with their neighbors; *
    with a smooth tongue they speak from a double heart.

3 Oh, that God would cut off all smooth tongues *
    and close the lips that utter proud boasts!

4 Those who say, "With our tongue will we prevail; *
    our lips are our own; who is ruler over us?"

5 "Because the needy are oppressed,
    and the poor cry out in misery, *
      I will rise up," says God,
      "and give them the help they long for."

6 The words of God are pure words, *
    like silver refined from ore
    and purified seven times in the fire.

7 O God, watch over us *
    and save us from this generation for ever.

8 The wicked prowl on every side, *
 and that which is worthless is highly prized by everyone.

Psalm 13

1 How long, O God?
 Will you forget me for ever; *
 how long will you hide your face from me?

2 How long shall I have perplexity in my mind
 and grief in my heart, day after day; *
 how long shall my enemy triumph over me?

3 Look upon me and answer me, O God, my God; *
 give light to my eyes, lest I sleep in death;

4 Lest my enemies say they have prevailed over me, *
 and my foes rejoice that I have fallen.

5 But I put my trust in your mercy; *
 my heart is joyful because of your saving help.

6 I will sing to the Holy One, who has dealt with me richly; *
 I will praise the Name of God Most High.

Psalm 14

1 The foolish have said in their hearts, "There is no God." *
 All are corrupt and commit abominable acts;
 there is none who does any good.

2 The Holy One looks down from heaven upon us all, *
 to see if there is any who is wise,
 if there is one who seeks after God.

3 Every one has proved faithless;
 all alike have turned bad; *
 there is none who does good; no, not one.

4 Have they no knowledge, all those evildoers *
 who eat up my people like bread
 and do not call upon God?

5 See how they tremble with fear, *
 because God is in the company of the righteous.

6 Their aim is to confound the plans of the afflicted, *
 but God is their refuge.

7 Oh, that Israel's deliverance would come out of Zion! *
   When God restores the fortunes of the people,
   Jacob will rejoice and Israel be glad.

Third Day: Morning Prayer

PSALM 15

1 O God, who may dwell in your tabernacle; *
   who may abide upon your holy hill?

2 Those who lead blameless lives and do what is right, *
   who speak truthfully from the heart.

3 There is no guile upon their tongues;
   they do no evil to their friends; *
      they do not heap contempt upon their neighbors;

4 In their sight the wicked are rejected, *
   but they honor those who fear God.

5 They have sworn to do no wrong *
   and do not take back their word.

6 They do not give their money in hope of gain, *
   nor do they take a bribe against the innocent.

7 Whoever does these things *
   shall never be overthrown.

PSALM 16

1 Protect me, O God, for I take refuge in you; *
   I have said to the Holy One, "You are my God,
   my good above all other."

2 All my delight is upon the godly that are in the land, *
   upon those who are noble among the people.

3 But those who run after other gods *
   shall have their troubles multiplied.

4 Their libations of blood I will not offer, *
   nor take the names of their gods upon my lips.

5 O God, you are my portion and my cup; *
   it is you who uphold my lot.

6 My boundaries enclose a pleasant land; *
   indeed, I have a goodly heritage.

7 I will bless you, O God who gives me counsel; *
   my heart teaches me, night after night.

8 I have set you always before me; *
   because you are at my right hand I shall not fall.

9 My heart, therefore, is glad and my spirit rejoices; *
   my body also shall rest in hope.

10 For you will not abandon me to the grave, *
   nor let your holy one see the Pit.

11 You will show me the path of life; *
   in your presence there is fullness of joy,
   and in your right hand are pleasures for evermore.

Psalm 17

1 Hear my plea of innocence, O God;
   give heed to my cry; *
   listen to my prayer, which does not come from lying lips.

2 Let my vindication come forth from your presence; *
   let your eyes be fixed on justice.

3 Weigh my heart, summon me by night, *
   melt me down; you will find no impurity in me.

4 I give no offense with my mouth as others do; *
   I have heeded the words of your lips.

5 My footsteps hold fast to the ways of your law; *
   in your paths my feet shall not stumble.

6 I call upon you, O God, for you will answer me; *
   incline your ear to me and hear my words.

7 Show me your marvelous loving-kindness, *
   O Savior of those who take refuge at your right hand
   from those who rise up against them.

8 Keep me as the apple of your eye; *
   hide me under the shadow of your wings,

9 From the wicked who assault me, *
   from my deadly enemies who surround me.

10 They have closed their heart to pity, *
   and their mouth speaks proud things.

11 They press me hard,
   now they surround me, *
   watching how they may cast me to the ground,

12 Like a lion, greedy for its prey, *
   and like a young lion lurking in secret places.

13 Arise, O God; confront them and bring them down; *
   deliver me from the wicked by your sword.

14 Deliver me, O God, by your hand, *
   from those whose portion in life is this world;

15 Whose bellies you fill with your treasure; *
   who are well supplied with children
   and leave their wealth to their little ones.

16 But at my vindication I shall see your face; *
   when I awake, I shall be satisfied, beholding your likeness.

Third Day: Evening Prayer

PSALM 18

PART I

1 I love you, O God, my strength, *
   my stronghold, my crag, and my haven,

2 My God, my rock in whom I put my trust, *
   my shield, the horn of my salvation, and my refuge;
   you are worthy of praise.

3 I will call upon you, O God, *
   and so shall I be saved from my enemies.

4 The breakers of death rolled over me, *
   and the torrents of oblivion made me afraid.

5 The cords of hell entangled me, *
   and the snares of death were set for me.

6 I called upon you, O God, in my distress; *
   I cried out to you for help.

7 You heard my voice from your heavenly dwelling; *
   my cry of anguish came to your ears.

8 The earth reeled and rocked; *
   the roots of the mountains shook;
   they reeled because of your anger.

9 Smoke rose from your nostrils
   and a consuming fire out of your mouth; *
   hot burning coals blazed forth from you.

10 You parted the heavens and came down *
   with a storm cloud under your feet.

11 You mounted on cherubim and flew; *
   you swooped on the wings of the wind.

12 You wrapped darkness about you; *
   you made dark waters and thick clouds your pavilion.

13 From the brightness of your presence, through the clouds, *
   burst hailstones and coals of fire.

14 O God, you thundered out of heaven; *
   O Most High, you uttered your voice.

15 You loosed your arrows and scattered them; *
   you hurled thunderbolts and routed them.

16 The beds of the seas were uncovered,
   and the foundations of the world laid bare, *
   at your battle cry, O God,
   at the blast of the breath of your nostrils.

17 You reached down from on high and grasped me; *
   you drew me out of great waters.

18 You delivered me from my strong enemies
   and from those who hated me, *
   for they were too mighty for me.

19 They confronted me in the day of my disaster, *
   but you were my support.

20 You brought me out into an open place; *
   you rescued me because you delighted in me.

PSALM 18: PART II

21 You rewarded me because of my righteous dealing; *
    because my hands were clean you rewarded me;

22 For I have kept your ways, O God, *
    and have not offended against you;

23 For all your judgments are before my eyes, *
    and your decrees I have not put away from me;

24 For I have been blameless with you *
    and have kept myself from iniquity;

25 Therefore you rewarded me according to my
        righteous dealing, *
    because of the cleanness of my hands in your sight.

26 With the faithful you show yourself faithful, O God; *
    with the forthright you show yourself forthright.

27 With the pure you show yourself pure, *
    but with the crooked you are wily.

28 You will save a lowly people, *
    but you will humble the haughty eyes.

29 You, O God, are my lamp; *
    my God, you make my darkness bright.

30 With you I will break down an enclosure; *
    with the help of my God I will scale any wall.

31 O God, your ways are perfect;
    your words are tried in the fire; *
    you are a shield to all who trust in you.

32 For who is God but you, O Holy One; *
    who is the Rock, except you, our God?

33 It is you who gird me about with strength *
    and make my way secure.

34 You make me sure-footed like a deer *
    and let me stand firm on the heights.

35 You train my hands for battle *
    and my arms for bending even a bow of bronze.

36 You have given me your shield of victory; *
    your right hand also sustains me;
    your loving care makes me great.

37 You lengthen my stride beneath me, *
 and my ankles do not give way.

38 I pursue my enemies and overtake them; *
 I will not turn back till I have destroyed them.

39 I strike them down, and they cannot rise; *
 they fall defeated at my feet.

40 You have girded me with strength for the battle; *
 you have cast down my adversaries beneath me;
 you have put my enemies to flight.

41 I destroy those who hate me;
 they cry out, but there is none to help them; *
 they cry to you, O God, but you do not answer.

42 I beat them small like dust before the wind; *
 I trample them like mud in the streets.

43 You deliver me from the strife of the peoples; *
 you put me at the head of the nations.

44 A people I have not known shall serve me;
 no sooner shall they hear than they shall obey me; *
 strangers will cringe before me.

45 The foreign peoples will lose heart; *
 they shall come trembling out of their strongholds.

46 You live, O God! You, my Rock, are blest; *
 exalted are you, O God of my salvation!

47 You are the one who gave me victory *
 and cast down the peoples beneath me.

48 You rescued me from the fury of my enemies;
 you exalted me above those who rose against me; *
 you saved me from my deadly foe.

49 Therefore will I extol you among the nations, O God, *
 and sing praises to your Name.

50 You multiply the victories of your king; *
 you show loving-kindness to your anointed,
 to David and his descendants for ever.

PSALM 19

1 The heavens declare your glory, O God, *
   and the firmament shows your handiwork.

2 One day tells its tale to another, *
   and one night imparts knowledge to another.

3 Although they have no words or language, *
   and their voices are not heard,

4 Their sound has gone out into all lands, *
   and their message to the ends of the world.

5 In the deep you have set a pavilion for the sun; *
   it comes forth like a bridegroom out of his chamber;
   it rejoices like a champion to run its course.

6 It goes forth from the uttermost edge of the heavens
   and runs about to the end of it again; *
   nothing is hidden from its burning heat.

7 Your law, O God, is perfect and revives the soul; *
   your testimony is sure and gives wisdom to the innocent.

8 Your statutes are just and rejoice the heart; *
   your commandment is clear and gives light to the eyes.

9 The fear of you is clean and endures for ever; *
   your judgments are true and righteous altogether.

10 More to be desired are they than gold,
      more than much fine gold; *
   sweeter far than honey, than honey in the comb.

11 By them also is your servant enlightened, *
   and in keeping them there is great reward.

12 Who can tell how often one offends? *
   Cleanse me from my secret faults.

13 Above all, keep your servant from presumptuous sins;
   let them not get dominion over me; *
    then shall I be whole and sound,
    and innocent of a great offense.

14 Let the words of my mouth and the meditation of my
         heart be acceptable in your sight, *
  O God, my strength and my redeemer.

Psalm 20

1 May the Most High answer you in the day of trouble, *
  the Name of the God of Jacob defend you;

2 Send you help from the holy place *
  and strengthen you out of Zion;

3 Remember all your offerings *
  and accept your burnt sacrifice;

4 Grant you your heart's desire *
  and prosper all your plans.

5 We will shout for joy at your victory
  and triumph in the Name of our God; *
  may the Most High grant all your requests.

6 Now I know that God gives victory to the anointed one; *
  out of the holy heaven God will answer,
  with a strong and victorious right hand.

7 Some put their trust in chariots and some in horses, *
  but we will call upon the Name of our God.

8 They collapse and fall down, *
  but we will arise and stand upright.

9 O God, give victory to our sovereign, *
  and answer us when we call.

Psalm 21

1 The king rejoices in your strength, O God; *
  how greatly he exults in your victory!

2 You have given him his heart's desire; *
  you have not denied him the request of his lips,

3 For you meet him with blessings of prosperity *
  and set a crown of fine gold upon his head.

4 He asked you for life, and you gave it to him: *
  length of days, for ever and ever.

5 His honor is great, because of your victory; *
  splendor and majesty have you bestowed upon him.

6 For you will give him everlasting felicity *
  and will make him glad with the joy of your presence.

7 For the king puts his trust in God; *
  because of the loving-kindness of the Most High,
      he will not fall.

8 Your hand will lay hold upon all your enemies; *
  your right hand will seize all those who hate you.

9 You will make them like a fiery furnace *
  at the time of your appearing, O God.

10 You will swallow them up in your wrath, *
   and fire shall consume them.

11 You will destroy their offspring from the land *
   and their descendants from among the peoples of the earth.

12 Though they intend evil against you
   and devise wicked schemes, *
       yet they shall not prevail.

13 For you will put them to flight *
   and aim your arrows at them.

14 Be exalted, O God, in your might; *
   we will sing and praise your power.

Fourth Day: Evening Prayer

PSALM 22

1 My God, my God, why have you forsaken me, *
  and are so far from my cry
  and from the words of my distress?

2 O my God, I cry in the daytime, but you do not answer; *
  by night as well, but I find no rest.

3 Yet you are the Holy One, *
  enthroned upon the praises of Israel.

4 Our forebears put their trust in you; *
  they trusted, and you delivered them.

5 They cried out to you and were delivered; *
    they trusted in you and were not put to shame.

6 But as for me, I am a worm, and less than human, *
    scorned by all and despised by the people.

7 All who see me laugh me to scorn; *
    they curl their lips and wag their heads, saying,

8 "You trusted in God for deliverance; *
    let God rescue you, if God delights in you."

9 Yet you, O God, are the one who took me out of the womb *
    and kept me safe upon my mother's breast.

10 I have been entrusted to you ever since I was born; *
    you were my God when I was still in my mother's womb.

11 Be not far from me, for trouble is near, *
    and there is none to help.

12 Many young bulls encircle me; *
    strong bulls of Bashan surround me.

13 They open wide their jaws at me, *
    like a ravening and a roaring lion.

14 I am poured out like water;
    all my bones are out of joint; *
    my heart within my breast is melting wax.

15 My mouth is dried out like a pot-sherd;
    my tongue sticks to the roof of my mouth, *
    and you have laid me in the dust of the grave.

16 Packs of dogs close me in,
    and gangs of evildoers circle around me; *
    they pierce my hands and my feet;
    I can count all my bones.

17 They stare and gloat over me; *
    they divide my garments among them;
    they cast lots for my clothing.

18 Be not far away, O God; *
    you are my strength; hasten to help me.

19 Save me from the sword, *
    my life from the power of the dog.

20 Save me from the lion's mouth, *
  my wretched body from the horns of wild bulls.

21 I will declare your Name to my people; *
  In the midst of the congregation I will praise you.

22 May all who fear you, O God, give praise; *
  may the offspring of Israel stand in awe
  and all of Jacob's line give glory.

23 For you do not despise nor abhor the poor in their poverty,
  neither do you hide your face from them, *
  but when they cry to you, you hear them.

24 My praise is of you in the great assembly; *
  I will perform my vows in the presence of those who
      worship you.

25 The poor shall eat and be satisfied,
  and those who seek you shall praise you: *
  "May your heart live for ever!"

26 All the ends of the earth shall remember and turn to you, *
  and all the families of the nations shall bow before you.

27 For yours is the royal power, O God; *
  you rule over the nations.

28 To you alone all who sleep in the earth bow down
      in worship; *
  all who go down to the dust fall before you.

29 My soul shall live for you;
  my descendants shall serve you; *
  they shall be known as yours for ever.

30 They shall come and make known to a people yet unborn *
  the saving deeds that you have done.

PSALM 23

1 O God, you are my shepherd; *
  I shall not be in want.

2 You make me lie down in green pastures *
  and lead me beside still waters.

3 You revive my soul *
    and guide me along right pathways
        for the sake of your Name.

4 Though I walk through the valley of the shadow of death,
    I shall fear no evil, *
        for you are with me;
        your rod and your staff, they comfort me.

5 You spread a table before me in the presence of those
        who trouble me; *
    you have anointed my head with oil,
    and my cup is running over.

6 Surely your goodness and mercy shall follow me
        all the days of my life, *
    and I will dwell in the house of God for ever.

Fifth Day: Morning Prayer

PSALM 24

1 The earth is God's and all that is in it, *
    the world and all who dwell therein.

2 For it is God who founded it upon the seas *
    and made it firm upon the rivers of the deep.

3 "Who can ascend the hill of the Most High, *
    and who can stand in God's holy place?"

4 "Those who have clean hands and a pure heart, *
    who have not pledged themselves to falsehood
    nor sworn by what is a fraud.

5 They shall receive a blessing from the Holy One *
    and a just reward from the God of their salvation."

6 Such is the generation of those who seek God, *
    of those who seek your face, O God of Jacob.

7 Lift up your heads, O gates;
    lift them high, O everlasting doors, *
    and the One who reigns in glory shall come in.

8 "Who is this who reigns in glory?" *
    "The Holy One, strong and mighty,
    the Holy One, mighty in battle."

9 Lift up your heads, O gates;
   lift them high, O everlasting doors, *
      and the One who reigns in glory shall come in.

10 "Who is this who reigns in glory?" *
   "This is God, the God of hosts,
      who reigns in glory."

PSALM 25

1 To you, O God, I lift up my soul;
   my God, I put my trust in you; *
      let me not be humiliated,
      nor let my enemies triumph over me.

2 Let none who look to you be put to shame; *
   let the treacherous be disappointed in their schemes.

3 Show me your ways, O God, *
   and teach me your paths.

4 Lead me in your truth and teach me, *
   for you are the God of my salvation;
      in you have I trusted all the day long.

5 Remember, O God, your compassion and love, *
   for they are from everlasting.

6 Remember not the sins of my youth and my transgressions; *
   remember me according to your love
      and for the sake of your goodness, O God.

7 Gracious and upright are you; *
   therefore you teach sinners in your way.

8 You guide the humble in doing right *
   and teach your way to the lowly.

9 All your paths are love and faithfulness *
   to those who keep your covenant and your testimonies.

10 For your Name's sake, O God, *
   forgive my sin, for it is great.

11 Who are they who fear you? *
   You will teach them the way that they should choose.

12 They shall dwell in prosperity, *
   and their offspring shall inherit the land.

13 You are a friend to those who fear you *
   and will show them your covenant.

14 My eyes are ever looking to you, *
   for you shall pluck my feet out of the net.

15 Turn to me and have pity on me, *
   for I am left alone and in misery.

16 The sorrows of my heart have increased; *
   bring me out of my troubles.

17 Look upon my adversity and misery, *
   and forgive me all my sin.

18 Look upon my enemies, for they are many, *
   and they bear a violent hatred against me.

19 Protect my life and deliver me; *
   let me not be put to shame, for I have trusted in you.

20 Let integrity and uprightness preserve me, *
   for my hope has been in you.

21 Deliver the people of Israel, O God, *
   out of all their troubles.

PSALM 26

1 Give judgment for me, O God,
   for I have lived with integrity; *
      I have trusted in you and have not faltered.

2 Test me, O God, and try me; *
   examine my heart and my mind.

3 For your love is before my eyes; *
   I have walked faithfully with you.

4 I have not sat with the worthless, *
   nor do I consort with the deceitful.

5 I have hated the company of evildoers; *
   I will not sit down with the wicked.

6 I will wash my hands in innocence, O God, *
   that I may go in procession round your altar,

7 Singing aloud a song of thanksgiving *
   and recounting all your wonderful deeds.

8 O God, I love the house in which you dwell *
   and the place where your glory abides.

9 Do not sweep me away with sinners *
   nor my life with those who thirst for blood,

10 Whose hands are full of evil plots *
   and their right hand full of bribes.

11 As for me, I will live with integrity; *
   redeem me, O God, and have pity on me.

12 My foot stands on level ground; *
   in the full assembly I will bless you, O God.

Fifth Day: Evening Prayer

Psalm 27

1 God is my light and my salvation;
   whom then shall I fear? *
      God is the strength of my life;
      of whom then shall I be afraid?

2 When evildoers came upon me to eat up my flesh, *
   it was they, my foes and my adversaries,
      who stumbled and fell.

3 Though an army should encamp against me, *
   yet my heart shall not be afraid;

4 And though war should rise up against me, *
   yet will I put my trust in God.

5 One thing have I asked of you, O God;
   one thing I seek: *
      that I may dwell in your house all the days of my life,

6 To behold your fair beauty, O God, *
   and to seek you in your temple.

7 For in the day of trouble you shall keep
      me safe in your shelter; *
   you shall hide me in the secrecy of your dwelling
   and set me high upon a rock.

8 Even now you lift up my head *
   above my enemies round about me.

9 Therefore I will offer in your dwelling an oblation
with sounds of great gladness; *
    I will sing and make music to you.

10 Hearken to my voice, O Most High, when I call; *
    have mercy on me and answer me.

11 You speak in my heart and say, "Seek my face." *
    Your face, O God, will I seek.

12 Hide not your face from me, *
    nor turn away your servant in displeasure.

13 You have been my helper;
cast me not away; *
    do not forsake me, O God of my salvation.

14 Though my father and my mother forsake me, *
    you will sustain me.

15 Show me your way, O God; *
    lead me on a level path, because of my enemies.

16 Deliver me not into the hand of my adversaries, *
    for false witnesses have risen up against me
    and also those who speak malice.

17 What if I had not believed
that I should see the goodness of my God *
    in the land of the living!

18 O tarry and await God's pleasure;
be strong, and let your heart take comfort; *
    wait patiently for God.

PSALM 28

1 O God, I call to you;
my Rock, do not be deaf to my cry; *
    lest, if you do not hear me,
    I become like those who go down to the Pit.

2 Hear the voice of my prayer when I cry out to you, *
    when I lift up my hands to your holy of holies.

3 Do not snatch me away with the wicked or with
            the evildoers, *
    who speak peaceably with their neighbors,
    while strife is in their hearts.

4 Repay them according to their deeds, *
　　and according to the wickedness of their actions.

5 According to the work of their hands repay them, *
　　and give them their just deserts.

6 They have no understanding of your doings
　nor of the works of your hands; *
　　therefore you will break them down and
　　　　not build them up.

7 Blest are you, O God, *
　　for you have heard the voice of my prayer.

8 You are my strength and my shield; *
　　my heart trusts in you, and I have been helped;

9 Therefore my heart dances for joy, *
　　and in my song will I praise you.

10 You are the strength of your people, *
　　a safe refuge for your anointed.

11 Save your people and bless your inheritance; *
　　shepherd them and carry them for ever.

PSALM 29

1 Ascribe to God, you heavenly beings, *
　　ascribe to God glory and strength.

2 Ascribe due honor to God's holy Name; *
　　worship the Most High in the beauty of holiness.

3 The voice of God is upon the waters;
　the God of glory thunders; *
　　God is upon the mighty waters.

4 The voice of God is a powerful voice; *
　　the voice of God is a voice of splendor.

5 The voice of God breaks the cedar trees; *
　　God breaks the cedars of Lebanon;

6 God makes Lebanon skip like a calf *
　　and Mount Hermon like a young wild ox.

7 The voice of God splits the flames of fire;
　the voice of God shakes the wilderness; *
　　God shakes the wilderness of Kadesh.

8 The voice of God makes the oak trees writhe *
   and strips the forests bare.

9 And in the temple of the Holy One, *
   all are crying, "Glory!"

10 God sits enthroned above the flood, *
   enthroned as Sovereign for evermore.

11 God shall give strength to the people; *
   God shall give the people the blessing of peace.

Sixth Day: Morning Prayer

Psalm 30

1 I will exalt you, O God,
   because you have lifted me up *
      and have not let my enemies triumph over me.

2 O my God, I cried out to you, *
   and you restored me to health.

3 You brought me up, O God, from the dead; *
   you restored my life as I was going down to the grave.

4 Sing to God, you servants of God, *
   and give thanks for the remembrance of God's holiness.

5 For divine wrath endures but the twinkling of an eye, *
   divine favor for a lifetime.

6 Weeping may spend the night, *
   but joy comes in the morning.

7 While I felt secure, I said,
   "I shall never be disturbed. *
      You, O God, with your favor, made me as strong as
         the mountains."

8 Then you hid your face, *
   and I was filled with fear.

9 I cried to you, O God; *
   I pleaded with you, saying,

10 "What profit is there in my blood, if I go down to the Pit; *
   will the dust praise you or declare your faithfulness?

11 Hear, O God, and have mercy upon me; *
    O God, be my helper."

12 You have turned my wailing into dancing; *
    you have put off my sack-cloth and clothed me with joy.

13 Therefore my heart sings to you without ceasing; *
    O God, my God, I will give you thanks for ever.

PSALM 31

1 In you, O God, have I taken refuge;
    let me never be put to shame; *
        deliver me in your righteousness.

2 Incline your ear to me; *
    make haste to deliver me.

3 Be my strong rock, a castle to keep me safe,
    for you are my crag and my stronghold; *
        for the sake of your Name, lead me and guide me.

4 Take me out of the net that they have secretly set for me, *
    for you are my tower of strength.

5 Into your hands I commend my spirit, *
    for you have redeemed me, O God of truth.

6 I hate those who cling to worthless idols, *
    and I put my trust in God.

7 I will rejoice and be glad because of your mercy, *
    for you have seen my affliction;
        you know my distress.

8 You have not shut me up in the power of the enemy; *
    you have set my feet in an open place.

9 Have mercy on me, O God, for I am in trouble; *
    my eye is consumed with sorrow,
        and also my throat and my belly.

10 For my life is wasted with grief
    and my years with sighing; *
        my strength fails me because of affliction,
        and my bones are consumed.

11 I have become a reproach to all my enemies and
                even to my neighbors,
   a dismay to those of my acquaintance; *
      when they see me in the street they avoid me.

12 I am forgotten like the dead, out of mind; *
   I am as useless as a broken pot.

13 For I have heard the whispering of the crowd;
   fear is all around; *
      they put their heads together against me;
      they plot to take my life.

14 But as for me, I have trusted in you, O God. *
   I have said, "You are my God.

15 My times are in your hand; *
   rescue me from the hand of my enemies
   and from those who persecute me.

16 Make your face to shine upon your servant, *
   and in your loving-kindness, save me."

17 O God, let me not be ashamed for having called upon you; *
   rather, let the wicked be put to shame;
   let them be silent in the grave.

18 Let the lying lips be silenced which speak against
            the righteous, *
   haughtily, disdainfully, and with contempt.

19 How great is your goodness, O God,
   which you have laid up for those who fear you, *
      which you have done in the sight of all
      for those who put their trust in you.

20 You hide them in the covert of your presence from those
            who slander them; *
   you keep them in your shelter from the strife of tongues.

21 Blessed be God! *
   For you have shown me the wonders of your love
      in a city under siege.

22 Yet I said in my alarm,
   "I have been cut off from the sight of your eyes." *
      Nevertheless, you heard the sound of my entreaty
      when I cried out to you.

23 Love God, all you who worship God; *
   God protects the faithful,
   but repays to the full those who act haughtily.

24 Be strong and let your heart take courage, *
   all you who wait for God.

Sixth Day: Evening Prayer

Psalm 32

1 Happy are they whose transgressions are forgiven *
   and whose sin is put away!

2 Happy are they to whom God imputes no guilt *
   and in whose spirit there is no guile!

3 While I held my tongue, my bones withered away, *
   because of my groaning all day long.

4 For your hand was heavy upon me day and night; *
   my moisture was dried up as in the heat of summer.

5 Then I acknowledged my sin to you *
   and did not conceal my guilt.

6 I said, "I will confess my transgressions to God." *
   Then you forgave me the guilt of my sin.

7 Therefore all the faithful will make their prayers to you
            in time of trouble; *
   when the great waters overflow, they shall not reach them.

8 You are my hiding-place;
   you preserve me from trouble; *
   you surround me with shouts of deliverance.

9 "I will instruct you and teach you in the way that you
            should go; *
   I will guide you with my eye.

10 Do not be like horse or mule, which have
            no understanding, *
   who must be fitted with bit and bridle,
   or else they will not stay near you."

11 Great are the tribulations of the wicked, *
   but mercy embraces those who trust in the Most High.

12 Be glad, you righteous, and rejoice in God; *
   shout for joy, all who are true of heart.

Psalm 33

1 Rejoice in God, you righteous; *
   it is good for the just to sing praises.

2 Praise God with the harp; *
   play upon the psaltery and lyre.

3 Sing for God a new song; *
   sound a fanfare with all your skill upon the trumpet.

4 For your word, O God, is right, *
   and all your works are sure.

5 You love righteousness and justice; *
   your loving-kindness fills the whole earth.

6 By your word, O God, were the heavens made, *
   by the breath of your mouth all the heavenly hosts.

7 You gather up the waters of the ocean as in a water-skin *
   and store up the depths of the sea.

8 Let all the earth fear you; *
   let all who dwell in the world stand in awe of you.

9 For you spoke, and it came to pass; *
   you commanded, and it stood fast.

10 You bring the will of the nations to naught *
   and thwart the designs of the peoples.

11 But your will stands fast for ever, *
   and the designs of your heart from age to age.

12 Happy is the nation that worships you, O Most High; *
   happy the people you have chosen to be your own!

13 You look down from heaven *
   and behold all the people in the world.

14 From where you sit enthroned you turn your gaze *
   on all who dwell on the earth.

15 You fashion all the hearts of them *
   and understand all their works.

16 There is no ruler that can be saved by a mighty army; *
　　the strong are not delivered by their great strength.

17 The horse is a vain hope for deliverance; *
　　for all its strength it cannot save.

18 But your eye, O God, is upon those who fear you, *
　　on those who wait upon your love,

19 To pluck their lives from death *
　　and to feed them in time of famine.

20 Our soul waits for you; *
　　you are our help and our shield.

21 Indeed, our heart rejoices in you, *
　　for in your holy Name we put our trust.

22 Let your loving-kindness, O God, be upon us, *
　　as we have put our trust in you.

PSALM 34

1 I will bless God at all times, *
　　and praise shall ever be in my mouth.

2 I will glory in the Most High; *
　　let the humble hear and rejoice.

3 Proclaim with me the greatness of God; *
　　let us exalt God's Name together.

4 I sought, and God answered me *
　　and delivered me out of all my terror.

5 Look upon the Most High and be radiant, *
　　and let not your faces be ashamed.

6 I called in my affliction, and God heard me *
　　and saved me from all my troubles.

7 The angels encompass those who fear God, *
　　and God will deliver them.

8 Taste and see that God is good; *
　　happy are they who trust in the Most High!

9 Fear the Most High, you that are God's saints, *
　　for those who fear God lack nothing.

10 The young lions lack and suffer hunger, *
 but those who seek God lack nothing that is good.

11 Come, children, and listen to me; *
 I will teach you the fear of God.

12 Who among you loves life *
 and desires long life to enjoy prosperity?

13 Keep your tongue from evil-speaking *
 and your lips from lying words.

14 Turn from evil and do good; *
 seek peace and pursue it.

15 The eyes of God are upon the righteous, *
 and the ears of God are open to their cry.

16 The face of God is against those who do evil, *
 to root out the remembrance of them from the earth.

17 The righteous cry, and God hears them *
 and delivers them from all their troubles.

18 God is near to the brokenhearted *
 and will save those whose spirits are crushed.

19 Many are the troubles of the righteous, *
 but God will deliver them out of them all.

20 God will keep safe all their bones; *
 not one of them shall be broken.

21 Evil shall slay the wicked, *
 and those who hate the righteous will be punished.

22 O God, you will ransom the life of your servants, *
 and none will be punished who trust in you.

Seventh Day: Morning Prayer

Psalm 35

1 Fight those who fight me, O God; *
 attack those who are attacking me.

2 Take up shield and armor, *
 and rise up to help me.

3 Draw the sword and bar the way against those
   who pursue me; *
   say to my soul, "I am your salvation."

4 Let those who seek after my life be shamed and humbled; *
   let those who plot my ruin fall back and be dismayed.

5 Let them be like chaff before the wind, *
   and let the angel of God drive them away.

6 Let their way be dark and slippery, *
   and let the angel of God pursue them.

7 For they have secretly spread a net for me without a cause; *
   without a cause they have dug a pit to take me alive.

8 Let ruin come upon them unawares; *
   let them be caught in the net they hid;
   let them fall into the pit they dug.

9 Then I will be joyful in you, O Most High; *
   I will glory in your victory.

10 My very bones will say, "O God, who is like you? *
   You deliver the poor from those who are too strong
       for them,
   the poor and needy from those who rob them."

11 Malicious witnesses rise up against me; *
   they charge me with matters I know nothing about.

12 They pay me evil in exchange for good; *
   my soul is full of despair.

13 But when they were sick I dressed in sack-cloth *
   and humbled myself by fasting;

14 I prayed with my whole heart,
   as one would for a friend or a neighbor; *
   I behaved like those who mourn for their mothers,
   bowed down and grieving.

15 But when I stumbled, they were glad and gathered together;
   they gathered against me; *
   strangers whom I did not know tore me to pieces and
       would not stop.

16 They put me to the test and mocked me; *
   they gnashed at me with their teeth.

17 O God, how long will you look on? *
  Rescue me from the roaring beasts,
  and my life from the young lions.

18 I will give you thanks in the great congregation; *
  I will praise you in the mighty throng.

19 Do not let my treacherous foes rejoice over me, *
  nor let those who hate me without a cause
        wink at each other.

20 For they do not plan for peace, *
  but invent deceitful schemes against the quiet in the land.

21 They opened their mouths at me and said, *
  "Aha! we saw it with our own eyes."

22 You saw it, O God; do not be silent; *
  O God, be not far from me.

23 Awake, arise, to my cause; *
  to my defense, my God and my Savior!

24 Give me justice, O my God,
  according to your righteousness; *
  do not let them triumph over me.

25 Do not let them say in their hearts,
  "Aha! just what we want!" *
  Do not let them say, "We have swallowed you up."

26 Let all who rejoice at my ruin be ashamed and disgraced; *
  let those who boast against me be clothed with
        dismay and shame.

27 Let those who favor my cause sing out with joy and be glad; *
  let them say always, "Great are you, O God,
  you desire the prosperity of your servant."

28 And my tongue shall be talking of your righteousness *
  and of your praise all the day long.

Psalm 36

1 There is a voice of rebellion deep in the heart of the wicked; *
  there is no fear of God before their eyes.

2 They flatter themselves in their own eyes *
  that their hateful sin will not be found out.

3 The words of their mouths are wicked and deceitful; *
   they have left off acting wisely and doing good.

4 They think up wickedness upon their beds
   and have set themselves in no good way; *
   they do not abhor that which is evil.

5 Your love, O God, reaches to the heavens, *
   and your faithfulness to the clouds.

6 Your righteousness is like the strong mountains,
   your justice like the great deep; *
   you save all your creatures, O God.

7 How priceless is your love, O God; *
   your people take refuge under the shadow of your wings.

8 They feast upon the abundance of your house; *
   you give them drink from the river of your delights.

9 For with you is the well of life, *
   and in your light we see light.

10 Continue your loving-kindness to those who know you, *
   and your favor to those who are true of heart.

11 Let not the foot of the proud come near me, *
   nor the hand of the wicked push me aside.

12 See how they are fallen, those who work wickedness; *
   they are cast down and shall not be able to rise.

Seventh Day: Evening Prayer

PSALM 37

PART I

1 Do not fret yourself because of evildoers; *
   do not be jealous of those who do wrong.

2 For they shall soon wither like the grass, *
   and like the green grass fade away.

3 Put your trust in God and do good; *
   dwell in the land and feed on its riches.

4 Take delight in God, *
   who shall give you your heart's desire.

5 Commit your way to God and put your trust in God, *
   who will bring it to pass.

6 God will make your righteousness as clear as the light *
   and your just dealing as the noonday.

7 Be still before God; *
   for God wait patiently.

8 Do not fret yourself over the one who prospers, *
   the one who succeeds in evil schemes.

9 Refrain from anger, leave rage alone; *
   do not fret yourself, it leads only to evil.

10 For evildoers shall be cut off, *
   but those who wait upon God shall possess the land.

11 In a little while the wicked shall be no more; *
   you shall search out their place, but they will not be there.

12 But the lowly shall possess the land; *
   they will delight in abundance of peace.

13 The wicked plot against the righteous *
   and gnash at them with their teeth.

14 God laughs at the wicked, *
   seeing that their day will come.

15 The wicked draw their sword and bend their bow
   to strike down the poor and needy, *
   to slaughter those who are upright in their ways.

16 Their sword shall go through their own heart, *
   and their bow shall be broken.

17 The little that the righteous has *
   is better than great riches of the wicked.

18 For the power of the wicked shall be broken, *
   but God upholds the righteous.

PSALM 37: PART II

19 God cares for the lives of the faithful, *
   and their inheritance shall last for ever.

20 They shall not be ashamed in bad times, *
   and in days of famine they shall have enough.

21 As for the wicked, they shall perish, *
    and the enemies of God, like the glory of
        the meadows, shall vanish;
    they shall vanish like smoke.

22 The wicked borrow and do not repay, *
    but the righteous are generous in giving.

23 Those who are blest by God shall possess the land, *
    but those who are cursed shall be destroyed.

24 Our steps are directed by God, *
    who strengthens those whose ways are upright.

25 If they stumble, they shall not fall headlong, *
    for God holds them by the hand.

26 I have been young and now I am old, *
    but never have I seen the righteous forsaken
    or their children begging bread.

27 The righteous are always generous in their lending, *
    and their children shall be a blessing.

28 Turn from evil and do good, *
    and dwell in the land for ever.

29 For God loves justice *
    and does not forsake the faithful ones.

30 They shall be kept safe for ever, *
    but the offspring of the wicked shall be destroyed.

31 The righteous shall possess the land *
    and dwell in it for ever.

32 The mouth of the righteous utters wisdom, *
    and their tongue speaks what is right.

33 The law of their God is in their heart, *
    and their footsteps shall not falter.

34 The wicked spy on the righteous *
    and seek occasion to kill them.

35 But God will not abandon them to their hand, *
    nor let them be found guilty when brought to trial.

36 Wait upon God and keep God's way; *
    you will be raised up to possess the land,
    and when the wicked are cut off, you will see it.

37 I have seen the wicked in their arrogance, *
  flourishing like a tree in full leaf.

38 I went by, and behold, they were not there; *
  I searched for them, but they could not be found.

39 Mark those who are honest;
  observe the upright, *
  for there is a future for the peaceable.

40 Transgressors shall be destroyed, one and all; *
  the future of the wicked is cut off.

41 But the deliverance of the righteous comes from God, *
  who is their stronghold in time of trouble.

42 God will help them and rescue them; *
  the Holy One will rescue them from the wicked
      and deliver them,
  because they seek refuge in God.

Eighth Day: Morning Prayer

PSALM 38

1 O God, do not rebuke me in your anger; *
  do not punish me in your wrath.

2 For your arrows have already pierced me, *
  and your hand presses hard upon me.

3 There is no health in my flesh
  because of your indignation; *
  there is no soundness in my body because of my sin.

4 For my iniquities overwhelm me; *
  like a heavy burden they are too much for me to bear.

5 My wounds stink and fester *
  by reason of my foolishness.

6 I am utterly bowed down and prostrate; *
  I go about in mourning all the day long.

7 My loins are filled with searing pain; *
  there is no health in my body.

8 I am utterly numb and crushed; *
  I wail, because of the groaning of my heart.

9 O God, you know all my desires, *
   and my sighing is not hidden from you.

10 My heart is pounding, my strength has failed me, *
   and the brightness of my eyes is gone from me.

11 My friends and companions draw back from my affliction; *
   my neighbors stand afar off.

12 Those who seek after my life lay snares for me; *
   those who strive to hurt me speak of my ruin
   and plot treachery all the day long.

13 But I am like the deaf who do not hear, *
   like those who are mute and do not open their mouth.

14 I have become like one who does not hear *
   and from whose mouth comes no defense.

15 For in you, O God, have I fixed my hope; *
   you will answer me, O my God.

16 For I said, "Do not let them rejoice at my expense, *
   those who gloat over me when my foot slips."

17 Truly, I am on the verge of falling, *
   and my pain is always with me.

18 I will confess my iniquity *
   and be sorry for my sin.

19 Those who are my enemies without cause are mighty, *
   and many in number are those who wrongfully hate me.

20 Those who repay evil for good slander me, *
   because I follow the course that is right.

21 O Holy One, do not forsake me; *
   be not far from me, O my God.

22 Make haste to help me, *
   O God of my salvation.

Psalm 39

1 I said, "I will keep watch upon my ways, *
   so that I do not offend with my tongue.

2 I will put a muzzle on my mouth *
   while the wicked are in my presence."

3 So I held my tongue and said nothing; *
    I refrained from rash words,
        but my pain became unbearable.

4 My heart was hot within me;
    while I pondered, the fire burst into flame; *
        I spoke out with my tongue:

5 O God, let me know my end and the number of my days, *
    so that I may know how short my life is.

6 You have given me a mere handful of days,
    and my lifetime is as nothing in your sight; *
        truly, even those who stand erect are but a puff of wind.

7 We walk about like a shadow,
    and in vain we are in turmoil; *
        we heap up riches and cannot tell who will gather them.

8 And now, what is my hope? *
    O God, my hope is in you.

9 Deliver me from all my transgressions, *
    and do not make me the taunt of the fool.

10 I fell silent and did not open my mouth, *
    for surely it was you that did it.

11 Take your affliction from me; *
    I am worn down by the blows of your hand.

12 With rebukes for sin you punish us;
    like a moth you eat away all that is dear to us; *
        truly, everyone is but a puff of wind.

13 Hear my prayer, O God,
    and give ear to my cry; *
        hold not your peace at my tears,

14 For I am but a sojourner with you, *
    a wayfarer, as all my forebears were.

15 Turn your gaze from me, that I may be glad again, *
    before I go my way and am no more.

Psalm 40

1 I waited patiently for you, O God; *
  you stooped to me and heard my cry.

2 You lifted me out of the desolate pit, out of the mire
        and clay; *
  you set my feet upon a high cliff and made
        my footing sure.

3 You put a new song in my mouth,
  a song of praise to our God; *
    many shall see, and stand in awe,
    and put their trust in you.

4 Happy are they who trust in you; *
  they do not resort to evil spirits or turn to false gods.

5 Great things are they that you have done, O God;
  how great your wonders and your plans for us; *
    there is none who can be compared with you.

6 Oh, that I could make them known and tell them, *
  but they are more than I can count.

7 In sacrifice and offering you take no pleasure *
  (you have given me ears to hear you);

8 Burnt-offering and sin-offering you have not required, *
  and so I said, "Behold, I come.

9 In the roll of the book it is written concerning me: *
  'I love to do your will, O my God;
  your law is deep in my heart.' "

10 I proclaimed righteousness in the great congregation; *
  behold, I did not restrain my lips,
  and that, O God, you know.

11 Your righteousness have I not hidden in my heart;
  I have spoken of your faithfulness and your deliverance; *
    I have not concealed your love and faithfulness from
        the great congregation.

12 You are the Holy One;
  do not withhold your compassion from me; *
    let your love and your faithfulness keep me safe for ever.

13 For innumerable troubles have crowded upon me;
  my sins have overtaken me, and I cannot see; *
    they are more in number than the hairs of my head,
    and my heart fails me.

14 Be pleased, O God, to deliver me; *
  O God, make haste to help me.

15 Let them be ashamed and altogether dismayed
  who seek after my life to destroy it; *
    let them draw back and be disgraced
    who take pleasure in my misfortune.

16 Let those who say "Aha!" and gloat over me be confounded,
  because they are ashamed.

17 Let all who seek you rejoice in you and be glad; *
  let those who love your salvation continually say,
    "Great is the Holy One!"

18 Though I am poor and afflicted, *
  you will have regard for me.

19 You are my helper and my deliverer; *
  do not tarry, O my God.

Eighth Day: Evening Prayer

PSALM 41

1 Happy are they who consider the poor and needy! *
  God will deliver them in the time of trouble.

2 God preserves them and keeps them alive,
  so that they may be happy in the land, *
    and does not hand them over to the will of their enemies.

3 God sustains them on their sickbed *
  and ministers to them in their illness.

4 I said, "O God, be merciful to me; *
  heal me, for I have sinned against you."

5 My enemies are saying wicked things about me, *
  wondering when I will die and my name perish.

6 Even if they come to see me, they speak empty words; *
  their heart collects false rumors;
    they go outside and spread them.

7 All my enemies whisper together about me *
　　and devise evil against me.

8 They say a deadly thing has fastened on me, *
　　that I have taken to my bed and will never get up again.

9 Even my best friend, whom I trusted,
　who broke bread with me, *
　　has spurned me and turned against me.

10 But you, O God, be merciful to me and raise me up, *
　　and I shall repay them.

11 By this I know you are pleased with me, *
　　that my enemy does not triumph over me.

12 In my integrity you hold me fast *
　　and shall set me before your face for ever.

13 Blessed be the God of Israel, *
　　from age to age. Amen. Amen.

Book Two

Psalm 42

1 As the deer longs for the water-brooks, *
　　so longs my soul for you, O God.

2 My soul is athirst for God, athirst for the living God; *
　　when shall I come to appear before the presence of God?

3 My tears have been my food day and night, *
　　while all day long they say to me,
　　"Where now is your God?"

4 I pour out my soul when I think on these things: *
　　how I went with the multitude and led them into the
　　　　house of God,

5 With the voice of praise and thanksgiving, *
　　among those who keep holy-day.

6 Why are you so full of heaviness, O my soul, *
　　and why are you so disquieted within me?

7 Put your trust in God, *
  for I will yet give thanks to the Holy One,
  who is the help of my countenance, and my God.

8 My soul is heavy within me; *
  therefore I will remember you from the land of Jordan,
  and from the peak of Mizar among the heights of Hermon.

9 One deep calls to another in the noise of your cataracts; *
  all your rapids and floods have gone over me.

10 You grant me your loving-kindness in the daytime; *
  in the night season your song is with me,
  a prayer to the God of my life.

11 I will say to the God of my strength,
  "Why have you forgotten me, *
  and why do I go so heavily while the enemy oppresses me?"

12 While my bones are being broken, *
  my enemies mock me to my face;

13 All day long they mock me *
  and say to me, "Where now is your God?"

14 Why are you so full of heaviness, O my soul, *
  and why are you so disquieted within me?

15 Put your trust in God, *
  for I will yet give thanks to the Holy One,
  who is the help of my countenance, and my God.

PSALM 43

1 Give judgment for me, O God,
  and defend my cause against an ungodly people; *
  deliver me from the deceitful and the wicked.

2 For you are the God of my strength;
  why have you put me from you, *
  and why do I go so heavily while the enemy oppresses me?

3 Send out your light and your truth, that they may lead me, *
  and bring me to your holy hill
  and to your dwelling;

4 That I may go to the altar of God,
  to the God of my joy and gladness, *
    and on the harp I will give thanks to you, O God,
      my God.

5 Why are you so full of heaviness, O my soul, *
  and why are you so disquieted within me?

6 Put your trust in God, *
  for I will yet give thanks to the Holy One,
  who is the help of my countenance, and my God.

Ninth Day: Morning Prayer

Psalm 44

1 We have heard with our ears, O God,
  our forebears have told us, *
    the deeds you did in their days,
    in the days of old;

2 How with your hand you drove the peoples out
  and planted our forebears in the land; *
    how you destroyed nations and made your people flourish.

3 For they did not take the land by their sword,
  nor did their arm win the victory for them; *
    but your right hand, your arm, and the
        light of your countenance,
    because you favored them.

4 You are my Ruler and my God; *
  you command victories for Jacob.

5 Through you we pushed back our adversaries; *
  through your Name we trampled on those who
      rose up against us.

6 For I do not rely on my bow, *
  and my sword does not give me the victory.

7 Surely, you gave us victory over our adversaries *
  and put those who hate us to shame.

8 Every day we gloried in God, *
  and we will praise your Name for ever.

9 Nevertheless, you have rejected and humbled us *
   and do not go forth with our armies.

10 You have made us fall back before our adversary, *
   and our enemies have plundered us.

11 You have made us like sheep to be eaten *
   and have scattered us among the nations.

12 You are selling your people for a trifle *
   and are making no profit on the sale of them.

13 You have made us the scorn of our neighbors, *
   a mockery and derision to those around us.

14 You have made us a byword among the nations, *
   a laughing-stock among the peoples.

15 My humiliation is daily before me, *
   and shame has covered my face,

16 Because of the taunts of the mockers and blasphemers, *
   because of the enemy and avenger.

17 All this has come upon us; *
   yet we have not forgotten you,
   nor have we betrayed your covenant.

18 Our heart never turned back, *
   nor did our footsteps stray from your path,

19 Though you thrust us down into a place of misery *
   and covered us over with deep darkness.

20 If we have forgotten the Name of our God *
   or stretched out our hands to some strange god,

21 Will God not find it out, *
   for God knows the secrets of the heart.

22 Indeed, for your sake we are killed all the day long; *
   we are accounted as sheep for the slaughter.

23 Awake, O God! Why are you sleeping? *
   Arise; do not reject us for ever.

24 Why have you hidden your face *
   and forgotten our affliction and oppression?

25 We sink down into the dust; *
  our body cleaves to the ground.

26 Rise up, and help us, *
  and save us, for the sake of your steadfast love.

Psalm 45

1 My heart is stirring with a noble song;
  let me recite what I have fashioned for the king; *
  my tongue shall be the pen of a skilled writer.

2 You are the fairest of men; *
  grace flows from your lips,
  because God has blessed you for ever.

3 Strap your sword upon your thigh, O mighty warrior, *
  in your pride and in your majesty.

4 Ride out and conquer in the cause of truth *
  and for the sake of justice.

5 Your right hand will show you marvelous things; *
  your arrows are very sharp, O mighty warrior.

6 The peoples are falling at your feet, *
  and the king's enemies are losing heart.

7 Your throne, O God, endures for ever and ever; *
  a scepter of righteousness is the scepter of your realm;
  you love righteousness and hate iniquity.

8 Therefore God, your God, has anointed you *
  with the oil of gladness above your companions.

9 All your garments are fragrant with myrrh, aloes and cassia, *
  and the music of strings from ivory palaces makes you glad.

10 The royal daughters stand among the ladies of the court; *
  on your right hand is the queen,
  adorned with the gold of Ophir.

11 "Hear, O daughter, consider and listen closely; *
  forget your people and your parents' house.

12 The king will have pleasure in your beauty; *
  you are committed to him; therefore do him honor.

13 The people of Tyre are here with a gift; *
  the rich among the people seek your favor."

14 All glorious is the princess as she enters; *
    her gown is cloth-of-gold.

15 In embroidered apparel she is brought to the king; *
    after her the bridesmaids follow in procession.

16 With joy and gladness they are brought *
    and enter into the palace of the king.

17 "In place of fathers, O king, you shall have sons; *
    you shall make them princes over all the earth.

18 I will make your name to be remembered
    from one generation to another; *
       therefore nations will praise you for ever and ever."

PSALM 46

1 God is our refuge and strength, *
    a very present help in trouble.

2 Therefore we will not fear, though the earth be moved, *
    and though the mountains be toppled into the depths
       of the sea;

3 Though its waters rage and foam, *
    and though the mountains tremble at its tumult.

4 The God of hosts is with us; *
    the God of Jacob is our stronghold.

5 There is a river whose streams make glad the city of God, *
    the holy habitation of the Most High.

6 God is in the midst of the city;
    it shall not be overthrown; *
       God shall help it at the break of day.

7 The nations make much ado, and the realms are shaken; *
    God has spoken, and the earth shall melt away.

8 The God of hosts is with us; *
    the God of Jacob is our stronghold.

9 Come now and look upon the works of the Most High, *
    who does awesome things on earth.

10 It is God who makes war to cease in all the world, *
    who breaks the bow and shatters the spear,
    and burns the shields with fire.

11 "Be still, then, and know that I am God; *
   I will be exalted among the nations;
   I will be exalted in the earth."

12 The God of hosts is with us; *
   the God of Jacob is our stronghold.

Ninth Day: Evening Prayer

PSALM 47

1 Clap your hands, all you peoples; *
   shout to God with a cry of joy.

2 For God Most High is to be feared; *
   God is the great Sovereign over all the earth.

3 God subdues the peoples under us *
   and the nations under our feet.

4 God chooses our inheritance for us, *
   the pride of Jacob whom God loves.

5 God has gone up with a shout, *
   the Most High with the sound of the ram's-horn.

6 Sing praises to God, sing praises; *
   sing praises to our Sovereign, sing praises.

7 For God is Sovereign over all the earth; *
   sing praises with all your skill.

8 God reigns over the nations; *
   God sits upon the holy throne.

9 The nobles of the peoples have gathered together *
   with the people of the God of Abraham.

10 The rulers of the earth belong to God, *
   who is highly exalted.

PSALM 48

1 God is great and highly to be praised; *
   in the city of our God is the holy hill.

2 Beautiful and lofty, the joy of all the earth, is the hill of Zion, *
   the very center of the world and the city
      of the great Sovereign.

3 God is in its citadels; *
   God is known to be its sure refuge.

4 Behold, the monarchs of the earth assembled *
   and marched forward together.

5 They looked and were astounded; *
   they retreated and fled in terror.

6 Trembling seized them there; *
   they writhed like a woman in childbirth,
   like ships of the sea when the east wind shatters them.

7 As we have heard, so have we seen,
   in the city of the God of hosts, in the city of our God; *
   God has established it for ever.

8 We have waited in silence on your loving-kindness, O God, *
   in the midst of your temple.

9 Your praise, like your Name, O God, reaches to
         the world's end; *
   your right hand is full of justice.

10 Let Mount Zion be glad
   and the cities of Judah rejoice, *
   because of your judgments.

11 Make the circuit of Zion;
   walk round about it; *
   count the number of its towers.

12 Consider well its bulwarks;
   examine its strongholds, *
   that you may tell those who come after:

13 This God is our God for ever and ever *
   and shall be our guide for evermore.

Psalm 49

1 Hear this, all you peoples;
   hearken, all you who dwell in the world, *
   you of high degree and low, rich and poor together.

2 My mouth shall speak of wisdom, *
   and my heart shall meditate on understanding.

3 I will incline my ear to a proverb *
   and set forth my riddle upon the harp.

4 Why should I be afraid in evil days, *
   when the wickedness of those at my heels surrounds me,

5 The wickedness of those who put their trust in their goods, *
   and boast of their great riches?

6 We can never ransom ourselves, *
   or deliver to God the price of our life;

7 For the ransom of our life is so great, *
   that we should never have enough to pay it,

8 In order to live for ever and ever, *
   and never see the grave.

9 For we see that the wise die also;
   like the dull and stupid they perish *
   and leave their wealth to those who come after them.

10 Their graves shall be their homes for ever,
   their dwelling places from generation to generation, *
   though they call the lands after their own names.

11 Even though honored, they cannot live for ever; *
   they are like the beasts that perish.

12 Such is the way of those who foolishly trust in themselves, *
   and the end of those who delight in their own words.

13 Like a flock of sheep they are destined to die;
   Death is their shepherd; *
   they go down straightway to the grave.

14 Their form shall waste away, *
   and the land of the dead shall be their home.

15 But God will ransom my life *
   and will snatch me from the grasp of death.

16 Do not be envious when some become rich *
   or when the grandeur of their house increases,

17 For they will carry nothing away at their death, *
   nor will their grandeur follow them.

18 Though they thought highly of themselves while they lived *
   and were praised for their success,

19 They shall join the company of their forebears, *
   who will never see the light again.

20 Those who are honored, but have no understanding, *
   are like the beasts that perish.

Tenth Day: Morning Prayer

PSALM 50

1 The God of gods has spoken; *
   God has called the earth from the rising of the sun to
      its setting.

2 Out of Zion, perfect in its beauty, *
   God is revealed in glory.

3 O God, you will come and will not keep silence; *
   before you there is a consuming flame,
   and round about you a raging storm.

4 You call the heavens and the earth from above *
   to witness the judgment of your people.

5 "Gather before me my loyal followers, *
   those who have made a covenant with me
   and sealed it with sacrifice."

6 Let the heavens declare the rightness of your cause, *
   for you alone are judge.

7 "Hear, O my people, and I will speak:
   O Israel, I will bear witness against you, *
   for I am God, your God.

8 I do not accuse you because of your sacrifices; *
   your offerings are always before me.

9 I will take no bull-calf from your stalls *
   nor he-goats out of your pens;

10 For all the beasts of the forest are mine, *
   the herds in their thousands upon the hills.

11 I know every bird in the sky, *
   and the creatures of the fields are in my sight.

12 If I were hungry, I would not tell you, *
   for the whole world is mine and all that is in it.

13 Do you think I eat the flesh of bulls *
   or drink the blood of goats?

14 Offer to God a sacrifice of thanksgiving, *
   and make good your vows to the Most High.

15 Call upon me in the day of trouble; *
   I will deliver you, and you shall honor me."

16 But to the wicked God says: *
   "Why do you recite my statutes
   and take my covenant upon your lips,

17 Since you refuse discipline *
   and toss my words behind your back?

18 When you see thieves, you make them your friends, *
   and you cast in your lot with adulterers.

19 You have loosed your lips for evil *
   and harnessed your tongue to a lie.

20 You are always speaking evil of your family *
   and slandering your own mother's child.

21 These things you have done, and I kept still, *
   and you thought that I am like you."

22 "I have made my accusation; *
   I have put my case in order before your eyes.

23 Consider this well, you who forget God, *
   lest I rend you and there be none to deliver you.

24 Whoever offers me the sacrifice of thanksgiving honors me; *
   but to those who keep in my way will I show
      the salvation of God."

Psalm 51

1 Have mercy on me, O God, according to
      your loving-kindness; *
   in your great compassion blot out my offenses.

2 Wash me through and through from my wickedness, *
   and cleanse me from my sin.

3 For I know my transgressions, *
   and my sin is ever before me.

4 Against you only have I sinned *
  and done what is evil in your sight.

5 And so you are justified when you speak *
  and upright in your judgment.

6 Indeed, I have been wicked from my birth, *
  a sinner from my mother's womb.

7 For behold, you look for truth deep within me *
  and will make me understand wisdom secretly.

8 Purge me from my sin, and I shall be pure; *
  wash me, and I shall be clean indeed.

9 Make me hear of joy and gladness, *
  that the body you have broken may rejoice.

10 Hide your face from my sins, *
  and blot out all my iniquities.

11 Create in me a clean heart, O God, *
  and renew a right spirit within me.

12 Cast me not away from your presence, *
  and take not your holy Spirit from me.

13 Give me the joy of your saving help again, *
  and sustain me with your bountiful Spirit.

14 I shall teach your ways to the wicked, *
  and sinners shall return to you.

15 Deliver me from death, O God, *
  and my tongue shall sing of your righteousness,
  O God of my salvation.

16 Open my lips, O God, *
  and my mouth shall proclaim your praise.

17 Had you desired it, I would have offered sacrifice, *
  but you take no delight in burnt-offerings.

18 The sacrifice of God is a troubled spirit; *
  a broken and contrite heart, O God, you will not despise.

19 Be favorable and gracious to Zion, *
  and rebuild the walls of Jerusalem.

20 Then you will be pleased with the appointed sacrifices,
  with burnt-offerings and oblations; *
  then shall they offer young bullocks upon your altar.

Psalm 52

1 You tyrant, why do you boast of wickedness *
    against the godly all day long?

2 You plot ruin;
    your tongue is like a sharpened razor, *
      O worker of deception.

3 You love evil more than good *
    and lying more than speaking the truth.

4 You love all words that hurt, *
    O you deceitful tongue.

5 Oh, that God would demolish you utterly, *
    topple you, and snatch you from your dwelling,
    and root you out of the land of the living!

6 The righteous shall see and tremble, *
    and they shall laugh at the tyrant, saying,

7 "This is the one who did not take God for a refuge, *
    but trusted in great wealth
    and relied upon wickedness."

8 But I am like a green olive tree in the house of God; *
    I trust in the mercy of God for ever and ever.

9 I will give you thanks for what you have done *
    and declare the goodness of your Name
      in the presence of the godly.

Tenth Day: Evening Prayer

Psalm 53

1 The foolish say in their hearts, "There is no God." *
    All are corrupt and commit abominable acts;
    there is none who does any good.

2 God looks down from heaven upon us all, *
    to see if there is any who is wise,
    if there is one who seeks after God.

3 Every one has proved faithless;
    all alike have turned bad; *
    there is none who does good; no, not one.

4 Have they no knowledge, those evildoers *
   who eat up my people like bread
   and do not call upon God?

5 See how greatly they tremble,
   such trembling as never was, *
      for God has scattered the bones of the enemy;
      they are put to shame, because God has rejected them.

6 Oh, that Israel's deliverance would come out of Zion! *
   When God restores the fortunes of the people,
   Jacob will rejoice and Israel be glad.

PSALM 54

1 Save me, O God, by your Name; *
   in your might, defend my cause.

2 Hear my prayer, O God; *
   give ear to the words of my mouth.

3 For the arrogant have risen up against me,
   and the ruthless have sought my life, *
      those who have no regard for God.

4 Behold, God is my helper; *
   it is God who sustains my life.

5 Render evil to those who spy on me; *
   in your faithfulness, destroy them.

6 I will offer you a freewill sacrifice *
   and praise your Name, O God, for it is good.

7 For you have rescued me from every trouble, *
   and my eye has seen the ruin of my foes.

PSALM 55

1 Hear my prayer, O God; *
   do not hide yourself from my petition.

2 Listen to me and answer me; *
   I have no peace, because of my cares.

3 I am shaken by the noise of the enemy *
   and by the pressure of the wicked;

4 For they have cast an evil spell upon me *
   and are set against me in fury.

5 My heart quakes within me, *
   and the terrors of death have fallen upon me.

6 Fear and trembling have come over me, *
   and horror overwhelms me.

7 And I said, "Oh, that I had wings like a dove! *
   I would fly away and be at rest.

8 I would flee to a far-off place *
   and make my lodging in the wilderness.

9 I would hasten to escape *
   from the stormy wind and tempest."

10 Swallow them up, O God; confound their speech, *
   for I have seen violence and strife in the city.

11 Day and night the sentries make their rounds upon its walls, *
   but trouble and misery are in the midst of it.

12 There is corruption at its heart; *
   its streets are never free of oppression and deceit.

13 For had it been an adversary who taunted me,
   then I could have borne it; *
   or had it been enemies who vaunted themselves against me,
   then I could have hidden from them.

14 But it was you, someone after my own heart, *
   my companion, my own familiar friend.

15 We took sweet counsel together *
   and walked with the throng in the house of God.

16 Let death come upon them suddenly;
   let them go down alive into the grave, *
   for wickedness is in their dwellings, in their very midst.

17 But I will call upon God, *
   and God will deliver me.

18 In the evening, in the morning, and at noonday,
   I will complain and lament, *
   and God will hear my voice.

19 God will bring me safely back from the battle
         waged against me, *
    for there are many who fight me.

20 God, who is enthroned of old, will hear me and
         bring them down; *
    they never change; they do not fear God.

21 My companions have stretched forth their hands
         against their comrade; *
    they have broken their covenant.

22 Their speech is softer than butter, *
    but war is in their hearts.

23 Their words are smoother than oil, *
    but they are drawn swords.

24 Cast your burden upon God
  who will sustain you; *
    God will never let the righteous stumble.

25 For you will bring the bloodthirsty and deceitful *
    down to the pit of destruction, O God.

26 They shall not live out half their days, *
    but I will put my trust in you.

Eleventh Day: Morning Prayer

PSALM 56

1 Have mercy on me, O God,
  for my enemies are hounding me; *
    all day long they assault and oppress me.

2 They hound me all the day long; *
    truly there are many who fight against me, O Most High.

3 Whenever I am afraid, *
    I will put my trust in you.

4 In God, whose word I praise,
  in God I trust and will not be afraid, *
    for what can flesh do to me?

5 All day long they damage my cause; *
    their only thought is to do me evil.

6 They band together; they lie in wait; *
   they spy upon my footsteps,
   because they seek my life.

7 Shall they escape despite their wickedness? *
   O God, in your anger, cast down the peoples.

8 You have noted my lamentation;
   put my tears into your bottle; *
   are they not recorded in your book?

9 Whenever I call upon you, my enemies will be put to flight; *
   this I know, for God is on my side.

10 In God, whose word I praise,
   in God I trust and will not be afraid, *
   for what can mortals do to me?

11 I am bound by the vow I made to you, O God; *
   I will present to you thank-offerings;

12 For you have rescued my soul from death and
            my feet from stumbling, *
   that I may walk before you in the light of the living.

PSALM 57

1 Be merciful to me, O God, be merciful,
   for I have taken refuge in you; *
   in the shadow of your wings will I take refuge
   until this time of trouble has gone by.

2 I will call upon you, O Most High God, *
   you who maintain my cause.

3 You will send from heaven and save me;
   you will confound those who trample upon me; *
   you will send forth your love and your faithfulness.

4 I lie in the midst of lions that devour the people; *
   their teeth are spears and arrows,
   their tongue a sharp sword.

5 They have laid a net for my feet,
   and I am bowed low; *
   they have dug a pit before me,
   but have fallen into it themselves.

6 Exalt yourself above the heavens, O God, *
  and your glory over all the earth.

7 My heart is firmly fixed, O God, my heart is fixed; *
  I will sing and make melody.

8 Wake up, my spirit;
  awake, lute and harp; *
  I myself will waken the dawn.

9 I will confess you among the peoples, O God; *
  I will sing praise to you among the nations.

10 For your loving-kindness is greater than the heavens, *
  and your faithfulness reaches to the clouds.

11 Exalt yourself above the heavens, O God, *
  and your glory over all the earth.

PSALM 58

1 Do you indeed decree righteousness, you rulers; *
  do you judge the peoples with equity?

2 No; you devise evil in your hearts, *
  and your hands deal out violence in the land.

3 The wicked are perverse from the womb; *
  liars go astray from their birth.

4 They are as venomous as a serpent; *
  they are like the deaf adder which stops its ears,

5 Which does not heed the voice of the charmer, *
  no matter how skillful the charming.

6 O God, break their teeth in their mouths; *
  pull the fangs of the young lions, O God.

7 Let them vanish like water that runs off; *
  let them wither like trodden grass.

8 Let them be like the snail that melts away, *
  like a stillborn child that never sees the sun.

9 Before they bear fruit, let them be cut down like a brier; *
  like thorns and thistles let them be swept away.

10 The righteous will be glad when they see the vengeance; *
  they will bathe their feet in the blood of the wicked.

11 And they will say,
  "Surely, there is a reward for the righteous; *
  surely, there is a God who rules in the earth."

Eleventh Day: Evening Prayer

PSALM 59

1 Rescue me from my enemies, O God; *
  protect me from those who rise up against me.

2 Rescue me from evildoers, *
  and save me from those who thirst for my blood.

3 See how they lie in wait for my life,
  how the mighty gather together against me; *
  not for any offense or fault of mine, O God.

4 Not because of any guilt of mine, *
  they run and prepare themselves for battle.

5 Rouse yourself, come to my side and see, *
  for you, O God of hosts, are Israel's God.

6 Awake, and punish all the ungodly; *
  show no mercy to those who are faithless and evil.

7 They go to and fro in the evening; *
  they snarl like dogs and run about the city.

8 Behold, they boast with their mouths,
  and taunts are on their lips; *
  "For who," they say, "will hear us?"

9 But you, O God, you laugh at them; *
  you laugh all the ungodly to scorn.

10 My eyes are fixed on you, O my Strength; *
  for you, O God, are my stronghold.

11 My merciful God comes to meet me; *
  God will let me look in triumph on my enemies.

12 Slay them, O God, lest my people forget; *
  send them reeling by your might,
  and put them down, O God our shield.

13 For the sins of their mouths, for the words of their lips,
    for the cursing and lies that they utter, *
        let them be caught in their pride.

14 Make an end of them in your wrath; *
    make an end of them, and they shall be no more.

15 Let everyone know that God rules in Jacob *
    and to the ends of the earth.

16 They go to and fro in the evening; *
    they snarl like dogs and run about the city.

17 They forage for food, *
    and if they are not filled, they howl.

18 For my part, I will sing of your strength; *
    I will celebrate your love in the morning;

19 For you have become my stronghold, *
    a refuge in the day of my trouble.

20 To you, O my Strength, will I sing; *
    for you, O God, are my stronghold and my merciful God.

PSALM 60

1 O God, you have cast us off and broken us; *
    you have been angry;
    oh, take us back to you again.

2 You have shaken the earth and split it open; *
    repair the cracks in it, for it totters.

3 You have made your people know hardship; *
    you have given us wine that makes us stagger.

4 You have set up a banner for those who fear you, *
    to be a refuge from the power of the bow.

5 Save us by your right hand and answer us, *
    that those who are dear to you may be delivered.

6 God spoke from the holy place and said: *
    "I will exult and parcel out Shechem;
    I will divide the valley of Succoth.

7 Gilead is mine and Manasseh is mine; *
    Ephraim is my helmet and Judah my scepter.

8 Moab is my wash-basin;
    on Edom I throw down my sandal to claim it, *
    and over Philistia will I shout in triumph."

9 Who will lead me into the strong city; *
    who will bring me into Edom?

10 Have you not cast us off, O God? *
    You no longer go out, O God, with our armies.

11 Grant us your help against the enemy, *
    for all human help is in vain.

12 With you, O God, we will do valiant deeds, *
    and you will tread our enemies under foot.

PSALM 61

1 Hear my cry, O God, *
    and listen to my prayer.

2 I call upon you from the ends of the earth
with heaviness in my heart; *
    set me upon the rock that is higher than I.

3 For you have been my refuge, *
    a strong tower against the enemy.

4 I will dwell in your house for ever; *
    I will take refuge under the cover of your wings.

5 For you, O God, have heard my vows; *
    you have granted me the heritage of those who
        fear your Name.

6 Add length of days to the king's life; *
    let his years extend over many generations.

7 Let him sit enthroned before God for ever; *
    bid love and faithfulness watch over him.

8 So will I always sing the praise of your Name, *
    and day by day I will fulfill my vows.

PSALM 62

1 For God alone my soul in silence waits; *
   from God comes my salvation.

2 God alone is my rock and my salvation, *
   my stronghold, so that I shall not be greatly shaken.

3 How long will you assail me to crush me,
   all of you together, *
   as if you were a leaning fence, a toppling wall?

4 They seek only to bring me down from my place of honor; *
   lies are their chief delight.

5 They bless with their lips, *
   but in their hearts they curse.

6 For God alone my soul in silence waits; *
   truly, there is my hope.

7 God alone is my rock and my salvation, *
   my stronghold, so that I shall not be shaken.

8 In God is my safety and my honor; *
   God is my strong rock and my refuge.

9 Put your trust in God always, O people; *
   pour out your hearts before the One who is our refuge.

10 Those of high degree are but a fleeting breath; *
   even those of low estate cannot be trusted.

11 On the scales they are lighter than a breath, *
   all of them together.

12 Put no trust in extortion;
   in robbery take no empty pride; *
   though wealth increase, set not your heart upon it.

13 God has spoken once, twice have I heard it, *
   that power belongs to God.

14 Steadfast love is yours, O God, *
   for you repay everyone according to their deeds.

PSALM 63

1 O God, you are my God; eagerly I seek you; *
　　my soul thirsts for you, my flesh faints for you,
　　as in a barren and dry land where there is no water.

2 Therefore I have gazed upon you in your holy place, *
　　that I might behold your power and your glory.

3 For your loving-kindness is better than life itself; *
　　my lips shall give you praise.

4 So will I bless you as long as I live *
　　and lift up my hands in your Name.

5 My soul is content, as with marrow and fatness, *
　　and my mouth praises you with joyful lips,

6 When I remember you upon my bed *
　　and meditate on you in the night watches.

7 For you have been my helper, *
　　and under the shadow of your wings I will rejoice.

8 My soul clings to you; *
　　your right hand holds me fast.

9 May those who seek my life to destroy it *
　　go down into the depths of the earth;

10 Let them fall upon the edge of the sword, *
　　and let them be food for jackals.

11 But the sovereign will rejoice in God;
　　all those who swear by God will be glad, *
　　for the mouth of those who speak lies shall be stopped.

PSALM 64

1 Hear my voice, O God, when I complain; *
　　protect my life from fear of the enemy.

2 Hide me from the conspiracy of the wicked, *
　　from the mob of evildoers.

3 They sharpen their tongue like a sword *
　　and aim their bitter words like arrows,

4 That they may shoot down the blameless from ambush; *
　　they shoot without warning and are not afraid.

5 They hold fast to their evil course; *
   they plan how they may hide their snares.

6 They say, "Who will see us;
   who will find out our crimes? *
   We have thought out a perfect plot."

7 The human mind and heart are a mystery, *
   but God will loose an arrow at them,
   and suddenly they will be wounded.

8 God will make them trip over their tongues, *
   and all who see them will shake their heads.

9 Everyone will stand in awe and declare God's deeds; *
   they will recognize the works of the Most High.

10 The righteous will rejoice and put their trust in God, *
   and all who are true of heart will glory.

Twelfth Day: Evening Prayer

Psalm 65

1 You are to be praised, O God, in Zion; *
   to you shall vows be performed in Jerusalem.

2 To you that hear prayer shall all flesh come, *
   because of their transgressions.

3 Our sins are stronger than we are, *
   but you will blot them out.

4 Happy are they whom you choose
   and draw to your courts to dwell there; *
   they will be satisfied by the beauty of your house,
   by the holiness of your temple.

5 Awesome things will you show us in your righteousness,
   O God of our salvation, *
   O Hope of all the ends of the earth
   and of the seas that are far away.

6 You make fast the mountains by your power; *
   they are girded about with might.

7 You still the roaring of the seas, *
   the roaring of their waves,
   and the clamor of the peoples.

8 Those who dwell at the ends of the earth will tremble
    at your marvelous signs; *
  you make the dawn and the dusk to sing for joy.

9 You visit the earth and water it abundantly;
  you make it very plenteous; *
    the river of God is full of water.

10 You prepare the grain, *
    for so you provide for the earth.

11 You drench the furrows and smooth out the ridges; *
    with heavy rain you soften the ground and bless its increase.

12 You crown the year with your goodness, *
    and your paths overflow with plenty.

13 May the fields of the wilderness be rich for grazing *
    and the hills be clothed with joy.

14 May the meadows cover themselves with flocks
  and the valleys cloak themselves with grain; *
    let them shout for joy and sing.

PSALM 66

1 Be joyful in God, all you lands; *
    sing the glory of God's Name;
    sing the glory of God's praise.

2 Say to God, "How awesome are your deeds; *
    because of your great strength your enemies
      cringe before you.

3 All the earth bows down before you, *
    sings to you, sings out your Name."

4 Come now and see the works of God, *
    how wonderful are these doings toward all people.

5 God turned the sea into dry land,
  so that they went through the water on foot, *
    and there we rejoiced in God,

6 Whose might rules for ever,
  whose eyes keep watch over the nations; *
    let not the rebellious lift up their heads.

7 Bless our God, you peoples; *
  let the sound of praise be heard;

8 God holds our souls in life *
  and will not allow our feet to slip.

9 For you, O God, have proved us; *
  you have tried us just as silver is tried.

10 You brought us into the snare *
  and laid heavy burdens upon our backs.

11 You let enemies ride over our heads;
  we went through fire and water, *
    but you brought us out into a place of refreshment.

12 I will enter your house with burnt-offerings
  and will pay you my vows, *
    which I promised with my lips
    and spoke with my mouth when I was in trouble.

13 I will offer you sacrifices of fat beasts
  with the smoke of rams; *
    I will give you oxen and goats.

14 Come and listen, all you who fear God, *
  and I will tell you what God has done for me.

15 I called out to God with my mouth, *
  and high praise was on my tongue.

16 If I had found evil in my heart, *
  God would not have heard me,

17 But in truth God has heard me *
  and has attended to the voice of my prayer.

18 Blessed be God, who has not rejected my prayer, *
  nor withheld steadfast love from me.

Psalm 67

1 Be merciful to us, O God, and bless us; *
  show us the light of your countenance and come to us.

2 Let your ways be known upon earth, *
  your saving health among all nations.

3 Let the peoples praise you, O God; *
  let all the peoples praise you.

4 Let the nations be glad and sing for joy, *
    for you judge the peoples with equity
    and guide all the nations upon earth.

5 Let the peoples praise you, O God; *
    let all the peoples praise you.

6 The earth has brought forth its increase; *
    may you, our own God, give us your blessing.

7 May you give us your blessing, *
    and may all the ends of the earth stand in awe of you.

Thirteenth Day: Morning Prayer

Psalm 68

1 Arise, O God, and let your enemies be scattered; *
    let those who hate you flee before you.

2 Let them vanish like smoke when the wind drives it away; *
    as the wax melts at the fire, so let the wicked perish at
        your presence, O God.

3 But let the righteous be glad and rejoice before you; *
    let them also be merry and joyful.

4 We sing praises to your holy Name;
    we exalt the One who rides upon the heavens; *
    yours is the Name in which we rejoice!

5 Guardian of orphans, defender of widows, *
    God, in your holy habitation!

6 You give the solitary a home and bring forth prisoners
        into freedom, *
    but the rebels shall live in dry places.

7 O God, when you went forth before your people, *
    when you marched through the wilderness,

8 The earth shook, and the skies poured down rain
    at the presence of God, the God of Sinai, *
    at the presence of God, the God of Israel.

9 You sent a gracious rain, O God, upon your inheritance; *
    you refreshed the land when it was weary.

10 Your people found their home in it; *
      in your goodness, O God, you have made provision
          for the poor.

11 You gave the word; *
      great was the company of those who bore the tidings:

12 "Rulers with their armies are fleeing away; *
      the ones at home are dividing the spoils."

13 Though you lingered among the sheepfolds, *
      you shall be like a dove whose wings
          are covered with silver,
      whose feathers are like green gold.

14 When the Almighty scattered rulers, *
      it was like snow falling in Zalmon.

15 O mighty mountain, O hill of Bashan! *
      O rugged mountain, O hill of Bashan!

16 Why do you look with envy, O rugged mountain,
      at the hill which God chose for a resting place? *
      Truly, God will dwell there for ever.

17 Your chariots, O God, are twenty thousand,
      even thousands of thousands; *
      you come in holiness from Sinai.

18 You have gone up on high and led captivity captive;
      you have received gifts even from your enemies, *
      that the Holy One might dwell among them.

19 Blest are you, O God, day by day, *
      the God of our salvation, who bears our burdens.

20 You are our God, the God of our salvation; *
      you are the one by whom we escape death.

21 You will crush the heads of your enemies *
      and the hairy scalp of those who go on still
          in their wickedness.

22 You have said, "I will bring my people back from Bashan; *
      I will bring them back from the depths of the sea;

23 That their feet may be dipped in blood, *
      the tongues of their dogs in the blood of their enemies."

24 They see your procession, O God, *
    your procession into the sanctuary, my God and
        my Sovereign.

25 The singers go before, musicians follow after, *
    in the midst of maidens playing upon the hand-drums.

26 Bless God in the congregation; *
    bless God, you that are of the fountain of Israel.

27 There is Benjamin, least of the tribes, at the head;
    the rulers of Judah in a company, *
    and the rulers of Zebulon and Naphtali.

28 Send forth your strength, O God; *
    establish, O God, what you have wrought for us.

29 Rulers shall bring gifts to you, *
    for your temple's sake at Jerusalem.

30 Rebuke the wild beast of the reeds, *
    and the peoples, a herd of wild bulls with its calves.

31 Trample down those who lust after silver; *
    scatter the peoples that delight in war.

32 Let tribute be brought out of Egypt; *
    let Ethiopia stretch out its hands to you.

33 Sing to God, O nations of the earth; *
    sing praises to the Holy One,

34 Who rides in the heavens, the ancient heavens, *
    who sends forth a voice, a mighty voice.

35 Ascribe power to God, *
    whose majesty is over Israel,
    whose strength is in the skies.

36 How wonderful is God in the holy places; *
    the God of Israel giving strength and power to the people;
    blessed be God!

PSALM 69

1 Save me, O God, *
    for the waters have risen up to my neck.

2 I am sinking in deep mire, *
    and there is no firm ground for my feet.

3 I have come into deep waters, *
    and the torrent washes over me.

4 I have grown weary with my crying;
    my throat is inflamed; *
    my eyes have failed from looking for my God.

5 Those who hate me without a cause are more than
        the hairs of my head;
    my lying foes who would destroy me are mighty. *
    Must I then give back what I never stole?

6 O God, you know my foolishness, *
    and my faults are not hidden from you.

7 Let not those who hope in you be put to shame through me,
        O God of hosts; *
    let not those who seek you be disgraced because of me,
        O God of Israel.

8 Surely for your sake have I suffered reproach, *
    and shame has covered my face.

9 I have become a stranger to my own kindred, *
    an outcast to my mother's children.

10 Zeal for your house has eaten me up; *
    the scorn of those who scorn you has fallen upon me.

11 I humbled myself with fasting, *
    but that was turned to my reproach.

12 I put on sack-cloth also *
    and became a byword among them.

13 Those who sit at the gate murmur against me, *
    and the drunkards make songs about me.

14 But as for me, this is my prayer to you *
    at the time you have set, O God.

15 "In your great mercy, O God, *
 answer me with your unfailing help.

16 Save me from the mire; do not let me sink; *
 let me be rescued from those who hate me
 and out of the deep waters.

17 Let not the torrent of waters wash over me,
 neither let the deep swallow me up; *
 do not let the Pit shut its mouth upon me.

18 Answer me, O God, for your love is kind; *
 in your great compassion, turn to me."

19 "Hide not your face from your servant; *
 be swift and answer me, for I am in distress.

20 Draw near to me and redeem me; *
 because of my enemies deliver me.

21 You know my reproach, my shame, and my dishonor; *
 my adversaries are all in your sight."

22 Reproach has broken my heart, and it cannot be healed; *
 I looked for sympathy, but there was none,
 for comforters, but I could find no one.

23 They gave me gall to eat, *
 and when I was thirsty, they gave me vinegar to drink.

24 Let the table before them be a trap *
 and their sacred feasts a snare.

25 Let their eyes be darkened, that they may not see, *
 and give them continual trembling in their loins.

26 Pour out your indignation upon them, *
 and let the fierceness of your anger overtake them.

27 Let their camp be desolate, *
 and let there be none to dwell in their tents.

28 For they persecute the one whom you have stricken *
 and add to the pain of those whom you have pierced.

29 Lay to their charge guilt upon guilt, *
 and let them not receive your vindication.

30 Let them be wiped out of the book of the living *
 and not be written among the righteous.

31 As for me, I am afflicted and in pain; *
   your help, O God, will lift me up on high.

32 I will praise your Name, O God, in song; *
   I will proclaim your greatness with thanksgiving.

33 This will please you more than an offering of oxen, *
   more than bullocks with horns and hoofs.

34 The afflicted shall see and be glad; *
   those who seek God, their heart shall live.

35 For you, O God, listen to the needy, *
   and your prisoners you do not despise.

36 Let the heavens and the earth praise you, *
   the seas and all that moves in them;

37 For you will save Zion and rebuild the cities of Judah; *
   your people shall live there and have it in possession.

38 The children of your servants will inherit it, *
   and those who love your Name will dwell therein.

Psalm 70

1 Be pleased, O God, to deliver me; *
   O God, make haste to help me.

2 Let those who seek my life be ashamed
   and altogether dismayed; *
      let those who take pleasure in my misfortune,
      draw back and be disgraced.

3 Let those who say to me "Aha!" and gloat over me turn back, *
   because they are ashamed.

4 Let all who seek you rejoice and be glad in you; *
      let those who love your salvation say for ever,
      "Great is the Holy One!"

5 But as for me, I am poor and needy; *
   come to me speedily, O God.

6 You are my helper and my deliverer; *
   O God, do not tarry.

PSALM 71

1 In you, O God, have I taken refuge; *
    let me never be ashamed.

2 In your righteousness, deliver me and set me free; *
    incline your ear to me and save me.

3 Be my strong rock, a castle to keep me safe; *
    you are my crag and my stronghold.

4 Deliver me, my God, from the hand of the wicked, *
    from the clutches of the evildoer and the oppressor.

5 For you are my hope, O God, *
    my confidence since I was young.

6 I have been sustained by you ever since I was born;
    from my mother's womb you have been my strength; *
    my praise shall be always of you.

7 I have become a portent to many, *
    but you are my refuge and my strength.

8 Let my mouth be full of your praise *
    and your glory all the day long.

9 Do not cast me off in my old age; *
    forsake me not when my strength fails.

10 For my enemies are talking against me, *
    and those who lie in wait for my life take counsel together.

11 They say that God has forsaken me,
    that they may pursue and seize me, *
    because there is none who will save.

12 O God, be not far from me; *
    come quickly to help me, O my God.

13 Let those who set themselves against me be put to shame
        and be disgraced; *
    let those who seek to do me evil be covered with scorn
        and reproach.

14 But I shall always wait in patience *
    and shall praise you more and more.

15 My mouth shall recount your mighty acts
and saving deeds all day long, *
  though I cannot know the number of them.

16 I will begin with your mighty works, O God; *
  I will recall your righteousness, yours alone.

17 O God, you have taught me since I was young, *
  and to this day I tell of your wonderful works.

18 And now that I am old and gray-headed, O God,
    do not forsake me, *
  till I make known your strength to this generation
  and your power to all who are to come.

19 Your righteousness, O God, reaches to the heavens; *
  you have done great things;
  who is like you, O God?

20 You have shown me great troubles and adversities, *
  but you will restore my life
  and bring me up again from the deep places of the earth.

21 You strengthen me more and more; *
  you enfold and comfort me;

22 Therefore I will praise you upon the lyre
    for your faithfulness, O my God; *
  I will sing to you with the harp, O Holy One of Israel.

23 My lips will sing with joy when I play to you *
  and so will my soul, which you have redeemed.

24 My tongue will proclaim your righteousness all day long, *
  for they are ashamed and disgraced who sought
    to do me harm.

PSALM 72

1 Give the King your justice, O God, *
  and your righteousness to the King's Son,

2 That he may rule your people righteously *
  and the poor with justice;

3 That the mountains may bring prosperity to the people, *
  and the little hills bring righteousness.

4 He shall defend the needy among the people; *
    he shall rescue the poor and crush the oppressor.

5 He shall live as long as the sun and moon endure, *
    from one generation to another.

6 He shall come down like rain upon the mown field, *
    like showers that water the earth.

7 In his time shall the righteous flourish; *
    there shall be abundance of peace till the moon shall
        be no more.

8 He shall rule from sea to sea *
    and from the River to the ends of the earth.

9 His foes shall bow down before him, *
    and his enemies lick the dust.

10 The rulers of Tarshish and of the isles shall pay tribute, *
    and the rulers of Arabia and Saba offer gifts.

11 All rulers shall bow down before him, *
    and all the nations do him service.

12 For he shall deliver the poor who cries out in distress *
    and the oppressed who has no helper.

13 He shall have pity on the lowly and poor; *
    he shall preserve the lives of the needy.

14 He shall redeem their lives from oppression and violence, *
    and dear shall their blood be in his sight.

15 Long may he live;
    and may there be given to him gold from Arabia; *
    may prayer be made for him always,
    and may they bless him all the day long.

16 May there be abundance of grain on the earth,
    growing thick even on the hilltops; *
    may its fruit flourish like Lebanon,
    and its grain like grass upon the earth.

17 May his Name remain for ever
    and be established as long as the sun endures; *
    may all the nations bless themselves in him and
        call him blest.

18 Blest are you, O God of Israel; *
   you alone do wondrous deeds!

19 And blest is your glorious Name for ever! *
   May all the earth be filled with your glory.
   Amen. Amen.

BOOK THREE

Fourteenth Day: Evening Prayer

PSALM 73

1 Truly, God is good to Israel, *
   to those who are pure in heart.

2 But as for me, my feet had nearly slipped; *
   I had almost tripped and fallen,

3 Because I envied the proud *
   and saw the prosperity of the wicked:

4 For they suffer no pain, *
   and their bodies are sleek and sound;

5 In the misfortunes of others they have no share; *
   they are not afflicted as others are;

6 Therefore they wear their pride like a necklace *
   and wrap their violence about them like a cloak.

7 Their iniquity comes from gross minds, *
   and their hearts overflow with wicked thoughts.

8 They scoff and speak maliciously; *
   out of their haughtiness they plan oppression.

9 They set their mouths against the heavens, *
   and their evil speech runs through the world.

10 And so the people turn to them *
   and find in them no fault.

11 They say, "How should God know; *
   is there knowledge in the Most High?"

12 So then, these are the wicked; *
 always at ease, they increase their wealth.

13 In vain have I kept my heart clean *
 and washed my hands in innocence.

14 I have been afflicted all day long *
 and punished every morning.

15 Had I gone on speaking this way, *
 I should have betrayed the generation of your children.

16 When I tried to understand these things, *
 it was too hard for me,

17 Until I entered the sanctuary of God *
 and discerned the end of the wicked.

18 Surely, you set them in slippery places; *
 you cast them down in ruin.

19 Oh, how suddenly do they come to destruction, *
 come to an end, and perish from terror!

20 Like a dream when one awakens, O God, *
 when you arise you will make their image vanish.

21 When my mind became embittered, *
 I was sorely wounded in my heart.

22 I was stupid and had no understanding; *
 I was like a brute beast in your presence.

23 Yet I am always with you; *
 you hold me by my right hand.

24 You will guide me by your counsel, *
 and afterwards receive me with glory.

25 Whom have I in heaven but you? *
 And having you I desire nothing upon earth.

26 Though my flesh and my heart should waste away, *
 God is the strength of my heart and my portion for ever.

27 Truly, those who forsake you will perish; *
 you destroy all who are unfaithful.

28 But it is good for me to be near God; *
 I have made the Most High my refuge.

29 I will speak of all your works *
 in the gates of the city of Zion.

PSALM 74

1 O God, why have you utterly cast us off; *
    why is your wrath so hot against the sheep of your pasture?

2 Remember your congregation that you purchased long ago, *
    the tribe you redeemed to be your inheritance,
    and Mount Zion where you dwell.

3 Turn your steps toward the endless ruins; *
    the enemy has laid waste everything in your sanctuary.

4 Your adversaries roared in your holy place; *
    they set up their banners as tokens of victory.

5 They were like men coming up with axes to a grove of trees; *
    they broke down all your carved work with hatchets
        and hammers.

6 They set fire to your holy place; *
    they defiled the dwelling-place of your Name
    and razed it to the ground.

7 They said to themselves, "Let us destroy them altogether." *
    They burned down all the meeting-places of God
        in the land.

8 There are no signs for us to see;
    there is no prophet left; *
    there is not one among us who knows how long.

9 How long, O God, will the adversary scoff; *
    will the enemy blaspheme your Name for ever?

10 Why do you draw back your hand; *
    why is your right hand hidden in your bosom?

11 Yet God is my Sovereign from ancient times, *
    victorious in the midst of the earth.

12 You divided the sea by your might *
    and shattered the heads of the dragons upon the waters;

13 You crushed the heads of Leviathan, *
    which you gave to the people of the desert for food.

14 You split open spring and torrent; *
    you dried up ever-flowing rivers.

15 Yours is the day, yours also the night; *
    you established the moon and the sun.

16 You fixed all the boundaries of the earth; *
  you made both summer and winter.

17 Remember, O God, how the enemy scoffed, *
  how a foolish people despised your Name.

18 Do not hand over the life of your dove to wild beasts; *
  never forget the lives of your poor.

19 Look upon your covenant; *
  the dark places of the earth are haunts of violence.

20 Let not the oppressed turn away ashamed; *
  let the poor and needy praise your Name.

21 Arise, O God, maintain your cause; *
  remember how fools revile you all day long.

22 Forget not the clamor of your adversaries, *
  the unending tumult of those who rise up against you.

Fifteenth Day: Morning Prayer

PSALM 75

1 We give you thanks, O God, we give you thanks, *
  calling upon your Name and declaring all your
    wonderful deeds.

2 "I will appoint a time," says God; *
  "I will judge with equity.

3 Though the earth and all its inhabitants are quaking, *
  I will make its pillars fast.

4 I will say to the boasters, 'Boast no more,' *
  and to the wicked, 'Do not toss your horns;

5 Do not toss your horns so high, *
  nor speak with a proud neck.'

6 For judgment is neither from the east nor from the west, *
  nor yet from the wilderness or the mountains."

7 You are judge, O God; *
  you put down one and lift up another.

8 For in your hand there is a cup,
  full of spiced and foaming wine, which you pour out, *
    and all the wicked of the earth shall drink and
      drain the dregs.

9 But I will rejoice for ever; *
  I will sing praises to you, O God of Jacob.

10 For you will break off all the horns of the wicked, *
  but the horns of the righteous shall be exalted.

PSALM 76

1 In Judah you are known, O God; *
  your Name is great in Israel.

2 At Salem is your tabernacle, *
  and your dwelling is in Zion.

3 There you broke the flashing arrows, *
  the shield, the sword, and the weapons of battle.

4 How glorious you are, *
  more splendid than the everlasting mountains!

5 The strong of heart have been despoiled;
  they sink into sleep; *
    none of the warriors can lift a hand.

6 At your rebuke, O God of Jacob, *
  both horse and rider lie stunned.

7 What terror you inspire; *
  who can stand before you when you are angry?

8 From heaven you pronounced judgment; *
  the earth was afraid and was still,

9 When God rose up to judgment *
  and to save all the oppressed of the earth.

10 Truly, wrathful Edom will give you thanks, *
  and the remnant of Hamath will keep your feasts.

11 Make a vow to your God and keep it; *
  let the nations bring gifts to the One who is worthy
    to be feared,

12 Who breaks the spirit of princes, *
  and strikes terror in the rulers of the earth.

PSALM 77

1 I will cry aloud to God; *
  I cry aloud to the One who will hear me.

2 In the day of my trouble I sought after God; *
  my hands were stretched out by night and did not tire;
  I refused to be comforted.

3 I think of God; I am restless; *
  I ponder and my spirit faints.

4 You will not let my eyelids close; *
  I am troubled and I cannot speak.

5 I consider the days of old; *
  I remember the years long past;

6 I commune with my heart in the night; *
  I ponder and search my mind.

7 Will you cast me off for ever; *
  will you no more show your favor?

8 Has your loving-kindness come to an end for ever; *
  has your promise failed for evermore?

9 Have you forgotten to be gracious; *
  have you, in your anger, withheld your compassion?

10 And I said, "My grief is this: *
  the right hand of the Most High has lost its power."

11 I will remember the works of God *
  and call to mind your wonders of old time.

12 I will meditate on all your acts *
  and ponder your mighty deeds.

13 Your way, O God, is holy; *
  who is so great a god as our God?

14 You are the God who works wonders *
  and have declared your power among the peoples.

15 By your strength you have redeemed your people, *
  the children of Jacob and Joseph.

16 The waters saw you, O God;
  the waters saw you and trembled; *
  the very depths were shaken.

17 The clouds poured out water;
the skies thundered; *
your arrows flashed to and fro;

18 The sound of your thunder was in the whirlwind;
your lightnings lit up the world; *
the earth trembled and shook.

19 Your way was in the sea,
and your paths in the great waters, *
yet your footsteps were not seen.

20 You led your people like a flock, *
by the hand of Moses and Aaron.

Fifteenth Day: Evening Prayer

PSALM 78

PART I

1 Hear my teaching, O my people; *
incline your ears to the words of my mouth.

2 I will open my mouth in a parable; *
I will declare the mysteries of ancient times.

3 That which we have heard and known,
and what our forebears have told us, *
we will not hide from their children.

4 We will recount to generations to come
your praiseworthy deeds and your power, O God, *
and the wonderful works you have done.

5 You gave your decrees to Jacob
and established a law for Israel, *
which you commanded them to teach their children;

6 That the generations to come might know,
and the children yet unborn, *
that they in their turn might tell it to their children;

7 So that they might put their trust in you *
and not forget your deeds,
but keep your commandments;

8 And not be like their forebears,
   a stubborn and rebellious generation, *
     a generation whose heart was not steadfast
     and whose spirit was not faithful to you.

9 The people of Ephraim, armed with the bow, *
   turned back in the day of battle;

10 They did not keep your covenant *
    and refused to walk in your law;

11 They forgot what you had done *
    and the wonders you had shown them.

12 You worked marvels in the sight of their forebears, *
    in the land of Egypt, in the field of Zoan.

13 You split open the sea and let them pass through; *
    you made the waters stand up like walls.

14 You led them with a cloud by day *
    and all the night through with a glow of fire.

15 You split the hard rocks in the wilderness *
    and gave them drink as from the great deep.

16 You brought streams out of the cliff, *
    and the waters gushed out like rivers.

17 But they went on sinning against you, *
    rebelling in the desert against the Most High.

18 They tested you in their hearts, *
    demanding food for their craving.

19 They railed against you and said, *
    "Can God set a table in the wilderness?

20 True, God struck the rock,
   the waters gushed out, and the gullies overflowed; *
    but is God able to give bread
    or to provide meat for the people?"

21 When you heard this, you were full of wrath; *
   a fire was kindled against Jacob,
    and your anger mounted against Israel;

22 For they had no faith in you, *
    nor did they put their trust in your saving power.

23 So you commanded the clouds above *
　　and opened the doors of heaven.

24 You rained down manna upon them to eat *
　　and gave them grain from heaven.

25 So mortals ate the bread of angels; *
　　you provided for them food enough.

26 You caused the east wind to blow in the heavens *
　　and led out the south wind by your might.

27 You rained down flesh upon them like dust *
　　and winged birds like the sand of the sea.

28 You let it fall in the midst of their camp *
　　and round about their dwellings.

29 So they ate and were well filled, *
　　for you gave them what they craved.

30 But they did not stop their craving, *
　　though the food was still in their mouths.

31 So your anger mounted against them; *
　　you slew the strongest among them
　　and laid low the youth of Israel.

32 In spite of all this, they went on sinning *
　　and had no faith in your wonderful works.

33 So you brought their days to an end like a breath *
　　and their years in sudden terror.

34 Whenever you slew them, they would seek you *
　　and repent, and diligently search for you.

35 They would remember that you were their rock, *
　　that you, the Most High, were their redeemer.

36 But they flattered you with their mouths *
　　and lied to you with their tongues.

37 Their heart was not steadfast toward you, *
　　and they were not faithful to your covenant.

38 But you were so merciful that you forgave their sins
　　and did not destroy them; *
　　　many times you held back your anger
　　　and did not permit your wrath to be roused.

39 For you remembered that they were but flesh, *
   a breath that goes forth and does not return.

PSALM 78: PART II

40 How often the people disobeyed you in the wilderness *
   and offended you in the desert!

41 Again and again they tempted you *
   and provoked you, the Holy One of Israel.

42 They did not remember your power *
   in the day when you ransomed them from the enemy;

43 How you wrought your signs in Egypt *
   and your omens in the field of Zoan.

44 You turned their rivers into blood, *
   so that they could not drink of their streams.

45 You sent swarms of flies among them, which ate them up, *
   and frogs, which destroyed them.

46 You gave their crops to the caterpillar, *
   the fruit of their toil to the locust.

47 You killed their vines with hail *
   and their sycamores with frost.

48 You delivered their cattle to hailstones *
   and their livestock to hot thunderbolts.

49 You poured out upon them your blazing anger: *
   fury, indignation, and distress,
   a troop of destroying angels.

50 You gave full rein to your anger;
   you did not spare their souls from death, *
   but delivered their lives to the plague.

51 You struck down all the firstborn of Egypt, *
   the first-fruits of their strength in the dwellings of Ham.

52 You led out your people like sheep *
   and guided them in the wilderness like a flock.

53 You led them to safety, and they were not afraid; *
   but the sea overwhelmed their enemies.

54 You brought them to your holy land, *
   the mountain your right hand had won.

55 You drove out the Canaanites before them
and apportioned an inheritance to them by lot; *
  you made the tribes of Israel to dwell in their tents.

56 But they tested you, O Most High, and defied you *
  and did not keep your commandments.

57 They turned away and were disloyal like their forebears; *
  they were undependable like a warped bow.

58 They grieved you with their hill-altars *
  and provoked your displeasure with their idols.

59 When you heard this, you were angry *
  and utterly rejected Israel.

60 You forsook the shrine at Shiloh, *
  the tabernacle where you had lived among your people.

61 You delivered the ark into captivity, *
  your glory into the adversary's hand.

62 You gave your people to the sword *
  and were angered against your inheritance.

63 The fire consumed their young men; *
  there were no wedding songs for their maidens.

64 Their priests fell by the sword, *
  and their widows made no lamentation.

65 Then you awoke, O God, as though from sleep, *
  like a warrior refreshed with wine.

66 You struck your enemies on the backside *
  and put them to perpetual shame.

67 You rejected the tent of Joseph *
  and did not choose the tribe of Ephraim;

68 You chose instead the tribe of Judah *
  and Mount Zion, which you loved.

69 You built your sanctuary like the heights of heaven, *
  like the earth which you founded for ever.

70 You chose David your servant *
  and took him away from the sheepfolds.

71 You brought him from following the ewes, *
    to be a shepherd over Jacob your people
    and over Israel your inheritance.

72 So he shepherded them with a faithful and true heart, *
    and guided them with the skillfulness of his hands.

Sixteenth Day: Morning Prayer

PSALM 79

1 O God, the nations have come into your inheritance;
    they have profaned your holy temple; *
    they have made Jerusalem a heap of rubble.

2 They have given the bodies of your servants as food for
        the birds of the air, *
    and the flesh of your faithful ones to the beasts
        of the field.

3 They have shed their blood like water on every side
        of Jerusalem, *
    and there was no one to bury them.

4 We have become a reproach to our neighbors, *
    an object of scorn and derision to those around us.

5 How long will you be angry, O God; *
    will your fury blaze like fire for ever?

6 Pour out your wrath upon the nations who have
        not known you *
    and upon the realms that have not called upon
        your Name.

7 For they have devoured Jacob *
    and made his dwelling a ruin.

8 Remember not our past sins;
    let your compassion be swift to meet us; *
    for we have been brought very low.

9 Help us, O God our Savior, for the glory of your Name; *
    deliver us and forgive us our sins, for your Name's sake.

10 Why should the nations say, "Where is their God?" *
    Let it be known among the nations and in our sight
    that you avenge the shedding of your servants' blood.

11 Let the sorrowful sighing of the prisoners come before you, *
    and by your great might spare those who are
        condemned to die.

12 May the revilings with which they reviled you, O God, *
    return seven-fold into their bosoms.

13 For we are your people and the sheep of your pasture; *
    we will give you thanks for ever
    and show forth your praise from age to age.

PSALM 80

1 Hear, O Shepherd of Israel, leading Joseph like a flock; *
    shine forth, you that are enthroned upon the cherubim.

2 In the presence of Ephraim, Benjamin, and Manasseh, *
    stir up your strength and come to help us.

3 Restore us, O God of hosts; *
    show the light of your countenance, and we shall be saved.

4 O God of hosts, *
    how long will you be angered
    despite the prayers of your people?

5 You have fed them with the bread of tears; *
    you have given them bowls of tears to drink.

6 You have made us the derision of our neighbors, *
    and our enemies laugh us to scorn.

7 Restore us, O God of hosts; *
    show the light of your countenance, and we shall be saved.

8 You have brought a vine out of Egypt; *
    you cast out the nations and planted it.

9 You prepared the ground for it; *
    it took root and filled the land.

10 The mountains were covered by its shadow *
    and the towering cedar trees by its boughs.

11 You stretched out its tendrils to the Sea *
    and its branches to the River.

12 Why have you broken down its wall, *
    so that all who pass by pluck off its grapes?

13 The wild boar of the forest has ravaged it, *
   and the beasts of the field have grazed upon it.

14 Turn now, O God of hosts, look down from heaven;
   behold and tend this vine; *
   preserve what your right hand has planted.

15 They burn it with fire like rubbish; *
   at the rebuke of your countenance let them perish.

16 Let your hand be upon the one at your right hand, *
   those whom you have made so strong for yourself.

17 And so will we never turn away from you, *
   give us life, that we may call upon your Name.

18 Restore us, O God of hosts; *
   show the light of your countenance, and we shall be saved.

PSALM 81

1 Sing with joy to God our strength, *
   and raise a loud shout to the God of Jacob.

2 Raise a song and sound the timbrel, *
   the merry harp, and the lyre.

3 Blow the ram's-horn at the new moon *
   and at the full moon, the day of our feast.

4 For this is a statute for Israel, *
   a law of the God of Jacob.

5 God laid it as a solemn charge upon Joseph, *
   when he came out of the land of Egypt.

6 I heard an unfamiliar voice saying, *
   "I eased Israel's shoulder from the burden;
   their hands were set free from bearing the load."

7 You called on me in trouble, and I saved you; *
   I answered you from the secret place of thunder
   and tested you at the waters of Meribah.

8 Hear, O my people, and I will admonish you: *
   O Israel, if you would but listen to me!

9 There shall be no strange god among you; *
   you shall not worship a foreign god.

10 I am your God,
    who brought you out of the land of Egypt and said, *
      "Open your mouth wide, and I will fill it."

11 And yet my people did not hear my voice, *
    and Israel would not obey me.

12 So I gave them over to the stubbornness of their hearts, *
    to follow their own devices.

13 Oh, that my people would listen to me, *
    that Israel would walk in my ways!

14 I should soon subdue their enemies *
    and turn my hand against their foes.

15 Those who hate me would cringe before me, *
    and their punishment would last for ever.

16 But Israel would I feed with the finest wheat *
    and satisfy them with honey from the rock.

Sixteenth Day: Evening Prayer

PSALM 82

1 God stands in the council of heaven *
    and gives judgment in the midst of the gods:

2 "How long will you judge unjustly *
    and show favor to the wicked?

3 Save the weak and the orphan; *
    defend the humble and needy;

4 Rescue the weak and the poor; *
    deliver them from the power of the wicked.

5 They do not know, neither do they understand;
    they go about in darkness; *
    all the foundations of the earth are shaken.

6 Now I say to you, 'You are gods, *
    and all of you children of the Most High;

7 Nevertheless, you shall die like mortals *
    and fall like any ruler.' "

8 Arise, O God, and rule the earth, *
    for you shall take all nations for your own.

PSALM 83

1 O God, do not be silent; *
   do not keep still nor hold your peace, O God;

2 For your enemies are in tumult, *
   and those who hate you have lifted up their heads.

3 They take secret counsel against your people *
   and plot against those whom you protect.

4 They have said, "Come, let us wipe them out from
         among the nations; *
   let the name of Israel be remembered no more."

5 They have conspired together; *
   they have made an alliance against you:

6 The tents of Edom and the Ishmaelites; *
   the Moabites and the Hagarenes;

7 Gebal, and Ammon, and Amalek; *
   the Philistines and those who dwell in Tyre.

8 The Assyrians also have joined them *
   and have come to help the people of Lot.

9 Do to them as you did to Midian, *
   to Sisera, and to Jabin at the river of Kishon:

10 They were destroyed at Endor; *
   they became like dung upon the ground.

11 Make their leaders like Oreb and Zeëb, *
   and all their commanders like Zebah and Zalmunna,

12 Who said, "Let us take for ourselves *
   the fields of God as our possession."

13 O my God, make them like whirling dust *
   and like chaff before the wind,

14 Like fire that burns down a forest, *
   like the flame that sets mountains ablaze.

15 Drive them with your tempest *
   and terrify them with your storm;

16 Cover their faces with shame, O God, *
   that they may seek your Name.

17 Let them be disgraced and terrified for ever; *
    let them be put to confusion and perish.

18 Let them know that you, whose Name is Holy, *
    you alone are the Most High over all the earth.

PSALM 84

1 How dear to me is your dwelling, O God of hosts! *
    My soul has a desire and longing for your courts;
    my heart and my flesh rejoice in the living God.

2 The sparrow has found her a house
    and the swallow a nest where she may lay her young, *
    by the side of your altars, O God of hosts,
    my Ruler and my God.

3 Happy are they who dwell in your house; *
    they will always be praising you.

4 Happy are the people whose strength is in you, *
    whose hearts are set on the pilgrims' way.

5 Those who go through the desolate valley will find
            it a place of springs, *
    for the early rains have covered it with pools of water.

6 They will climb from height to height; *
    the God of gods will be revealed in Zion.

7 O God of hosts, hear my prayer; *
    hearken, O God of Jacob.

8 Behold our defender, O God, *
    and look upon the face of your Anointed,

9 For one day in your courts is better than
            a thousand in my own room, *
    and to stand at the threshold of the house of my God
    than to dwell in the tents of the wicked;

10 For God is both sun and shield *
    and will give grace and glory.

11 No good thing will God withhold *
    from those who walk with integrity.

12 O God of hosts, *
    happy are they who put their trust in you!

PSALM 85

1 You have been gracious to your land, O God;*
   you have restored the good fortune of Jacob.

2 You have forgiven the iniquity of your people *
   . and blotted out all their sins.

3 You have withdrawn all your fury *
   and turned yourself from your wrathful indignation.

4 Restore us then, O God our Savior; *
   let your anger depart from us.

5 Will you be displeased with us for ever; *
   will you prolong your anger from age to age?

6 Will you not give us life again, *
   that your people may rejoice in you?

7 Show us your mercy, O God, *
   and grant us your salvation.

8 I will listen to what you are saying, *
   for you are speaking peace to your faithful people
   and to those who turn their hearts to you.

9 Truly, your salvation is very near to those who fear you, *
   that your glory may dwell in our land.

10 Mercy and truth have met together; *
   righteousness and peace have kissed each other.

11 Truth shall spring up from the earth, *
   and righteousness shall look down from heaven.

12 You, O God, will indeed grant prosperity, *
   and our land will yield its increase.

13 Righteousness shall go before you, *
   and peace shall be a pathway for your feet.

Seventeenth Day: Morning Prayer

PSALM 86

1 Bow down your ear, O God, and answer me, *
   for I am poor and in misery.

2 Keep watch over my life, for I am faithful; *
   save your servant, for I put my trust in you.

3 Be merciful to me, O God, for you are my God; *
　　I call upon you all the day long.

4 Gladden the soul of your servant, *
　　for to you, O God, I lift up my soul.

5 For you, O God, are good and forgiving, *
　　and great is your love toward all who call upon you.

6 Give ear, O God, to my prayer, *
　　and attend to the voice of my supplications.

7 In the time of my trouble I will call upon you, *
　　for you will answer me.

8 Among the gods there is none like you, O God, *
　　nor anything like your works.

9 All nations you have made will come and worship you,
　　　　O God, *
　　and glorify your Name.

10 For you are great; you do wondrous things; *
　　and you alone are God.

11 Teach me your way, O God, and I will walk in your truth; *
　　knit my heart to you that I may fear your Name.

12 I will thank you, my God, with all my heart, *
　　and glorify your Name for evermore.

13 For great is your love toward me; *
　　you have delivered me from the nethermost Pit.

14 The arrogant rise up against me, O God,
　　and a band of the violent seeks my life; *
　　they have not set you before their eyes.

15 But you, O God, are gracious and full of compassion, *
　　slow to anger, and full of kindness and truth.

16 Turn to me and have mercy upon me; *
　　give your strength to your servant
　　and save the child of your handmaid.

17 Show me a sign of your favor,
　　so that those who hate me may see it and be ashamed, *
　　because you, O God, have helped me and comforted me.

PSALM 87

1 On the holy mountain stands the city God has founded; *
   God loves the gates of Zion
   · more than all the dwellings of Jacob.

2 Glorious things are spoken of you, *
   O city of our God.

3 I count Egypt and Babylon among those who know me; *
   behold Philistia, Tyre, and Ethiopia:
   in Zion were they born.

4 Of Zion it shall be said, "Everyone was born there, *
   and the Most High God shall sustain it."

5 God will record in the roll of the peoples, *
   "These also were born there."

6 The singers and the dancers will say, *
   "All my fresh springs are in you."

PSALM 88

1 O my God, my Savior, *
   by day and night I cry to you.

2 Let my prayer enter into your presence; *
   incline your ear to my lamentation.

3 For I am full of trouble; *
   my life is at the brink of the grave.

4 I am counted among those who go down to the Pit; *
   I have become like one who has no strength;

5 Lost among the dead, *
   like the slain who lie in the grave,

6 Whom you remember no more, *
   for they are cut off from your hand.

7 You have laid me in the depths of the Pit, *
   in dark places, and in the abyss.

8 Your anger weighs upon me heavily, *
   and all your great waves overwhelm me.

9 You have put my friends far from me;
   you have made me to be abhorred by them; *
   I am in prison and cannot get free.

10 My sight has failed me because of trouble; *
   O God, I have called upon you daily;
   I have stretched out my hands to you.

11 Do you work wonders for the dead; *
   will those who have died stand up and give you thanks?

12 Will your loving-kindness be declared in the grave *
   or your faithfulness in the land of destruction?

13 Will your wonders be known in the dark *
   or your righteousness in the country where all is forgotten?

14 But as for me, O God, I cry to you for help; *
   in the morning my prayer comes before you.

15 O God, why have you rejected me; *
   why have you hidden your face from me?

16 Ever since my youth, I have been wretched and at the
         point of death; *
   I have borne your terrors with a troubled mind.

17 Your blazing anger has swept over me; *
   your terrors have destroyed me;

18 They surround me all day long like a flood; *
   they encompass me on every side.

19 My friend and my neighbor you have put away from me, *
   and darkness is my only companion.

Seventeenth Day: Evening Prayer

PSALM 89

PART I

1 Your love, O God, for ever will I sing; *
   from age to age my mouth will proclaim your faithfulness.

2 For I am persuaded that your love is established for ever; *
   you have set your faithfulness firmly in the heavens.

3 "I have made a covenant with my chosen one; *
   I have sworn an oath to David my servant:

4 'I will establish your line for ever, *
   and preserve your throne for all generations.' "

5 The heavens bear witness to your wonders, O God, *
   and to your faithfulness in the assembly of the holy ones;

6 For who in the skies can be compared to you, O God; *
   who is like you among the gods?

7 You are much to be feared in the council of the holy ones, *
   great and terrible to all those round about you.

8 Who is like you, O God of hosts? *
   O Mighty One, your faithfulness is all around you.

9 You rule the raging of the sea *
   and still the surging of its waves.

10 You have crushed Rahab of the deep with a deadly wound; *
   you have scattered your enemies with your mighty arm.

11 Yours are the heavens; the earth also is yours; *
   you laid the foundations of the world and all that is in it.

12 You have made the north and the south; *
   Tabor and Hermon rejoice in your Name.

13 You have a mighty arm; *
   strong is your hand and high is your right hand.

14 Righteousness and justice are the foundations
      of your throne; *
   love and truth go before your face.

15 Happy are the people who know the festal shout; *
   they walk, O God, in the light of your presence.

16 They rejoice daily in your Name; *
   they are jubilant in your righteousness.

17 For you are the glory of their strength, *
   and by your favor our might is exalted.

18 Truly, God is our Ruler; *
   the Holy One of Israel is our Sovereign.

PSALM 89: PART II

19 You spoke once in a vision and said to your faithful people: *
   "I have set the crown upon a warrior
   and have exalted one chosen out of the people.

20 I have found David my servant; *
   with my holy oil have I anointed him.

21 My hand will hold him fast, *
    and my arm will make him strong.

22 No enemy shall deceive him *
    nor any adversary bring him down.

23 I will crush his foes before him *
    and strike down those who hate him.

24 My faithfulness and love shall be with him, *
    and he shall be victorious through my Name.

25 I shall make his dominion extend *
    from the Great Sea to the River.

26 He will say to me, 'You are my Creator, *
    my God, and the rock of my salvation.'

27 I will make him my firstborn *
    and higher than the rulers of the earth.

28 I will keep my love for him for ever, *
    and my covenant will stand firm for him.

29 I will establish his line for ever *
    and his throne as the days of heaven."

30 "If his children forsake my law *
    and do not walk according to my judgments;

31 If they break my statutes *
    and do not keep my commandments;

32 I will punish their transgressions with a rod *
    and their iniquities with the lash;

33 But I will not take my love from him *
    nor let my faithfulness prove false.

34 I will not break my covenant *
    nor change what has gone out of my lips.

35 Once for all I have sworn by my holiness: *
    'I will not lie to David.

36 His line shall endure for ever *
    and his throne as the sun before me;

37 It shall stand fast for evermore like the moon, *
    the abiding witness in the sky.' "

38 But you have cast off and rejected your anointed; *
    you have become enraged at him.

39 You have broken your covenant with your servant, *
    defiled his crown, and hurled it to the ground.

40 You have breached all his walls *
    and laid his strongholds in ruins.

41 All who pass by despoil him; *
    he has become the scorn of his neighbors.

42 You have exalted the right hand of his foes *
    and made all his enemies rejoice.

43 You have turned back the edge of his sword *
    and have not sustained him in battle.

44 You have put an end to his splendor *
    and cast his throne to the ground.

45 You have cut short the days of his youth *
    and have covered him with shame.

46 How long will you hide yourself, O God,
    will you hide yourself for ever; *
    how long will your anger burn like fire?

47 Remember, O God, how short life is, *
    how frail you have made all flesh.

48 Who can live and not see death; *
    who can be saved from the power of the grave?

49 Where, O God, are your loving-kindnesses of old, *
    which you promised David in your faithfulness?

50 Remember how your servant is mocked, *
    how I carry in my bosom the taunts of many peoples,

51 The taunts your enemies have hurled, O God, *
    which they hurled at the heels of your anointed.

52 Blessed be God for evermore! *
    Amen, I say, Amen.

Book Four

Psalm 90

1 O God, you have been our refuge *
 from one generation to another.

2 Before the mountains were brought forth,
 or the land and the earth were born, *
 from age to age you are God.

3 You turn us back to the dust and say, *
 "Go back, O child of earth."

4 For a thousand years in your sight are like yesterday
 when it is past *
 and like a watch in the night.

5 You sweep us away like a dream; *
 we fade away suddenly like the grass.

6 In the morning it is green and flourishes; *
 in the evening it is dried up and withered.

7 For we consume away in your displeasure; *
 we are afraid because of your wrathful indignation.

8 Our iniquities you have set before you *
 and our secret sins in the light of your countenance.

9 When you are angry, all our days are gone; *
 we bring our years to an end like a sigh.

10 The span of our life is seventy years,
 perhaps in strength even eighty; *
 yet the sum of them is but labor and sorrow,
 for they pass away quickly and we are gone.

11 Who regards the power of your wrath; *
 who rightly fears your indignation?

12 So teach us to number our days *
 that we may apply our hearts to wisdom.

13 Return, O God; how long will you tarry? *
 Be gracious to your servants.

14 Satisfy us by your loving-kindness in the morning; *
  so shall we rejoice and be glad all the days of our life.

15 Make us glad by the measure of the days that you afflicted us *
  and the years in which we suffered adversity.

16 Show your servants your works *
  and your splendor to their children.

17 May the graciousness of our God be upon us; *
  prosper the work of our hands;
  prosper our handiwork.

PSALM 91

1 They who dwell in the shelter of the Most High *
  abide under the shadow of the Almighty.

2 They shall say to God, "You are my refuge and
      my stronghold, *
  my God in whom I put my trust."

3 For God shall deliver you from the snare of the hunter *
  and from the deadly pestilence.

4 God's pinions shall cover you,
  and under God's wings you shall find refuge; *
  God's faithfulness shall be a shield and buckler.

5 You shall not be afraid of any terror by night *
  nor of the arrow that flies by day;

6 Of the plague that stalks in the darkness *
  nor of the sickness that lays waste at mid-day.

7 A thousand shall fall at your side
  and ten thousand at your right hand, *
  but it shall not come near you.

8 Your eyes have only to behold, *
  to see the reward of the wicked.

9 Because you have made God your refuge *
  and the Most High your habitation,

10 There shall no evil happen to you, *
  neither shall any plague come near your dwelling.

11 For God shall give the angels charge over you, *
  to keep you in all your ways.

12 They shall bear you in their hands, *
    lest you dash your foot against a stone.

13 You shall tread upon the lion and adder; *
    you shall trample the young lion and the serpent
        under your feet.

14 Because you are bound to me in love,
    therefore will I deliver you; *
    I will protect you, because you know my Name.

15 You shall call upon me, and I will answer you; *
    I am with you in trouble; I will rescue you and
        bring you honor.

16 With long life will I satisfy you *
    and show you my salvation.

PSALM 92

1 It is a good thing to give thanks to God *
    and to sing praises to your Name, O Most High;

2 To tell of your loving-kindness early in the morning *
    and of your faithfulness in the night season;

3 On the psaltery, and on the lyre, *
    and to the melody of the harp,

4 For you have made me glad by your acts, O God, *
    and I shout for joy because of the works of your hands.

5 O God, how great are your works; *
    your thoughts are very deep.

6 The dullard does not know
    nor does the fool understand, *
    that though the wicked grow like weeds
    and all the workers of iniquity flourish,

7 They flourish only to be destroyed for ever; *
    but you, O God, are exalted for evermore.

8 For lo, your enemies, O God,
    lo, your enemies shall perish, *
    and all the workers of iniquity shall be scattered.

9 But my horn you have exalted like the horns of wild bulls; *
    I am anointed with fresh oil.

10 My eyes also gloat over my enemies, *
 and my ears rejoice to hear the doom of
  the wicked who rise up against me.

11 The righteous shall flourish like a palm tree *
 and shall spread abroad like a cedar of Lebanon.

12 Those who are planted in the house of God *
 shall flourish in the heavenly courts.

13 They shall still bear fruit in old age; *
 they shall be green and succulent,

14 That they may show how upright God is, *
 my Rock, in whom there is no fault.

Eighteenth Day: Evening Prayer

PSALM 93

1 God is Sovereign,
 clothed in splendid apparel; *
 God is robed in majesty
 and is girded with strength.

2 God has made the whole world so sure *
 that it cannot be moved;

3 Ever since the world began,
 your throne has been established; *
 you are from everlasting.

4 The waters have lifted up, O God,
 the waters have lifted up their voice; *
 the waters have lifted up their pounding waves.

5 Mightier than the sound of many waters,
 mightier than the breakers of the sea, *
 mightier is the Holy One who dwells on high.

6 Your testimonies are very sure, *
 and holiness adorns your house, O God,
 for ever and for evermore.

PSALM 94

1 O mighty God of vengeance, *
   O God of vengeance, show yourself.

2 Rise up, O Judge of the world; *
   give the arrogant their just deserts.

3 How long shall the wicked, O God, *
   how long shall the wicked triumph?

4 They bluster in their insolence; *
   all evildoers are full of boasting.

5 They crush your people, O God, *
   and afflict your chosen nation.

6 They murder the widow and the stranger *
   and put the orphans to death.

7 Yet they say, "God does not see, *
   the God of Jacob takes no notice."

8 Consider well, you dullards among the people; *
   when will you fools understand?

9 Does the one who planted the ear not hear; *
   does the one who formed the eye not see?

10 Will the one who admonishes the nations not punish; *
   does the one who teaches all the world have no knowledge?

11 God knows our human thoughts, *
   how like a puff of wind they are.

12 Happy are they whom you instruct, O God, *
   whom you teach out of your law,

13 To give them rest in evil days, *
   until a pit is dug for the wicked.

14 For you will not abandon your people *
   nor will you forsake your own.

15 For judgment will again be just, *
   and all the true of heart will follow it.

16 Who rose up for me against the wicked; *
   who took my part against the evildoers?

17 If you had not come to my help, *
   I should soon have dwelt in the land of silence.

18 As often as I said, "My foot has slipped," *
    your love, O God, upheld me.

19 When many cares fill my mind, *
    your consolations cheer my soul.

20 Can a corrupt tribunal have any part with you, *
    one which frames evil into law?

21 They conspire against the life of the just *
    and condemn the innocent to death.

22 But you have become my stronghold; *
    you are the rock of my trust.

23 You will turn their wickedness back upon them
    and destroy them in their own malice; *
    you, O Most High, will destroy them.

Nineteenth Day: Morning Prayer

Psalm 95

1 Come, let us sing to the Holy One; *
    let us shout for joy to the Rock of our salvation.

2 Let us come before God's presence with thanksgiving *
    and raise a loud shout with psalms.

3 For you, O God, are a great God; *
    you are great above all gods.

4 In your hand are the caverns of the earth, *
    and the heights of the hills are yours also.

5 The sea is yours, for you made it, *
    and your hands have molded the dry land.

6 Come, let us bow down and bend the knee, *
    and kneel before God, our Maker,

7 For you are our God,
    and we are the people of your pasture and the sheep
        of your hand. *
    Oh, that today we would hearken to your voice!

8 Harden not your hearts,
as your forebears did in the wilderness, *
at Meribah, and on that day at Massah,
when they tempted me;

9 They put me to the test, *
though they had seen my works.

10 Forty years long I detested that generation and said, *
"This people are wayward in their hearts;
they do not know my ways."

11 So I swore in my wrath, *
"They shall not enter into my rest."

PSALM 96

1 Sing to God a new song; *
sing to God all the whole earth.

2 Sing and bless God's holy Name; *
proclaim the good news of salvation from day to day.

3 Declare God's glory among the nations, *
God's wonders among all peoples.

4 For God is great and greatly to be praised, *
more to be feared than all gods.

5 As for all the gods of the nations, they are but idols, *
but it is God who made the heavens.

6 Oh, the majesty and magnificence of God's presence! *
Oh, the power and the splendor of God's sanctuary!

7 Ascribe to God, you families of the peoples, *
ascribe to God honor and power.

8 Ascribe due honor to God's holy Name; *
bring offerings and come into God's courts.

9 Worship the Most High in the beauty of holiness; *
let the whole earth tremble before God.

10 Tell it out among the nations that God reigns! *
God has made the world so firm that it cannot be moved,
and will judge the peoples with equity.

11 Let the heavens rejoice, and let the earth be glad;
  let the sea thunder and all that is in it; *
    let the field be joyful and all that is therein.

12 Then shall all the trees of the wood shout for joy
  before God, who will come, *
    who will come to judge the earth.

13 God will judge the world with righteousness *
  and the peoples with truth.

PSALM 97

1 You reign, O God; let the earth rejoice; *
  let the multitude of the isles be glad.

2 Clouds and darkness are round about you; *
  righteousness and justice are the
    foundations of your throne.

3 A fire goes before you *
  and burns up your enemies on every side.

4 Your lightnings light up the world; *
  the earth sees it and is afraid.

5 The mountains melt like wax at your presence, O God, *
  at your presence, O God of the whole earth.

6 The heavens declare your righteousness, *
  and all the peoples see your glory.

7 Confounded be all who worship carved images
  and delight in false gods! *
    Let all gods bow down before you.

8 Zion hears and is glad, and the cities of Judah rejoice, *
  because of your judgments, O God.

9 For you are God,
  most high over all the earth; *
    you are exalted far above all gods.

10 You love those who hate evil; *
  you preserve the lives of your saints
    and deliver them from the hand of the wicked.

11 Light has sprung up for the righteous *
    and joyful gladness for those who are truehearted.

12 Rejoice in God, you righteous, *
    and give thanks to God's holy Name.

Nineteenth Day: Evening Prayer

PSALM 98

1 Sing a new song to God, *
    who has done marvelous things.

2 With your right hand, O God, and your holy arm, *
    you have won for yourself the victory.

3 You have made known your victory; *
    your righteousness have you openly shown in
        the sight of the nations.

4 You remember your mercy and faithfulness to
        the house of Israel, *
    and all the ends of the earth have seen the
        victory of our God.

5 Shout with joy to God, all you lands; *
    lift up your voice, rejoice, and sing.

6 Sing to God with the harp, *
    with the harp and the voice of song.

7 With trumpets and the sound of the horn, *
    shout with joy before God who reigns in majesty.

8 Let the sea make a noise and all that is in it, *
    the lands and those who dwell therein.

9 Let the rivers clap their hands, *
    and let the hills ring out with joy before God,
    who will come to judge the earth.

10 God shall judge the world in righteousness *
    and the peoples with equity.

Psalm 99

1 God reigns; let the people tremble; *
  God is enthroned upon the cherubim;
  let the earth shake.

2 God is great in Zion *
  and is high above all peoples.

3 Let them confess God's Name, which is great and awesome; *
  God is the Holy One.

4 "O mighty Ruler, lover of justice,
  you have established equity; *
  you have executed justice and righteousness in Jacob."

5 We proclaim your greatness, O God,
  and fall down before your footstool; *
  you are the Holy One.

6 Moses and Aaron among your priests,
  and Samuel among those who call upon your Name, *
  they called upon you, and you answered them.

7 You spoke to them out of the pillar of cloud; *
  they kept your testimonies and the decree that
      you gave them.

8 "O Holy God, you answered them indeed; *
  you were a God who forgave them,
  yet punished them for their evil deeds."

9 Proclaim the greatness of our God,
  and worship on God's holy hill, *
  for our God is the Holy One.

Psalm 100

1 May all lands be joyful before you, O God, *
  serve you with gladness
  and come before your presence with a song.

2 For we know that you are God; *
  you yourself have made us, and we are yours;
  we are your people and the sheep of your pasture.

3 We shall enter your gates with thanksgiving,
  go into your courts with praise, *
  give thanks to you and call upon your Name.

4 For you are good;
   your mercy is everlasting, *
      and your faithfulness endures from age to age.

Psalm 101

1 I will sing of mercy and justice; *
   to you, O God, will I sing praises.

2 I will strive to follow a blameless course;
   oh, when will you come to me? *
      I will walk with sincerity of heart within my house.

3 I will set no worthless thing before my eyes; *
   I hate the doers of evil deeds;
      they shall not remain with me.

4 A crooked heart shall be far from me; *
   I will not know evil.

5 Those who in secret slander their neighbors I will destroy; *
   those who have a haughty look and a proud
      heart I cannot abide.

6 My eyes are upon the faithful in the land, that they may
      dwell with me, *
   and only those who lead a blameless life shall
      be my servants.

7 Those who act deceitfully shall not dwell in my house, *
   and those who tell lies shall not continue in my sight.

8 I will soon destroy all the wicked in the land, *
   that I may root out all evildoers from the city of God.

Twentieth Day: Morning Prayer

Psalm 102

1 O God, hear my prayer, and let my cry come before you; *
   hide not your face from me in the day of my trouble.

2 Incline your ear to me; *
   when I call, make haste to answer me,

3 For my days drift away like smoke, *
   and my bones are hot as burning coals.

4 My heart is smitten like grass and withered, *
 so that I forget to eat my bread.

5 Because of the voice of my groaning, *
 I am but skin and bones.

6 I have become like a vulture in the wilderness, *
 like an owl among the ruins.

7 I lie awake and groan; *
 I am like a sparrow, lonely on a house-top.

8 My enemies revile me all day long, *
 and those who scoff at me have taken an oath against me.

9 For I have eaten ashes for bread *
 and mingled my drink with weeping.

10 Because of your indignation and wrath, *
 you have lifted me up and thrown me away.

11 My days pass away like a shadow, *
 and I wither like the grass.

12 But you, O God, endure for ever, *
 and your Name from age to age.

13 You will arise and have compassion on Zion,
 for it is time to have mercy; *
 indeed, the appointed time has come.

14 For your servants love its very rubble *
 and are moved to pity even for its dust.

15 The nations shall fear your Name, O God, *
 and all the rulers of the earth your glory.

16 You, O God, will build up Zion, *
 and your glory will appear.

17 You will look with favor on the prayer of the homeless *
 and will not despise their plea.

18 Let this be written for a future generation, *
 so that a people yet unborn may praise you, O God.

19 For you looked down from your holy place on high; *
 from the heavens you beheld the earth,

20 That you might hear the groan of the captive *
 and set free those condemned to die,

21 That they may declare in Zion your Name, O God, *
       and your praise in Jerusalem,

22 When the peoples are gathered together, *
       and the nations also, to serve you.

23 You have brought down my strength before my time; *
       you have shortened the number of my days.

24 And I said, "O my God,
       do not take me away in the midst of my days; *
       your years endure throughout all generations.

25 In the beginning, O God, you laid the foundations
               of the earth, *
       and the heavens are the work of your hands.

26 They shall perish, but you will endure;
       they all shall wear out like a garment; *
           as clothing you will change them,
           and they shall be changed,

27 But you are always the same, *
       and your years will never end.

28 The children of your servants shall continue, *
       and their offspring shall stand fast in your sight."

Psalm 103

 1 Bless the Holy One, O my soul, *
       and all that is within me, bless God's holy Name.

 2 Bless the Holy One, O my soul, *
       and forget not all the gifts of God.

 3 O God, you forgive all our sins, *
       and you heal all our infirmities;

 4 You redeem our life from the grave *
       and crown us with mercy and loving-kindness;

 5 You satisfy us with good things, *
       and our youth is renewed like an eagle's.

 6 O God, you execute righteousness *
       and judgment for all who are oppressed.

 7 You made your ways known to Moses *
       and your works to the children of Israel.

8 You are full of compassion and mercy, *
    slow to anger and of great kindness.

9 You will not always accuse us, *
    nor will you keep your anger for ever.

10 You have not dealt with us according to our sins, *
    nor rewarded us according to our wickedness.

11 For as the heavens are high above the earth, *
    so is your mercy great upon those who fear you.

12 As far as the east is from the west, *
    so far have you removed our sins from us.

13 As a parent cares for a child, *
    so do you care for those who fear you.

14 For you yourself know whereof we are made; *
    you remember that we are but dust.

15 Our days are like the grass; *
    we flourish like a flower of the field;

16 When the wind goes over it, it is gone, *
    and its place shall know it no more.

17 But your merciful goodness endures for ever
        on those who fear you, *
    and your righteousness on children's children;

18 On those who keep your covenant *
    and remember your commandments and do them.

19 You have set your throne in heaven, *
    and you have dominion over all.

20 Bless God, all you angels,
    you mighty ones who do God's bidding, *
    and hearken to the voice of God's word.

21 Bless God, all you heavenly hosts, *
    you ministers who do God's will.

22 Bless God, all creation,
    in all places of God's dominion; *
    bless the Holy One, O my soul.

Psalm 104

1 Bless the Holy One, O my soul; *
  O God, how excellent is your greatness;
  you are clothed with majesty and splendor.

2 You wrap yourself with light as with a cloak; *
  you spread out the heavens like a curtain.

3 You lay the beams of your chambers in the waters above; *
  you make the clouds your chariot;
  you ride on the wings of the wind.

4 You make the winds your messengers *
  and flames of fire your servants.

5 You have set the earth upon its foundations, *
  so that it never shall move at any time.

6 You covered it with the Deep as with a mantle; *
  the waters stood higher than the mountains.

7 At your rebuke they fled; *
  at the voice of your thunder they hastened away.

8 They went up into the hills and down to
      the valleys beneath, *
  to the places you had appointed for them.

9 You set the limits that they should not pass; *
  they shall not again cover the earth.

10 You send the springs into the valleys; *
  they flow between the mountains.

11 All the beasts of the field drink their fill from them, *
  and the wild asses quench their thirst.

12 Beside them the birds of the air make their nests *
  and sing among the branches.

13 You water the mountains from your dwelling on high; *
  the earth is fully satisfied by the fruit of your works.

14 You make grass grow for flocks and herds *
  and plants to serve all people;

15 That they may bring forth food from the earth, *
  and wine to gladden our hearts,

16 Oil to make a cheerful countenance, *
   and bread to strengthen the heart.

17 The trees of the Holy One are full of sap, *
   the cedars of Lebanon which God planted,

18 In which the birds build their nests, *
   and in whose tops the storks make their dwellings.

19 The high hills are a refuge for the mountain goats,*
   and the stony cliffs for the rock badgers.

20 You appointed the moon to mark the seasons,*
   and the sun knows the time of its setting.

21 You make darkness that it may be night,*
   in which all the beasts of the forest prowl.

22 The lions roar after their prey *
   and seek their food from God.

23 The sun rises, and they slip away *
   and lay themselves down in their dens.

24 We go forth to our work*
   and to our labor until the evening.

25 O Holy One, how manifold are your works;*
   in wisdom you have made them all;
   the earth is full of your creatures.

26 Yonder is the great and wide sea
   with its living things too many to number,*
   creatures both small and great.

27 There move the ships,
   and there is that Leviathan, *
   which you have made for the sport of it.

28 All of them look to you *
   to give them their food in due season.

29 You give it to them; they gather it; *
   you open your hand, and they are filled with good things.

30 You hide your face, and they are terrified; *
   you take away their breath,
   and they die and return to their dust.

31 You send forth your Spirit, and they are created; *
   and so you renew the face of the earth.

32 May the glory of God endure for ever; *
    may the Holy One rejoice in all creation.

33 God looks at the earth and it trembles; *
    God touches the mountains and they smoke.

34 I will sing to God as long as I live; *
    I will praise my God while I have my being.

35 May these words of mine find favor; *
    I will rejoice in the Holy One.

36 Let sinners be consumed out of the earth, *
    and the wicked be no more.

37 Bless the Holy One, O my soul. *
    Alleluia!

Twenty-first Day: Morning Prayer

Psalm 105

Part I

1 We give you thanks, O God, and call upon your Name; *
    we make known your deeds among the peoples.

2 We sing to you; we sing your praise *
    and speak of all your marvelous works.

3 We glory in your holy Name; *
    let the hearts of those who seek you rejoice.

4 We search for you and your strength; *
    we continue to seek your face.

5 We remember the marvels you have done, *
    the wonders and the judgments of your mouth,

6 We, the offspring of Abraham, your servant, *
    we, the children of Jacob, the chosen ones.

7 You are our God indeed; *
    your judgments prevail in all the world.

8 You have always been mindful of your covenant, *
    the promise you made for a thousand generations:

9 The covenant you made with Abraham, *
    the oath that you swore to Isaac,

10 Which you established as a statute for Jacob, *
    an everlasting covenant for Israel,

11 Saying, "To them will I give the land of Canaan *
    to be their allotted inheritance."

12 When they were few in number, *
    of little account, and sojourners in the land,

13 Wandering from nation to nation *
    and from one realm to another,

14 You let no one oppress them *
    and rebuked monarchs for their sake,

15 Saying, "Do not touch my anointed *
    and do my prophets no harm."

16 Then you called for a famine in the land *
    and destroyed the supply of bread.

17 You sent a man before them, *
    Joseph, who was sold as a slave.

18 They bruised his feet in fetters; *
    his neck they put in an iron collar.

19 Until his prediction came to pass, *
    your word, O Most High, tested him.

20 The king sent and released him; *
    the ruler of the peoples set him free.

21 He set him as a master over his household, *
    as a ruler over all his possessions,

22 To instruct his princes according to his will *
    and to teach his elders wisdom.

PSALM 105: PART II

23 Israel came into Egypt, *
    and Jacob became a sojourner in the land of Ham.

24 You made your people exceedingly fruitful; *
    you made them stronger than their enemies,

25 Whose hearts you turned, so that they hated your people *
    and dealt unjustly with your servants.

26 You sent Moses your servant, *
    and Aaron whom you had chosen.

27 They worked your signs among them, *
    and portents in the land of Ham.

28 You sent darkness, and it grew dark; *
    but the Egyptians rebelled against your words.

29 You turned their waters into blood *
    and caused their fish to die.

30 Their land was overrun by frogs, *
    in the very chambers of their rulers.

31 You spoke, and there came swarms of insects *
    and gnats within all their borders.

32 You gave them hailstones instead of rain, *
    and flames of fire throughout their land.

33 You blasted their vines and their fig trees *
    and shattered every tree in their country.

34 You spoke, and the locust came, *
    and young locusts without number,

35 Which ate up all the green plants in their land *
    and devoured the fruit of their soil.

36 You struck down the firstborn of their land, *
    the firstfruits of all their strength.

37 You led out your people with silver and gold; *
    in all their tribes there was not one that stumbled.

38 Egypt was glad of their going, *
    because they were afraid of them.

39 You spread out a cloud for a covering *
    and a fire to give light in the night season.

40 They asked, and quails appeared, *
    and you satisfied them with bread from heaven.

41 You opened the rock, and water flowed, *
    so the river ran in the dry places.

42 For you remembered your holy word *
    and Abraham your servant.

43 So you led forth your people with gladness, *
    your chosen with shouts of joy.

44 You gave your people the lands of the nations, *
    and they took the fruit of others' toil,

45 That they might keep your statutes *
    and observe your laws. Alleluia!

Twenty-first Day: Evening Prayer

PSALM 106

PART I

1 Alleluia! Give thanks, for the Holy One is good; *
    God's mercy endures for ever.

2 Who can declare the mighty acts of God *
    or show forth rightful praise?

3 Happy are they who act with justice *
    and always do what is right!

4 Remember me, O God, with the favor you have
        for your people, *
    and visit me with your saving help,

5 That I may see the prosperity of your elect
    and be glad with the gladness of your people; *
    that I may glory with your inheritance.

6 We have sinned as our forebears did; *
    we have done wrong and dealt wickedly.

7 In Egypt they did not consider your marvelous works
    nor remember the abundance of your love; *
    they defied you, O Most High, at the Red Sea.

8 But you saved them for your Name's sake, *
    to make your power known.

9 You rebuked the Red Sea, and it dried up, *
    and you led them through the deep as through a desert.

10 You saved them from the hand of those who hated them *
    and redeemed them from the hand of the enemy.

11 The waters covered their oppressors; *
    not one of them was left.

12 Then they believed your words *
    and sang you songs of praise.

13 But they soon forgot your deeds *
    and did not wait for your counsel.

14 A craving seized them in the wilderness, *
    and they put you to the test in the desert.

15 You gave them what they asked, *
    but sent leanness into their soul.

16 They envied Moses in the camp, *
    and Aaron, the holy one of God.

17 The earth opened and swallowed Dathan *
    and covered the company of Abiram.

18 Fire blazed up against their company, *
    and flames devoured the wicked.

PSALM 106: PART II

19 Israel made a bull-calf at Horeb *
    and worshiped a molten image;

20 And so they exchanged their Glory *
    for the image of an ox that feeds on grass.

21 They forgot you, their Savior, *
    who had done great things in Egypt,

22 Wonderful deeds in the land of Ham, *
    and fearful things at the Red Sea.

23 So you would have destroyed them,
    had not Moses your chosen stood before you in the breach, *
    to turn away your wrath from consuming them.

24 They refused the pleasant land *
    and would not believe your promise.

25 They grumbled in their tents *
    and would not listen to your voice, O God.

26 So you lifted your hand against them, *
    to overthrow them in the wilderness,

27 To cast out their seed among the nations, *
    and to scatter them throughout the lands.

28 They joined themselves to Baal-Peor *
    and ate sacrifices offered to the dead.

29 They provoked you to anger with their actions, *
and a plague broke out among them.

30 Then Phinehas stood up and interceded, *
and the plague came to an end.

31 This was reckoned to him as righteousness *
throughout all generations for ever.

32 Again they provoked your anger at the waters of Meribah, *
so that you punished Moses because of them;

33 For they so embittered his spirit *
that he spoke rash words with his lips.

34 They did not destroy the peoples *
as you had commanded them.

35 They intermingled with the nations *
and learned their foreign ways,

36 So that they worshiped their idols, *
which became a snare to them.

37 They sacrificed their sons *
and their daughters to evil spirits.

38 They shed innocent blood,
the blood of their sons and daughters, *
which they offered to the idols of Canaan,
and the land was defiled with blood.

39 Thus they were polluted by their actions *
and went whoring in their evil deeds.

40 Therefore your wrath was kindled against your people, *
and you abhorred your inheritance.

41 You gave them over to the hand of the nations, *
and those who hated them ruled over them.

42 Their enemies oppressed them, *
and they were humbled under their hand.

43 Many a time did you deliver them,
but they rebelled through their own devices *
and were brought down in their iniquity.

44 Nevertheless, you saw their distress, *
when you heard their lamentation.

45 You remembered your covenant with them *
    and relented in accordance with your great mercy.

46 You caused them to be pitied *
    by those who held them captive.

47 Save us, O God,
    and gather us from among the nations, *
    that we may give thanks to your holy Name
    and glory in your praise.

48 Blest be the God of Israel,
    from everlasting and to everlasting, *
    and let all the people say, "Amen!" Alleluia!

BOOK FIVE

Twenty-second Day: Morning Prayer

PSALM 107

PART I

1 We give you thanks, O God, for you are good; *
    your mercy endures for ever.

2 Let all those whom you have redeemed proclaim *
    that you redeemed them from the hand of the foe.

3 You gathered them out of the lands, *
    from the east and from the west,
    from the north and from the south.

4 Some wandered in desert wastes; *
    they found no way to a city where they might dwell.

5 They were hungry and thirsty; *
    their spirits languished within them.

6 Then they cried to you in their trouble, *
    and you delivered them from their distress.

7 You put their feet on a straight path *
    to go to a city where they might dwell.

8 Let them give thanks to you for your mercy *
and the wonders you do for your children.

9 For you satisfy the thirsty *
and fill the hungry with good things.

10 Some sat in darkness and deep gloom, *
bound fast in misery and iron,

11 Because they rebelled against your words, O God, *
and despised your counsel, O Most High.

12 So you humbled their spirits with hard labor; *
they stumbled, and there was none to help.

13 Then they cried to you in their trouble, *
and you delivered them from their distress.

14 You led them out of darkness and deep gloom, *
and broke their bonds asunder.

15 Let them give thanks to you for your mercy *
and the wonders you do for your children,

16 For you shatter the doors of bronze *
and break in two the iron bars.

17 Some were fools and took to rebellious ways; *
they were afflicted because of their sins.

18 They abhorred all manner of food *
and drew near to death's door.

19 Then they cried to you in their trouble, *
and you delivered them from their distress.

20 You sent forth your word and healed them, *
and saved them from the grave.

21 Let them give thanks to you for your mercy *
and the wonders you do for your children.

22 Let them offer a sacrifice of thanksgiving, *
and tell of your acts with shouts of joy.

23 Some went down to the sea in ships *
and plied their trade in deep waters;

24 They beheld your works, O God, *
and your wonders in the deep.

25 Then you spoke, and a stormy wind arose, *
which tossed high the waves of the sea.

26 They mounted up to the heavens and fell back to the depths; *
   their hearts melted because of their peril.

27 They reeled and staggered like drunkards *
   and were at their wits' end.

28 Then they cried to you in their trouble, *
   and you delivered them from their distress.

29 You stilled the storm to a whisper *
   and quieted the waves of the sea.

30 Then were they glad because of the calm, *
   and you brought them to the harbor they were bound for.

31 Let them give thanks to you for your mercy *
   and the wonders you do for your children.

32 Let them exalt you in the congregation of the people *
   and praise you in the council of the elders.

PSALM 107: PART II

33 You changed rivers into deserts *
   and water-springs into thirsty ground,

34 A fruitful land into salt flats, *
   because of the wickedness of those who dwell there.

35 You changed deserts into pools of water *
   and dry land into water-springs.

36 You settled the hungry there, *
   and they founded a city to dwell in.

37 They sowed fields and planted vineyards, *
   and brought in a fruitful harvest.

38 You blessed them, so that they increased greatly; *
   you did not let their herds decrease.

39 Yet when they were diminished and brought low *
   through stress of adversity and sorrow,

40 (You pour contempt on princes *
   and make them wander in trackless wastes),

41 You lifted up the poor out of misery *
   and multiplied their families like flocks of sheep.

42 The upright will see this and rejoice, *
   but all wickedness will shut its mouth.

43 Whoever is wise will ponder these things *
   and consider well your mercies, O God.

Twenty-second Day: Evening Prayer

PSALM 108

1 My heart is firmly fixed, O God, my heart is fixed; *
   I will sing and make melody.

2 Wake up, my spirit;
   awake, lute and harp; *
   I myself will waken the dawn.

3 I will confess you among the peoples, O God; *
   I will sing praises to you among the nations.

4 For your loving-kindness is greater than the heavens, *
   and your faithfulness reaches to the clouds.

5 Exalt yourself above the heavens, O God, *
   and your glory over all the earth.

6 So that those who are dear to you may be delivered, *
   save with your right hand and answer me.

7 God spoke from the holy place and said: *
   "I will exult and parcel out Shechem;
   I will divide the valley of Succoth.

8 Gilead is mine and Manasseh is mine; *
   Ephraim is my helmet and Judah my scepter.

9 Moab is my wash-basin;
   on Edom I throw down my sandal to claim it, *
   and over Philistia will I shout in triumph."

10 Who will lead me into the strong city; *
   who will bring me into Edom?

11 Have you not cast us off, O God? *
   You no longer go out, O God, with our armies.

12 Grant us your help against the enemy, *
   for all human help is in vain.

13 With you, O God, we will do valiant deeds, *
   and you will tread our enemies under foot.

PSALM 109

1 Hold not your tongue, O God of my praise, *
   for the mouth of the wicked,
   the mouth of the deceitful, is opened against me.

2 They speak to me with a lying tongue; *
   they encompass me with hateful words
   and fight against me without a cause.

3 Despite my love, they accuse me, *
   but as for me, I pray for them.

4 They repay evil for good *
   and hatred for my love.

5 Set wicked ones against them, *
   and let accusers stand at their right hand.

6 When they are judged, let them be found guilty, *
   and let their appeals be in vain.

7 Let their days be few, *
   and let others take their office.

8 Let their children be fatherless *
   and their wives become widows.

9 Let their children be waifs and beggars; *
   let them be driven from the ruins of their homes.

10 Let the creditor seize everything they have; *
   let strangers plunder their gains.

11 Let there be no one to show them kindness, *
   and none to pity their fatherless children.

12 Let their descendants be destroyed, *
   and their names be blotted out in the next generation.

13 Let the wickedness of their parents be remembered
         before God, *
   and their forebears' sin not be blotted out;

14 Let their sin be always before God, *
   but let God root out their names from the earth;

15 Because they did not remember to show mercy, *
     but persecuted the poor and needy
     and sought to kill the brokenhearted.

16 They loved cursing,
   let it come upon them; *
     they took no delight in blessing,
     let it depart from them.

17 They put on cursing like a garment; *
     let it soak into their bodies like water
     and into their bones like oil;

18 Let it be to them like the cloak which they wrap
          around themselves *
     and like the belt that they wear continually.

19 Let this be the recompense from God to my accusers *
     and to those who speak evil against me.

20 But you, O God, my God,
   oh, deal with me according to your Name; *
     for your tender mercy's sake, deliver me.

21 For I am poor and needy, *
     and my heart is wounded within me.

22 I have faded away like a shadow when it lengthens; *
     I am shaken off like a locust.

23 My knees are weak through fasting, *
     and my flesh is wasted and gaunt.

24 I have become a reproach to them; *
     they see and shake their heads.

25 Help me, O God, my God; *
     save me for your mercy's sake.

26 Let them know that this is your hand, *
     that you, O God, have done it.

27 They may curse, but you will bless; *
     let those who rise up against me be put to shame,
     and your servant will rejoice.

28 Let my accusers be clothed with disgrace *
     and wrap themselves in their shame as in a cloak.

29 I will give great thanks to you with my mouth; *
    in the midst of the multitude will I praise you,

30 Because you stand at the right hand of the needy, *
    to save their lives from those who would condemn them.

Twenty-third Day: Morning Prayer

PSALM 110

1 The Holy One said to my Ruler, "Sit at my right hand, *
    until I make your enemies your footstool."

2 The Holy One will send the scepter of your power
        out of Zion, *
    saying, "Rule over your enemies round about you.

3 Royal state has been yours from the day of your birth; *
    in the beauty of holiness have I begotten you,
    like dew from the womb of the morning."

4 The Holy One has sworn and will not recant: *
    "You are a priest for ever after the order of Melchizedek."

5 The Ruler who is at your right hand
  will smite monarchs in the day of wrath *
    and will rule over the nations;

6 Will heap high the corpses *
    and will smash heads over the wide earth.

7 The Ruler will drink from the brook beside the road, *
    and therefore will stand victorious.

PSALM 111

1 Alleluia! I will give thanks to you, O God, with
        my whole heart, *
    in the assembly of the upright, in the congregation.

2 Great are your deeds, O God; *
    they are studied by all who delight in them.

3 Your work is full of majesty and splendor, *
    and your righteousness endures for ever.

4 You make your marvelous works to be remembered; *
    you are gracious and full of compassion.

5 You give food to those who fear you; *
   you are ever mindful of your covenant.

6 You have shown your people the power of your works *
   in giving them the lands of the nations.

7 The works of your hands are faithfulness and justice; *
   all your commandments are sure.

8 They stand fast for ever and ever, *
   because they are done in truth and equity.

9 You sent redemption to your people;
   you commanded your covenant for ever; *
   holy and awesome is your Name.

10 The fear of God is the beginning of wisdom; *
   those who act accordingly have a good understanding;
   God's praise endures for ever.

PSALM 112

1 Alleluia! Happy are they who fear God *
   and have great delight in the commandments!

2 Their descendants will be mighty in the land; *
   the generation of the upright will be blest.

3 Wealth and riches will be in their house, *
   and their righteousness will last for ever.

4 Light shines in the darkness for the upright; *
   the righteous are merciful and full of compassion.

5 It is good for them to be generous in lending *
   and to manage their affairs with justice.

6 For they will never be shaken; *
   the righteous will be kept in everlasting remembrance.

7 They will not be afraid of any evil rumors; *
   their heart is right;
   they put their trust in God.

8 Their heart is established and will not shrink, *
   until they see their desire upon their enemies.

9 They have given freely to the poor, *
   and their righteousness stands fast for ever;
   they will hold up their head with honor.

10 The wicked will see it and be angry;
   they will gnash their teeth and pine away; *
   the desires of the wicked will perish.

PSALM 113

1 Alleluia! Give praise, you servants of God; *
  praise the Name of the Most High.

2 Let God's Name be blest, *
  from this time forth for evermore.

3 From the rising of the sun to its going down, *
  let God's holy Name be praised.

4 God is high above all nations, *
  and God's glory above the heavens.

5 Who is like our God, who sits enthroned on high, *
  but stoops to behold the heavens and the earth?

6 God takes up the weak out of the dust *
  and lifts up the poor from the ashes,

7 To set them up on high, *
  with the rulers of the people.

8 God makes the woman of a childless house *
  to be a joyful mother of children.

Twenty-third Day: Evening Prayer

PSALM 114

1 Alleluia! When Israel came out of Egypt, *
  the house of Jacob from a people of strange speech,

2 Judah became God's sanctuary *
  and Israel God's dominion.

3 The sea beheld it and fled; *
  Jordan turned and went back.

4 The mountains skipped like rams, *
  and the little hills like young sheep.

5 What ailed you, O sea, that you fled; *
  O Jordan, that you turned back?

6 You mountains, that you skipped like rams; *
    you little hills, like young sheep?

7 Tremble, O earth, at the presence of God, *
    at the presence of the God of Jacob,

8 Who turned the hard rock into a pool of water *
    and flint-stone into a flowing spring.

Psalm 115

1 Not to us, O God, not to us,
    but to your Name give glory, *
        because of your love and because of your faithfulness.

2 Why should the nations say, *
    "Where then is their God?"

3 Our God is in heaven, *
    and whatever God wills to do comes to pass.

4 Their idols are silver and gold, *
    the work of human hands.

5 They have mouths, but they cannot speak; *
    eyes have they, but they cannot see;

6 They have ears, but they cannot hear; *
    noses, but they cannot smell;

7 They have hands, but they cannot feel;
    feet, but they cannot walk; *
        they make no sound with their throat.

8 Those who make them are like them, *
    and so are all who put their trust in them.

9 O Israel, trust in God, *
    who is their help and their shield.

10 O house of Aaron, trust in God, *
    who is their help and their shield.

11 You who fear God, trust in God, *
    who is their help and their shield.

12 God has been mindful of us and will bless us; *
    God will bless the house of Israel
    and will bless the house of Aaron;

13 God will bless those who stand in awe, *
  both small and great together.

14 May God increase you more and more, *
  you and your children after you.

15 May you be blessed by God, *
  the maker of heaven and earth.

16 The heaven of heavens belongs to God, *
  who entrusted the earth to its peoples.

17 The dead do not praise God, *
  nor all those who go down into silence;

18 But we will bless God, *
  from this time forth for evermore. Alleluia!

Twenty-fourth Day: Morning Prayer

PSALM 116

1 I love you, O God, because you have heard the voice
    of my supplication, *
  because you have inclined your ear to me whenever
    I called upon you.

2 The cords of death entangled me;
  the grip of the grave took hold of me; *
  I came to grief and sorrow.

3 Then I called upon your holy Name: *
  "O God, I pray you, save my life."

4 Gracious are you and righteous; *
  you are full of compassion.

5 You watch over the innocent; *
  I was brought very low, and you helped me.

6 Turn again to your rest, O my soul, *
  for God has treated you well.

7 For you, O God, have rescued my life from death, *
  my eyes from tears, and my feet from stumbling.

8 I will walk in the presence of God, *
  in the land of the living.

9 I believed, even when I said,
   "I have been brought very low." *
      In my distress I said, "No one can be trusted."

10 How shall I repay God *
   for all the good things done for me?

11 I will lift up the cup of salvation *
   and call upon the Name of God.

12 I will fulfill my vows to God *
   in the presence of all people.

13 Precious in your sight, O God, *
   is the death of your servants.

14 O God, I am your servant; *
   I am your servant and the child of your handmaid;
      you have freed me from my bonds.

15 I will offer you the sacrifice of thanksgiving *
   and call upon your holy Name.

16 I will fulfill my vows to you *
   in the presence of all your people,

17 In the courts of God's house, *
   in the midst of you, O Jerusalem. Alleluia!

PSALM 117

1 Praise God, all you nations; *
   laud the Most High, all you peoples.

2 For God's loving-kindness toward us is great, *
   and the faithfulness of God endures for ever. Alleluia!

PSALM 118

1 Give thanks to God who is good; *
   God's mercy endures for ever.

2 Let Israel now proclaim: *
   "God's mercy endures for ever."

3 Let the house of Aaron now proclaim: *
   "God's mercy endures for ever."

4 Let those who fear God now proclaim: *
   "God's mercy endures for ever."

5 I called out in my distress; *
   God answered by setting me free.

6 The Mighty One is at my side, therefore I will not fear; *
   what can anyone do to me?

7 God is at my side to help me; *
   I will triumph over those who hate me.

8 It is better to rely on God *
   than to put any trust in flesh.

9 It is better to rely on God *
   than to put any trust in rulers.

10 All the ungodly encompass me; *
   in the name of God I will repel them.

11 They hem me in, they hem me in on every side; *
   in the name of God I will repel them.

12 They swarm about me like bees;
   they blaze like a fire of thorns; *
   in the name of God I will repel them.

13 I was pressed so hard that I almost fell, *
   but God came to my help.

14 God is my strength and my song *
   and has become my salvation.

15 There is a sound of exultation and victory *
   in the tents of the righteous:

16 "The right hand of the Most High has triumphed; *
   the right hand of the Most High is exalted;
   the right hand of the Most High has triumphed!"

17 I shall not die, but live *
   and declare the works of God.

18 God has punished me sorely, *
   but did not hand me over to death.

19 Open for me the gates of righteousness; *
   I will enter them;
   I will offer thanks to God.

20 "This is the gate of the Holy One; *
   those who are righteous may enter."

21 I will give thanks to you, for you answered me *
   and have become my salvation.

22 The same stone which the builders rejected *
   has become the chief cornerstone.

23 This is God's doing, *
   and it is marvelous in our eyes.

24 On this day the Holy One has acted; *
   we will rejoice and be glad in it.

25 Hosanna, O God, hosanna! *
   O Holy One, send us now success.

26 Blest is the one who comes in the name of God; *
   we bless you from the house of God.

27 God is the Holy One who has shined upon us; *
   form a procession with branches up to
      the horns of the altar.

28 "You are my God, and I will thank you; *
   you are my God, and I will exalt you."

29 Give thanks to God who is good; *
   God's mercy endures for ever.

Twenty-fourth Day: Evening Prayer

PSALM 119:1-32

ALEPH

1 Happy are they whose way is blameless, *
   who walk in your law, O God!

2 Happy are they who observe your decrees *
   and seek you with all their hearts;

3 Who never do any wrong, *
   but always walk in your ways.

4 You laid down your commandments, *
   that we should fully keep them.

5 Oh, that my ways were made so direct *
   that I might keep your statutes!

6 Then I should not be put to shame *
  when I regard all your commandments.

7 I will thank you with an unfeigned heart *
  when I have learned your righteous judgments.

8 I will keep your statutes; *
  do not utterly forsake me.

BETH

9 How shall young ones cleanse their ways? *
  By keeping to your words.

10 With my whole heart I seek you; *
   let me not stray from your commandments.

11 I treasure your promise in my heart, *
   that I may not sin against you.

12 Blest are you, O God; *
   instruct me in your statutes.

13 With my lips will I recite *
   all the judgments of your mouth.

14 I have taken greater delight in the way of your decrees *
   than in all manner of riches.

15 I will meditate on your commandments *
   and give attention to your ways.

16 My delight is in your statutes; *
   I will not forget your word.

GIMEL

17 Deal bountifully with your servant, *
   that I may live and keep your word.

18 Open my eyes, that I may see *
   the wonders of your law.

19 I am a stranger here on earth; *
   do not hide your commandments from me.

20 My soul is consumed at all times *
   with longing for your judgments.

21 You have rebuked the insolent; *
   cursed are they who stray from your commandments!

22 Turn from me shame and rebuke, *
　　for I have kept your decrees.

23 Even though rulers sit and plot against me, *
　　I will meditate on your statutes.

24 For your decrees are my delight, *
　　and they are my counselors.

DALETH

25 My soul cleaves to the dust; *
　　give me life according to your word.

26 I have confessed my ways, and you answered me; *
　　instruct me in your statutes.

27 Make me understand the way of your commandments, *
　　that I may meditate on your marvelous works.

28 My soul melts away for sorrow; *
　　strengthen me according to your word.

29 Take from me the way of lying; *
　　let me find grace through your law.

30 I have chosen the way of faithfulness; *
　　I have set your judgments before me.

31 I hold fast to your decrees; *
　　O God, let me not be put to shame.

32 I will run the way of your commandments, *
　　for you have set my heart at liberty.

Twenty-fifth Day: Morning Prayer

PSALM 119:33-72

HE

33 Teach me, O God, the way of your statutes, *
　　and I shall keep it to the end.

34 Give me understanding, and I shall keep your law; *
　　I shall keep it with all my heart.

35 Make me go in the path of your commandments, *
　　for that is my desire.

36 Incline my heart to your decrees *
    and not to unjust gain.

37 Turn my eyes from watching what is worthless; *
    give me life in your ways.

38 Fulfill your promise to your servant, *
    which you make to those who fear you.

39 Turn away the reproach which I dread, *
    because your judgments are good.

40 Behold, I long for your commandments; *
    in your righteousness preserve my life.

WAW

41 Let your loving-kindness come to me, O God, *
    and your salvation, according to your promise.

42 Then shall I have a word for those who taunt me, *
    because I trust in your words.

43 Do not take the word of truth out of my mouth, *
    for my hope is in your judgments.

44 I shall continue to keep your law; *
    I shall keep it for ever and ever.

45 I will walk at liberty, *
    because I study your commandments.

46 I will tell of your decrees before rulers *
    and will not be ashamed.

47 I delight in your commandments, *
    which I have always loved.

48 I will lift up my hands to your commandments, *
    and I will meditate on your statutes.

ZAYIN

49 Remember your word to your servant, *
    because you have given me hope.

50 This is my comfort in my trouble: *
    that your promise gives me life.

51 The proud have derided me cruelly, *
    but I have not turned from your law.

52 When I remember your judgments of old, *
　　O God, I take great comfort.

53 I am filled with a burning rage, *
　　because of the wicked who forsake your law.

54 Your statutes have been like songs to me *
　　wherever I have lived as a stranger.

55 I remember your Name in the night, O God, *
　　and dwell upon your law.

56 This is how it has been with me, *
　　because I have kept your commandments.

Heth

57 You only are my portion, O God; *
　　I have promised to keep your words.

58 I entreat you with all my heart: *
　　be merciful to me according to your promise.

59 I have considered my ways *
　　and turned my feet toward your decrees.

60 I hasten and do not tarry *
　　to keep your commandments.

61 Though the cords of the wicked entangle me, *
　　I do not forget your law.

62 At midnight I will rise to give you thanks, *
　　because of your righteous judgments.

63 I am a companion of all who fear you *
　　and of those who keep your commandments.

64 The earth, O God, is full of your love; *
　　instruct me in your statutes.

Teth

65 O God, you have dealt graciously with your servant, *
　　according to your word.

66 Teach me discernment and knowledge, *
　　for I have believed in your commandments.

67 Before I was afflicted I went astray, *
　　but now I keep your word.

68 You are good and you bring forth good; *
    instruct me in your statutes.

69 The proud have smeared me with lies, *
    but I will keep your commandments with my whole heart.

70 Their heart is gross and fat, *
    but my delight is in your law.

71 It is good for me that I have been afflicted, *
    that I might learn your statutes.

72 The law of your mouth is dearer to me *
    than thousands in gold and silver.

Twenty-fifth Day: Evening Prayer

PSALM 119:73-104

YODH

73 Your hands have made me and fashioned me; *
    give me understanding, that I may learn your
        commandments.

74 Those who fear you will be glad when they see me, *
    because I trust in your word.

75 I know, O God, that your judgments are right, *
    and that in faithfulness you have afflicted me.

76 Let your loving-kindness be my comfort, *
    as you have promised to your servant.

77 Let your compassion come to me, that I may live, *
    for your law is my delight.

78 Let the arrogant be put to shame, for they wrong me
        with lies, *
    but I will meditate on your commandments.

79 Let those who fear you turn to me *
    and also those who know your decrees.

80 Let my heart be sound in your statutes, *
    that I may not be put to shame.

KAPH

81 My soul has longed for your salvation; *
 I have put my hope in your word.

82 My eyes have failed from watching for your promise, *
 and I say, "When will you comfort me?"

83 I have become like a leather flask in the smoke, *
 but I have not forgotten your statutes.

84 How much longer must I wait; *
 when will you give judgment against those who
 persecute me?

85 The proud have dug pits for me; *
 they do not keep your law.

86 All your commandments are true; *
 help me, for they persecute me with lies.

87 They had almost made an end of me on earth, *
 but I have not forsaken your commandments.

88 In your loving-kindness, revive me, *
 that I may keep the decrees of your mouth.

LAMEDH

89 O God, your word is everlasting; *
 it stands firm in the heavens.

90 Your faithfulness remains from one generation to another; *
 you established the earth, and it abides.

91 By your decree these continue to this day, *
 for all things are your servants.

92 If my delight had not been in your law, *
 I should have perished in my affliction.

93 I will never forget your commandments, *
 because by them you give me life.

94 I am yours; oh, that you would save me, *
 for I study your commandments.

95 Though the wicked lie in wait for me to destroy me, *
 I will apply my mind to your decrees.

96 I see that all things come to an end, *
 but your commandment has no bounds.

97 Oh, how I love your law; *
   all the day long it is in my mind.

98 Your commandment has made me wiser than my enemies, *
   and it is always with me.

99 I have more understanding than all my teachers, *
   for your decrees are my study.

100 I am wiser than the elders, *
   because I observe your commandments.

101 I restrain my feet from every evil way, *
   that I may keep your word.

102 I do not shrink from your judgments, *
   because you yourself have taught me.

103 How sweet are your words to my taste; *
   they are sweeter than honey to my mouth.

104 Through your commandments I gain understanding; *
   therefore I hate every lying way.

Twenty-sixth Day: Morning Prayer

PSALM 119:105-144

NUN

105 Your word is a lantern to my feet *
   and a light upon my path.

106 I have sworn and am determined *
   to keep your righteous judgments.

107 I am deeply troubled; *
   preserve my life, O God, according to your word.

108 Accept, O God, the willing tribute of my lips, *
   and teach me your judgments.

109 My life is always in my hand, *
   yet I do not forget your law.

110 The wicked have set a trap for me, *
   but I have not strayed from your commandments.

111 Your decrees are my inheritance for ever; *
    truly, they are the joy of my heart.

112 I have applied my heart to fulfill your statutes *
    for ever and to the end.

Samekh

113 I hate those who have a divided heart, *
    but your law do I love.

114 You are my refuge and shield; *
    my hope is in your word.

115 Away from me, you wicked! *
    I will keep the commandments of my God.

116 Sustain me according to your promise, that I may live, *
    and let me not be disappointed in my hope.

117 Hold me up, and I shall be safe, *
    and my delight shall be ever in your statutes.

118 You spurn all who stray from your statutes; *
    their deceitfulness is in vain.

119 In your sight all the wicked of the earth are but dross; *
    therefore I love your decrees.

120 My flesh trembles with dread of you; *
    I am afraid of your judgments.

Ayin

121 I have done what is just and right; *
    do not deliver me to my oppressors.

122 Be surety for your servant's good; *
    let not the proud oppress me.

123 My eyes have failed from watching for your salvation *
    and for your righteous promise.

124 Deal with your servant according to your loving-kindness, *
    and teach me your statutes.

125 I am your servant; grant me understanding, *
    that I may know your decrees.

126 It is time for you to act, O God, *
    for they have broken your law.

127 Truly, I love your commandments *
   more than gold and precious stones.

128 I hold all your commandments to be right for me; *
   all paths of falsehood I abhor.

PE

129 Your decrees are wonderful; *
   therefore I obey them with all my heart.

130 When your word goes forth it gives light; *
   it gives understanding to the simple.

131 I open my mouth and pant; *
   I long for your commandments.

132 Turn to me in mercy, *
   as you always do to those who love your Name.

133 Steady my footsteps in your word; *
   let no iniquity have dominion over me.

134 Rescue me from those who oppress me, *
   and I will keep your commandments.

135 Let your countenance shine upon your servant, *
   and teach me your statutes.

136 My eyes shed streams of tears, *
   because people do not keep your law.

SADHE

137 You are righteous, O God, *
   and upright are your judgments.

138 You have issued your decrees *
   with justice and in perfect faithfulness.

139 My indignation has consumed me, *
   because my enemies forget your words.

140 Your word has been tested to the uttermost, *
   and your servant holds it dear.

141 I am small and of little account, *
   yet I do not forget your commandments.

142 Your justice is an everlasting justice, *
   and your law is the truth.

143 Trouble and distress have come upon me, *
    yet your commandments are my delight.

144 The righteousness of your decrees is everlasting; *
    grant me understanding, that I may live.

Twenty-sixth Day: Evening Prayer

PSALM 119:145-176

QOPH

145 I call with my whole heart; *
    answer me, O God, that I may keep your statutes.

146 I call to you;
    oh, that you would save me! *
    I will keep your decrees.

147 Early in the morning I cry out to you, *
    for in your word is my trust.

148 My eyes are open in the night watches, *
    that I may meditate upon your promise.

149 Hear my voice, O God, according to your loving-kindness; *
    according to your judgments, give me life.

150 They draw near who in malice persecute me; *
    they are very far from your law.

151 You, O God, are near at hand, *
    and all your commandments are true.

152 Long have I known from your decrees *
    that you have established them for ever.

RESH

153 Behold my affliction and deliver me, *
    for I do not forget your law.

154 Plead my cause and redeem me; *
    according to your promise, give me life.

155 Deliverance is far from the wicked, *
    for they do not study your statutes.

156 Great is your compassion, O God; *
    preserve my life, according to your judgments.

157 There are many who persecute and oppress me, *
       yet I have not swerved from your decrees.

158 I look with loathing at the faithless, *
       for they have not kept your word.

159 See how I love your commandments! *
       O God, in your mercy, preserve me.

160 The heart of your word is truth; *
       all your righteous judgments endure for evermore.

SHIN

161 Rulers have persecuted me without a cause, *
       but my heart stands in awe of your word.

162 I am as glad because of your promise *
       as one who finds great spoils.

163 As for lies, I hate and abhor them, *
       but your law is my love.

164 Seven times a day do I praise you, *
       because of your righteous judgments.

165 Great peace have they who love your law; *
       for them there is no stumbling block.

166 I have hoped for your salvation, O God, *
       and I have fulfilled your commandments.

167 I have kept your decrees, *
       and I have loved them deeply.

168 I have kept your commandments and decrees, *
       for all my ways are before you.

TAW

169 Let my cry come before you, O God; *
       give me understanding, according to your word.

170 Let my supplication come before you; *
       deliver me, according to your promise.

171 My lips shall pour forth your praise, *
       when you teach me your statutes.

172 My tongue shall sing of your promise, *
       for all your commandments are righteous.

173 Let your hand be ready to help me, *
   for I have chosen your commandments.

174 I long for your salvation, O God, *
   and your law is my delight.

175 Let me live, and I will praise you, *
   and let your judgments help me.

176 I have gone astray like a sheep that is lost; *
   search for your servant,
   for I do not forget your commandments.

Twenty-seventh Day: Morning Prayer

PSALM 120

1 When I was in trouble, I called out to God; *
   I called out to God, who answered me.

2 Deliver me, O God, from lying lips *
   and from the deceitful tongue.

3 What shall be done to you, and what more besides, *
   O you deceitful tongue?

4 The sharpened arrows of a warrior, *
   along with hot glowing coals.

5 How hateful it is that I must lodge in Meshech *
   and dwell among the tents of Kedar!

6 Too long have I had to live *
   among the enemies of peace.

7 I am on the side of peace, *
   but when I speak of it, they are for war.

PSALM 121

1 I lift up my eyes to the hills; *
   from where is my help to come?

2 My help comes from God, *
   the maker of heaven and earth.

3 God will not let your foot be moved; *
   the One who watches over you will not fall asleep.

4 Behold, the One who keeps watch over Israel *
    shall neither slumber nor sleep;

5 The Holy One watches over you *
    and is your shade at your right hand,

6 So that the sun shall not strike you by day, *
    nor the moon by night.

7 God shall preserve you from all evil, *
    and is the One who shall keep you safe.

8 God shall watch over your going out and your coming in, *
    from this time forth for evermore.

PSALM 122

1 I was glad when they said to me, *
    "Let us go to the house of God."

2 Now our feet are standing *
    within your gates, O Jerusalem.

3 Jerusalem is built as a city *
    that is at unity with itself;

4 To which the tribes go up,
  the tribes of the Holy One, *
    the assembly of Israel,
    to praise the Name of God.

5 For there are the thrones of judgment, *
    the thrones of the house of David.

6 Pray for the peace of Jerusalem: *
    "May they prosper who love you.

7 Peace be within your walls *
    and quietness within your towers.

8 For my kindred and companions' sake, *
    I pray for your prosperity.

9 Because of the house of the Holy One our God, *
    I will seek to do you good."

PSALM 123

1 To you I lift up my eyes, *
    to you enthroned in the heavens.

2 As the eyes of servants look to the hand of their masters, *
    and the eyes of a maid to the hand of her mistress,

3 So our eyes look to the Holy One our God, *
    until God shows us mercy.

4 Have mercy upon us, O God, have mercy, *
    for we have had more than enough of contempt,

5 Too much of the scorn of the indolent rich, *
    and of the derision of the proud.

PSALM 124

1 If God had not been on our side, *
    let Israel now say;

2 If God had not been on our side, *
    when enemies rose up against us,

3 Then would they have swallowed us up alive *
    in their fierce anger toward us;

4 Then would the waters have overwhelmed us *
    and the torrent gone over us;

5 Then would the raging waters *
    have gone right over us.

6 Blessed be God, *
    who has not given us over to be a prey for their teeth.

7 We have escaped like a bird from the snare of the fowler; *
    the snare is broken, and we have escaped.

8 Our help is in the Name of God, *
    the maker of heaven and earth.

PSALM 125

1 They who trust in God are like Mount Zion, *
    which cannot be moved, but stands fast for ever.

2 The hills stand about Jerusalem; *
    so does God stand round about the people,
    from this time forth for evermore.

3 The scepter of the wicked shall not hold sway over
the land allotted to the just, *
so that the just shall not put their hands to evil.

4 Show your goodness, O God, to those who are good *
and to those who are true of heart.

5 As for those who turn aside to crooked ways,
God will lead them away with the evildoers; *
but peace be upon Israel.

Twenty-seventh Day: Evening Prayer

PSALM 126

1 When God restored the fortunes of Zion, *
then were we like those who dream.

2 Then was our mouth filled with laughter, *
and our tongue with shouts of joy.

3 Then they said among the nations, *
"God has done great things for them."

4 God has done great things for us, *
and we are glad indeed.

5 Restore our fortunes, O God, *
like the watercourses of the Negev.

6 Those who sowed with tears *
will reap with songs of joy.

7 Those who go out weeping, carrying the seed, *
will come again with joy, shouldering their sheaves.

PSALM 127

1 Unless God builds the house, *
their labor is in vain who build it.

2 Unless God watches over the city, *
in vain the sentries keep their vigil.

3 It is in vain that you rise so early and go to bed so late; *
vain, too, to eat the bread of toil,
for God gives to the beloved sleep.

4 Children are a heritage from God, *
  and the fruit of the womb is a gift.

5 Like arrows in the hand of a warrior *
  are the children of one's youth.

6 Happy are they who have their quivers full of them; *
  they shall not be put to shame
  when they contend with their enemies in the gate.

PSALM 128

1 Happy are they all who fear God, *
  and who follow in God's ways!

2 You shall eat the fruit of your labor; *
  happiness and prosperity shall be yours.

3 Your wife shall be like a fruitful vine within your house, *
  your children like olive shoots round about your table.

4 They who fear God *
  shall thus indeed be blest.

5 May God bless you from Zion, *
  and may you see the prosperity of Jerusalem all the
  days of your life.

6 May you live to see your children's children; *
  may peace be upon Israel.

PSALM 129

1 "Greatly have they oppressed me since my youth," *
  let Israel now say;

2 "Greatly have they oppressed me since my youth, *
  but they have not prevailed against me."

3 They scored my back as with a ploughshare *
  and made their furrows long.

4 Our God, the Righteous One, *
  has cut the cords of the wicked.

5 Let them be put to shame and thrown back, *
  all those who are enemies of Zion.

6 Let them be like grass upon the housetops, *
  which withers before it can be plucked;

7 Which does not fill the hand of the reaper, *
    nor the bosom of one who binds the sheaves;

8 So that those who go by say not so much as,
    "May God prosper you. *
    We wish you well in the Name of our God."

PSALM 130

1 Out of the depths have I called to you;
    O God, hear my voice; *
    let your ears consider well the voice of my supplication.

2 If you were to note what is done amiss, *
    O God, who could stand?

3 For there is forgiveness with you; *
    therefore you shall be feared.

4 I wait for you, O God; my soul waits for you; *
    in your word is my hope.

5 My soul waits for you,
    more than sentries for the morning, *
    more than sentries for the morning.

6 O Israel, wait upon God, *
    for with God there is mercy.

7 With God there is plenteous redemption; *
    God shall redeem Israel from all their sins.

PSALM 131

1 O God, I am not proud; *
    I have no haughty looks.

2 I do not occupy myself with great matters, *
    or with things that are too hard for me.

3 But I still my soul and make it quiet,
    like a child upon its mother's breast; *
    my soul is quieted within me.

4 O Israel, wait upon God, *
    from this time forth for evermore.

PSALM 132

1 O God, remember David *
 and all the hardships he endured;

2 How he swore an oath to God *
 and vowed a vow to the Mighty One of Jacob:

3 "I will not come under the roof of my house, *
 nor climb up into my bed;

4 I will not allow my eyes to sleep, *
 nor let my eyelids slumber;

5 Until I find a place for you, O God, *
 a dwelling for you, O Mighty One of Jacob."

6 "The ark! We heard it was in Ephratah; *
 we found it in the fields of Jearim.

7 Let us go to God's dwelling place; *
 let us fall upon our knees before God's footstool."

8 Arise, O God, into your resting-place, *
 you and the ark of your strength.

9 Let your priests be clothed with righteousness; *
 let your faithful people sing with joy.

10 For your servant David's sake, *
 do not turn away the face of your Anointed.

11 You have sworn an oath to David; *
 in truth, you will not break it:

12 "A son, the fruit of your body, *
 will I set upon your throne.

13 If your children keep my covenant
 and my testimonies that I shall teach them, *
 their children will sit upon your throne for evermore.

14 For God has chosen Zion *
 and has desired it for a habitation:

15 "This shall be my resting-place for ever; *
 here will I dwell, for I delight in it.

16 I will surely bless its provisions, *
 and satisfy its poor with bread.

17 I will clothe its priests with salvation, *
  and its faithful people will rejoice and sing.

18 There will I make the horn of David flourish; *
  I have prepared a lamp for my Anointed.

19 As for his enemies, I will clothe them with shame; *
  but as for him, his crown will shine."

PSALM 133

1 Oh, how good and pleasant it is, *
  when kindred live together in unity!

2 It is like fine oil upon the head *
  that runs down upon the beard,

3 Upon the beard of Aaron, *
  and runs down upon the collar of his robe.

4 It is like the dew of Hermon *
  that falls upon the hills of Zion.

5 For there has God ordained the blessing: *
  life for evermore.

PSALM 134

1 Behold now, bless God, all you servants of God, *
  you that stand by night in the house of God.

2 Lift up your hands in the holy place and bless God; *
  God who made heaven and earth bless you out of Zion.

PSALM 135

1 Alleluia! Praise the Name of the Holy One; *
  give praise, you servants of the Most High.

2 You who stand in the house of the Holy One, *
  in the courts of the house of our God.

3 Praise God, for God is good; *
  sing praises to the holy Name, for it is lovely.

4 For you, O God, have chosen Jacob for yourself *
  and Israel for your own possession.

5 For I know that you are great, *
  that you are above all gods.

6 You do whatever pleases you, in heaven and on earth, *
   in the seas and all the deeps.

7 You bring up rain clouds from the ends of the earth; *
   you send out lightning with the rain;
   you bring the winds out of your storehouse.

8 It was you who struck down the firstborn of Egypt, *
   the firstborn of all creatures.

9 You sent signs and wonders into the midst of Egypt, *
   against Pharaoh and all his servants.

10 You overthrew many nations *
   and put mighty kings to death:

11 Sihon, king of the Amorites,
   and Og, the king of Bashan, *
   and all the kingdoms of Canaan.

12 You gave their land to be an inheritance, *
   an inheritance for Israel your people.

13 O God, your Name is everlasting; *
   your renown endures from age to age.

14 For you give your people justice *
   and show compassion to your servants.

15 The idols of the nations are silver and gold, *
   the work of human hands.

16 They have mouths, but they cannot speak; *
   eyes have they, but they cannot see.

17 They have ears, but they cannot hear; *
   neither is there any breath in their mouth.

18 Those who make them are like them, *
   and so are all who put their trust in them.

19 Bless God, O house of Israel; *
   O house of Aaron, bless God.

20 Bless God, O house of Levi; *
   you who fear God, bless God.

21 Blest be the Most High out of Zion, *
   who dwells in Jerusalem. Alleluia!

PSALM 136

1 Give thanks to the Holy One who is good, *
  for God's mercy endures for ever.

2 Give thanks to the God of gods, *
  for God's mercy endures for ever.

3 Give thanks to the Ruler of rulers, *
  for God's mercy endures for ever;

4 Who only does great wonders, *
  for God's mercy endures for ever;

5 Who by wisdom made the heavens, *
  for God's mercy endures for ever;

6 Who spread out the earth upon the waters, *
  for God's mercy endures for ever;

7 Who created great lights, *
  for God's mercy endures for ever;

8 The sun to rule the day, *
  for God's mercy endures for ever;

9 The moon and the stars to govern the night, *
  for God's mercy endures for ever;

10 Who struck down the firstborn of Egypt, *
  for God's mercy endures for ever;

11 And brought out Israel from among them, *
  for God's mercy endures for ever;

12 With a mighty hand and a stretched-out arm, *
  for God's mercy endures for ever;

13 Who divided the Red Sea in two, *
  for God's mercy endures for ever;

14 And made Israel to pass through the midst of it, *
  for God's mercy endures for ever;

15 But swept Pharaoh and his army into the Red Sea, *
  for God's mercy endures for ever;

16 Who led the people through the wilderness, *
  for God's mercy endures for ever;

17 Who struck down great kings, *
   for God's mercy endures for ever;

18 And slew mighty kings, *
   for God's mercy endures for ever;

19 Sihon, king of the Amorites, *
   for God's mercy endures for ever;

20 And Og, the king of Bashan, *
   for God's mercy endures for ever;

21 And gave away their lands for an inheritance, *
   for God's mercy endures for ever;

22 An inheritance for Israel God's servant, *
   for God's mercy endures for ever;

23 Who remembered us in our low estate, *
   for God's mercy endures for ever;

24 And delivered us from our enemies, *
   for God's mercy endures for ever;

25 Who gives food to all creatures, *
   for God's mercy endures for ever.

26 Give thanks to the God of heaven, *
   for God's mercy endures for ever.

PSALM 137

1 By the waters of Babylon we sat down and wept *
  when we remembered you, O Zion.

2 As for our harps, we hung them up *
  on the trees in the midst of that land.

3 For those who led us away captive asked us for a song,
  and our oppressors called for mirth: *
     "Sing us one of the songs of Zion."

4 How shall we sing God's holy song *
  upon a foreign soil?

5 If I forget you, O Jerusalem, *
  let my right hand forget its skill.

6 Let my tongue cleave to the roof of my mouth
  if I do not remember you, *
     if I do not set Jerusalem above my highest joy.

7 Remember the day of Jerusalem, O God,
against the people of Edom, *
    who said, "Down with it! Down with it,
    even to the ground!"

8 O Offspring of Babylon, doomed to destruction, *
    happy the one who pays you back
    for what you have done to us!

9 Happy shall be the one who takes your little ones *
    and dashes them against the rock!

Psalm 138

1 I will give thanks to you, O God, with my whole heart; *
    before the gods I will sing your praise.

2 I will bow down toward your holy temple
and praise your Name, *
    because of your love and faithfulness;

3 For you have glorified your Name *
    and your word above all things.

4 When I called, you answered me; *
    you increased my strength within me.

5 All the rulers of the earth will praise you, O God, *
    when they have heard the words of your mouth.

6 They will sing of the ways of God, *
    that great is the glory of God.

7 Although on high, God cares for the lowly *
    and perceives the haughty from afar.

8 Though I walk in the midst of trouble, you keep me safe; *
    you stretch forth your hand against the fury of my enemies;
    your right hand shall save me.

9 You will make good your purpose for me; *
    O God, your love endures for ever;
    do not abandon the works of your hands.

PSALM 139

1 O God, you have searched me out and known me; *
you know my sitting down and my rising up;
you discern my thoughts from afar.

2 You trace my journeys and my resting-places, *
and are acquainted with all my ways.

3 Indeed, there is not a word on my lips, *
but you, O God, know it altogether.

4 You press upon me behind and before, *
and lay your hand upon me.

5 Such knowledge is too wonderful for me; *
it is so high that I cannot attain to it.

6 Where can I go then from your Spirit; *
where can I flee from your presence?

7 If I climb up to heaven, you are there; *
if I make the grave my bed, you are there also.

8 If I take the wings of the morning *
and dwell in the uttermost parts of the sea,

9 Even there your hand will lead me, *
and your right hand hold me fast.

10 If I say, "Surely the darkness will cover me, *
and the light around me turn to night,"

11 Darkness is not dark to you;
the night is as bright as the day; *
darkness and light to you are both alike.

12 For you yourself created my inmost parts; *
you knit me together in my mother's womb.

13 I will thank you because I am marvelously made; *
your works are wonderful, and I know it well.

14 My body was not hidden from you, *
while I was being made in secret
and woven in the depths of the earth.

15 Your eyes beheld my limbs, yet unfinished in the womb;
all of them were written in your book; *
they were fashioned day by day,
when as yet there was none of them.

16 How deep I find your thoughts, O God; *
how great is the sum of them!

17 If I were to count them, they would be more in number
than the sand; *
to count them all, my life span would need to
be like yours.

18 Oh, that you would slay the wicked, O God! *
You that thirst for blood, depart from me.

19 They speak despitefully against you; *
your enemies take your Name in vain.

20 Do I not hate those, O God, who hate you; *
and do I not loathe those who rise up against you?

21 I hate them with a perfect hatred; *
they have become my own enemies.

22 Search me out, O God, and know my heart; *
try me and know my restless thoughts.

23 Look well whether there be any wickedness in me, *
and lead me in the way that is everlasting.

PSALM 140

1 Deliver me, O God, from evildoers; *
protect me from the violent,

2 Who devise evil in their hearts *
and stir up strife all day long.

3 They have sharpened their tongues like a serpent; *
adder's poison is under their lips.

4 Keep me, O God, from the hands of the wicked; *
protect me from the violent,
who are determined to trip me up.

5 The proud have hidden a snare for me
and stretched out a net of cords; *
they have set traps for me along the path.

6 I have said to God, "You are my God; *
    listen to my supplication.

7 O God, the strength of my salvation, *
    you have covered my head in the day of battle.

8 Do not grant the desires of the wicked, O God,*
    nor let their evil plans prosper.

9 Let not those who surround me lift up their heads; *
    let the evil of their lips overwhelm them.

10 Let hot burning coals fall upon them; *
    let them be cast into the mire, never to rise up again."

11 A slanderer shall not be established on the earth, *
    and evil shall hunt down the lawless.

12 I know that God will maintain the cause of the poor *
    and render justice to the needy.

13 Surely, the righteous will give thanks to your Name, *
    and the upright shall continue in your sight.

Twenty-ninth Day: Evening Prayer

PSALM 141

1 O God, I call to you; come to me quickly; *
    hear my voice when I cry to you.

2 Let my prayer be set forth in your sight as incense, *
    the lifting up of my hands as the evening sacrifice.

3 Set a watch before my mouth, O God,
    and guard the door of my lips; *
    let not my heart incline to any evil thing.

4 Let me not be occupied in wickedness with evildoers, *
    nor eat of their choice foods.

5 Let the righteous smite me in friendly rebuke;
    let not the oil of the unrighteous anoint my head, *
    for my prayer is continually against their wicked deeds.

6 Let their rulers be overthrown in stony places, *
    that they may know my words are true.

7 As when a ploughshare turns over the earth in furrows, *
    let their bones be scattered at the mouth of the grave.

8 But my eyes are turned to you, O God; *
    in you I take refuge;
    do not strip me of my life.

9 Protect me from the snare which they have laid for me *
    and from the traps of the evildoers.

10 Let the wicked fall into their own nets, *
    while I myself escape.

PSALM 142

1 I cry to you, O God, with my voice; *
    to you I make loud supplication.

2 I pour out my complaint before you *
    and tell you all my trouble.

3 When my spirit languishes within me, you know my path; *
    in the way wherein I walk they have hidden a trap for me.

4 I look to my right hand and find no one who knows me; *
    I have no place to flee to, and no one cares for me.

5 I cry out to you, O God; *
    I say, "You are my refuge,
    my portion in the land of the living."

6 Listen to my cry for help, for I have been brought very low; *
    save me from those who pursue me,
    for they are too strong for me.

7 Bring me out of prison, that I may give
            thanks to your Name; *
    when you have dealt bountifully with me,
    the righteous will gather around me.

PSALM 143

1 O God, hear my prayer,
    and in your faithfulness heed my supplications; *
    answer me in your righteousness.

2 Enter not into judgment with your servant, *
    for in your sight shall no one living be justified.

3 For my enemy has sought my life,
has crushed me to the ground, *
    and has made me live in dark places like those who
        are long dead.

4 My spirit faints within me; *
my heart within me is desolate.

5 I remember the time past;
I muse upon all your deeds; *
    I consider the works of your hands.

6 I spread out my hands to you; *
my soul gasps to you like a thirsty land.

7 O God, make haste to answer me; my spirit fails me; *
do not hide your face from me,
or I shall be like those who go down to the Pit.

8 Let me hear of your loving-kindness in the morning,
for I put my trust in you; *
    show me the road that I must walk,
    for I lift up my soul to you.

9 Deliver me from my enemies, O God, *
for I flee to you for refuge.

10 Teach me to do what pleases you, for you are my God; *
let your good Spirit lead me on level ground.

11 Revive me, O God, for your Name's sake; *
for your righteousness' sake, bring me out of trouble.

12 Of your goodness, destroy my enemies
and bring all my foes to naught, *
    for truly I am your servant.

Thirtieth Day: Morning Prayer

PSALM 144

1 Blessed be my God, my rock, *
who trains my hands to fight and my fingers to battle;

2 My help and my fortress, my stronghold and my deliverer, *
my shield in whom I trust,
who subdues the peoples under me.

3 O God, what are we that you should care for us, *
mere mortals that you should think of us?

4 We are like a puff of wind; *
     our days are like a passing shadow.

5 Bow your heavens, O God, and come down; *
     touch the mountains, and they shall smoke.

6 Hurl the lightning and scatter them; *
     shoot out your arrows and rout them.

7 Stretch out your hand from on high; *
     rescue me and deliver me from the great waters,
     from the hand of foreign peoples,

8 Whose mouths speak deceitfully *
     and whose right hand is raised in falsehood.

9 O God, I will sing to you a new song; *
     I will play to you on a ten-stringed lyre.

10 You give victory to rulers *
     and have rescued David your servant.

11 Rescue me from the hurtful sword, *
     and deliver me from the hand of foreign peoples,

12 Whose mouths speak deceitfully *
     and whose right hand is raised in falsehood.

13 May our sons be like plants well nurtured from their youth, *
     and our daughters like sculptured corners of a palace.

14 May our barns be filled to overflowing with all manner
          of crops; *
     may the flocks in our pastures increase by thousands
          and tens of thousands;
     may our cattle be fat and sleek.

15 May there be no breaching of the walls, no going into exile, *
     no wailing in the public squares.

16 Happy are the people of whom this is so; *
     happy are the people who worship God!

Psalm 145

1 I will exalt you, O holy God, *
     and bless your Name for ever and ever.

2 Every day will I bless you *
     and praise your Name for ever and ever.

3 Great are you, O God, and greatly to be praised; *
     there is no end to your greatness.

4 One generation shall praise your works to another *
     and shall declare your power.

5 I will ponder the glorious splendor of your majesty *
     and all your marvelous works.

6 They shall speak of the might of your wondrous acts, *
     and I will tell of your greatness.

7 They shall publish the remembrance of your great goodness; *
     they shall sing of your righteous deeds.

8 You are gracious and full of compassion, *
     slow to anger and of great kindness.

9 You are loving to everyone, *
     and your compassion is over all your works.

10 All your works praise you, O God, *
     and your faithful servants bless you.

11 They make known the glory of your realm *
     and speak of your power,

12 That the peoples may know of your power *
     and the glorious splendor of your dominion.

13 Yours, O God, is an everlasting reign; *
     your dominion endures throughout all ages.

14 You are faithful in all your words *
     and merciful in all your deeds.

15 You uphold all those who fall; *
     you lift up those who are bowed down.

16 The eyes of all wait upon you, O God, *
     and you give them their food in due season.

17 You open wide your hand *
     and satisfy the needs of every living creature.

18 You are righteous in all your ways *
     and loving in all your works.

19 You are near to those who call upon you, *
     to all who call upon you faithfully.

20 You fulfill the desire of those who fear you; *
     you hear their cry and help them.

21 You preserve all those who love you, *
    but you destroy all the wicked.

22 My mouth shall speak your praise, O God; *
    let all flesh bless your holy Name for ever and ever.

PSALM 146

1 Alleluia! Praise God, O my soul! *
    I will praise God as long as I live;
    I will sing praises to my God while I have my being.

2 Put not your trust in rulers, nor in any child of earth, *
    for there is no help in them.

3 When they breathe their last, they return to earth, *
    and in that day their thoughts perish.

4 Happy are they who have the God of Jacob for their help, *
    whose hope is in their God;

5 Who made heaven and earth, the seas, and all that is in them; *
    whose promise abides for ever;

6 Who gives justice to those who are oppressed *
    and food to those who hunger.

7 God sets the prisoners free
    and opens the eyes of the blind; *
    God lifts up those who are bowed down;

8 God loves the righteous
    and cares for the stranger; *
    God sustains the orphan and widow,
    but frustrates the way of the wicked.

9 God shall reign for ever, *
    your God, O Zion, throughout all generations. Alleluia!

Thirtieth Day: Evening Prayer

PSALM 147

1 Alleluia! How good it is to sing praises to you, O God; *
    how pleasant it is to honor you with praise!

2 For you rebuild Jerusalem *
    and gather the exiles of Israel.

3 You heal the brokenhearted *
   and bind up their wounds.

4 You count the number of the stars *
   and call them all by their names.

5 Great are you and mighty in power; *
   there is no limit to your wisdom.

6 You lift up the lowly, *
   but cast the wicked to the ground.

7 We sing to you, Most High, with thanksgiving; *
   we make music to you upon the harp,

8 For you cover the heavens with clouds *
   and prepare rain for the earth;

9 You make grass to grow upon the mountains *
   and green plants to serve humankind.

10 You provide food for flocks and herds *
   and for the young ravens when they cry.

11 You are not impressed by the might of a horse; *
   you have no pleasure in human strength;

12 But you have pleasure in those who fear you, *
   in those who await your gracious favor.

13 Jerusalem will worship you, O God, *
   and Zion will praise your name.

14 For you have strengthened the bars of our gates *
   and have blest our children within us.

15 You have established peace on our borders *
   and satisfied us with the finest wheat.

16 You send out your command to the earth, *
   and your word runs very swiftly.

17 You give snow like wool *
   and scatter hoarfrost like ashes.

18 You scatter your hail like bread crumbs; *
   who can stand against your cold?

19 You send forth your word and melt them; *
   you blow with your wind and the waters flow.

20 You declare your word to Jacob, *
  your statutes and your judgments to Israel.

21 You have not done so to any other nation; *
  to them you have not revealed your judgments. Alleluia!

PSALM 148

1 Alleluia! Praise God from the heavens; *
  sing praise in the heights.

2 Praise God, all you angels; *
  sing praise, all the heavenly host.

3 Praise God, sun and moon; *
  sing praise, all you shining stars.

4 Praise God, heaven of heavens *
  and you waters above the heavens.

5 Let them praise the Name of God, *
  by whose command they were created.

6 God made them stand fast for ever and ever, *
  and gave them a law which shall not pass away.

7 Praise God from the earth, *
  you sea-monsters and all deeps;

8 Fire and hail, snow and fog, *
  tempestuous wind, doing God's will;

9 Mountains and all hills, *
  fruit trees and all cedars;

10 Wild beasts and all cattle, *
  creeping things and winged birds;

11 Sovereigns of the earth and all peoples, *
  leaders and all rulers of the world;

12 Young men and maidens, *
  old and young together.

13 Let them praise your Name, O God, *
  for your Name only is exalted;
  your splendor is over earth and heaven.

14 You have raised up strength for your people
  and praise for all your loyal servants, *
  the children of Israel, a people who are near you. Alleluia!

Psalm 149

1 Alleluia! Sing to God a new song; *
  sing praise in the congregation of the faithful.

2 Let the people of Israel rejoice in their Maker; *
  let the children of Zion be joyful in their Monarch.

3 Let them praise God's Name in the dance; *
  let them sing praise with timbrel and harp.

4 God takes pleasure in the people *
  and adorns the poor with victory.

5 Let the faithful rejoice in triumph; *
  let them be joyful on their beds.

6 Let the praises of God be in their throat *
  and a two-edged sword in their hand,

7 To wreak vengeance on the nations *
  and punishment on the peoples;

8 To bind their rulers in chains *
  and their nobles with links of iron;

9 To inflict on them the judgment decreed; *
  this is glory for all God's faithful people. Alleluia!

Psalm 150

1 Alleluia! Praise God in the holy temple; *
  praise God in the firmament of power.

2 Praise God for every mighty act; *
  praise God's excellent greatness.

3 Praise God with the blast of the ram's-horn; *
  praise God with lyre and harp.

4 Praise God with timbrel and dance; *
  praise God with strings and pipe.

5 Praise God with resounding cymbals; *
  praise God with loud-clanging cymbals.

6 Let everything that has breath *
  praise God. Alleluia!

Acknowledgments and Background History

This book is clearly the offspring of *A Monastic Breviary*, edited by the Order of the Holy Cross and the Order of Saint Helena (Holy Cross Publications, West Park NY, distributed by Morehouse Barlow Co, 1976). Brother David Bryan Hoopes, OHC, Superior of the Order of the Holy Cross, has graciously given permission for *The Saint Helena Breviary* to include "anything needed from *The Monastic Breviary*".

Many individuals have contributed to the making of this breviary. We are grateful for editorial comments, for proofreading, for assistance in small work groups, and for all kinds of suggestions to help make a better and more user-friendly book. In particular we would like to thank Louise Abbot, Louisville, GA; Judith Barrett, New York City; the Rev. Talmadge Bowden, MD, Augusta, GA; the Rev. Carole Johannsen, Bedford Hills, NY; Liz Peacock, Charlotte, NC; Dr Stephen Plank, Oberlin, OH; the Rev. Nancy Roth, Oberlin, OH; and Sister Pamela, CSJB.

A special word of thanks must be extended to Frank Tedeschi, Vice President and Executive Editor at Church Publishing, Inc. His friendship with the Order of St. Helena and his guidance and advice on matters technical and editorial have been invaluable.

Special thanks are also extended to Phoebe Pettingell for her sensitive editorial hand in preparing this personal edition of the *Breviary*.

Within the Order, the original Breviary Committee, appointed in 2000, consisted of Sisters Cintra Pemberton (convener), Ruth, Ellen Stephen, Carol Andrew, Ann Prentice, and Ellen Francis. They worked for a year and a half, and by Advent of 2002, the first draft of the complete book was in use. That committee then disbanded, and a small work group consisting of Sisters Cintra Pemberton, Carol Andrew and Ann Prentice completed the details, while other sisters continued to offer help and invaluable suggestions.

Sister Carol Andrew's impressive theological understanding and memory with regard to biblical passages and the location of material, both textual and musical, in the current as well as in past breviaries has been of great value. Sister

Ellen Stephen's poetic gifts with the revised hymn texts and Sister Cintra Pemberton's musical gifts in the revised and sometimes totally new antiphons, hymn tunes, and canticles merit special recognition. Linda Brooks also deserves credit for countless hours creating the design and layout of the personal edition of the *Breviary*.

However, *The Saint Helena Breviary* is far more than the work of a few dedicated and gifted sisters; it has resulted from the shared gifts of the entire community. All sisters were involved and made contributions. Most important, the book has been prayed by sisters and guests alike in the Daily Office for the several years before it was accepted in its final form. To all involved in the project, we offer a heartfelt thanks.

A Note on the Process

Regarding text changes in the psalms, the most obvious ones were those that eliminated all references to God as masculine. Wherever possible, a phrase was reworked, either avoiding a masculine pronoun for God or substituting another term, such as "Holy One" or "Mighty One", or something similar. Sometimes substituting "who" for "he", or moving from the singular to plural ("he" to "they"), offered a graceful solution. A few psalms were put into the second person, but that option was followed only as a last resort. After much debate, the committee felt they could not maintain the distinction between LORD (YHWH), Lord (*Adonai*), and God (*Elohim*) and still remain inclusive because of the need for the text to be both poetic and singable.

There was also an attempt to eliminate other specifically masculine nouns, for example, substituting "sentries" for "watchmen", "ruler" for "prince", and "monarch" or "sovereign" for "king" (except where the king was clearly a reference to David). In addition to the masculine references, the committee tried to use alternate terms for such words as "heathen" or "alien" (which have negative connotations today), using instead "nations" or "foreigners".

Since all the psalms or psalm groups in previous breviaries ended with the traditional doxology: "Glory to the Father, and to the Son, and to the Holy Spirit", the committee wanted to find a substitute for this. Drawing on the doxology suggested in *Enriching Our Worship* (supplemental liturgical materials authorized by the General Convention of the Episcopal Church), they modified it slightly and chose "Glory to the holy and undivided Trinity, one God". However, a number of sisters preferred a slightly adapted version of the doxology used by the Franciscan community in England, "Glory to God, Source of all being, Incarnate Word, and Holy Spirit". Thus two doxologies are used in *The Saint Helena Breviary*, the Franciscan one at Matins and the *Enriching Our Worship* one at the other three Offices.

In addition to the psalms, the committee worked on the texts of hymns, canticles, antiphons, and other parts of the Office, following the same principles. Here more freedom was permissible, allowing the committee to eliminate unnecessary war imagery, many punitive and vindictive adjectives, and to emphasize instead God's love and mercy. In many instances, biblical verses from the NRSV were substituted for older translations, and even with biblical texts the committee worked to avoid the use of masculine language and imagery. In some cases, totally new biblical selections were substituted for previous ones.

In the New Testament, a suitable substitute for "Father" might be either "Creator" or "Maker", but what was most difficult was finding a substitute for "Son". The committee used a number of different options, sometimes simply "Word", but also "Holy One", "Anointed One", "Promised One", "Beloved One" or "Only-begotten One". Usually the context, plus musical considerations, determined the ultimate choice.

Since the Offices of Diurnum, Vespers, and Compline are ordinarily sung, the antiphons assigned to the Diurnum and Vespers Psalter throughout the church year posed a particular challenge, as did the Vespers canticles. Every text change in an antiphon or canticle affected the music, which then had to be re-written or adjusted to fit the new texts. The inclusion of over forty totally new canticles necessitated the writing of new music in the medieval modes for those assigned to Vespers.

In working with revised hymn texts, much effort went into updating archaic theology and phraseology, especially emphasizing God as love rather than God as judge, and stressing redemption rather than sin. Furthermore, not only did the rhythm of the poetry in the hymns have to be kept, but all text changes had to fit the existing medieval hymn tunes.

The Order of St. Helena follows the liturgical year of the Episcopal Church, keeping all the saints included in *Lesser Feasts and Fasts 2003* in addition to some of particular interest to the community, such as John of the Cross (December 14), Pachomius (May 14), Helena (August 18), and the Founding of the Order of St. Helena (November 8). However, many of the collects from *Lesser Feasts and Fasts 2003* were reworded or replaced with entirely new ones, such as the ones for Brigid (February 1) and Sergius of Moscow (September 25). All reworded collects followed the same principles mentioned above.

One of the most rewarding aspects of the whole revision process was the degree of involvement and participation by all the sisters. At every stage of trial use, all members of the community were invited to make suggestions, to comment and to critique. Although this inevitably caused frustration at times, we know it has produced a better book, and we would not have had it any other way. The present *Saint Helena Breviary* is indeed a work of the entire community. The committee members unanimously agree that it has been a truly rewarding work that the Order of St. Helena is pleased to make available to all who would "sing to God a new song" in the Daily Office.

The 2-Week Distribution of Psalms
Used by the Order of St. Helena

WEEK	MATINS	DIURNUM	VESPERS	COMPLINE
		SUNDAY		
I	32; 146; 118; 99	84; 1; 8	110; 111; 104; 93	4; 91; 134
II	42; 43; 26; 116; 98	19; 15; 23	112; 107; 150	61; 34
		MONDAY		
I	3; 6; 9; 76; 87	14; 13; 119:1-16	7; 37	12; 16; 11
II	53; 10; 5; 64; 24; 100	120; 121; 119:97-112	114; 18	17; 30
		TUESDAY		
I	40; 57; 21; 144	36; 119:17-32	78:1-39; 66	31; 133
II	39; 70;132; 145	123; 119:113-128; 122	25; 68	82; 33
		WEDNESDAY		
I	58; 38; 80; 60; 108	41; 119:33-48	78:40-72; 94	49; 47
II	109; 102; 148	124; 119:129-144; 125	69; 71	54; 50
		THURSDAY		
I	63; 27; 81; 92	119:49-64; 48	20; 106	59; 62
II	52; 72; 147; 29	126; 127; 119:145-160	75; 105	90; 115
		FRIDAY		
I	22; 83; 149	79; 119:65-80	89; 137	55; 131
II	142; 51; 77; 138	129; 119:161-176; 128	139; 28; 103	88; 140
		SATURDAY		
I	130; 101; 113; 45; 96	56; 119:81-96	35; 135; 67	141; 86
II	143; 85; 2; 46; 97	44; 117	74; 65; 136	73

I Vespers of Major Feasts: 96; 97; 98; 99; 148
Matins of Major Feasts   24; 29; 72; 93; 100
II Vespers of Major Feasts   135:1-5,19-21; 111; 112; 113; 150

DAILY OFFICE
LECTIONARY

CONCERNING THE DAILY OFFICE LECTIONARY

The Daily Office Lectionary is arranged in a two-year cycle. Year One begins on the First Sunday of Advent preceding odd-numbered years, and Year Two begins on the First Sunday of Advent preceding even-numbered years. (Thus, on the First Sunday of Advent, 2006, the Lectionary for Year One is begun.)

Three Readings are provided for each Sunday and weekday in each of the two years. Two of the Readings may be used in the morning and one in the evening; or, if the Office is read only once in the day, all three Readings may be used. When the Office is read twice in the day, it is suggested that the Gospel Reading be used in the evening in Year One, and in the morning in Year Two. If two Readings are desired at both Offices, the Old Testament Reading for the alternate year is used as the First Reading at Evening Prayer.

When more than one Reading is used at an Office, the first is always from the Old Testament (or the Apocrypha).

When a Major Feast interrupts the sequence of Readings, they may be re-ordered by lengthening, combining, or omitting some of them, to secure continuity or avoid repetition.

Any Reading may be lengthened at discretion. Suggested lengthenings are shown in parentheses.

In this Lectionary (except in the weeks from 4 Advent to 1 Epiphany, and Palm Sunday to 2 Easter), the Psalms are arranged in a seven-week pattern which recurs throughout the year, except for appropriate variations in Lent and Easter Season.

In the citation of the Psalms, those for the morning are given first, and then those for the evening.

Brackets and parentheses are used (brackets in the case of whole Psalms, parentheses in the case of verses) to indicate Psalms and verses of Psalms which may be omitted. In some instances, the entire portion of the Psalter assigned to a given Office has been bracketed, and alternative Psalmody provided. Those who desire to recite the Psalter in its entirety should, in each instance, use the bracketed Psalms rather than the alternatives.

The Proper to be used on each of the Sundays after Pentecost (except for Trinity Sunday) is determined by the calendar date of that Sunday. Thus, in any year, the Proper for the Sunday after Trinity Sunday (the Second Sunday after Pentecost) is the numbered Proper (number 3 through number 8), the calendar date of which falls on that Sunday, or is closest to it, whether before or after. Thereafter, the Propers are used consecutively. For example, if the Sunday after Trinity Sunday is May 26, the sequence begins with Proper 3 (Propers 1 and 2 being used on the weekdays of Pentecost and Trinity weeks). If the Sunday after Trinity Sunday is June 13, the sequence begins with Proper 6 (Propers I through 3 being omitted that year, and Propers 4 and 5 being used in Pentecost and Trinity weeks).

WEEK OF 1 ADVENT

Sunday   146, 147   ❖   111, 112, 113
              Isa. 1:1-9   2 Pet. 3:1-10   Matt. 25:1-18

Monday   1, 2, 3   ❖   4, 7
              Isa. 1:10-20   1 Thess. 1:1-10   Luke 20:1-8

Tuesday   5, 6   ❖   10, 11
              Isa. 1:21-31   1 Thess. 2:1-12   Luke 20:9-18

Wednesday   119:1-24   ❖   12, 13, 14
              Isa. 2:1-11   1 Thess. 2:13-20   Luke 20:19-26

Thursday   18:1-20   ❖   18:21-50
              Isa. 2:12-22   1 Thess. 3:1-13   Luke 20:27-40

Friday   16, 17   ❖   22
              Isa. 3:8-15   I Thess. 4:1-12   Luke 20:41—21:4

Saturday   20, 21:1-7(8-14)   ❖   110:5(6-7), 116, 117
              Isa. 4:2-6   1 Thess. 4:13-18   Luke 21:5-19

WEEK OF 2 ADVENT

Sunday   148, 149, 150   ❖   114, 115
              Isa. 5:1-7   2 Pet. 3:11-18   Luke 7:28-35

Monday   25   ❖   9, 15
              Isa. 5:8-12, 18-23   1 Thess. 5:1-11   Luke 21:20-28

Tuesday   26, 28   ❖   36, 39
              Isa. 5:13-17, 24-25   1 Thess. 5:12-28   Luke 21:29-38

Wednesday   38   ❖   119:25-48
              Isa. 6:1-13   2 Thess. 1:1-12   John 7:53—8:11

Thursday   37:1-18   ❖   37:19-42
              Isa. 7:1-9   2 Thess. 2:1-12   Luke 22:1-13

Friday   31   ❖   35
              Isa. 7:10-25   2 Thess. 2:13—3:5   Luke 22:14-30

Saturday   30, 32   ❖   42, 43
              Isa. 8:1-15   2 Thess. 3:6-18   Luke 22:31-38

Week of 1 Advent

Sunday	146, 147 ❖ 111, 112, 113	
	Amos 1:1-5, 13—2:8 1 Thess. 5:1-11 Luke 21:5-19	
Monday	1, 2, 3 ❖ 4, 7	
	Amos 2:6-16 2 Pet. 1:1-11 Matt. 21:1-11	
Tuesday	5, 6 ❖ 10, 11	
	Amos 3:1-11 2 Pet. 1:12-21 Matt. 21:12-22	
Wednesday	119:1-24 ❖ 12, 13, 14	
	Amos 3:12—4:5 2 Pet. 3:1-10 Matt. 21:23-32	
Thursday	18:1-20 ❖ 18:21-50	
	Amos 4:6-13 2 Pet. 3:11-18 Matt. 21:33-46	
Friday	16, 17 ❖ 22	
	Amos 5:1-17 Jude 1-16 Matt. 22:1-14	
Saturday	20, 21:1-7(8-14) ❖ 110:1-5(6-7), 116, 117	
	Amos 5:18-27 Jude 17-25 Matt. 22:15-22	

Week of 2 Advent

Sunday	148, 149, 150 ❖ 114, 115
	Amos 6:1-14 2 Thess. 1:5-12 Luke 1:57-68
Monday	25 ❖ 9, 15
	Amos 7:1-9 Rev. 1:1-8 Matt. 22:23-33
Tuesday	26, 28 ❖ 36, 39
	Amos 7:10-17 Rev. 1:9-16 Matt. 22:34-46
Wednesday	38 ❖ 119:25-48
	Amos 8:1-14 Rev. 1:17—2:7 Matt. 23:1-12
Thursday	37:1-18 ❖ 37:19-42
	Amos 9:1-10 Rev. 2:8-17 Matt. 23:13-26
Friday	31 ❖ 35
	Haggai 1:1-15 Rev. 2:18-29 Matt. 23:27-39
Saturday	30, 32 ❖ 42, 43
	Haggai 2:1-9 Rev. 3:1-6 Matt. 24:1-14

WEEK OF 3 ADVENT

Sunday   63:1-8(9-11), 98   ❖   103
Isa. 13:6-13   Heb. 12:18-29   John 3:22-30

Monday   41, 52   ❖   44
Isa. 8:16—9:1   2 Pet. 1:1-11   Luke 22:39-53

Tuesday   45   ❖   47, 48
Isa. 9:1-7   2 Pet. 1:12-21   Luke 22:54-69

Wednesday   119:49-72   ❖   49, [53]
Isa. 9:8-17   2 Pet. 2:1-10a   Mark 1:1-8

Thursday   50   ❖   [59, 60] *or* 33
Isa. 9:18—10:4   2 Pet. 2:10b-16   Matt. 3:1-12

Friday   40, 54   ❖   51
Isa. 10:5-19   2 Pet. 2:17-22   Matt. 11:2-15

Saturday   55   ❖   138, 139:1-17(18-23)
Isa. 10:20-27   Jude 17-25   Luke 3:1-9

WEEK OF 4 ADVENT

Sunday   24, 29   ❖   8, 84
Isa. 42:1-12   Eph. 6:10-20   John 3:16-21

Monday   61, 62   ❖   112, 115
Isa. 11:1-9   Rev. 20:1-10   John 5:30-47

Tuesday   66, 67   ❖   116, 117
Isa. 11:10-16   Rev. 20:11—21:8   Luke 1:5-25

Wednesday   72   ❖   111, 113
Isa. 28:9-22   Rev. 21:9-21   Luke 1:26-38

Thursday   80   ❖   146, 147
Isa. 29:13-24   Rev. 21:22—22:5   Luke 1:39-48a(48b-56)

Friday   93, 96   ❖   148, 150
Isa. 33:17-22   Rev. 22:6-11, 18-20   Luke 1:57-66

Dec. 24   45, 46   ❖   ——
Isa. 35:1-10   Rev. 22:12-17, 21   Luke 1:67-80

Christmas Eve   ——   ❖   89:1-29
Isa. 59:15b-21   Phil. 2:5-11

WEEK OF 3 ADVENT

Sunday   63:1-8(9-11), 98   ❖   103
Amos 9:11-15   2 Thess. 2:1-3, 13-17   John 5:30-47

Monday   41, 52   ❖   44
Zech. 1:7-17   Rev. 3:7-13   Matt. 24:15-31

Tuesday   45   ❖   47, 48
Zech. 2:1-13   Rev. 3:14-22   Matt. 24:32-44

Wednesday   119:49-72   ❖   49, [53]
Zech. 3:1-10   Rev. 4:1-8   Matt. 24:45-51

Thursday   50   ❖   [59, 60] *or* 33
Zech. 4:1-14   Rev. 4:9—5:5   Matt. 25:1-13

Friday   40, 54   ❖   51
Zech. 7:8—8:8   Rev. 5:6-14   Matt. 25:14-30

Saturday   55   ❖   138, 139:1-17(18-23)
Zech. 8:9-17   Rev. 6:1-17   Matt. 25:31-46

WEEK OF 4 ADVENT

Sunday   24, 29   ❖   8, 84
Gen. 3:8-15   Rev. 12:1-10   John 3:16-21

Monday   61, 62   ❖   112, 115
Zeph. 3:14-20   Titus 1:1-16   Luke 1:1-25

Tuesday   66, 67   ❖   116, 117
1 Samuel 2:1b-10   Titus 2:1-10   Luke 1:26-38

Wednesday   72   ❖   111, 113
2 Samuel 7:1-17   Titus 2:11—3:8a   Luke 1:39-48a(48b-56)

Thursday   80   ❖   146, 147
2 Samuel 7:18-29   Gal. 3:1-14   Luke 1:57-66

Friday   93, 96   ❖   148, 150
Baruch 4:21-29   Gal. 3:15-22   Luke 1:67-80 *or* Matt. 1:1-17

Dec. 24   45, 46   ❖   ——
Baruch 4:36—5:9   Gal. 3:23—4:7   Matt. 1:18-25

Christmas Eve   ——   ❖   89:1-29
Isa. 59:15b-21   Phil. 2:5-11

Christmas Day   2, 85   ❖   110:1-5(6-7), 132
Zech. 2:10-13   1 John 4:7-16   John 3:31-36

First Sunday after Christmas   93, 96   ❖   34
Isa. 62:6-7, 10-12   Heb. 2:10-18   Matt. 1:18-25

Dec. 29   18:1-20   ❖   18:21-50 *
Isa. 12:1-6   Rev. 1:1-8   John 7:37-52

Dec. 30   20, 21:1-7(8-14)   ❖   23, 27
Isa. 25:1-9   Rev. 1:9-20   John 7:53—8:11

Dec. 31   46, 48   ❖   ——
Isa. 26:1-9   2 Cor. 5:16—6:2   John 8:12-19

Eve of Holy Name   ——   ❖   90
Isa. 65:15b-25   Rev. 21:1-6

Holy Name   103   ❖   148
Gen. 17:1-12a, 15-16   Col. 2:6-12   John 16:23b-30

Second Sunday after Christmas   66, 67   ❖   145
Ecclus. 3:3-9, 14-17   1 John 2:12-17   John 6:41-47

Jan. 2   34   ❖   33
Gen. 12:1-7   Heb. 11:1-12   John 6:35-42, 48-51

Jan. 3   68   ❖   72 **
Gen. 28:10-22   Heb. 11:13-22   John 10:7-17

Jan. 4   85, 87   ❖   89:1-29
Exod. 3:1-12   Heb. 11:23-31   John 14:6-14

Jan. 5   2, 110:1-5(6-7)   ❖   ——
Joshua 1:1-9   Heb. 11:32—12:2   John 15:1-16

Eve of Epiphany   ——   ❖   29, 98
Isa. 66:18-23   Rom. 15:7-13

* If today is Saturday, use Psalms 23 and 27 at Evening Prayer.
** If today is Saturday, use Psalm 136 at Evening Prayer.

Christmas Day   2, 85   ❖   110:1-5(6-7), 132
         Micah 4:1-5; 5:2-4   1 John 4:7-16   John 3:31-36

First Sunday after Christmas   93, 96   ❖   34
         1 Samuel 1:1-2, 7b-28   Col. 1:9-20   Luke 2:22-40

Dec. 29   18:1-20   ❖   18:21-50 *
         2 Samuel 23:13-17b   2 John 1-13   John 2:1-11

Dec. 30   20, 21:1-7(8-14)   ❖   23, 27
         1 Kings 17:17-24   3 John 1-15   John 4:46-54

Dec. 31   46, 48   ❖   ——
         1 Kings 3:5-14   James 4:13-17; 5:7-11   John 5:1-15

Eve of Holy Name   ——   ❖   90
         Isa. 65:15b-25   Rev. 21:1-6

Holy Name   103   ❖   148
         Isa. 62:1-5, 10-12   Rev. 19:11-16   Matt. 1:18-25

Second Sunday after Christmas   66, 67   ❖   145
         Wisdom 7:3-14   Col. 3:12-17   John 6:41-47

Jan. 2   34   ❖   33
         1 Kings 19:1-8   Eph. 4:1-16   John 6:1-14

Jan. 3   68   ❖   72 **
         1 Kings 19:9-18   Eph. 4:17-32   John 6:15-27

Jan. 4   85, 87   ❖   89:1-29 **
         Joshua 3:14 4:7   Eph. 5:1-20   John 9:1-12, 35-38

Jan. 5   2, 110:1-5(6-7)   ❖   ——
         Jonah 2:2-9   Eph. 6:10-20   John 11:17-27, 38-44

Eve of Epiphany   ——   ❖   29, 98
         Isa. 66:18-23   Rom. 15:7-13

* If today is Saturday, use Psalms 23 and 27 at Evening Prayer.
** If today is Saturday, use Psalm 136 at Evening Prayer.

THE EPIPHANY AND FOLLOWING

Epiphany   46, 97 ❖ 96, 100
          Isa. 52:7-10   Rev. 21:22-27   Matt. 12:14-21

Jan. 7 *   103 ❖ 114, 115
          Isa. 52:3-6   Rev. 2:1-7   John 2:1-11

Jan. 8   117, 118 ❖ 112, 113
          Isa. 59:15-21   Rev. 2:8-17   John 4:46-54

Jan. 9   121, 122, 123 ❖ 131, 132
          Isa. 63:1-5   Rev. 2:18-29   John 5:1-15

Jan. 10   138, 139:1-17(18-23) ❖ 147
          Isa. 65:1-9   Rev. 3:1-6   John 6:1-14

Jan. 11   148, 150 ❖ 91, 92
          Isa. 65:13-16   Rev. 3:7-13   John 6:15-27

Jan. 12   98, 99, [100] ❖ ——
          Isa. 66:1-2, 22-23   Rev. 3:14-22   John 9:1-12, 35-38

Eve of 1 Epiphany   —— ❖ 104
          Isa. 61:1-9   Gal. 3:23-29; 4:4-7

WEEK OF 1 EPIPHANY

Sunday   146, 147 ❖ 111, 112, 113
          Isa. 40:1-11   Heb. 1:1-12   John 1:1-7, 19-20, 29-34

Monday   1, 2, 3 ❖ 4, 7
          Isa. 40:12-23   Eph. 1:1-14   Mark 1:1-13

Tuesday   5, 6 ❖ 10, 11
          Isa. 40:25-31   Eph. 1:15-23   Mark 1:14-28

Wednesday 119:1-24 ❖ 12, 13, 14
          Isa. 41:1-16   Eph. 2:1-10   Mark 1:29-45

Thursday   18:1-20 ❖ 18:21-50
          Isa. 41:17-29   Eph. 2:11-22   Mark 2:1-12

Friday   16, 17 ❖ 22
          Isa. 42:(1-9)10-17   Eph. 3:1-13   Mark 2:13-22

Saturday   20, 21:1-7(8-14) ❖ 110:1-5(6-7), 116, 117
          Isa. 43:1-13   Eph. 3:14-21   Mark 2:23—3:6

* The Psalms and Readings for the dated days after the Epiphany are used only until the following Saturday evening.

The Epiphany and Following

Epiphany	46, 97 ❖ 96, 100		
	Isa. 49:1-7	Rev. 21:22-27	Matt. 12:14-21
Jan. 7*	103 ❖ 114, 115		
	Deut. 8:1-3	Col. 1:1-14	John 6:30-33, 48-51
Jan. 8	117, 118 ❖ 112, 113		
	Exod. 17:1-7	Col. 1:15-23	John 7:37-52
Jan. 9	121, 122, 123 ❖ 131, 132		
	Isa. 45:14-19	Col. 1:24—2:7	John 8:12-19
Jan. 10	138, 139:1-17(18-23) ❖ 147		
	Jer. 23:1-8	Col. 2:8-23	John 10:7-17
Jan. 11	148, 150 ❖ 91, 92		
	Isa. 55:3-9	Col. 3:1-17	John 14:6-14
Jan. 12	98, 99, [100] ❖ ———		
	Gen. 49:1-2, 8-12	Col. 3:18—4:6	John 15:1-16
Eve of 1 Epiphany	——— ❖ 104		
	Isa. 61:1-9	Gal. 3:23-29; 4:4-7	

Week of 1 Epiphany

Sunday	146, 147 ❖ 111, 112, 113		
	Gen. 1:1—2:3	Eph. 1:3-14	John 1:29-34
Monday	1, 2, 3 ❖ 4, 7		
	Gen. 2:4-9(10-15)16-25	Heb. 1:1-14	John 1:1-18
Tuesday	5, 6 ❖ 10, 11		
	Gen. 3:1-24	Heb. 2:1-10	John 1:19-28
Wednesday	119:1-24 ❖ 12, 13, 14		
	Gen. 4:1-16	Heb. 2:11-18	John 1:(29-34)35-42
Thursday	18:1-20 ❖ 18:21-50		
	Gen. 4:17-26	Heb. 3:1-11	John 1:43-51
Friday	16, 17 ❖ 22		
	Gen. 6:1-8	Heb. 3:12-19	John 2:1-12
Saturday	20, 21:1-7(8-14) ❖ 110:1-5(6-7), 116, 117		
	Gen. 6:9-22	Heb. 4:1-13	John 2:13-22

* The Psalms and Readings for the dated days after the Epiphany are used only until the following Saturday evening.

Week of 2 Epiphany

Sunday   148, 149, 150   ❖   114, 115
Isa. 43:14—44:5   Heb. 6:17—7:10   John 4:27-42

Monday   25   ❖   9, 15
Isa. 44:6-8, 21-23   Eph. 4:1-16   Mark 3:7-19a

Tuesday   26, 28   ❖   36, 39
Isa. 44:9-20   Eph. 4:17-32   Mark 3:19b-35

Wednesday 38   ❖   119:25-48
Isa. 44:24—45:7   Eph. 5:1-14   Mark 4:1-20

Thursday   37:1-18   ❖   37:19-42
Isa. 45:5-17   Eph. 5:15-33   Mark 4:21-34

Friday   31   ❖   35
Isa. 45:18-25   Eph. 6:1-9   Mark 4:35-41

Saturday   30, 32   ❖   42, 43
Isa. 46:1-13   Eph. 6:10-24   Mark 5:1-20

Week of 3 Epiphany

Sunday   63:1-8(9-11), 98   ❖   103
Isa. 47:1-15   Heb. 10:19-31   John 5:2-18

Monday   41, 52   ❖   44
Isa. 48:1-11   Gal. 1:1-17   Mark 5:21-43

Tuesday   45   ❖   47, 48
Isa. 48:12-21   Gal. 1:18—2:10   Mark 6:1-13

Wednesday 119:49-72   ❖   49, [53]
Isa. 49:1-12   Gal. 2:11-21   Mark 6:13-29

Thursday   50   ❖   [59, 60] *or* 118
Isa. 49:13-23   Gal. 3:1-14   Mark 6:30-46

Friday   40, 54   ❖   51
Isa. 50:1-11   Gal. 3:15-22   Mark 6:47-56

Saturday   55   ❖   138, 139:1-17(18-23)
Isa. 51:1-8   Gal. 3:23-29   Mark 7:1-23

WEEK OF 2 EPIPHANY

| Sunday | 148, 149, 150 ❖ 114, 115 |
| | Gen. 7:1-10, 17-23   Eph. 4:1-16   Mark 3:7-19 |

Sunday 148, 149, 150 ❖ 114, 115
Gen. 7:1-10, 17-23   Eph. 4:1-16   Mark 3:7-19

Monday 25 ❖ 9, 15
Gen. 8:6-22   Heb. 4:14—5:6   John 2:23—3:15

Tuesday 26, 28 ❖ 36, 39
Gen. 9:1-17   Heb. 5:7-14   John 3:16-21

Wednesday 38 ❖ 119:25-48
Gen. 9:18-29   Heb. 6:1-12   John 3:22-36

Thursday 37:1-18 ❖ 37:19-42
Gen. 11:1-9   Heb. 6:13-20   John 4:1-15

Friday 31 ❖ 35
Gen. 11:27—12:8   Heb. 7:1-17   John 4:16-26

Saturday 30, 32 ❖ 42, 43
Gen. 12:9—13:1   Heb. 7:18-28   John 4:27-42

WEEK OF 3 EPIPHANY

Sunday 63:1-8(9-11), 98 ❖ 103
Gen. 13:2-18   Gal. 2:1-10   Mark 7:31-37

Monday 41, 52 ❖ 44
Gen. 14(1-7)8-24   Heb. 8:1-13   John 4:43-54

Tuesday 45 ❖ 47, 48
Gen. 15:1-11, 17-21   Heb. 9:1-14   John 5:1-18

Wednesday 119:49-72 ❖ 49, [53]
Gen. 16:1-14   Heb. 9:15-28   John 5:19-29

Thursday 50 ❖ [59, 60] or 118
Gen. 16:15—17:14   Heb. 10:1-10   John 5:30-47

Friday 40, 54 ❖ 51
Gen. 17:15-27   Heb. 10:11-25   John 6:1-15

Saturday 55 ❖ 138, 139:1-17(18-23)
Gen. 18:1-16   Heb. 10:26-39   John 6:16-27

Week of 4 Epiphany

Sunday   24, 29   ❖   8, 84
              Isa. 51:9-16   Heb. 11:8-16   John 7:14-31

Monday   56, 57, [58]   ❖   64, 65
              Isa. 51:17-23   Gal. 4:1-11   Mark 7:24-37

Tuesday   61, 6   ❖   68:1-20(21-23)24-36
              Isa. 52:1-12   Gal. 4:12-20   Mark 8:1-10

Wednesday   72   ❖   119:73-96
              Isa. 54:1-10(11-17)   Gal. 4:21-31   Mark 8:11-26

Thursday   [70], 71   ❖   74
              Isa. 55:1-13   Gal. 5:1-15   Mark 8:27—9:1

Friday   69:1-23(24-30)31-38   ❖   73
              Isa. 56:1-8   Gal. 5:16-24   Mark 9:2-13

Saturday   75, 76   ❖   23, 27
              Isa. 57:3-13   Gal. 5:25—6:10   Mark 9:14-29

Week of 5 Epiphany

Sunday   93, 96   ❖   34
              Isa. 57:14-21   Heb. 12:1-6   John 7:37-46

Monday   80   ❖   77, [79]
              Isa. 58:1-12   Gal. 6:11-18   Mark 9:30-41

Tuesday   78:1-39   ❖   78:40-72
              Isa. 59:1-15a   2 Tim. 1:1-14   Mark 9:42-50

Wednesday   119:97-120   ❖   81, 82
              Isa. 59:15b-21   2 Tim. 1:15—2:13   Mark 10:1-16

Thursday   [83] *or* 146, 147   ❖   85, 86
              Isa. 60:1-17   2 Tim. 2:14-26   Mark 10:17-31

Friday   88   ❖   91, 92
              Isa. 61:1-9   2 Tim. 3:1-17   Mark 10:32-45

Saturday   87, 90   ❖   136
              Isa. 61:10—62:5   2 Tim. 4:1-8   Mark 10:46-52

WEEK OF 4 EPIPHANY

Sunday   24, 29   ❖   8, 84
            Gen. 18:16-33   Gal. 5:13-25   Mark 8:22-30

Monday   56, 57, [58]   ❖   64, 65
            Gen. 19:1-17(18-23)24-29   Heb. 11:1-12   John 6:27-40

Tuesday   61, 62   ❖   68:1-20(21-23)24-36
            Gen. 21:1-21   Heb. 11:13-22   John 6:41-51

Wednesday   72   ❖   119:73-96
            Gen. 22:1-18   Heb. 11:23-31   John 6:52-59

Thursday   [70], 71   ❖   74
            Gen. 23:1-20   Heb. 11:32—12:2   John 6:60-71

Friday   69:1-23(24-30)31-38   ❖   73
            Gen. 24:1-27   Heb. 12:3-11   John 7:1-13

Saturday   75, 76   ❖   23, 27
            Gen. 24:28-38, 49-51   Heb. 12:12-29   John 7:14-36

WEEK OF 5 EPIPHANY

Sunday   93, 96   ❖   34
            Gen. 24:50-67   2 Tim. 2:14-21   Mark 10:13-22

Monday   80   ❖   77, [79]
            Gen. 25:19-34   Heb. 13:1-16   John 7:37-52

Tuesday   78:1-39   ❖   78:40-72
            Gen. 26:1-6, 12-33   Heb. 13:17-25   John 7:53—8:11

Wednesday   119:97-120   ❖   81, 82
            Gen. 27:1-29   Rom. 12:1-8   John 8:12-20

Thursday   [83] *or* 146, 147   ❖   85, 86
            Gen. 27:30-45   Rom. 12:9-21   John 8:21-32

Friday   88   ❖   91, 92
            Gen. 27:46—28:4, 10-22   Rom. 13:1-14   John 8:33-47

Saturday   87, 90   ❖   136
            Gen. 29:1-20   Rom. 14:1-23   John 8:47-59

Week of 6 Epiphany

Sunday 66, 67 ❖ 19, 46
Isa. 62:6-12   1 John 2:3-11   John 8:12-19

Monday 89:1-18 ❖ 89:19-52
Isa. 63:1-6   1 Tim. 1:1-17   Mark 11:1-11

Tuesday 97, 99, [100] ❖ 94, [95]
Isa. 63:7-14   1 Tim. 1:18—2:8   Mark 11:12-26

Wednesday 101, 109:1-4(5-19)20-30 ❖ 119:121-144
Isa. 63:15—64:9   1 Tim. 3:1-16   Mark 11:27—12:12

Thursday 105:1-22 ❖ 105:23-45
Isa. 65:1-12   1 Tim. 4:1-16   Mark 12:13-27

Friday 102 ❖ 107:1-32
Isa. 65:17-25   1 Tim 5:17-22(23-25)   Mark 12:28-34

Saturday 107:33-43, 108:1-6(7-13) ❖ 33
Isa. 66:1-6   1 Tim. 6:6-21   Mark 12:35-44

Week of 7 Epiphany

Sunday 118 ❖ 145
Isa. 66:7-14   1 John 3:4-10   John 10:7-16

Monday 106:1-18 ❖ 106:19-48
Ruth 1:1-14   2 Cor. 1:1-11   Matt. 5:1-12

Tuesday [120], 121, 122, 123 ❖ 124, 125, 126, [127]
Ruth 1:15-22   2 Cor. 1:12-22   Matt. 5:13-20

Wednesday 119:145-17 ❖ 128, 129, 130
Ruth 2:1-13   2 Cor. 1:23—2:17   Matt. 5:21-26

Thursday 131, 132, [133] ❖ 134, 135
Ruth 2:14-23   2 Cor. 3:1-18   Matt. 5:27-37

Friday 140, 142 ❖ 141, 143:1-11(12)
Ruth 3:1-18   2 Cor. 4:1-12   Matt. 5:38-48

Saturday 137:1-6(7-9), 144 ❖ 104
Ruth 4:1-17   2 Cor. 4:13—5:10   Matt. 6:1-6

WEEK OF 6 EPIPHANY

Sunday   66, 67   ❖   19, 46
              Gen. 29:20-35   1 Tim. 3:14—4:10   Mark 10:23-31

Monday   89:1-18   ❖   89:19-52
              Gen. 30:1-24   1 John 1:1-10   John 9:1-17

Tuesday   97, 99, [100]   ❖   94, [95]
              Gen. 31:1-24   1 John 2:1-11   John 9:18-41

Wednesday   101,109:1-4(5-19)20-30   ❖   119:121-144
              Gen. 31:25-50   1 John 2:12-17   John 10:1-18

Thursday   105:1-22   ❖   105:23-45
              Gen. 32:3-21   1 John 2:18-29   John 10:19-30

Friday   102   ❖   107:1-32
              Gen. 32:22—33:17   1 John 3:1-10   John 10:31-42

Saturday   107:33-43, 108:1-6(7-13)   ❖   33
              Gen. 35:1-20   1 John 3:11-18   John 11:1-16

WEEK OF 7 EPIPHANY

Sunday   118   ❖   145
              Prov. 1:20-33   2 Cor. 5:11-21   Mark 10:35-45

Monday   106:1-18   ❖   106:19-48
              Prov. 3:11-20   1 John 3:18—4:6   John 11:17-29

Tuesday   [120], 121, 122, 123   ❖   124, 125, 126, [127]
              Prov. 4:1-27   1 John 4:7-21   John 11:30-44

Wednesday   119:145-176   ❖   128, 129, 130
              Prov. 6:1-19   1 John 5:1-12   John 11:45-54

Thursday   131, 132, [133]   ❖   134, 135
              Prov. 7:1-27   1 John 5:13-21   John 11:55—12:8

Friday   140, 142   ❖   141, 143:1-11(12)
              Prov. 8:1-21   Philemon 1-25   John 12:9-19

Saturday   137:1-6(7-9), 144   ❖   104
              Prov. 8:22-36   2 Tim. 1:1-14   John 12:20-26

WEEK OF 8 EPIPHANY

Sunday	146, 147 ❖ 111, 112, 113	
	Deut. 4:1-9	2 Tim. 4:1-8	John 12:1-8

Sunday 146, 147 ❖ 111, 112, 113
Deut. 4:1-9 2 Tim. 4:1-8 John 12:1-8

Monday 1, 2, 3 ❖ 4, 7
Deut. 4:9-14 2 Cor. 10:1-18 Matt. 6:7-15

*Tues*day 5, 6 ❖ 10, 11
Deut. 4:15-24 2 Cor. 11:1-21a Matt. 6:16-23

Wednesday 119:1-24 ❖ 12, 13, 14
Deut. 4:25-31 2 Cor. 11:21b-33 Matt. 6:24-34

*Thurs*day 18:1-20 ❖ 18:21-50
Deut. 4:32-40 2 Cor. 12:1-10 Matt. 7:1-12

Friday 16, 17 ❖ 22
Deut. 5:1-22 2 Cor. 12:11-21 Matt. 7:13-21

Saturday 20, 21:1-7(8-14) ❖ 110:1-5(6-7), 116, 117
Deut. 5:22-33 2 Cor. 13:1-14 Matt. 7:22-29

WEEK OF LAST EPIPHANY

Sunday 148, 149, 150 ❖ 114, 115
Deut. 6:1-9 Heb. 12:18-29 John 12:24-32

Monday 25 ❖ 9, 15
Deut. 6:10-15 Heb. 1:1-14 John 1:1-18

Tuesday 26, 28 ❖ 36, 39
Deut. 6:16-25 Heb. 2:1-10 John 1:19-28

Ash Wednesday 95* & 32, 143 ❖ 102, 130
Jonah 3:1—4:11 Heb. 12:1-14 Luke 18:9-14

Thursday 37:1-18 ❖ 37:19-42
Deut. 7:6-11 Titus 1:1-16 John 1:29-34

Friday 95* & 31 ❖ 35
Deut. 7:12-16 Titus 2:1-15 John 1:35-42

Saturday 30, 32 ❖ 42, 43
Deut. 7:17-26 Titus 3:1-15 John 1:43-51

* For the Invitatory

Week of 8 Epiphany

Sunday 146, 147 ❖ 111, 112, 113
Prov. 9:1-12   2 Cor. 9:6b-15   Mark 10:46-52

Monday 1, 2, 3 ❖ 4, 7
Prov. 10:1-12   2 Tim. 1:15—2:13   John 12:27-36a

Tuesday 5, 6 ❖ 10, 11
Prov. 15:16-33   2 Tim. 2:14-26   John 12:36b-50

Wednesday 119:1-24 ❖ 12, 13, 14
Prov. 17:1-20   2 Tim 3:1-17   John 13:1-20

Thursday 18:1-20 ❖ 18:21-50
Prov. 21:30—22:6   2 Tim. 4:1-8   John 13:21-30

Friday 16, 17 ❖ 22
Prov. 23:19-21, 29—24:2   2 Tim. 4:9-22   John 13:31-38

Saturday 20, 21:1-7(8-14) ❖ 110:1-5(6-7), 116, 117
Prov. 25:15-28   Phil. 1:1-11   John 18:1-14

Week of Last Epiphany

Sunday 148, 149, 150 ❖ 114, 115
Ecclus. 48:1-11   2 Cor. 3:7-18   Luke 9:18-27

Monday 25 ❖ 9, 15
Prov. 27:1-6, 10-12   Phil. 2:1-13   John 18:15-18, 25-27

Tuesday 26, 28 ❖ 36, 39
Prov. 30:1-4, 24-33   Phil. 3:1-11   John 18:28-38

Ash Wednesday 95* & 32, 143 ❖ 102, 130
Amos 5:6-15   Heb. 12:1-14   Luke 18:9-14

Thursday 37:1-18 ❖ 37:19-42
Hab. 3:1-10(11-15)16-18   Phil. 3:12-21   John 17:1-8

Friday 95* & 31 ❖ 35
Ezek. 18:1-4, 25-32   Phil. 4:1-9   John 17:9-19

Saturday 30, 32 ❖ 42, 43
Ezek. 39:21-29   Phil. 4:10-20   John 17:20-26

* For the Invitatory

WEEK OF 1 LENT

Sunday   63:1-8(9-11), 98 ❖ 103
Deut. 8:1-10   1 Cor. 1:17-31   Mark 2:18-22

Monday   41, 52 ❖ 44
Deut. 8:11-20   Heb. 2:11-18   John 2:1-12

Tuesday   45 ❖ 47, 48
Deut. 9:4-12   Heb. 3:1-11   John 2:13-22

Wednesday   119:49-72 ❖ 49, [53]
Deut. 9:13-21   Heb. 3:12-19   John 2:23—3:15

Thursday   50 ❖ [59, 60] *or* 19, 46
Deut. 9:23—10:5   Heb. 4:1-10   John 3:16-21

Friday   95* & 40, 54 ❖ 51
Deut. 10:12-22   Heb. 4:11-16   John 3:22-36

Saturday   55 ❖ 138, 139:1-17(18-23)
Deut. 11:18-28   Heb. 5:1-10   John 4:1-26

WEEK OF 2 LENT

Sunday   24, 29 ❖ 8, 84
Jer. 1:1-10   1 Cor. 3:11-23   Mark 3:31—4:9

Monday   56, 57, [58] ❖ 64, 65
Jer. 1:11-19   Rom. 1:1-15   John 4:27-42

Tuesday   61, 62 ❖ 68:1-20(21-23)24-36
Jer. 2:1-13   Rom. 1:16-25   John 4:43-54

Wednesday   72 ❖ 119:73-96
Jer. 3:6-18   Rom. 1:28—2:11   John 5:1-18

Thursday   [70], 71 ❖ 74
Jer. 4:9-10, 19-28   Rom. 2:12-24   John 5:19-29

Friday   95* & 69:1-23(24-30)31-38 ❖ 73
Jer. 5:1-9   Rom. 2:25—3:18   John 5:30-47

Saturday   75, 76 ❖ 23, 27
Jer. 5:20-31   Rom. 3:19-31   John 7:1-13

* For the Invitatory

WEEK OF 1 LENT

Sunday	63:1-8(9-11), 98 ❖ 103	
	Dan. 9:3-10 Heb. 2:10-18 John 12:44-50	

Sunday   63:1-8(9-11), 98 ❖ 103
Dan. 9:3-10   Heb. 2:10-18   John 12:44-50

Monday   41, 52 ❖ 44
Gen. 37:1-11   1 Cor. 1:1-19   Mark 1:1-13

Tuesday   45 ❖ 47, 48
Gen. 37:12-24   1 Cor. 1:20-31   Mark 1:14-28

Wednesday   119:49-72 ❖ 49, [53]
Gen. 37:25-36   1 Cor. 2:1-13   Mark 1:29-45

Thursday   50 ❖ [59, 60] *or* 19, 46
Gen. 39:1-23   1 Cor. 2:14—3:15   Mark 2:1-12

Friday   95* & 40, 54 ❖ 51
Gen. 40:1-23   1 Cor. 3:16-23   Mark 2:13-22

Saturday   55 ❖ 138, 139:1-17(18-23)
Gen. 41:1-13   1 Cor. 4:1-7   Mark 2:23—3:6

WEEK OF 2 LENT

Sunday   24, 29 ❖ 8, 84
Gen. 41:14-45   Rom. 6:3-14   John 5:19-24

Monday   56, 57, [58] ❖ 64, 65
Gen. 41:46-57   1 Cor. 4:8-20(21)   Mark 3:7-19a

Tuesday   61, 62 ❖ 68:1-20(21-23)24-36
Gen. 42:1-17   1 Cor. 5:1-8   Mark 3:19b-35

Wednesday   72 ❖ 119:73-96
Gen. 42:18-28   1 Cor. 5:9—6:8   Mark 4:1-20

Thursday   [70], 71 ❖ 74
Gen. 42:29-38   1 Cor. 6:12-20   Mark 4:21-34

Friday   95* & 69:1-23(24-30)31-38 ❖ 73
Gen. 43:1-15   1 Cor. 7:1-9   Mark 4:35-41

Saturday   75, 76 ❖ 23, 27
Gen. 43:16-34   1 Cor. 7:10-24   Mark 5:1-20

* For the Invitatory

Sunday 93, 96 ❖ 34
Jer. 6:9-15   1 Cor. 6:12-20   Mark 5:1-20

Monday 80 ❖ 77, [79]
Jer. 7:1-15   Rom. 4:1-12   John 7:14-36

Tuesday 78:1-39 ❖ 78:40-72
Jer. 7:21-34   Rom. 4:13-25   John 7:37-52

Wednesday 119:97-120 ❖ 81, 82
Jer. 8:18—9:6   Rom. 5:1-11   John 8:12-20

Thursday [83] *or* 42, 43 ❖ 85, 86
Jer. 10:11-24   Rom. 5:12-21   John 8:21-32

Friday 95* & 88 ❖ 91, 92
Jer. 11:1-8, 14-20   Rom. 6:1-11   John 8:33-47

Saturday 87, 90 ❖ 136
Jer. 13:1-11   Rom. 6:12-23   John 8:47-59

WEEK OF 4 LENT

Sunday 66, 67 ❖ 19, 46
Jer. 14:1-9, 17-22   Gal. 4:21—5:1   Mark 8:11-21

Monday 89:1-18 ❖ 89:19-52
Jer. 16:10-21   Rom. 7:1-12   John 6:1-15

Tuesday 97, 99, [100] ❖ 94, [95]
Jer. 17:19-27   Rom. 7:13-25   John 6:16-27

Wednesday 101, 109:1-4(5-19)20-30 ❖ 119:121-144
Jer. 18:1-11   Rom. 8:1-11   John 6:27-40

Thursday 69:1-23(24-30)31-38 ❖ 73
Jer. 22:13-23   Rom. 8:12-27   John 6:41-51

Friday 95* & 102 ❖ 107:1-32
Jer. 23:1-8   Rom. 8:28-39   John 6:52-59

Saturday 107:33-43, 108:1-6(7-13) ❖ 33
Jer. 23:9-15   Rom. 9:1-18   John 6:60-71

* For the Invitatory

Sunday	93, 96 ❖ 34	
	Gen. 44:1-17 Rom. 8:1-10 John 5:25-29	
Monday	80 ❖ 77, [79]	
	Gen. 44:18-34 1 Cor. 7:25-31 Mark 5:21-43	
Tuesday	78:1-39 ❖ 78:40-72	
	Gen. 45:1-15 1 Cor. 7:32-40 Mark 6:1-13	
Wednesday	119:97-120 ❖ 81, 82	
	Gen. 45:16-28 1 Cor. 8:1-13 Mark 6:13-29	
Thursday	[83] *or* 42, 43 ❖ 85, 86	
	Gen. 46:1-7, 28-34 1 Cor. 9:1-15 Mark 6:30-46	
Friday	95* & 88 ❖ 91, 92	
	Gen. 47:1-26 1 Cor. 9:16-27 Mark 6:47-56	
Saturday	87, 90 ❖ 136	
	Gen. 47:27—48:7 1 Cor. 10:1-13 Mark 7:1-23	

WEEK OF 4 LENT

Sunday	66, 67 ❖ 19, 46	
	Gen. 48:8-22 Rom. 8:11-25 John 6:27-40	
Monday	89:1-18 ❖ 89:19-52	
	Gen. 49:1-28 1 Cor. 10:14—11:1 Mark 7:24-37	
Tuesday	97, 99, [100] ❖ 94, [95]	
	Gen. 49:29—50:14 1 Cor. 11:17-34 Mark 8:1-10	
Wednesday	101, 109:1-4(5-19)20-30 ❖ 119:121-144	
	Gen. 50:15-26 1 Cor. 12:1-11 Mark 8:11-26	
Thursday	69:1-23(24-30)31-38 ❖ 73	
	Exod. 1:6-22 1 Cor. 12:12-26 Mark 8:27—9:1	
Friday	95* & 102 ❖ 107:1-32	
	Exod. 2:1-22 1 Cor. 12:27—13:3 Mark 9:2-13	
Saturday	107:33-43, 108:1-6(7-13) ❖ 33	
	Exod. 2:23—3:15 1 Cor. 13:1-13 Mark 9:14-29	

* For the Invitatory

Week of 5 Lent

Sunday 118 ❖ 145
Jer. 23:16-32   1 Cor. 9:19-27   Mark 8:31—9:1

Monday 31 ❖ 35
Jer. 24:1-10   Rom. 9:19-33   John 9:1-17

Tuesday [120], 121, 122, 123 ❖ 124, 125, 126, [127]
Jer. 25:8-17   Rom. 10:1-13   John 9:18-41

Wednesday 119:145-176 ❖ 128, 129, 130
Jer. 25:30-38   Rom. 10:14-21   John 10:1-18

Thursday 131,132, [133] ❖ 140, 142
Jer. 26:1-16   Rom. 11:1-12   John 10:19-42

Friday 95* & 22 ❖ 141, 143:1-11(12)
Jer. 29:1, 4-13   Rom. 11:13-24   John 11:1-27, *or* 12:1-10

Saturday 137:1-6(7-9), 144 ❖ 42, 43
Jer. 31:27-34   Rom. 11:25-36   John 11:28-44, *or* 12:37-50

Holy Week

Palm Sunday 24, 29 ❖ 103
Zech. 9:9-12**   1 Tim. 6:12-16**
Zech. 12:9-11, 13:1, 7-9***   Matt. 21:12-17***

Monday 51:1-18(19-20) ❖ 69:1-23
Jer. 12:1-16   Phil. 3:1-14   John 12:9-19

Tuesday 6, 12 ❖ 94
Jer. 15:10-21   Phil. 3:15-21   John 12:20-26

Wednesday 55 ❖ 74
Jer. 17:5-10, 14-17   Phil. 4:1-13   John 12:27-36

Maundy Thursday 102 ❖ 142, 143
Jer. 20:7-11   1 Cor. 10:14-17; 11:27-32   John 17:1-11(12-26)

Good Friday 95* & 22 ❖ 40:1-14(15-19), 54
Wisdom 1:16—2:1, 12-22   1 Peter 1:10-20   John 13:36-38**
or Gen. 22:1-14   John 19:38-42***

Holy Saturday 95* & 88 ❖ 27
Job 19:21-27a   Heb. 4:1-16**   Rom. 8:1-11***

* For the Invitatory   ** Intended for use in the morning   *** Intended for use in the evening

WEEK OF 5 LENT

Sunday 118 ❖ 145
Exod. 3:16—4:12 Rom. 12:1-21 John 8:46-59

Monday 31 ❖ 35
Exod. 4:10-20(21-26)27-31 1 Cor. 14:1-19 Mark 9:30-41

Tuesday [120], 121, 122, 123 ❖ 124, 125, 126, [127]
Exod. 5:1—6:1 1 Cor. 14:20-33a, 39-40 Mark 9:42-50

Wednesday 119:145-176 ❖ 128, 129, 130
Exod. 7:8-24 2 Cor. 2:14—3:6 Mark 10:1-16

Thursday 131, 132, [133] ❖ 140, 142
Exod. 7:25—8:19 2 Cor. 3:7-18 Mark 10:17-31

Friday 95* & 22 ❖ 141, 143:1-11(12)
Exod. 9:13-35 2 Cor. 4:1-12 Mark 10:32-45

Saturday 137:1-6(7-9), 144 ❖ 42, 43
Exod. 10:21—11:8 2 Cor. 4:13-18 Mark 10:46-52

HOLY WEEK

Palm Sunday 24, 29 ❖ 103
Zech. 9:9-12** 1 Tim. 6:12-16**
Zech. 12:9-11; 13:1, 7-9*** Luke 19:41-48***

Monday 51:1-18(19-20) ❖ 69:1-23
Lam. 1:1-2, 6-12 2 Cor. 1:1-7 Mark 11:12-25

Tuesday 6, 12 ❖ 94
Lam. 1:17-22 2 Cor. 1:8-22 Mark 11:27-33

Wednesday 55 ❖ 74
Lam. 2:1-9 2 Cor. 1:23—2:11 Mark 12:1-11

Maundy Thursday 102 ❖ 142, 143
Lam. 2:10-18 1 Cor. 10:14-17; 11:27-32 Mark 14:12-25

Good Friday 95* & 22 ❖ 40:1-14(15-19), 54
Lam. 3:1-9, 19-33 1 Pet. 1:10-20 John 13:36-38**
John 19:38-42***

Holy Saturday 95* & 88 ❖ 27
Lam. 3:37-58 Heb. 4:1-16** Rom. 8:1-11***

* For the Invitatory ** Intended for use in the morning *** Intended for use in the evening

EASTER WEEK

Easter Day 148, 149, 150 ❖ 113, 114, *or* 118
Exod. 12:1-14** —— John 1:1-18**
Isa. 51:9-11*** Luke 24:13-35, *or* John 20:19-23***

Monday 93, 98 ❖ 66
Jonah 2:1-9 Acts 2:14, 22-32* John 14:1-14

Tuesday 103 ❖ 111, 114
Isa. 30:18-21 Acts 2:36-41(42-47)* John 14:15-31

Wednesday 97, 99 ❖ 115
Micah 7:7-15 Acts 3:1-10* John 15:1-11

Thursday 146, 147 ❖ 148, 149
Ezek. 37:1-14 Acts 3:11-26* John 15:12-27

Friday 136 ❖ 118
Dan. 12:1-4, 13 Acts 4:1-12* John 16:1-15

Saturday 145 ❖ 104
Isa. 25:1-9 Acts 4:13-21(22-31)* John 16:16-33

WEEK OF 2 EASTER

Sunday 146, 147 ❖ 111, 112, 113
Isa. 43:8-13 1 Pet. 2:2-10 John 14:1-7

Monday 1, 2, 3 ❖ 4, 7
Dan. 1:1-21 1 John 1:1-10 John 17:1-11

Tuesday 5, 6 ❖ 10, 11
Dan. 2:1-16 1 John 2:1-11 John 17:12-19

Wednesday 119:1-24 ❖ 12, 13, 14
Dan. 2:17-30 1 John 2:12-17 John 17:20-26

Thursday 18:1-20 ❖ 18:21-50
Dan. 2:31-49 1 John 2:18-29 Luke 3:1-14

Friday 16, 17 ❖ 134, 135
Dan. 3:1-18 1 John 3:1-10 Luke 3:15-22

Saturday 20, 21:1-7(8-14) ❖ 110:1-5(6-7), 116, 117
Dan. 3:19-30 1 John 3:11-18 Luke 4:1-13

** Intended for use in the morning * Duplicates the First Lesson at the Eucharist.
*** Intended for use in the evening Readings from Year Two may be substituted.

EASTER WEEK

Easter Day   148, 149, 150   ❖   113, 114, *or* 118
Exod. 12:1-1 4**   ——   John 1:1-18**
Isa. 51:9-11***   Luke 24:13-35, *or* John 20:19-23***

Monday   93, 98   ❖   66
Exod. 12:14-27   1 Cor. 15:1-11   Mark 16:1-8

Tuesday   103   ❖   111, 114
Exod. 12:28-39   1 Cor. 15:12-28   Mark 16:9-20

Wednesday   97, 99   ❖   115
Exod. 12:40-51   1 Cor. 15:(29)30-41   Matt. 28:1-16

Thursday   146, 147   ❖   148, 149
Exod. 13:3-10   1 Cor. 15:41-50   Matt. 28:16-20

Friday   136   ❖   118
Exod. 13:1-2, 11-16   1 Cor. 15:51-58   Luke 24:1-12

Saturday   145   ❖   104
Exod. 13:17—14:4   2 Cor. 4:16—5:10   Mark 12:1 8-27

WEEK OF 2 EASTER

Sunday   146, 147   ❖   111, 112, 113
Exod. 14:5-22   1 John 1:1-7   John 14:1-7

Monday   1, 2, 3   ❖   4, 7
Exod. 14:21-31   1 Pet. 1:1-12   John 14:(1-7)8-17

Tuesday   5, 6   ❖   10, 11
Exod. 15:1-21   1 Pet. 1:13-25   John 14:18-31

Wednesday   119:1-24   ❖   12, 13, 14
Exod. 15:22—16:10   1 Pet. 2:1-10   John 15:1-11

Thursday   18:1-20   ❖   18:21-50
Exod. 16:10-22   1 Pet. 2:11-25   John 15:12-27

Friday   16,17   ❖   134, 135
Exod. 16:23-36   1 Pet. 3:13—4:6   John 16:1-15

Saturday   20, 21:1-7(8-14)   ❖   110:1-5(6-7), 116, 117
Exod. 17:1-16   1 Pet. 4:7-19   John 16:16-33

** Intended for use in the morning   *** Intended for use in the evening

WEEK OF 3 EASTER

Sunday   148, 149, 150 ❖ 114, 115
          Dan. 4:1-18   1 Pet. 4:7-11   John 21:15-25

Monday   25 ❖ 9, 15
          Dan. 4:19-27   1 John 3:19—4:6   Luke 4:14-30

Tuesday   26, 28 ❖ 36, 39
          Dan. 4:28-37   1 John 4:7-21   Luke 4:31-37

Wednesday 38 ❖ 119:25-48
          Dan. 5:1-12   1 John 5:1-12   Luke 4:38-44

Thursday   37:1-18 ❖ 37:19-42
          Dan. 5:13-30   1 John 5:13-20(21)   Luke 5:1-11

Friday   105:1-22 ❖ 105:23-45
          Dan. 6:1-15   2 John 1-13   Luke 5:12-26

Saturday   30, 32 ❖ 42, 43
          Dan. 6:16-28   3 John 1-15   Luke 5:27-39

WEEK OF 4 EASTER

Sunday   63:1-8(9-11), 98 ❖ 103
          Wisdom 1:1-15   1 Pet. 5:1-11   Matt. 7:15-29

Monday   41, 52 ❖ 44
          Wisdom 1:16—2:11, 21-24   Col. 1:1-14   Luke 6:1-11

Tuesday   45 ❖ 47, 48
          Wisdom 3:1-9   Col. 1:15-23   Luke 6:12-26

Wednesday 119:49-72 ❖ 49, [53]
          Wisdom 4:16—5:8   Col. 1:24—2:7   Luke 6:27-38

Thursday   50 ❖ [59, 60] *or* 114, 115
          Wisdom 5:9-23   Col. 2:8-23   Luke 6:39-49

Friday   40, 54 ❖ 51
          Wisdom 6:12-23   Col. 3:1-11   Luke 7:1-17

Saturday   55 ❖ 138, 139:1-17(18-23)
          Wisdom 7:1-14   Col. 3:12-17   Luke 7:18-28(29-30)31-35

Week of 3 Easter

Sunday   148, 149, 150 ❖ 114, 115
Exod. 18:1-12   1 John 2:7-17   Mark 16:9-20

Monday   25 ❖ 9, 15
Exod. 18:13-27   1 Pet. 5:1-14   Matt. (1:1-17); 3:1-6

Tuesday   26, 28 ❖ 36, 39
Exod. 19:1-16   Col. 1:1-14   Matt. 3:7-12

Wednesday   38 ❖ 119:25-48
Exod. 19:16-25   Col. 1:15-23   Matt. 3:13-17

Thursday   37:1-18 ❖ 37:19-42
Exod. 20:1-21   Col. 1:24—2:7   Matt. 4:1-11

Friday   105:1-22 ❖ 105:23-45
Exod. 24:1-18   Col. 2:8-23   Matt. 4:12-17

Saturday   30, 32 ❖ 42, 43
Exod. 25:1-22   Col. 3:1-17   Matt. 4:18-25

Week of 4 Easter

Sunday   63:1-8(9-11), 98 ❖ 103
Exod. 28:1-4, 30-38   1 John 2:18-29   Mark 6:30-44

Monday   41, 52 ❖ 44
Exod. 32:1-20   Col. 3:18—4:6(7-18)   Matt. 5:1-10

Tuesday   45 ❖ 47, 48
Exod. 32:21-34   1 Thess. 1:1-10   Matt. 5:11-16

Wednesday   119:49-72 ❖ 49, [53]
Exod. 33:1-23   1 Thess. 2:1-12   Matt. 5:17-20

Thursday   50 ❖ [59, 60] *or* 114, 115
Exod. 34:1-17   1 Thess. 2:13-20   Matt. 5:21-26

Friday   40, 54 ❖ 51
Exod. 34:18-35   1 Thess. 3:1-13   Matt. 5:27-37

Saturday   55 ❖ 138, 139:1-17(18-23)
Exod. 40:18-38   1 Thess. 4:1-12   Matt. 5:38-48

Sunday	24, 29 ❖ 8, 84	
	Wisdom 7:22—8:1 2 Thess. 2:13-17 Matt. 7:7-14	
Monday	56, 57, [58] ❖ 64, 65	
	Wisdom 9:1, 7-18 Col. (3:18—4:1)2-18 Luke 7:36-50	
Tuesday	61, 62 ❖ 68:1-20(21-23)24-36	
	Wisdom 10:1-4(5-12)13-21 Rom. 12:1-21 Luke 8:1-15	
Wednesday	72 ❖ 119:73-96	
	Wisdom 13:1-9 Rom. 13:1-14 Luke 8:16-25	
Thursday	[70], 71 ❖ 74	
	Wisdom 14:27—15:3 Rom. 14:1-12 Luke 8:26-39	
Friday	106:1-18 ❖ 106:19-48	
	Wisdom 16:15—17:1 Rom. 14:13-23 Luke 8:40-56	
Saturday	75, 76 ❖ 23, 27	
	Wisdom 19:1-8, 18-22 Rom. 15:1-13 Luke 9:1-17	

WEEK OF 6 EASTER

Sunday	93, 96 ❖ 34	
	Ecclus. 43:1-12, 27-32 1 Tim. 3:14—4:5 Matt. 13:24-34a	
Monday	80 ❖ 77, [79]	
	Deut. 8:1-10 James 1:1-15 Luke 9:18-27	
Tuesday	78:1-39 ❖ 78:40-72	
	Deut. 8:11-20 James 1:16-27 Luke 11:1-13	
Wednesday	119:97-120 ❖ ——	
	Baruch 3:24-37 James 5:13-18 Luke 12:22-31	
Eve of Ascension	—— ❖ 68:1-20	
	2 Kings 2:1-15 Rev. 5:1-14	
Ascension Day	8, 47 ❖ 24, 96	
	Ezek. 1:1-14, 24-28b Heb. 2:5-18 Matt. 28:16-20	
Friday	85, 86 ❖ 91, 92	
	Ezek. 1:28—3:3 Heb. 4:14—5:6 Luke 9:28-36	
Saturday	87, 90 ❖ 136	
	Ezek. 3:4-17 Heb. 5:7-14 Luke 9:37-50	

WEEK OF 5 EASTER

Sunday	24, 29 ❖ 8, 84	
	Lev. 8:1-13, 30-36 Heb. 12:1-14 Luke 4:16-30	
Monday	56, 57, [58] ❖ 64, 65	
	Lev. 16:1-19 1 Thess. 4:13-18 Matt. 6:1-6,16-18	
Tuesday	61, 62 ❖ 68:1-20(21-23)24-36	
	Lev. 16:20-34 1 Thess. 5:1-11 Matt. 6:7-15	
Wednesday	72 ❖ 119:73-96	
	Lev. 19:1-18 1 Thess. 5:12-28 Matt. 6:19-24	
Thursday	[70], 71 ❖ 74	
	Lev. 19:26-37 2 Thess. 1:1-12 Matt. 6:25-34	
Friday	106:1-18 ❖ 106:19-48	
	Lev. 23:1-22 2 Thess. 2:1-17 Matt. 7:1-12	
Saturday	75, 76 ❖ 23, 27	
	Lev. 23:23-44 2 Thess. 3:1-18 Matt. 7:13-21	

WEEK OF 6 EASTER

Sunday	93, 96 ❖ 34	
	Lev. 25:1-17 James 1:2-8, 16-18 Luke 12:13-21	
Monday	80 ❖ 77, [79]	
	Lev. 25:35-55 Col. 1:9-14 Matt. 13:1-16	
Tuesday	78:1-39 ❖ 78:40-72	
	Lev. 26:1-20 1 Tim. 2:1-6 Matt. 13:18-23	
Wednesday	119:97-120 ❖ ——	
	Lev. 26:27-42 Eph. 1:1-10 Matt. 22:41-46	
Eve of Ascension	—— ❖ 68:1-20	
	2 Kings 2:1-15 Rev. 5:1-14	
Ascension Day	8, 47 ❖ 24, 96	
	Dan. 7:9-14 Heb. 2:5-18 Matt. 28:16-20	
Friday	85, 86 ❖ 91, 92	
	1 Sam. 2:1-10 Eph. 2:1-10 Matt. 7:22-27	
Saturday	87, 90 ❖ 136	
	Num. 11:16-17, 24-29 Eph. 2:11-22 Matt. 7:28—8:4	

Sunday	66, 67 ❖ 19, 46	
	Ezek. 3:16-27 Eph. 2:1-10 Matt. 10:24-33, 40-42	
Monday	89:1-18 ❖ 89:19-52	
	Ezek. 4:1-17 Heb. 6:1-12 Luke 9:51-62	
Tuesday	97, 99, [100] ❖ 94, [95]	
	Ezek. 7:10-15, 23b-27 Heb. 6:13-20 Luke 10:1-17	
Wednesday	101, 109:1-4(5-19)20-30 ❖ 119:121-144	
	Ezek. 11:14-25 Heb. 7:1-17 Luke 10:17-24	
Thursday	105:1-22 ❖ 105:23-45	
	Ezek. 18:1-4, 19-32 Heb. 7:18-28 Luke 10:25-37	
Friday	102 ❖ 107:1-32	
	Ezek. 34:17-31 Heb. 8:1-13 Luke 10:38-42	
Saturday	107:33-43, 108:1-6(7-13) ❖ ——	
	Ezek. 43:1-12 Heb. 9:1-14 Luke 11:14-23	
Eve of Pentecost	—— ❖ 33	
	Exod. 19:3-8a, 16-20 1 Pet. 2:4-10	
The Day of Pentecost 118 ❖ 145		
	Isa. 11:1-9 1 Cor. 2:1-13 John 14:21-29	

On the weekdays which follow, the Readings are taken from the numbered Proper (one through six) which corresponds most closely to the date of Pentecost.

Eve of Trinity Sunday	—— ❖ 104
	Ecclus. 42:15-25 Eph. 3:14-21
Trinity Sunday 146, 147 ❖ 111, 112, 113	
	Ecclus. 43:1-12(27-33) Eph. 4:1-16 John 1:1-18

On the weekdays which follow, the Readings are taken from the numbered Proper (two through seven) which corresponds most closely to the date of Trinity Sunday.

Sunday   66, 67   ❖   19, 46
              Exod. 3:1-12   Heb. 12:18-29   Luke 10:17-24

Monday   89:1-18   ❖   89:19-52
              Joshua 1:1-9   Eph. 3:1-13   Matt. 8:5-17

Tuesday   97, 99, [100]   ❖   94, [95]
              1 Sam. 16:1-13a   Eph. 3:14-21   Matt. 8:18-27

Wednesday   101, 109:1-4(5-19)20-30   ❖   119:121-144
              Isa. 4:2-6   Eph. 4:1-16   Matt. 8:28-34

Thursday   105:1-22   ❖   105: 23-45
              Zech. 4:1-14   Eph. 4:17-32   Matt. 9:1-8

Friday   102   ❖   107:1-32
              Jer. 31:27-34   Eph. 5:1-20   Matt. 9:9-17

Saturday   107:33-43, 108:1-6(7-13)   ❖   ——
              Ezek. 36:22-27   Eph. 6:10-24   Matt. 9:18-26

Eve of Pentecost   ——   ❖   33
              Exod. 19:3-8a, 16-20   1 Pet. 2:4-10

The Day of Pentecost 118   ❖   145
              Deut. 16:9-12   Acts 4:18-21, 23-33   John 4:19-26

On the weekdays which follow, the Readings are taken from the numbered Proper (one through six) which corresponds most closely to the date of Pentecost.

Eve of Trinity Sunday   ——   ❖   104
              Ecclus. 42:15-25   Eph. 3:14-21

Trinity Sunday 146, 147   ❖   111, 112, 113
              Job 38:1-11; 42:1-5   Rev. 19:4-16   John 1:29-34

On the weekdays which follow, the Readings are taken from the numbered Proper (two through seven) which corresponds most closely to the date of Trinity Sunday.

The Season after Pentecost

Directions for the use of the Propers which follow are on page 194.

PROPER 1   *Week of the Sunday closest to May 11*

Monday   106:1-18   ❖   106:19-48
              Isa. 63:7-14   2 Tim. 1:1-14   Luke 11:24-36

Tuesday   [120], 121, 122, 123   ❖   124, 125, 126, [127]
              Isa. 63:15—64:9   2 Tim. 1:15—2:13   Luke 11:37-52

Wednesday   119:145-176   ❖   128, 129, 130
              Isa. 65:1-12   2 Tim. 2:14-26   Luke 11:53—12:12

Thursday   131, 132, [133]   ❖   134, 135
              Isa. 65:17-25   2 Tim. 3:1-17   Luke 12:13-31

Friday   140, 142   ❖   141, 143:1-11(12)
              Isa. 66:1-6   2 Tim. 4:1-8   Luke 12:32-48

Saturday   137:1-6(7-9), 144   ❖   104
              Isa. 66:7-14   2 Tim. 4:9-22   Luke 12:49-59

PROPER 2   *Week of the Sunday closest to May 18*

Monday   1, 2, 3   ❖   4, 7
              Ruth 1:1-18   1 Tim. 1:1-17   Luke 13:1-9

Tuesday   5, 6   ❖   10, 11
              Ruth 1:19—2:13   1 Tim. 1:18—2:8   Luke 13:10-17

Wednesday   119:1-24   ❖   12, 13, 14
              Ruth 2:14-23   1 Tim. 3:1-16   Luke 13:18-30

Thursday   18:1-20   ❖   18:21-50
              Ruth 3:1-18   1 Tim. 4:1-16   Luke 13:31-35

Friday   16, 17   ❖   22
              Ruth 4:1-17   1 Tim. 5:17-22(23-25)   Luke 14:1-11

Saturday   20, 21:1-7(8-14)   ❖   110:1-5(6-7), 116, 117
              Deut. 1:1-8   1 Tim. 6:6-21   Luke 14:12-24

The Season after Pentecost

Directions for use of the Propers which follow are on page 194.

PROPER 1   *Week of the Sunday closest to May 11*

Monday
106:1-18   ❖   106:19-48
Ezek. 33:1-11   1 John 1:1-10   Matt. 9:27-34

Tuesday
[120], 121, 122, 123   ❖   124, 125, 126, [127]
Ezek. 33:21-33   1 John 2:1-11   Matt. 9:35—10:4

Wednesday
119:145-176   ❖   128, 129, 130
Ezek. 34:1-16   1 John 2:12-17   Matt. 10:5-15

Thursday
131, 132, [133]   ❖   134, 135
Ezek. 37:21b-28   1 John 2:18-29   Matt. 10:16-23

Friday
140, 142   ❖   141, 143:1-11(12)
Ezek. 39:21-29   1 John 3:1-10   Matt. 10:24-33

Saturday
137:1-6(7-9), 144   ❖   104
Ezek. 47:1-12   1 John 3:11-18   Matt. 10:34-42

PROPER 2   *Week of the Sunday closest to May 18*

Monday
1, 2, 3   ❖   4, 7
Prov. 3:11-20   1 John 3:18—4:6   Matt. 11:1-6

Tuesday
5, 6   ❖   10, 11
Prov. 4:1-27   1 John 4:7-21   Matt. 11:7-15

Wednesday
119:1-24   ❖   12, 13, 14
Prov. 6:1-19   1 John 5:1-12   Matt. 11:16-24

Thursday
18:1-20   ❖   18:21-50
Prov. 7:1-27   1 John 5:13-21   Matt. 11:25-30

Friday
16, 17   ❖   22
Prov. 8:1-21   2 John 1-13   Matt. 12:1-14

Saturday
20, 21:1-7(8-14)   ❖   110:1-5(6-7), 116, 117
Prov. 8:22-36   3 John 1-15   Matt. 12:15-21

PROPER 3   *Week of the Sunday closest to May 25*

Sunday
148, 149, 150   ❖   114, 115
Deut. 4:1-9   Rev. 7:1-4, 9-17   Matt. 12:33-45

Monday
25   ❖   9, 15
Deut. 4:9-14   2 Cor. 1:1-11   Luke 14:25-35

Tuesday
26, 28   ❖   36, 39
Deut. 4:15-24   2 Cor. 1:12-22   Luke 15:1-10

Wednesday
38   ❖   119:25-48
Deut. 4:25-31   2 Cor. 1:23—2:17   Luke 15:1-2, 11-32

Thursday
37:1-18   ❖   37:19-42
Deut. 4:32-40   2 Cor. 3:1-18   Luke 16:1-9

Friday
31   ❖   35
Deut. 5:1-22   2 Cor. 4:1-12   Luke 16:10-17(18)

Saturday
30, 32   ❖   42, 43
Deut. 5:22-33   2 Cor. 4:13—5:10   Luke 16:19-31

PROPER 4   *Week of the Sunday closest to June 1*

Sunday
63:1-8(9-11), 98   ❖   103
Deut. 11:1-12   Rev. 10:1-11   Matt. 13:44-58

Monday
41, 52   ❖   44
Deut. 11:13-19   2 Cor. 5:11—6:2   Luke 17:1-10

Tuesday
45   ❖   47, 48
Deut. 12:1-12   2 Cor. 6:3-13 (14—7:1)   Luke 17:11-19

Wednesday
119:49-72   ❖   49, [53]
Deut. 13:1-11   2 Cor. 7:2-16   Luke 17:20-37

Thursday
50   ❖   [59, 60] *or* 8, 84
Deut. 16:18-20; 17:14-20   2 Cor. 8:1-16   Luke 18:1-8

Friday
40, 54   ❖   51
Deut. 26:1-11   2 Cor. 8:16-24   Luke 18:9-14

Saturday
55   ❖   138, 139:1-17(18-23)
Deut. 29:2-15   2 Cor. 9:1-15   Luke 18:15-30

PROPER 3 *Week of the Sunday closest to May 25*

Sunday 148, 149, 150 ❖ 114, 115
Prov. 9:1-12 Acts 8:14-25 Luke 10:25-28, 38-42

Monday 25 ❖ 9, 15
Prov. 10:1-12 1 Tim. 1:1-17 Matt. 12:22-32

Tuesday 26, 28 ❖ 36, 39
Prov. 15:16-33 1 Tim. 1:18—2:8 Matt. 12:33-42

Wednesday 38 ❖ 119:25-48
Prov. 17:1-20 1 Tim. 3:1-16 Matt. 12:43-50

Thursday 37:1-18 ❖ 37:19-42
Prov. 21:30—22:6 1 Tim. 4:1-16 Matt. 13:24-30

Friday 31 ❖ 35
Prov. 23:19-21, 29—24:2 1 Tim. 5:17-22(23-25) Matt. 13:31-35

Saturday 30, 32 ❖ 42, 43
Prov. 25:15-28 1 Tim. 6:6-21 Matt. 13:36-43

PROPER 4 *Week of the Sunday closest to June 1*

Sunday 63:1-8(9-11), 98 ❖ 103
Eccles. 1:1-11 Acts 8:26-40 Luke 11:1-13

Monday 41, 52 ❖ 44
Eccles. 2:1-15 Gal. 1:1-17 Matt. 13:44-52

Tuesday 45 ❖ 47, 48
Eccles. 2:16-26 Gal. 1:18—2:10 Matt. 13:53-58

Wednesday 119:49-72 ❖ 49, [53]
Eccles. 3:1-15 Gal. 2:11-21 Matt. 14:1-12

Thursday 50 ❖ [59, 60] *or* 8, 84
Eccles. 3:16—4:3 Gal. 3:1-14 Matt. 14:13-21

Friday 40, 54 ❖ 51
Eccles. 5:1-7 Gal. 3:15-22 Matt. 14:22-36

Saturday 55 ❖ 138, 139:1-17(18-23)
Eccles. 5:8-20 Gal. 3:23—4:11 Matt. 15:1-20

PROPER 5 *Week of the Sunday closest to June 8*

Sunday   24, 29   ❖   8, 84
            Deut. 29:16-29   Rev. 12:1-12   Matt. 15:29-39

Monday   56, 57, [58]   ❖   64, 65
            Deut. 30:1-10   2 Cor. 10:1-18   Luke 18:31-43

Tuesday   61, 62   ❖   68:1-20(21-23)24-36
            Deut. 30:11-20   2 Cor. 11:1-21a   Luke 19:1-10

Wednesday 72   ❖   119:73-96
            Deut. 31:30—32:14   2 Cor. 11:21b-33   Luke 19:11-27

Thursday   [70], 71   ❖   74
            Ecclus. 44:19—45:5   2 Cor. 12:1-10   Luke 19:28-40

Friday   69:1-23(24-30)31-38   ❖   73
            Ecclus. 45:6-16   2 Cor. 12-21   Luke 19:41-48

Saturday   75, 76   ❖   23, 27
            Ecclus. 46:1-10   2 Cor. 13:1-14   Luke 20:1-8

PROPER 6 *Week of the Sunday closest to June 15*

Sunday   93, 96   ❖   34
            Ecclus. 46:11-20   Rev. 15:1-8   Matt. 18:1-14

Monday   80   ❖   77, [79]
            1 Samuel 1:1-20   Acts 1:1-14   Luke 20:9-19

Tuesday   78:1-39   ❖   78:40-72
            1 Samuel 1:21—2:11   Acts 1:15-26   Luke 20:19-26

Wednesday 119:97-120   ❖   81, 82
            1 Samuel 2:12-26   Acts 2:1-21   Luke 20:27-40

Thursday   [83] *or* 34   ❖   85, 86
            1 Samuel 2:27-36   Acts 2:22-36   Luke 20:41—21:4

Friday   88   ❖   91, 92
            1 Samuel 3:1-21   Acts 2:37-47   Luke 21:5-19

Saturday   87, 90   ❖   136
            1 Samuel 4:1b-11   Acts 4:32—5:11   Luke 21:20-28

PROPER 5 *Week of the Sunday closest to June 8*

Sunday   24, 29   ❖   8, 84
            Eccles. 6:1-12   Acts 10:9-23   Luke 12:32-40

Monday   56, 57, [58]   ❖   64, 65
            Eccles. 7:1-14   Gal. 4:12-20   Matt. 15:21-28

Tuesday   61, 62   ❖   68:1-20(21-23)24-36
            Eccles. 8:14—9:10   Gal. 4:21-31   Matt. 15:29-39

Wednesday   72   ❖   119:73-96
            Eccles. 9:11-18   Gal. 5:1-15   Matt. 16:1-12

Thursday   [70], 71   ❖   74
            Eccles. 11:1-8   Gal. 5:16-24   Matt. 16:13-20

Friday   69:1-23(24-30)31-38   ❖   73
            Eccles. 11:9—12:14   Gal. 5:25—6:10   Matt. 16:21-28

Saturday   75, 76   ❖   23, 27
            Num. 3:1-13   Gal. 6:11-18   Matt. 17:1-13

PROPER 6 *Week of the Sunday closest to June 15*

Sunday   93, 96   ❖   34
            Num. 6:22-27   Acts 13:1-12   Luke 12:41-48

Monday   80   ❖   77, [79]
            Num. 9:15-23; 10:29-36   Rom. 1:1-15   Matt. 17:14-21

Tuesday   78:1-39   ❖   78:40-72
            Num. 11:1-23   Rom. 1:16-25   Matt. 17:22-27

Wednesday   119:97-120   ❖   81, 82
            Num. 11:24-33(34-35)   Rom. 1:28—2:11   Matt. 18:1-9

Thursday   [83] *or* 34   ❖   85, 86
            Num. 12:1-16   Rom. 2:12-24   Matt. 18:10-20

Friday   88   ❖   91, 92
            Num. 13:1-3, 21-30   Rom. 2:25—3:8   Matt. 18:21-35

Saturday   87, 90   ❖   136
            Num. 13:31—14:25   Rom. 3:9-20   Matt. 19:1-12

PROPER 7 *Week of the Sunday closest to June 22*

Sunday   66, 67   ❖   19, 46
1 Samuel 4:12-22   James 1:1-18   Matt. 19:23-30

Monday   89:1-18   ❖   89:19-52
1 Samuel 5:1-12   Acts 5:12-26   Luke 21:29-36

Tuesday   97, 99, [100]   ❖   94, [95]
1 Samuel 6:1-16   Acts 5:27-42   Luke 21:37—22:13

Wednesday   101, 109:1-4(5-19) 20-30   ❖   119:121-144
1 Samuel 7:2-17   Acts 6:1-15   Luke 22:14-23

Thursday   105:1-22   ❖   105:23-45
1 Samuel 8:1-22   Acts 6:15—7:16   Luke 22:24-30

Friday   102   ❖   107:1-32
1 Samuel 9:1-14   Acts 7:17-29   Luke 22:31-38

Saturday   107:33-43, 108:1-6(7-13)   ❖   33
1 Samuel 9:15—10:1   Acts 7:30-43   Luke 22:39-51

PROPER 8 *Week of the Sunday closest to June 29*

Sunday   118   ❖   145
1 Samuel 10:1-16   Rom. 4:13-25   Matt. 21:23-32

Monday   106:1-18   ❖   106:19-48
1 Samuel 10:17-27   Acts 7:44—8:1a   Luke 22:52-62

Tuesday   [120], 121, 122, 123   ❖   124, 125, 126, [127]
1 Samuel 11:1-15   Acts 8:1-13   Luke 22:63-71

Wednesday   119:145-176   ❖   128, 129, 130
1 Samuel 12:1-6, 16-25   Acts 8:14-25   Luke 23:1-12

Thursday   131, 132, [133]   ❖   134, 135
1 Samuel 13:5-18   Acts 8:26-40   Luke 23:13-25

Friday   140, 142   ❖   141, 143:1-11(12)
1 Samuel 13:19—14:15   Acts 9:1-9   Luke 23:26-31

Saturday   137:1-6(7-9), 144   ❖   104
1 Samuel 14:16-30   Acts 9:10-19a   Luke 23:32-43

PROPER 7   *Week of the Sunday closest to June 7*2

Sunday	66, 67 ❖ 19, 46		
	Num. 14:26-45 Acts 15:1-12 Luke 12:49-56		
Monday	89:1-18 ❖ 89:19-52		
	Num. 16:1-19 Rom. 3:21-31 Matt. 19:13-22		
Tuesday	97, 99, [100] ❖ 94, [95]		
	Num. 16:20-35 Rom. 4:1-12 Matt. 19:23-30		
Wednesday	101, 109: 1-4(5-19)20-30 ❖ 119: 121-144		
	Num. 16: 36-50 Rom. 4:13-25 Matt. 20:1-16		
Thursday	105:1-22 ❖ 105:23-45		
	Num. 17:1-11 Rom. 5:1-11 Matt. 20:17-28		
Friday	102 ❖ 107:1-32		
	Num. 20:1-13 Rom. 5:12-21 Matt. 20:29-34		
Saturday	107:33-43, 108:1-6(7-13) ❖ 33		
	Num. 20:14-29 Rom. 6:1-11 Matt. 21:1-11		

PROPER 8   *Week of the Sunday closest to June 29*

Sunday	118 ❖ 145		
	Num. 21:4-9, 21-35 Acts 17:(12-21)22-34 Luke 13:10-17		
Monday	106:1-18 ❖ 106:19-48		
	Num. 22:1-21 Rom. 6:12-23 Matt. 21:12-22		
Tuesday	[120], 121, 122, 123 ❖ 124, 125, 126, [127]		
	Num. 22:21-38 Rom. 7:1-12 Matt. 21:23-32		
Wednesday	119:145-176 ❖ 128, 129, 130		
	Num. 22:41—23:12 & Rom. 7:13-25 Matt. 21:33-46		
Thursday	131, 132, [133] ❖ 134, 135		
	Num. 23:11-26 Rom. 8:1-11 Matt. 22:1-14		
Friday	140, 142 ❖ 141, 143:1-11(12)		
	Num. 24:1-13 Rom. 8:12-17 Matt. 22:15-22		
Saturday	137:1-6(7-9), 144 ❖ 104		
	Num. 24:12-25 Rom. 8:18-25 Matt. 22:23-40		

PROPER 9 *Week of the Sunday closest to July 6*

Sunday	146, 147 ❖ 111, 112, 113	
	1 Samuel 14:36-45 Rom. 5:1-11 Matt. 22:1-14	
Monday	1, 2, 3 ❖ 4, 7	
	1 Samuel 15:1-3, 7-23 Acts 9:19b-31 Luke 23:44-56a	
Tuesday	5, 6 ❖ 10, 11	
	1 Samuel 15:24-35 Acts 9:32-43 Luke 23:56b—24:11	
Wednesday	119:1-24 ❖ 12, 13, 14	
	1 Samuel 16:1-13 Acts 10:1-16 Luke 24:12-35	
Thursday	18:1-20 ❖ 18:21-50	
	1 Samuel 16:14—17:11 Acts 10:17-33 Luke 24:36-53	
Friday	16, 17 ❖ 22	
	1 Samuel 17:17-30 Acts 10:34-48 Mark 1:1-13	
Saturday	20, 21:1-7(8-14) ❖ 110:1-5(6-7), 116, 117	
	1 Samuel 17:31-49 Acts 11:1-18 Mark 1:14-28	

PROPER 10 *Week of the Sunday closest to July 13*

Sunday	148, 149, 150 ❖ 114, 115	
	1 Samuel 17:50—18:4 Rom. 10:4-17 Matt. 23:29-39	
Monday	25 ❖ 9, 15	
	1 Samuel 18:5-16, 27b-30 Acts 11:19-30 Mark 1:29-45	
Tuesday	26, 28 ❖ 36, 39	
	1 Samuel 19:1-18 Acts 12:1-17 Mark 2:1-12	
Wednesday	38 ❖ 119:25-48	
	1 Samuel 20:1-23 Acts 12:18-25 Mark 2:13-22	
Thursday	37:1-18 ❖ 37:19-42	
	1 Samuel 20:24-42 Acts 13:1-12 Mark 2:23—3:6	
Friday	31 ❖ 35	
	1 Samuel 21:1-15 Acts 13:13-25 Mark 3:7-19a	
Saturday	30, 32 ❖ 42, 43	
	1 Samuel 22:1-23 Acts 13:26-43 Mark 3:19b-35	

PROPER 9   *Week of the Sunday closest to July 6*

Sunday   146, 147   ❖   111, 112, 113
              Num. 27:12-23   Acts 19:11-20   Mark 1:14-20

Monday   1, 2, 3   ❖   4, 7
              Num. 32:1-6,16-27   Rom. 8:26-30   Matt. 23:1-12

Tuesday   5, 6   ❖   10, 11
              Num. 35:1-3, 9-15, 30-34   Rom. 8:31-39   Matt. 23:13-26

Wednesday   119:1-24   ❖   12, 13, 14
              Deut. 1:1-18   Rom. 9:1-18   Matt. 23:27-39

Thursday   18:1-20   ❖   18:21-50
              Deut. 3:18-28   Rom. 9:19-33   Matt. 24:1-14

Friday   16, 17   ❖   22
              Deut. 31:7-13, 24—32:4   Rom. 10:1-13   Matt. 24:15-31

Saturday   20, 21:1-7(8-14)   ❖   110:1-5(6-7), 116, 117
              Deut. 34:1-12   Rom. 10:14-21   Matt. 24:32-51

PROPER 10   *Week of the Sunday closest to July 13*

Sunday   148, 149, 150   ❖   114, 115
              Joshua 1:1-18   Acts 21:3-15   Mark 1:21-27

Monday   25   ❖   9, 15
              Joshua 2:1-14   Rom. 11:1-12   Matt. 25:1-13

Tuesday   26, 28   ❖   36, 39
              Joshua 2:15-24   Rom. 11:13-24   Matt. 25:14-30

Wednesday   38   ❖   119:25-48
              Joshua 3:1-13   Rom. 11:25-36   Matt. 25:31-46

Thursday   37:1-18   ❖   37:19-42
              Joshua 3:14—4:7   Rom. 12:1-8   Matt. 26:1-16

Friday   31   ❖   35
              Joshua 4:19—5:1, 10-15   Rom. 12:9-21   Matt. 26:17-25

Saturday   30, 32   ❖   42, 43
              Joshua 6:1-14   Rom. 13:1-7   Matt. 26:26-35

PROPER 11 *Week of the Sunday closest to July 20*

Sunday   63:1-8(9-11), 98   ❖   103
             1 Samuel 23:7-18   Rom. 11:33—12:2   Matt. 25:14-30

Monday   41, 52   ❖   44
             1 Samuel 24:1-22   Acts 13:44-52   Mark 4:1-20

Tuesday   45   ❖   47, 48
             1 Samuel 25:1-22   Acts 14:1-18   Mark 4:21-34

Wednesday   119:49-72   ❖   49, [53]
             1 Samuel 25:23-44   Acts 14:19-28   Mark 4:35-41

Thursday   50   ❖   [59, 60] *or* 66, 67
             1 Samuel 28:3-20   Acts 15:1-11   Mark 5:1-20

Friday   40, 54   ❖   51
             1 Samuel 31:1-13   Acts 15:12-21   Mark 5:21-43

Saturday   55   ❖   138, 139:1-17(18-23)
             2 Samuel 1:1-16   Acts 15:22-35   Mark 6:1-13

PROPER 12 *Week of the Sunday closest to July 27*

Sunday   24, 29   ❖   8, 84
             2 Samuel 1:17-27   Rom. 12:9-21   Matt. 25:31-46

Monday   56, 57, [58]   ❖   64, 65
             2 Samuel 2:1-11   Acts 15:36—16:5   Mark 6:14-29

Tuesday   61, 62   ❖   68:1-20(21-23)24-36
             2 Samuel 3:6-21   Acts 16:6-15   Mark 6:30-46

Wednesday   72   ❖   119:73-96
             2 Samuel 3:22-39   Acts 16:16-24   Mark 6:47-56

Thursday   [70], 71   ❖   74
             2 Samuel 4:1-12   Acts 16:25-40   Mark 7:1-23

Friday   69:1-23(24-30)31-38   ❖   73
             2 Samuel 5:1-12   Acts 17:1-15   Mark 7:24-37

Saturday   75, 76   ❖   23, 27
             2 Samuel 5:22—6:11   Acts 17:16-34   Mark 8:1-10

Sunday	63:1-8(9-11), 98 ❖ 103		
	Joshua 6:15-27	Acts 22:30—23:11	Mark 2:1-12
Monday	41, 52 ❖ 44		
	Joshua 7:1-13	Rom. 13:8-14	Matt. 26:36-46
Tuesday	45 ❖ 47, 48		
	Joshua 8:1-22	Rom. 14:1-12	Matt. 26:47-56
Wednesday	119:49-72 ❖ 49, [53]		
	Joshua 8:30-35	Rom. 14:13-23	Matt. 26:57-68
Thursday	50 ❖ [59, 60] *or* 66, 67		
	Joshua 9:3-21	Rom. 15:1-13	Matt. 26:69-75
Friday	40, 54 ❖ 51		
	Joshua 9:22—10:15	Rom. 15:14-24	Matt. 27:1-10
Saturday	55 ❖ 138, 139:1-17(18-23)		
	Joshua 23:1-16	Rom. 15:25-33	Matt. 27:11-23

PROPER 12 *Week of the Sunday closest to July 27*

Sunday	24, 29 ❖ 8, 84		
	Joshua 24:1-15	Acts 28:23-31	Mark 2:23-28
Monday	56, 57, [58] ❖ 64, 65		
	Joshua 24:16-33	Rom. 16:1-16	Matt. 27:24-31
Tuesday	61, 62 ❖ 68:1-20(21-23)24-36		
	Judges 2:1-5, 11-23	Rom. 16:17-27	Matt. 27:32-44
Wednesday	72 ❖ 119:73-96		
	Judges 3:12-30	Acts 1:1-14	Matt. 27:45-54
Thursday	[70], 71 ❖ 74		
	Judges 4:4-23	Acts 1:15-26	Matt. 27:55-66
Friday	69:1-23(24-30)31-38 ❖ 73		
	Judges 5:1-18	Acts 2:1-21	Matt. 28:1-10
Saturday	75, 76 ❖ 23, 27		
	Judges 5:19-31	Acts 2:22-36	Matt. 28:11-20

PROPER 13 *Week of the Sunday closest to August 3*

Sunday	93, 96 ❖ 34		
	2 Samuel 6:12-23	Rom. 14:7-12	John 1:43-51

Monday	80 ❖ 77, [79]		
	2 Samuel 7:1-17	Acts 18:1-11	Mark 8:11-21

Tuesday	78:1-39 ❖ 78:40-72		
	2 Samuel 7:18-29	Acts 18:12-28	Mark 8:22-33

Wednesday	119:97-120 ❖ 81, 82		
	2 Samuel 9:1-13	Acts 19:1-10	Mark 8:34—9:1

Thursday	[83] *or* 145 ❖ 85, 86		
	2 Samuel 11:1-27	Acts 19:11-20	Mark 9:2-13

Friday	88 ❖ 91, 92		
	2 Samuel 12:1-14	Acts 19:21-41	Mark 9:14-29

Saturday	87, 90 ❖ 136		
	2 Samuel 12:15-31	Acts 20:1-16	Mark 9:30-41

PROPER 14 *Week of the Sunday closest to August 10*

Sunday	66, 67 ❖ 19, 46		
	2 Samuel 13:1-22	Rom. 15:1-13	John 3:22-36

Monday	89:1-18 ❖ 89:19-52		
	2 Samuel 13:23-39	Acts 20:17-38	Mark 9:42-50

Tuesday	97, 99, [100] ❖ 94, [95]		
	2 Samuel 14:1-20	Acts 21:1-14	Mark 10:1-16

Wednesday	101, 109:1-4(5-19)20-30 ❖ 119:121-144		
	2 Samuel 14:21-33	Acts 21:15-26	Mark 10:17-31

Thursday	105:1-22 ❖ 105:23-45		
	2 Samuel 15:1-18	Acts 21: 27-36	Mark 10:32-45

Friday	102 ❖ 107:1-32		
	2 Samuel 15:19-37	Acts 21:37—22:16	Mark 10:46-52

Saturday	107:33-43, 108:1-6(7-13) ❖ 33		
	2 Samuel 16:1-23	Acts 22:17-29	Mark 11:1-11

Sunday   93, 96 ❖ 34
Judges 6:1-24   2 Cor. 9:6-15   Mark 3:20-30

Monday   80 ❖ 77, [79]
Judges 6:25-40   Acts 2:37-47   John 1:1-18

Tuesday   78:1-39 ❖ 78:40-72
Judges 7:1-18   Acts 3:1-11   John 1:19-28

Wednesday   119:97-120 ❖ 81, 82
Judges 7:19—8:12   Acts 3:12-26   John 1:29-42

Thursday   [83] *or* 145 ❖ 85, 86
Judges 8:22-35   Acts 4:1-12   John 1:43-51

Friday   88 ❖ 91, 92
Judges 9:1-16, 19-21   Acts 4:13-31   John 2:1-12

Saturday   87, 90 ❖ 136
Judges 9:22-25, 50-57   Acts 4:32—5:11   John 2:13-25

Sunday   66, 67 ❖ 19, 46
Judges 11:1-11, 29-40   2 Cor. 11:21b-31   Mark 4:35-41

Monday   89:1-18 ❖ 89:19-52
Judges 12:1-7   Acts 5:12-26   John 3:1-21

Tuesday   97, 99, [100] ❖ 94, [95]
Judges 13:1-15   Acts 5:27-42   John 3:22-36

Wednesday   101, 109:1-4(5-19)20-30 ❖ 119:121-144
Judges 13:15-24   Acts 6:1-15   John 4:1-26

Thursday   105:1-22 ❖ 105:23-45
Judges 14:1-19   Acts 6:15—7:16   John 4:27-42

Friday   102 ❖ 107:1-32
Judges 14:20—15:20   Acts 7:17-29   John 4:43-54

Saturday   107:33-43, 108:1-6(7-13) ❖ 33
Judges 16:1-14   Acts 7:30-43   John 5:1-18

PROPER 15 *Week of the Sunday closest to August 17*

Sunday   118   ❖   145
          2 Samuel 17:1-23   Gal. 3:6-14   John 5:30-47

Monday   106:1-18   ❖   106:19-48
          2 Samuel 17:24—18:8   Acts 22:30—23:11   Mark 11:12-26

Tuesday   [120], 121, 122, 123   ❖   124, 125, 126, [127]
          2 Samuel 18:9-18   Acts 23:12-24   Mark 11:27—12:12

Wednesday 119:145-176   ❖   128, 129, 130
          2 Samuel 18:19-33   Acts 23:23-35   Mark 12:13-27

Thursday 131, 132, [133]   ❖   134, 135
          2 Samuel 19:1-23   Acts 24:1-23   Mark 12:28-34

Friday   140, 142   ❖   141, 143:1-11(12)
          2 Samuel 19:24-43   Acts 24:24—25:12   Mark 12:35-44

Saturday 137:1-6(7-9), 144   ❖   104
          2 Samuel 23:1-7, 13-17   Acts 25:13-27   Mark 13:1-13

PROPER 16 *Week of the Sunday closest to August 24*

Sunday   146, 147   ❖   111 , 112, 113
          2 Samuel 24:1-2, 10-25   Gal. 3:23—4:7   John 8:12-20

Monday   1, 2, 3   ❖   4, 7
          1 Kings 1:5-31   Acts 26:1-23   Mark 13:14-27

Tuesday   5, 6   ❖   10, 11
          1 Kings 1:38—2:4   Acts 26:24—27:8   Mark 13:28-37

Wednesday 119:1-24   ❖   12, 13, 14
          1 Kings 3:1-15   Acts 27:9-26   Mark 14:1-11

Thursday 18:1-20   ❖   18:21-50
          1 Kings 3:16-28   Acts 27:27-44   Mark 14:12-26

Friday   16, 17   ❖   22
          1 Kings 5:1—6:1, 7   Acts 28:1-16   Mark 14:27-42

Saturday 20, 21:1-7(8-14)   ❖   110:1-5(6-7), 116, 117
          1 Kings 7:51—8:21   Acts 28:17-31   Mark 14:43-52

PROPER 15 *Week of the Sunday closest to August 17*

Sunday
118 ❖ 145
Judges 16:15-31   2 Cor. 13:1-11   Mark 5:25-34

Monday
106:1-18 ❖ 106:19-48
Judges 17:1-13   Acts 7:44—8:1a   John 5:19-29

Tuesday
[120], 121, 122, 123 ❖ 124, 125, 126, [127]
Judges 18:1-15   Acts 8:1-13   John 5:30-47

Wednesday
119:145-176 ❖ 128, 129, 130
Judges 18:16-31   Acts 8:14-25   John 6:1-15

Thursday
131, 132, [133] ❖ 134, 135
Job 1:1-22   Acts 8:26-40   John 6:16-27

Friday
140, 142 ❖ 141, 143:1-11(12)
Job 2:1-13   Acts 9:1-9   John 6:27-40

Saturday
137:1-6(7-9), 144 ❖ 104
Job 3:1-26   Acts 9:10-19a   John 6:41-51

PROPER 16 *Week of the Sunday closest to August 24*

Sunday
146, 147 ❖ 111, 112, 113
Job 4:1-6, 12-21   Rev. 4:1-11   Mark 6:1-6a

Monday
1, 2, 3 ❖ 4, 7
Job 4:1; 5:1-11, 17-21, 26-27   Acts 9:19b-31   John 6:52-59

Tuesday
5, 6 ❖ 10, 11
Job 6:1-4, 8-15, 21   Acts 9:32-43   John 6:60-71

Wednesday
119:1-24 ❖ 12, 13, 14
Job 6:1; 7:1-21   Acts 10:1-16   John 7:1-13

Thursday
18:1-20 ❖ 18:21-50
Job 8:1-10, 20-22   Acts 10:17-33   John 7:14-36

Friday
16, 17 ❖ 22
Job 9:1-15, 32-35   Acts 10:34-48   John 7:37-52

Saturday
20, 21:1-7(8-14) ❖ 110:1-5(6-7), 116, 117
Job 9:1; 10:1-9, 16-22   Acts 11:1-18   John 8:12-20

PROPER 17 *Week of the Sunday closest to August 31*

Sunday   148, 149, 150 ❖ 114, 115
           1 Kings 8:22-30(31-40)   1 Tim. 4:7b-16   John 8:47-59

Monday   25 ❖ 9, 15
           2 Chron. 6:32—7:7   James 2:1-13   Mark 14:53-65

Tuesday   26, 28 ❖ 36, 39
           1 Kings 8:65—9:9   James 2:14-26   Mark 14:66-72

Wednesday   38 ❖ 119:25-48
           1 Kings 9:24—10:13   James 3:1-12   Mark 15:1-11

Thursday   37:1-18 ❖ 37:19-42
           1 Kings 11:1-13   James 3:13—4:12   Mark 15:12-21

Friday   31 ❖ 35
           1 Kings 11:26-43   James 4:13—5:6   Mark 15:22-32

Saturday   30, 32 ❖ 42, 43
           1 Kings 12:1-20   James 5:7-12, 19-20   Mark 15:33-39

PROPER 18 *Week of the Sunday closest to September 7*

Sunday   63:1-8(9-11), 98 ❖ 103
           1 Kings 12:21-33   Acts 4:18-31   John 10:31-42

Monday   41, 52 ❖ 44
           1 Kings 13:1-10   Phil. 1:1-11   Mark 15:40-47

Tuesday   45 ❖ 47, 48
           1 Kings 16:23-34   Phil. 1:12-30   Mark 16:1-8(9-20)

Wednesday   119:49-72 ❖ 49, [53]
           1 Kings 17:1-24   Phil. 2:1-11   Matt. 2:1-12

Thursday   50 ❖ [59, 60] *or* 93, 96
           1 Kings 18:1-19   Phil. 2:12-30   Matt. 2:13-23

Friday   40, 54 ❖ 51
           1 Kings 18:20-40   Phil. 3:1-16   Matt. 3:1-12

Saturday   55 ❖ 138, 139:1-17(18-23)
           1 Kings 18:41—19:8   Phil. 3:17—4:7   Matt. 3:13-17

PROPER 17 *Week of the Sunday closest to August 31*

Sunday   148, 149, 150   ❖   114, 115
              Job 11:1-9, 13-20   Rev. 5:1-14   Matt. 5:1-12

Monday   25   ❖   9, 15
              Job 12:1-6, 13-25   Acts 11:19-30   John 8:21-32

Tuesday   26, 28   ❖   36, 39
              Job 12:1;13:3-17, 21-27   Acts 12:1-17   John 8:33-47

Wednesday   38   ❖   119:25-48
              Job 12:1;14:1-22   Acts 12:18-25   John 8:47-59

Thursday   37:1-18   ❖   37:19-42
              Job 16:16-22; 17:1, 13-16   Acts 13:1-12   John 9:1-17

Friday   31   ❖   35
              Job 19:1-7, 14-27   Acts 13:13-25   John 9:18-41

Saturday   30, 32   ❖   42, 43
              Job 22:1-4, 21—23:7   Acts 13:26-43   John 10:1-18

PROPER 18 *Week of the Sunday closest to September 7*

Sunday   63:1-8(9-11), 98   ❖   103
              Job 25:1-6; 27:1-6   Rev. 14:1-7, 13   Matt. 5:13-20

Monday   41, 52   ❖   44
              Job 32:1-10, 19—33:1, 19-28   Acts 13:44-52   John 10:19-30

Tuesday   45   ❖   47, 48
              Job 29:1-20   Acts 14:1-18   John 10:31-42

Wednesday   119:49-72   ❖   49, [53]
              Job 29:1;30:1-2, 16-31   Acts 14:19-28   John 11:1-16

Thursday   50   ❖   [59, 60] *or* 93, 96
              Job 29:1;31:1-23   Acts 15:1-11   John 11:17-29

Friday   40, 54   ❖   51
              Job 29:1; 31:24-40   Acts 15:12-21   John 11:30-44

Saturday   55   ❖   138, 139:1-17(18-23)
              Job 38:1-17   Acts 15:22-35   John 11:45-54

PROPER 19 *Week of the Sunday closest to September 14*

Sunday   24, 29   ❖   8, 84
              1 Kings 19:8-21   Acts 5:34-42   John 11:45-57

Monday   56, 57, [58]   ❖   64, 65
              1 Kings 21:1-16   1 Cor. 1:1-19   Matt. 4:1-11

Tuesday   61, 62   ❖   68:1-20(21-23)24-36
              1 Kings 21:17-29   1 Cor. 1:20-31   Matt. 4:12-17

Wednesday   72   ❖   119:73-96
              1 Kings 22:1-28   1 Cor. 2:1-13   Matt. 4:18-25

Thursday   [70], 71   ❖   74
              1 Kings 22:29-45   1 Cor. 2:14—3:15   Matt. 5:1-10

Friday   69:1-23(24-30)31-38   ❖   73
              2 Kings 1:2-17   1 Cor. 3:16-23   Matt. 5:11-16

Saturday   75, 76   ❖   23, 27
              2 Kings 2:1-18   1 Cor. 4:1-7   Matt. 5:17-20

PROPER 20 *Week of the Sunday closest to September 21*

Sunday   93, 96   ❖   34
              2 Kings 4:8-37   Acts 9:10-32   Luke 3:7-18

Monday   80   ❖   77, [79]
              2 Kings 5:1-19   1 Cor. 4:8-21   Matt. 5:21-26

Tuesday   78:1-3 9   ❖   78:40-72
              2 Kings 5:19-27   1 Cor. 5:1-8   Matt. 5:27-37

Wednesday   119:97-120   ❖   81, 82
              2 Kings 6:1-23   1 Cor. 5:9—6:8   Matt. 5:38-48

Thursday   [83] *or* 116, 117   ❖   85, 86
              2 Kings 9:1-16   1 Cor. 6:12-20   Matt. 6:1-6, 16-18

Friday   88   ❖   91, 92
              2 Kings 9:17-37   1 Cor. 7:1-9   Matt. 6:7-15

Saturday   87, 90   ❖   136
              2 Kings 11:1-20a   1 Cor. 7:10-24   Matt. 6:19-24

PROPER 19 *Week of the Sunday closest to September 14*

Sunday   24, 29 ❖ 8, 84
Job 38:1, 18-41   Rev. 18:1-8   Matt. 5:21-26

Monday   56, 57, [58] ❖ 64, 65
Job 40:1-24   Acts 15:36—16:5   John 11:55—12:8

Tuesday   61, 62 ❖ 68:1-20(21-23)24-36
Job 40:1; 41:1-11   Acts 16:6-15   John 12:9-19

Wednesday 72 ❖ 119:73-96
Job 42:1-17   Acts 16:16-24   John 12:20-26

Thursday   [70], 71 ❖ 74
Job 28:1-28   Acts 16:25-40   John 12:27-36a

Friday   69:1-23(24-30)31-38 ❖ 73
Esther 1:1-4, 10-19*   Acts 17:1-15   John 12:36b-43

Saturday   75, 76 ❖ 23, 27
Esther 2:5-8, 15-23*   Acts 17:16-34   John 12:44-50

PROPER 20 *Week of the Sunday closest to September 21*

Sunday   93, 96 ❖ 34
Esther 3:1—4:3*   James 1:19-27   Matt. 6:1-6, 16-18

Monday   80 ❖ 77, [79]
Esther 4:4-17*   Acts 18:1-11   Luke (1:1-4); 3:1-14

Tuesday   78:1-39 ❖ 78:40-72
Esther 5:1-14*   Acts 18:12-28   Luke 3:15-22

Wednesday 119:97-120 ❖ 81, 82
Esther 6:1-14*   Acts 19:1-10   Luke 4:1-13

Thursday   [83] *or* 116, 117 ❖ 85, 86
Esther 7:1-10*   Acts 19:11-20   Luke 4:14-30

Friday   88 ❖ 91, 92
Esther 8:1-8, 15-17*   Acts 19:21-41   Luke 4:31-37

Saturday   87, 90 ❖ 136
Hosea 1:1—2:1   Acts 20:1-16   Luke 4:38-44

* In place of Esther may be read Judith:
  F 4:1-15   Su 5:22–6:4, 10-21   Tu 8:9-17; 9:1, 7-10   Th 12:1-20
  Sa 5:1-21   M 7:1-7, 19-32   W 10:1-23   F 13:1-20

PROPER 21 *Week of the Sunday closest to September 28*

Sunday   66, 67 ❖ 19, 46
            2 Kings 17:1-18   Acts 9:36-43   Luke 5:1-11

Monday   89:1-18 ❖ 89:19-52
            2 Kings 17:24-41   1 Cor. 7:25-31   Matt. 6:25-34

Tuesday   97, 99, [100] ❖ 94, [95]
            2 Chron. 29:1-3;   1 Cor. 7:32-40   Matt. 7:1-12
                30:1(2-9) 10-27

Wednesday   101, 109:1-4(5-19)20-30 ❖ 119:121-144
            2 Kings 18:9-25   1 Cor. 8:1-13   Matt. 7:13-21

Thursday   105:1-22 ❖ 105:23-45
            2 Kings 18:28-37   1 Cor. 9:1-15   Matt. 7:22-29

Friday   102 ❖ 107:1-32
            2 Kings 19:1-20   1 Cor. 9:16-27   Matt. 8:1-17

Saturday   107:33-43, 108:1-6(7-13) ❖ 33
            2 Kings 19:21-36   1 Cor. 10:1-13   Matt. 8:18-27

PROPER 22 *Week of the Sunday closest to October 5*

Sunday   118 ❖ 145
            2 Kings 20:1-21   Acts 12:1-17   Luke 7:11-17

Monday   106:1-18 ❖ 106:19-48
            2 Kings 21:1-18   1 Cor. 10:14—11:1   Matt. 8:28-34

Tuesday   [120], 121, 122, 123 ❖ 124, 125, 126, [127]
            2 Kings 22:1-13   1 Cor. 11:2, 17-22   Matt. 9:1-8

Wednesday   119:145-176 ❖ 128, 129, 130
            2 Kings 22:14—23:3   1 Cor. 11:23-34   Matt. 9:9-17

Thursday   131, 132, [133] ❖ 134, 135
            2 Kings 23:4-25   1 Cor. 12:1-11   Matt. 9:18-26

Friday   140, 142 ❖ 141, 143:1-11(12)
            2 Kings 23:36—24:17   1 Cor. 12:12-26   Matt. 9:27-34

Saturday   137:1-6(7-9), 144 ❖ 104
            Jer. 35:1-19   1 Cor. 12:27—13:3   Matt. 9:35—10:4

PROPER 21 *Week of the Sunday closest to September 28*

Sunday   66, 67 ❖ 19, 46
          Hosea 2:2-14   James 3:1-13   Matt. 13:44-52

Monday   89:1-18 ❖ 89:19-52
          Hosea 2:14-23   Acts 20:17-38   Luke 5:1-11

Tuesday   97, 99, [100] ❖ 94, [95]
          Hosea 4:1-10   Acts 21:1-14   Luke 5:12-26

Wednesday 101, 109:1-4(5-19)20-30 ❖ 119:121-144
          Hosea 4:11-19   Acts 21:15-26   Luke 5:27-39

Thursday 105:1-22 ❖ 105:23-45
          Hosea 5:8—6:6   Acts 21:27-36   Luke 6:1-11

Friday   102 ❖ 107:1-32
          Hosea 10:1-15   Acts 21:37—22:16   Luke 6:12-26

Saturday 107:33-43, 108:1-6(7-13) ❖ 33
          Hosea 11:1-9   Acts 22:17-29   Luke 6:27-38

PROPER 22 *Week of the Sunday closest to October 5*

Sunday   118 ❖ 145
          Hosea 13:4-14   1 Cor. 2:6-16   Matt. 14:1-12

Monday   106:1-18 ❖ 106:19-48
          Hosea 14:1-9   Acts 22:30—23:11   Luke 6:39-49

Tuesday   [120], 121, 122, 123 ❖ 124, 125, 126, [127]
          Micah 1:1-9   Acts 23:12-24   Luke 7:1-17

Wednesday 119:145-176 ❖ 128, 129, 130
          Micah 2:1-13   Acts 23:23-35   Luke 7:18-35

Thursday 131, 132, [133] ❖ 134, 135
          Micah 3:1-8   Acts 24:1-23   Luke 7:36-50

Friday   140, 142 ❖ 141, 143:1-11(12)
          Micah 3:9—4:5   Acts 24:24—25:12   Luke 8:1-15

Saturday 137:1-6(7-9), 144 ❖ 104
          Micah 5:1-4, 10-15   Acts 25:13-27   Luke 8:16-25

PROPER 23 *Week of the Sunday closest to October 12*

Sunday   146, 147   ❖   111, 112, 113
Jer. 36:1-10   Acts 14:8-18   Luke 7:36-50

Monday   1, 2, 3   ❖   4, 7
Jer. 36:11-26   1 Cor. 13:(1-3)4-13   Matt. 10:5-15

Tuesday   5, 6   ❖   10, 11
Jer. 36:27—37:2   1 Cor. 14:1-12   Matt. 10:16-23

Wednesday   119:1-24   ❖   12, 13, 14
Jer. 37:3-21   1 Cor. 14:13-25   Matt. 10:24-33

Thursday   18:1-20   ❖   18:21-50
Jer. 38:1-13   1 Cor. 14:26-33a, 37-40   Matt. 10:34-42

Friday   16, 17   ❖   22
Jer. 38:14-28   1 Cor. 15:1-11   Matt. 11:1-6

Saturday   20, 21:1-7(8-14)   ❖   110:1-5(6-7), 116, 117
2 Kings 25:8-12, 22-26   1 Cor. 15:12-29   Matt. 11:7-15

PROPER 24 *Week of the Sunday closest to October 19*

Sunday   148, 149, 15   ❖   114, 115
Jer. 29:1, 4-14   Acts 16:6-15   Luke 10:1-12, 17-20

Monday   25   ❖   9, 15
Jer. 44:1-14   1 Cor. 15:30-41   Matt. 11:16-24

Tuesday   26, 28   ❖   36, 39
Lam. 1:1-5(6-9)10-12   1 Cor. 15:41-50   Matt. 11:25-30

Wednesday   38   ❖   119:25-48
Lam. 2:8-15   1 Cor. 15:51-58   Matt. 12:1-14

Thursday   37:1-18   ❖   37:19-42
Ezra 1:1-11   1 Cor. 16:1-9   Matt. 12:15-21

Friday   31   ❖   35
Ezra 3:1-13   1 Cor. 16:10-24   Matt. 12:22-32

Saturday   30, 32   ❖   42, 43
Ezra 4:7, 11-24   Philemon 1-25   Matt. 12:33-42

PROPER 23 *Week of the Sunday closest to October 12*

Sunday   146, 147   ❖   111 , 112, 113
Micah 6:1-8   1 Cor. 4:9-16   Matt. 15:21-28

Monday   1, 2, 3   ❖   4, 7
Micah 7:1-7   Acts 26:1-23   Luke 8:26-39

Tuesday   5, 6   ❖   10, 11
Jonah 1:1-17a   Acts 26:24—27:8   Luke 8:40-56

Wednesday   119:1-24   ❖   12, 13, 14
Jonah 1:17—2:10   Acts 27:9-26   Luke 9:1-17

Thursday   18:1-20   ❖   18:21-50
Jonah 3:1—4:11   Acts 27:27-44   Luke 9:18-27

Friday   16, 17   ❖   22
Ecclus. 1:1-10, 18-27   Acts 28:1-16   Luke 9:28-36

Saturday   20, 21:1-7(8-14)   ❖   110:1-5(6-7), 116, 117
Ecclus. 3:17-31   Acts 28:17-31   Luke 9:37-50

PROPER 24 *Week of the Sunday closest to October 19*

Sunday   148, 149, 150   ❖   114, 115
Ecclus. 4:1-10   1 Cor. 10:1-13   Matt. 16:13-20

Monday   25   ❖   9, 15
Ecclus. 4:20—5:7   Rev. 7:1-8   Luke 9:51-62

Tuesday   26, 28   ❖   36, 39
Ecclus. 6:5-17   Rev. 7:9-17   Luke 10:1-16

Wednesday   38   ❖   119:25-48
Ecclus. 7:4-14   Rev. 8:1-13   Luke 10:17-24

Thursday   37:1-18   ❖   37:19-42
Ecclus. 10:1-18   Rev. 9:1-12   Luke 10:25-37

Friday   31   ❖   35
Ecclus. 11:2-20   Rev. 9:13-21   Luke 10:38-42

Saturday   30, 32   ❖   42, 43
Ecclus. 15:9-20   Rev. 10:1-11   Luke 11:1-13

PROPER 25 *Week of the Sunday closest to October 26*

Sunday   63:1-8(9-11), 98   ❖   103
              Haggai 1:1—2:9   Acts 18:24—19:7   Luke 10:2S-37

Monday   41, 52   ❖   44
              Zech. 1:7-17   Rev. 1:4-20   Matt. 12:43-50

Tuesday   45   ❖   47, 48
              Ezra 5:1-17   Rev. 4:1-11   Matt. 13:1-9

Wednesday   119:49-72   ❖   49, [53]
              Ezra 6:1-22   Rev. 5:1-10   Matt. 13:10-17

Thursday   50   ❖   [59, 60] *or* 103
              Neh. 1:1-11   Rev. 5:11—6:11   Matt. 13:18-23

Friday   40, 54   ❖   51
              Neh. 2:1-20   Rev. 6:12—7:4   Matt. 13:24-30

Saturday   55   ❖   138, 139:1-17(18-23)
              Neh. 4:1-23   Rev. 7:(4-8)9-17   Matt. 13:31-35

PROPER 26 *Week of the Sunday closest to November 2*

Sunday   24, 29   ❖   8, 84
              Neh. 5:1-19   Acts 20:7-12   Luke 12:22-31

Monday   56, 57, [58]   ❖   64, 65
              Neh. 6:1-19   Rev. 10:1-11   Matt. 13:36-43

Tuesday   61, 62   ❖   68:1-20(21-23)24-36
              Neh. 12:27-31a, 42b-47   Rev. 11:1-19   Matt. 13:44-52

Wednesday   72   ❖   119:73-96
              Neh. 13:4-22   Rev. 12:1-12   Matt. 13:53-58

Thursday   [70], 71   ❖   74
              Ezra 7:(1-10)11-26   Rev. 14:1-13   Matt. 14:1-12

Friday   69:1-23(24-30)31-38   ❖   73
              Ezra 7:27-28; 8:21-36   Rev. 15:1-8   Matt. 14:13-21

Saturday   75, 76   ❖   23, 27
              Ezra 9:1-15   Rev. 17:1-14   Matt. 14:22-36

Sunday   63:1-8(9-11), 98   ❖   103
             Ecclus. 18:19-33   1 Cor. 10:15-24   Matt. 18:15-20

Monday   41, 52   ❖   44
             Ecclus. 19:4-17   Rev. 11:1-14   Luke 11:14-26

Tuesday   45   ❖   47, 48
             Ecclus. 24:1-12   Rev. 11:14-19   Luke 11:27-36

Wednesday 119:49-72   ❖   49, [53]
             Ecclus. 28:14-26   Rev. 12:1-6   Luke 11:37-52

Thursday   50   ❖   [59, 60] *or* 103
             Ecclus. 31:12-18, 25—32:2   Rev. 12:7-17   Luke 11:53—12:12

Friday   40, 54   ❖   51
             Ecclus. 34:1-8, 18-22   Rev. 13:1-10   Luke 12:13-31

Saturday   55   ❖   138, 139:1-17(18-23)
             Ecclus. 35:1-17   Rev. 13:11-18   Luke 12:32-48

PROPER 26 *Week of the Sunday closest to November 2*

Sunday   24, 29   ❖   8, 84
             Ecclus. 36:1-17   1 Cor. 12:27—13:13   Matt. 18:21-35

Monday   56, 57, [58]   ❖   64, 65
             Ecclus. 38:24-34   Rev. 14:1-13   Luke 12:49-59

Tuesday   61, 62   ❖   68:1-20(21-23)24-36
             Ecclus. 43:1-22   Rev. 14:14—15:8   Luke 13:1-9

Wednesday 72   ❖   119:73-96
             Ecclus. 43:23-33   Rev. 16:1-11   Luke 13:10-17

Thursday   [70] 71   ❖   74
             Ecclus. 44:1-15   Rev. 16:12-21   Luke 13:18-30

Friday   69:1-23(24-30)31-38   ❖   73
             Ecclus. 50:1, 11-24   Rev. 17:1-18   Luke 13:31-35

Saturday   75, 76   ❖   23, 27
             Ecclus. 51:1-12   Rev. 18:1-14   Luke 14:1-11

PROPER 27 *Week of the Sunday closest to November 9*

Sunday
93, 96 ❖ 34
Ezra 10:1-17   Acts 24:10-21   Luke 14:12-24

Monday
80 ❖ 77, [79]
Neh. 9:1-15(16-25)   Rev. 18:1-8   Matt. 15:1-20

Tuesday
78:1-39 ❖ 78:40-72
Neh. 9:26-38   Rev. 18:9-20   Matt. 15:21-28

Wednesday
119:97-120 ❖ 81, 82
Neh. 7:73b—8:3, 5-18   Rev. 18:21-24   Matt. 15:29-39

Thursday
[83] *or* 23, 27 ❖ 85, 86
1 Macc. 1:1-28   Rev. 19:1-10   Matt. 16:1-12

Friday
88 ❖ 91, 92
1 Macc. 1:41-63   Rev. 19:11-16   Matt. 16:13-20

Saturday
87, 90 ❖ 136
1 Macc. 2:1-28   Rev. 20:1-6   Matt. 16:21-28

PROPER 28 *Week of the Sunday closest to November 16*

Sunday
66, 67 ❖ 19, 46
1 Macc. 2:29-43, 49-50   Acts 28:14b-23   Luke 16:1-13

Monday
89:1-18 ❖ 89:19-52
1 Macc. 3:1-24   Rev. 20:7-15   Matt. 17:1-13

Tuesday
97, 99, [100] ❖ 94, [95]
1 Macc. 3:25-41   Rev. 21:1-8   Matt. 17:14-21

Wednesday
101, 109:1-4(5-19)20-30 ❖ 119:121-144
1 Macc. 3:42-60   Rev. 21:9-21   Matt. 17:22-27

Thursday
105:1-22 ❖ 105:23-45
1 Macc. 4:1-25   Rev.21:22—22:5   Matt.18:1-9

Friday
102 ❖ 107:1-32
1 Macc. 4:36-59   Rev. 22:6-13   Matt. 18:10-20

Saturday
107:33-43, 108:1-6(7-13) ❖ 33
Isa. 65:17-25   Rev. 22:14-21   Matt. 18:21-35

PROPER 27 *Week of the Sunday closest to November 9*

Sunday   93, 96   ❖   34
Ecclus. 51:13-22   1 Cor. 14:1-12   Matt. 20:1-16

Monday   80   ❖   77, [79]
Joel 1:1-13   Rev. 18:15-24   Luke 14:12-24

Tuesday   78:1-39   ❖   78:40-72
Joel 1:15—2:2(3-11)   Rev. 19:1-10   Luke 14:25-35

Wednesday 119:97-120   ❖   81, 82
Joel 2:12-19   Rev. 19:11-21   Luke 15:1-10

Thursday   [83] *or* 23, 27   ❖   85, 86
Joel 2:21-27   James 1:1-15   Luke 15:1-2, 11-32

Friday   88   ❖   91, 92
Joel 2:28—3:8   James 1:16-27   Luke 16:1-9

Saturday   87, 90   ❖   136
Joel 3:9-17   James 2:1-13   Luke 16:10-17(18)

PROPER 28 *Week of the Sunday closest to November 16*

Sunday   66, 67   ❖   19, 46
Hab. 1:1-4(5-11)12—2:1   Phil. 3:13—4:1   Matt. 23:13-24

Monday   89:1-18   ❖   89:19-52
Hab. 2:1-4, 9-20   James 2:14-26   Luke 16:19-31

Tuesday   97, 99, [100]   ❖   94, [95]
Hab. 3:1-10(11-15)16-18   James 3:1-12   Luke 17:1-10

Wednesday 101, 109:1-4(5-19)20-30   ❖   119:121-144
Mal. 1:1, 6-14   James 3:13—4:12   Luke 17:11-19

Thursday   105:1-22   ❖   105:23-45
Mal. 2:1-16   James 4:13—5:6   Luke 17:20-37

Friday   102   ❖   107:1-32
Mal. 3:1-12   James 5:7-12   Luke 18:1-8

Saturday   107:33-43, 108:1-6(7-13)   ❖   33
Mal. 3:13—4:6   James 5:13-20   Luke 18:9-14

PROPER 29 *Week of the Sunday closest to November 23*

Sunday   118   ❖   145
               Isa. 19:19-25   Rom. 15:5-13   Luke 19:11-27

Monday   106:1-18   ❖   106:19-48
               Joel 3:1-2, 9-17   1 Pet. 1:1-12   Matt. 19:1-12

Tuesday   [120], 121, 122, 123   ❖   124, 125, 126, [127]
               Nahum 1:1-13   1 Pet. 1:13-25   Matt. 19:13-22

Wednesday   119:145-17   ❖   128, 129, 130
               Obadiah 15-21   1 Pet. 2:1-10   Matt. 19:23-30

Thursday   131, 132, [133]   ❖   134, 135
               Zeph. 3:1-13   1 Pet. 2:11-25   Matt. 20:1-16

Friday   140, 142   ❖   141, 143:1-11(12)
               Isa. 24:14-23   1 Pet. 3:13—4:6   Matt. 20:17-28

Saturday   137:1-6(7-9), 144   ❖   104
               Micah 7:11-20   1 Pet. 4:7-19   Matt. 20:29-34

PROPER 29 *Week of the Sunday closest to November 23*

Sunday	118 ❖ 145		
	Zech. 9:9-16	1 Pet. 3:13-22	Matt. 21:1-13
Monday	106:1-18 ❖ 106:19-48		
	Zech. 10:1-12	Gal. 6:1-10	Luke 18:15-30
Tuesday	[120], 121, 122, 123 ❖ 124, 125, 126, [127]		
	Zech. 11:4-17	1 Cor. 3:10-23	Luke 18:31-43
Wednesday	119:145-176 ❖ 128, 129,130		
	Zech. 12:1-10	Eph. 1:3-14	Luke 19:1-10
Thursday	131, 132, [133] ❖ 134, 135		
	Zech. 13:1-9	Eph. 1:15-23	Luke 19:11-27
Friday	140, 142 ❖ 141, 143:1-11(12)		
	Zech. 14:1-11	Rom. 15:7-13	Luke 19:28-40
Saturday	137:1-6(7-9), 144 ❖ 104		
	Zech. 14:12-21	Phil. 2:1-11	Luke 19:41-48

Holy Days

	MORNING PRAYER	EVENING PRAYER
ST. ANDREW *November 30*	34 Isaiah 49:1-6 1 Corinthians 4:1-16	96, 100 Isaiah 55:1-5 John 1:35-42
ST. THOMAS *December 21*	23, 121 Job 42:1-6 1 Peter 1:3-9	27 Isaiah 43:8-13 John 14:1-7
ST. STEPHEN *December 26*	28, 30 2 Chronicles 24:17-22 Acts 6:1-7	118 Wisdom 4:7-15 Acts 7:59—8:8
ST. JOHN *December 27*	97, 98 Proverbs 8:22-30 John 13:20-35	145 Isaiah 44:1-8 1 John 5:1-12
HOLY INNOCENTS *December 28*	2, 26 Isaiah 49:13-23 Matthew 18:1-14	19, 126 Isaiah 54:1-13 Mark 10:13-16
CONFESSION OF **ST. PETER** *January 18*	66, 67 Ezekiel 3:4-11 Acts 10:34-44	118 Ezekiel 34:11-16 John 21:15-22
CONVERSION OF **ST. PAUL** *January 25*	19 Isaiah 45:18-25 Philippians 3:4b-11	119:89-112 Ecclesiasticus 39:1-10 Acts 9:1-22
EVE OF THE **PRESENTATION**		113, 122 1 Samuel 1:20-28a Romans 8:14-21

	MORNING PRAYER	EVENING PRAYER
THE PRESENTATION *February 2*	42, 43 1 Samuel 2:1-10 John 8:31-36	48, 87 Haggai 2:1-9 1 John 3:1-8
ST. MATTHIAS *February 24*	80 1 Samuel 16:1-13 1 John 2:18-25	33 1 Samuel 12:1-5 Acts 20:17-35
ST. JOSEPH *March 19*	132 Isaiah 63:7-16 Matthew 1:18-25	34 2 Chronicles 6:12-17 Ephesians 3:14-21
EVE OF THE **ANNUNCIATION**		8, 138 Genesis 3:1-15 Romans 5:12-21 *or* Galatians 4:1-7
ANNUNCIATION *March 25*	85, 87 Isaiah 52:7-12 Hebrews 2:5-10	110:1-5(6-7), 132 Wisdom 9:1-12 John 1:9-14
ST. MARK *April 25*	145 Ecclesiasticus 2:1-11 Acts 12:25—13:3	67, 96 Isaiah 62:6-12 2 Timothy 4:1-11
SS. PHILIP & JAMES *May 1*	119:137-160 Job 23:1-12 John 1:43-51	139 Proverbs 4:7-18 John 12:20-26
EVE OF THE **VISITATION**		132 Isaiah 11:1-10 Hebrews 2:11-18
THE VISITATION *May 31*	72 1 Samuel 1:1-20 Hebrews 3:1-6	146, 147 Zechariah 2:10-13 John 3:25-30

	MORNING PRAYER	EVENING PRAYER
ST. BARNABAS *June 11*	15, 67 Ecclesiasticus 31:3-11 Acts 4:32-37	19, 146 Job 29:1-16 Acts 9:26-31
EVE OF ST. JOHN THE BAPTIST		103 Ecclesiasticus 48:1-11 Luke 1:5-23
NATIVITY OF ST. JOHN THE BAPTIST *June 24*	82, 98 Malachi 3:1-5 John 3:22-30	80 Malachi 4:1-6 Matthew 11:2-19
SS. PETER & PAUL *June 29*	66 Ezekiel 2:1-7 Acts 11:1-18	97, 138 Isaiah 49:1-6 Galatians 2:1-9
INDEPENDENCE DAY *July 4*	33 Ecclesiasticus 10:1-8, 12-18 James 5:7-10	107:1-32 Micah 4:1-5 Revelation 21:1-7
ST. MARY MAGDALENE *July 22*	116 Zephaniah 3:14-20 Mark 15:47—16:7	30, 149 Exodus 15:19-21 2 Corinthians 1:3-7
ST. JAMES *July 25*	34 Jeremiah 16:14-21 Mark 1:14-20	33 Jeremiah 26:1-15 Matthew 10:16-32
EVE OF THE TRANSFIGURATION		84 1 Kings 19:1-12 2 Corinthians 3:1-9, 18
THE TRANSFIGURATION *August 6*	2, 24 Exodus 24:12-18 2 Corinthians 4:1-6	72 Daniel 7:9-10, 13-14 John 12:27-36a

	MORNING PRAYER	EVENING PRAYER

ST. MARY
THE VIRGIN
August 15
	113, 115
	1 Samuel 2:1-10
	John 2:1-12
		45, *or* 138, 149
		Jeremiah 31:1-14
		  or Zechariah 2:10-13
		John 19:23-27
		  or Acts 1:6-14

ST. BARTHOLOMEW *August 24*	86 Genesis 28:10-17 John 1:43-51	15, 67 Isaiah 66:1-2, 18-23 1 Peter 5:1-11
EVE OF HOLY CROSS		46, 87 1 Kings 8:22-30 Ephesians 2:11-22
HOLY CROSS DAY *September 14*	66 Numbers 21:4-9 John 3:11-17	118 Genesis 3:1-15 1 Peter 3:17-22
ST. MATTHEW *September 21*	119:41-64 Isaiah 8:11-20 Romans 10:1-15	19, 112 Job 28:12-28 Matthew 13:44-52

ST. MICHAEL &
ALL ANGELS
September 29
	8, 148
	Job 38:1-7
	Hebrews 1:1-14
		34, 150, *or* 104
		Daniel 12:1-3
		  or 2 Kings 6:8-17
		Mark 13:21-27
		  or Revelation 5:1-14

ST. LUKE *October 18*	103 Ezekiel 47:1-12 Luke 1:1-4	67, 96 Isaiah 52:7-10 Acts 1:1-8
ST. JAMES **OF JERUSALEM** *October 23*	119:145-168 Jeremiah 11:18-23 Matthew 10:16-22	122, 125 Isaiah 65:17-25 Hebrews 12:12-24

	MORNING PRAYER	EVENING PRAYER
SS. SIMON & JUDE *October 28*	66 Isaiah 28:9-16 Ephesians 4:1-16	116, 117 Isaiah 4:2-6 John 14:15-31
EVE OF ALL SAINTS		34 Wisdom 3:1-9 Revelation 19:1, 4-10
ALL SAINTS' DAY *November 1*	111, 112 2 Esdras 2:42-47 Hebrews 11:32—12:2	48, 150 Wisdom 5:1-5, 14-16 Revelation 21:1-4, 22—22:5
THANKSGIVING DAY	147 Deuteronomy 26:1-11 John 6:26-35	145 Joel 2:21-27 1 Thessalonians 5:12-24

www.ingramcontent.com/pod-product-compliance
Lightning Source LLC
Chambersburg PA
CBHW071854090426
42811CB00004B/606

* 9 7 8 1 6 4 0 6 5 2 7 5 0 *